Nation-States and Indians
in Latin America

Symposia on Latin America Series
Institute of Latin American Studies
University of Texas at Austin

Nation-States and Indians in Latin America

**Edited by Greg Urban
and Joel Sherzer**

University of Texas Press, Austin

First Edition, 1991

Requests for permission to reproduce material from this work should be sent to:

Permissions
University of Texas Press
P.O. Box 7819
Austin, Texas 78713-7819

♾ The paper used in this publication meets the minimum requirements of American National Standard for Information Sciences—Permanence of Paper for Printed Library Materials, ANSI Z39.48–1984.

Library of Congress Cataloging-in-Publication Data

Nation-states and Indians in Latin America / edited by Greg Urban and
    Joel Sherzer.
       p.   cm. — (Symposia on Latin America series)
       Includes bibliographical references and index.
       ISBN 0-292-75545-7
       1. Indians—Ethnic identity. 2. Nationalism—Latin America.
3. Indians—Government relations. I. Urban, Greg, 1949– II. Sherzer, Joel.
III. Series.
E59.E75N38 1991
305.898—dc20   91–4460
                                                        CIP

Contents

Nation-States and Indians
in Latin America

Introduction:
Indians, Nation-States, and Culture

Greg Urban and Joel Sherzer

There is a growing recognition in the social sciences, and especially in anthropology, that traditional and seemingly isolated communities of the world are no longer in fact isolated, that new webs are constantly being spun between such communities and broader national and international arenas, and that in many cases the assumption of community isolation seriously distorts research results. The effects of linkage with the outside world are evident in numerous phenomena, from indigenous movements and projects to political protests to forms of discourse. They may furthermore and most interestingly be reflected in the persistence and shape of autochthonous forms, such as language, ritual, myth, and clothing style. As a result of interest in the role such linkages play, new theoretical concerns have been spawned. The essays in this volume constitute a set of reflections on these issues from the point of view of relations between nation-states and Amerindian populations in Latin America.

What is the status of culture when Amerindian peoples and their customs are viewed not as isolated, but rather as parts of nation-states and larger international networks? This question motivates these essays, which are concerned, however, not just with the overall and abstract mechanism of culture, but also with its concrete manifestations—Kuna molas, the fiesta-cargo system of ayllu K'ulta in Bolivia, the *kenas* (or end-notched flutes) of highland Peru, the Guatemalan *huipil* blouse, the Nheêngatú language of Brazil. In what measure can culture be understood as handed down across the generations? In what measure must we invoke a relational approach grounded in cultural differences (Barth 1969), which views the mola not just as a legacy of the past, but as part of a struggle between Kuna and the Panamanian state, which views the *huipil* not just as Mayan, but as a nationally appropriated mark of Guatemalan distinctiveness with respect to other countries?

The study of Indian and nation-state relations challenges received theoretical and methodological perspectives. It raises the question of whether anthropology as a discipline, as many of its practitioners have been trained to do it, is capable of dealing with the issue of linkage. By focusing attention on culture as something received from the past, anthropology has actually in some measure trained us to ignore the possible role of outside influence and to turn away from the fast-changing situations of the kind described in this book. The processes of self-definition and external characterization of indigenous groups are ongoing ones, involving more changes and occurring more rapidly than we think.

Given this challenge to (some have called it a crisis in) anthropology's ability to come to terms with contemporary situations, especially those involving relationships between native peoples and nation-states, two solutions emerge, both of which are reflected in the papers in this volume. One solution is to recognize that our work must be interdisciplinary, involving, in addition to anthropology, linguistics, political science, economics, ethnomusicology, history, and other areas. A second solution is to recognize that basic changes must be made in the theoretical models and categories we employ within anthropology in coming to terms with Indian nation-state relations. Both solutions involve attention to a global system, within which native peoples cannot be viewed as isolated entities, and both involve a historical perspective, which sheds significant light on contemporary actions and actors. They also involve attention to the privileged and yet sensitive and critical role that anthropology plays in relation to native peoples.

Some of the essays draw inspiration from the work of Michael Taussig (1980, 1987), who argued that "certain fantastic and magical reactions to our nonfantastic reality," such as Colombian peasant beliefs about money and compacts made with the devil, are "part of a critique of the modern mode of production" (1980: 10). They cannot be correctly interpreted as isolated cultural phenomena. This is true even in the case of beliefs and practices that appear to be autochthonous—Sibundoy valley shamanism, for instance—but are in fact the product of colonial encounter, "an invented tradition" (1987: 377), which covertly criticizes the dominant culture.

The role of assimilation and reattribution in cultural encounter is especially apparent in Abercrombie's (chap. 4) Bolivian examples, where the fiesta-cargo system appears as a Spanish colonial residue now reinterpreted as "Indian." Not a legacy of the pre-Columbian past but rather a relatively recent historical creation—handed-downness being in this sense in part illusory—this element of Indian culture was fused in the crucible of cultural contact, with its fiery clash of differences. Abercrombie goes so far as to claim that "'indigenous ethnic groups' and 'indigenous cosmologies' are unintelligible apart from their struggle with the state. . . ." In other words, our ability to interpret culture from the standpoint of tradition or continuity over time is undermined by the force of colonially imposed difference, which becomes the principal ground for cultural understanding.

We are reminded of Friedlander's (1975: 71) study of the central Mexican village of Hueyapan, where the Indians have "primarily a negative identity," "filling in the 'void' of their Indian-ness by accumulating symbols identified with the hispanic elite," which in turn constantly acquired new symbols, demoting "characteristics previously associated with its prestigious high status to the low level of nonculture or Indianness." Hueyapan Indian culture, for Friedlander, was not so much a legacy of the pre-Columbian past, understandable in terms of cultural continuity, as a diacritic of low socioeconomic status within a national system of social stratification.

But not all examples presented here are of this sort. In many areas of lowland South America, Indian peoples were never effectively colonized, did not develop a colonial mentality, and in some cases eluded outside domination and contact until recently. The Shuar of Ecuador (Hendricks, chap. 2), Tukanoans in parts of the Vaupés region of northwest Amazonia (Jackson, chap. 5), and the Kuna of Panama (Howe, chap. 1) are cases in point. Their cultural forms are the continuation of precontact patterns. Nevertheless, even here the effects of cultural difference are evident. In the Kuna case, the period between 1915 and 1925 witnessed an intense struggle with the Panamanian state wherein some aspects of traditional Kuna culture disappeared, while others (such as the mola) persisted. The persisting elements that were contested took on a new value as not simply legacies of the past but now also symbols of a hard-won victory against the Panamanian state. This is not covert resistance to domination through the modification of colonially imposed forms, but an overt flaunting of the failure of the state to effect its domination through forced assimilation, simultaneously as it is a continuation of tradition. The mola is particularly interesting, since in recent years it has become simultaneously a symbol of "Kunaness" and "Panamaness," while at the same time developing in particular aesthetic directions as a result of its place in the contemporary tourist and Latin American ethnic arts world (Sherzer and Sherzer 1976). In any case, we cannot achieve a full interpretive understanding of cultural forms without reference to the effects of cultural contact and difference.

The issue is not just how native peoples represent their experience of the "white man"—the theme of many papers in the recent volume by Jonathan Hill (1988)—although this plays a role as well, especially in the papers by Hendricks and by Jane Hill (chap. 3). Rather, what is involved is the interpretation of Amerindian cultures more generally. In what measure can we understand them internally, without reference to their nation-state contexts; in what measure must we interpret them relationally, as functioning within the modern world (cf. Whitten 1981)?

To illuminate these questions, several of the authors use the concept of ethnicity, which has assumed increasing importance in anthropological discussions (Barth 1969; A. Cohen 1974; R. Cohen 1978a; Stutzman 1981; Williams 1989), intersecting with the concepts of class (Nash 1979; Smith 1984) and race (Banton 1983; Stutzman 1981; Williams 1989). In one strand of this work (Williams 1989), to which Adams's formulation of ethnicities—as "subgroups within the purview of the state whose members use the subgroup to promote their collective interest"—is related, the key aspect of the ethnic group concept is situatedness with respect to a state. Ethnic groups are interest groups competing for resources, and they mobilize language, rituals, and other aspects of culture to do so. Their manipulations, however, already presuppose that they accede to state sovereignty, that they are self-organizing groups within the purview of an external authority, although their perception of self-interest may motivate them to overthrow the regime in power, or to seek some form of autonomy, as in the case of the Nicaraguan Miskitu during the 1980s, discussed in this volume by Diskin (chap. 6).

In formulating important similarities among diverse situations of cultural difference, however, the ethnicity concept also obscures important differences, making it appear as if the situation of Japanese or German settlers in Brazil were the same as that of the Uru-eu-wau-wau Indians of the western Brazilian state of Rondônia, first "contacted" in the early 1980s. In describing the pre-1980 situation of the latter, even the term *autonomy* is misleading, since there was then no notion of a heteronomy to which it might be opposed, no self-awareness that they might be but one subordinate unit within an encompassing, hierarchically organized structure. Watching Adrian Cowell's (1984) celebrated film documentary, *The Decade of Destruction*, which shows the first encounters between members of the tribe and representatives of the Brazilian government Indian agency (FUNAI), we appreciate, as the camera peers out at the Indians from its concealment within the attraction hut, that they cannot possibly comprehend the vastness of the system that has now engulfed them.

The starting point for the Uru-eu-wau-wau is distinct from that of the Japanese or Germans who migrated to Brazil. The latter voluntarily submitted to state authority, and organized—insofar as they did so—within the jurisdictional bounds established by the state. While the Uru-eu-wau-wau were not conquered militarily, as the Incas or Aztecs had been, they were nevertheless ferreted out by the Brazilian state, which hoped to open indigenous lands to settlement by other Brazilians. The state, in other words, sought to impose a heteronymous condition; the Uru-eu-wau-wau were not given the right to accept or reject it. From an objective point of view, the Uru-eu-wau-wau may end up the same as the Japanese or Germans—interest groups within the purview of the state. Subjectively, however, their situation is different. If we are to understand the course of future events, we need to appreciate the subjective self-understanding of the ethnic group—how the group views its own present situation—as well as its objective circumstances understood in terms of interests, resources, and competition.

It is for this reason that some anthropologists, such as Jean Jackson in this volume, have preferred a broader definition of the ethnic group "as a recognizably distinct group of people substantially embedded in a larger society," whose "inventory of culturally distinct traits [has] been produced to a significant extent by interaction with other sectors of the society." Her conception builds on Fredrik Barth's (1969) earlier examination of boundaries and boundary maintenance of interacting social groups. Jackson's concern in particular is to understand the process whereby a relatively isolated culture becomes an ethnic group and self-awareness transforms in the direction of ethnic consciousness.

From this perspective, Indians within Latin America can be located on a continuum from isolated, uncontacted Indian populations to full-fledged ethnic groups, on a par with other recognized ethnic groups within the nation-state. The just-contacted Uru-eu-wau-wau are at the extreme Indian end of the continuum. Jackson situates the Tukanoans near the Indian end of the continuum, since they are just beginning to move out of their isolated status. The Panamanian Kuna are further along on the continuum, with a history of developed relations with nation-states (Colombia, Panama, and the United States), fine-tuned through treaties and congresses. [Similarly, the Shuar, through their federation, which is as important to the Ecuadorian state as to the Shuar themselves, have developed into an ethnic group, in ways that sometimes conflict with their sense of themselves as an Indian population] The highland Andean groups, because of the peculiar histories and social, political, and economic realities of the region, seem to be farthest along the continuum.

The focus on the isolated culture-into-ethnic group transformation recalls the indigenism of early-twentieth-century Brazil (Stauffer 1955), discussed in this book by Antonio Carlos de Souza Lima (chap. 9). Based on Comtean notions of progress and unilinear evolution, the idea was that indigenous cultures were bound to disappear, assimilated into the mainstream of nation-state life. Souza Lima maps the Brazilian voices that articulated this early understanding, which is reflected even much later in such anthropological classics as Darcy Ribeiro's (1970) *Os índios e a civilização brasileira* and Roberto Cardoso de Oliveira's (1972) *O índio e o mundo dos brancos*, as well as in North American acculturation studies. Ribeiro (1970: 229–262), in particular, viewed the assimilation process as consisting of five stages: isolation, intermittent contact, permanent contact, integration, and extinction, where "isolated" referred to "tribes that, living in zones not reached by Brazilian society, had only experienced accidental and rare contacts with civilized people" (Ribeiro 1970: 231), and "extinct" to "those that disappeared in the middle of this century as tribal groups differentiated from the Brazilian population," whatever vestiges of an Indian past their descendants may have maintained.

The understanding of cultural contact and the clash of difference as leading inexorably toward homogenization and sameness was firmly entrenched in Mexican indigenism (Nolasco Armas 1981; Briones 1973; Caso 1958; Villa Rojas 1971; Wright 1988) as well: "indigenism . . . has as its objective the integration of indigenous communities into the economic, social, and political life of the nation" (Caso 1958: 27). Wright (1988: 370) adds that this "necessarily implied the denial of an autonomous [Indian] identity." Erasure rather than highlighting of cultural differences would be the outcome of cultural encounters.

By the 1970s, however, it had become clear to Brazilian researchers that the force driving assimilation also met with a countervailing force—resistance. The clear-sighted Eduardo Galvão (1961: 10) recognized this early on: "There are many indigenous tribes that have, up to the present, resisted, and there is nothing to indicate that they will not continue to resist in the future, the process of integration into the Brazilian community," although the outcome, he foresaw, might not always be a happy one. In some cases, resistance would result in the decimation of the resisting tribe.

The notion that cultural forms play a role in resistance, when interpreted through the lens of local cultural difference rather than or in addition to continuity over time, is central to many of the essays in this volume, but especially to those by Howe, Hendricks, and Hill. As described by Hendricks, the Ecuadorian Shuar have developed an explicit political rhetoric critical of the beliefs and practices of the neighboring non-Shuar Ecuadorians—"when my child is disobedient, I don't hit him with a stick to punish him, like an animal." This is not an implicit critique of capitalism, as in Taussig's work, but a differential valuation of cultural norms, and the valorized Shuar norms are continuous with a precontact past: they are culture as handed down across the generations.

A related valorization occurs among the Mexicanos of the Malinche, as described by Hill, in the story of Pillo, who fights "the government of

Puebla." Here, however, it is not precontact norms that are valorized so much as the act of resistance itself, the Malinche people being characterized by appropriated Spanish forms, as in Abercrombie's Bolivian examples. Local resistance to state sovereignty is lauded, but there is no celebration of cultural differences rooted in distinctive time-honored traditions. Here is an explicit ideology of resistance that may need to invent a tradition to justify itself.

To take provisional stock of the processes at work at the interface of cultural difference, there is a basic distinction between assimilation (erasure of contrasts) and differentiation (highlighting of contrasts), which applies primarily to culture understood as embodied practices—wearing molas, playing *kenas*, participating in the fiesta-cargo system, physically disciplining children. But we need to distinguish embodiment from consciousness, where the latter is manifested in talk about similarity and difference, such as political rhetoric valorizing Shuar as against non-Shuar ways of knowing or child-rearing practices. Indeed, the Malinche case reminds us that there can be a consciousness of difference that does not focus explicitly on embodiment, so that the phenomenon of cultural difference does not presuppose the existence of objectively distinct social groups. Consciousness may function as well as a lever to bring about group differentiation, which in turn stimulates differentiation at the level of embodiment.

What role do particular embodied forms play in this process? They can be, in the first place, overt markers of differentiation or assimilation, when they have been explicitly contested, as in the Kuna case or in the long history of Peruvian music described by Turino (chap. 10), and the historical memory of the contestation has been preserved through stories, or when they become objects of what Hendricks calls "counterhegemonic rhetoric," as among the Shuar. But they can also function, in the second place, covertly, as in Taussig's Colombian devil stories, which serve to criticize monetary accumulation for its own sake and the life that goes along with it. In some cases, however, it is difficult to distinguish covert differentiation—where the meaning of a form depends on cultural difference—from persistence or continuity that has not been contested. Turino notes that "it may have been precisely *because* Andean arts were ignored or marginalized in the context of a rigid hierarchy that they have been maintained to the surprising degree still evident today." At the same time, that difficult-to-determine quality is precisely what makes the covert approach so effective for powerless people in situations of domination. It is less susceptible to overt repression.

In Barth's (1969) formulation of ethnicity, there is no special role given to the state; ethnicity is a characteristic of culture contact more generally. In Adams's conception—ethnicities as "subgroups within the purview of the state"—as in Williams's (1989) view, however, the processes operating at the interface of difference are special, characteristic of the last few hundred years of world history, when the globe has been chopped up into a recognized system of differences, each unit territorially defined and controlled by a state. The "nation-state and Indian" problem cannot be understood just in terms of the idea of culture contact. Many Amerindian societies may not be ethnic groups, but the state still looms for them like storm clouds gathering on the horizon, darkening the skies, and threatening apocalyptic destruction.

Our usage of the term *nation-state* is limited to the social formations that originated in Europe during the fifteenth and sixteenth centuries, in their absolutist form (P. Anderson 1979), transforming during the eighteenth and nineteenth centuries in the direction of modern nation-states, with the development of notions of citizenship (Bendix 1977, 1978) and of administration subordinated to the rule of law. Anthropologists (Lowie 1927; Service 1971, 1975; Claessen and Skalník 1978; R. Cohen 1978b) have long used the term *state* to refer to societies of an advanced degree of complexity—characterized by a relatively continuous administrative apparatus distinct from the broader population coupled with incipient urbanism and control of force by a central authority—so that it has been possible to speak of pre-Columbian states, especially among the Incas and Aztecs. However, the specific characteristics of indigenous encounters with nation-states are linked to the peculiarities of the state system that grew up in Europe and took root in the New World.

Three characteristics of the state are especially important in this regard: (1) its claim to monopoly over the legitimate use of force within its territorial boundaries, (2) its assertion of autonomy relative to other states (cf. Held 1989: 215–216; Giddens 1987: 121; Weber 1978: 56), and (3) its gradual development of citizenship (Bendix 1977, 1978) as the form of membership in the collectivity. The implications of this for formerly autonomous Indian groups, within the territorial boundaries claimed by the state, are made plain by David Maybury-Lewis (chap. 8) for Argentina, Brazil, and Chile: "over the centuries the conquerors and settlers have been trying to break up Indian communities and abolish the very category of Indian, arguing that Indians should cease to be Indian and become undifferentiated citizens of their respective countries," subject to the rule of the state and recognizing its claim to monopoly over force. We are not dealing with autonomous groups, each recognizing the other's right to exist autonomously within distinct territorial bounds. Here one group has a historical autonomy (the Indian group) that the other (the state) seeks to curtail, insisting on its own sovereignty.

In numerous instances, Latin American states have in fact used superior military force to gain control over indigenous peoples, as Maybury-Lewis describes for Argentina and Chile and Adams for Central America. But there are also the more subtle mechanisms of indigenism, which Souza Lima describes for the Brazilian case. Without intervening militarily, the state, through its agents, nevertheless brings about the gradual attraction and "pacification" of its Indian populations, smoothing their assimilation into the national society. Since the state possesses superior military force, it always has a fall-back position, but it is a position that Brazil, at least, has been loathe to assume. While the colonial states sought to directly subjugate Indian populations for labor—throughout Latin America, but especially in the Andes and Mexico—the purpose of the postcolonial nation-states has been more regularly to transform the Indians into citizens and to gain sovereignty simultaneously over their lands, and these goals could be accomplished, in some cases more effectively, through means other than the direct application of force.

At the same time, for Indians, recognizing the inferiority of their own military might, "there is only one quick way . . . to obtain an advantageous position of power with respect to the state: [they] must obtain support from a third power, an alternative source that can provide sufficient backing that the state must, in a sense, at least pause and pay attention" (Adams, chap. 7). Howe describes this for the Kuna between 1915 and 1925, who received support in their struggle against the Panamanian state from the United States. And this has happened in the 1970s and 1980s with backing that Indian groups in Brazil and elsewhere have received from organizations in Europe and the United States (notably, IWGIA, Survival International, and Cultural Survival). The attempt by Indians and their supporters is to deny one of the pillars of the state, namely, its autonomy with respect to other states. By bringing international pressure to bear—the appeal being to a global public opinion, to which, it is hoped, the state will be responsive—the goal is to secure Indian rights, up to and including the kind of relative autonomy achieved by the Kuna.

While Indians from one perspective are but one of many social, cultural, and ethnic groups in each of the countries of Latin America, part of the peasant population in Mexico and Guatemala, agricultural workers in Panama and Colombia, and urban working class poor and unemployed in Bolivia, they have had and will always have a special place in Latin America. Indians are special because they are the original owners of the land. They continue to represent and embody the preconquest past of the region. Moreover, they actually and symbolically provide much of the unique nature of Latin America. In certain countries (Guatemala, Bolivia) they are a majority; but even in a country such as Brazil where they are but a tiny minority, they have a significance far beyond their numbers.

It is no doubt for this reason that, while Latin American states have been historically opposed to Indians on the question of autonomy, they have not always been opposed to Indianness (i.e., to the persistence of traits understood to be of Indian origin). Hendrickson (chap. 11) describes the role of Mayan-derived clothing in Guatemalan national identity, especially the *"Miss Universo"* beauty pageant, whose winner "represents her country in the world competition decked out in Guatemala's 'national costume'—*traje*," or indigenous dress. The key issue here is the local identity of Guatemala relative to other countries within the state system, embodied diacritics of Indianness (in opposition to non-Indian Guatemalans) being appropriated nationally. The force of difference is at work not at the interface of Indian and nation-state—as in the Kuna example discussed by Howe or the Shuar case studied by Hendricks—but rather at that between state and state, "Indianness" being valorized as national symbol.

The nation-state, as a peculiar social formation distinguishable from other state forms, requires a sense of nationalism on the part of its citizens, a sense of belonging to what B. Anderson (1983) felicitously dubbed an "imagined community." The latter relies on the media—originally print, but more and more in the twentieth century radio and television—to fuse itself into a single entity. Internal processes of pulling together the diverse elements of the nation were complemented by external processes of differentiating the nation from others, especially the parent European states out of which the new Latin American nations were born. Indianness played a critical role in this complex process, contributing to the formation of a national identity.

The process of internal pulling together goes hand in hand with what Turino calls, for Andean music, *folklorization*—the relocation of native customs (typically music and dance, but other art forms as well) from their original contexts to new urban contexts, usually under the direct sponsorship of the state. What were formerly manifestations of continuity with a pre-Columbian past, or diacritics of ethnicity, distinguishing a subgroup within a national context, become now markers of a folk tradition—one of a number of such traditions—making up the nation. Despite their association with one sector of society, the cultural elements come to be identified with the whole society, metonyms of the imagined community.

Hobsbawm (1983) and his colleagues have coined the expression "invented tradition" to refer to practices "of a ritual or symbolic nature" that were formally instituted or emerged "within a brief and dateable period—a matter of a few years perhaps" (1983: 1). Folklorization shares some properties with invented traditions, but, whereas in the latter emphasis is on the creation of a common historical past for the collectivity, in folklorization the tradition is regarded as part of a menagerie, one of several semi-independent traditions that taken together make up the whole. Folklorization allows the distinct parts of the nation to be juxtaposed, without suggesting that any one of them defines the totality.

A related but distinguishable process is *exoticization*, which is connected with touristic interest. Hendrickson describes the exotic image the tourist industry builds up in promoting Guatemala. Where folklorization is part of the process of internal pulling together—assembling in the city the different traditions of which the nation is made—exoticization is part of the external process of differentiation, wherein difference holds an allure or appeal, exercises an attractive force. Exoticism can be linked to the interest that one part of a nation has in another, distinct part, but it also pertains to the external image of the state relative to other states. What motivates the exoticized nation or ethnic group is in part the economic benefits accruing to tourism; but the motivation for the tourist is the attractive force—an almost aesthetic fascination—exercised by the difference itself.

Folklorization and exoticization are two processes operating within the nation-state that tend to preserve aspects of indigenous culture. These processes run counter to the basic interests of the state in assimilating ethnic groups and effacing cultural difference. Yet while the state has interests in effacing differences, it also has interests in fostering them; while it may seek to expunge native customs, it also has a stake in perpetuating them. In the encounter between states and Indians, we cannot judge on a priori grounds in what measure a given cultural element functions in terms of continuity or resistance, and in what measure in terms of exoticization or folklorization. The issue demands empirical investigation on a case by case basis.

The shifting ideological valences of sameness and difference are the focus of Urban's (chap. 12) study of Amerindian languages in Brazil, Paraguay, and Peru. While states seek to homogenize and efface language differences as a means of fashioning imagined communities— the monolingual standard, in which the language becomes "an index of one culture and of one people"—they also make use of the attractive potential of difference, seeing "the relationship between languages as meaningful, and, in particular, as signaling the basis of social cohesion in the newly emergent collectivity formed from the fusion of the two previous ones." The state's relationship to difference is thus ambivalent. On the one hand, it understands its basis of cohesion to lie in homogenization and sameness, but that homogeneity can be stifling and provoke resistance. On the other hand, it recognizes the attractive potential of difference, which, however, is also potentially threatening to the sovereign jurisdiction of the state. The two tendencies are in dynamic tension, forcing perpetual reconfigurations at the level of the nation-state itself.

The concept of emergence is central to theoretical understanding of the issues raised in this book. None of the terms in our title, *Indians*, *nation-states*, and *culture*, are monolithic and static categories, but rather dynamic, in that they are constantly changing and adapting and, in this sense, emerging. Nation-states, in particular the Latin American nation-states examined here, are an amalgamation and conglomeration of peoples, languages, lands, histories, politics, and economies. Competing groups within the state apparatus pursue their own strategies in attempting to influence it. From the point of view of native peoples, states do not appear to be monolithic or goal-driven, but rather heterogeneous and random, guided by impenetrable and changing motives. The non-Indian is perceived to have a complicated, diverse nature that includes competing ideologies as manifested in ideas with regard to practices needed to be carried out toward Indians. The state is heterogeneous, composed of different and conflicting factions, intertwined with local power groups.

The concept of Indian is, even more strikingly than that of nation-state, constantly emerging and changing. Until the arrival of Europeans, there were no "Indians." The concept is a European invention. In the Americas, before 1492, there were only individual groups, Kuna, Shuar, Shavante, and so on. One of the interesting developments of the last five hundred years, and one that is focused on in many of the papers in this volume with regard to contemporary Latin America, is the way in which the concept of Indian has emerged and is emerging in the awareness and practices, not only of nation-states, but of the Indian peoples themselves.

Since both nation-state and Indian are emerging concepts and entities within Latin America, the relationship between them is, all the more so, an emerging one. Because the various actors in the relationship between Indians and nation-states are so different from one another in outlook, viewpoint, and action, their interrelationships make state-Indian relations inherently dynamic. Among the actors, there are ongoing major institutions such as the church and missionary organizations, educational institutions, and the military. There are also the press and the media, more generally. While regarded traditionally as observers, even anthropologists prove to be actors in the unfolding drama.

As we have argued here, a most fruitful way to conceive of the emergent quality of nation-state and Indian relationships is in terms of a continuum from Indian population to ethnic group. In addition to historical factors, one important aspect of the transformation from Indian to ethnic group seems to be geography and ecology, including demography. Thus, an important distinction is that between highland and lowland. Lowland Indian groups are numerically much smaller than highland groups. They are closer to the ecology, and they are dependant on natural resources. These Indian groups are the only populations in Latin America that are not actively destroying the environment. As a rule, lowland populations are more isolated and closer to traditional precontact situations than are highland Indians, since many of them have disappeared altogether under the pressure of acculturation. In contrast to lowland Indians, highland Indians are numerically much larger populations, and they have been part of the definition of the state and intimately linked to everything associated with it (from language to occupation to goods purchased) since the early colonial period. They are often landless, and can be classified as peasants, urban working class, or migrants.

Another useful geographic distinction for approaching Indian and nation-state relations is that between the Atlantic and the Pacific coasts, a distinction particularly relevant to Central America. The Pacific side is the side of mestizoized, ladinoized populations, committed to the developing nation-state, and of the large urban centers that are the fast-growing capitals of nation-states. The Atlantic side, strikingly so in countries such as Nicaragua and Panama, is the side of Indian populations that are relatively independent of the nation-state as defined and practiced on the Pacific side. The Atlantic side is also the side of relations and alliances with other international entities, beyond the boundaries of the local nation-state.

If anthropology must change in order to take account of Indian nation-state relations, as argued in several of the essays in this book but especially in the one by Diskin, it is also the case that to fully understand these relations we need anthropology. Anthropologists have developed ways of understanding symbolic behavior, and its methods are relevant to understanding not only Indian cultures and ethnic groups, but to analyzing strategies employed by states and to comprehending state-Indian-ethnic group relations as well.

The anthropological perspective is also important in another way. While some and perhaps many aspects of Amerindian culture formerly attributed to autochthonous developments can and must be reanalyzed in terms of state-Indian encounters, we should not imagine in our exuberance at this discovery that all aspects of Amerindian culture can be understood in this light, or, conversely, that classical culture theory and ethnographic research have nothing to offer. In fact, from a political, as well as an anthropological perspective, it is as pernicious and "colonial" and solipsistic to imagine that everything about the Amerindian experience can be explained by the state-Indian encounter as it is to ignore the role of the state altogether. With that caveat, however, the state-Indian encounter offers fresh insights and new vistas of research, which are reinvigorating anthropology simultaneously as they are challenging it.

No amount of crystal ball gazing reveals to us the shape of our future world, much as we would like to know how difference and similarity will play themselves out. As modern nation-states have consolidated over the past two centuries, they have on balance favored assimilation and homogenization as integrative mechanisms—the Paraguayan linguistic situation and the folklorizing/exoticizing trends notwithstanding. Stutzman (1981: 47) put this very well for Ecuador: "from the perspective of the nation, contemporary ethnic and cultural diversity is interpreted as a burdensome residue of the republic's colonial past and as an impediment to its future progress." At the same time, such self-understandings on the part of states of their own bases of integration may be historically specific and subject to change—residues of nineteenth-century evolutionism à la Comte, rather than intrinsic characteristics of the state.

When the state's goal is homogenization, difference appears as resistance. The "ethnic discourse," described by Diskin, is inherently a discourse of resistance. At the same time, homogenization is the attendant of powerful and captivating ideas about equality and rights, which emerged in the seventeenth and eighteenth centuries and served as shining ideals for generations of thinkers motivated to construct a just world. The equality of citizens entailed their interchangeability and hence sameness, with its attendant ideal of homogenization. As we approach the new millennium, one wonders whether new ideals are taking shape. If the world has grown weary of the abuses stemming from the overconcentration of power in states, from their efforts at integration through forced assimilation, can we imagine a new set of ideals in which difference is not only protected, but also positively regarded as integrative, where cultural variability is possible without strife and degradation—which it was the goal of the Hobbesian absolutist state to overcome—and where the positive ideals of citizenship and access can be protected without its incumbent oppression through leveling?

Many intellectuals during the 1970s and 1980s made preliminary moves in this direction. One thinks of Foucault and the attack on power, and we can see the problematic running through the debate over the canon within the humanities. But there is also the parallel turn toward indigenous advocacy on the part of anthropologists and others, which resulted in the creation of international support groups (Survival International, Cultural Survival, and IWGIA—International Work Group for Indigenous Affairs), as well as organizations within Latin America and especially Brazil (Wright 1988; Urban 1985). Several contributors to this volume, indeed, came to the nation-state and Indian question through their practical activities on behalf of native peoples. Here we find the implicit celebration of difference as a normative ideal.

But it is a far cry from such celebrations to a vision of the role of cultural difference within the modern state-centered world. The essays in the present volume modestly propose, as a precursor to such a vision, empirical studies of state-Indian relations in Latin America. At the same time, there is the continuing hope that an intuitive appreciation of difference has been kept alive in the real world, and that it can be nurtured through a vision (or visions) of a just world. Judith Friedlander ended her work, *Being Indian in Hueyapan*, with an anecdote about an Indian woman named Doña Zeferina, who, while in Mexico City, met a man—the proud owner of a Mexican hairless dog:

> Never having seen one before, Doña Zeferina told the gentleman that she thought the dog was very ugly . . . The owner . . . was quite surprised by Doña Zeferina's reaction and told her that this was a real Aztec dog, domesticated by *her* ancestors; she should be proud of it. Doña Zeferina replied that first of all she was *not* Aztec and secondly the dog was *still* ugly! (1975: 184)

The incident effectively summed up Friedlander's argument that, in Hueyapan understanding, Indianness is not linked to continuity with a pre-Columbian past, but is instead defined in terms of social class. At the same time, one wonders lingeringly about the anonymous man in the story. Was he only engaged in a marginal form of exoticization, or did he also keep alive an appreciation of cultural difference, conjoined with a sense of tradition? Should we see in him the shadow of colonial domination, his remarks a covert form of superciliousness, or are they glimmerings of hope that the Mexican nation can be construed from the point of view of difference, if only as a museum housing artifacts of the tribes of humanity? And, more generally, do the smoky images in the crystal ball foretell the tightening grip of forced assimilation, or can we glimpse in their hazy shapes a great garden of lushly flourishing pluralism? One hopes that the future is not foreordained, that it depends, in part, at least, on us as scholars and intellectuals, that we can fashion visions of a just world, much as earlier thinkers developed an understanding grounded in human rights, that that world is one in which differences can prosper without degenerating into Hobbesian chaos, and that, finally, in peering into crystal balls, we are really peering into ourselves, taking control over the cultural forces that are, after all, partly of our own making.

Note

Because the situations described in this book are rapidly changing, it is important to note that all of the papers were in final form by 1989, some of them as early as 1988. It is impossible in a scholarly work of this sort to be completely au courant. We beg the reader's indulgence.

References

Anderson, Benedict
  1983   *Imagined communities: reflections on the origin and spread of na-
          tionalism.* London: Verso Editions.
Anderson, Perry
  1979   *Lineages of the absolutist state.* London: Verso Editions.
Banton, Michael
  1983   *Racial and ethnic competition.* Cambridge: Cambridge University
          Press.
Barth, Fredrik
  1969   Introduction to *Ethnic groups and boundaries: the social organization
          of cultural differences,* F. Barth (ed.), 9–38. London: Allen & Unwin.
Bendix, Reinhard
  1977   *Nation building and citizenship.* Berkeley: University of California
          Press.
  1978   *Kings or people.* Berkeley: University of California Press.
Briones, José de Jesús Montoya
  1973   Hacia un nuevo planteamiento y fundamentación del indigenismo.
          América Indígena 33(1): 13–43.
Cardoso de Oliveira, Roberto
  1972   *O índio e o mundo dos brancos: uma interpretação sociológica da
          situação dos Tukúna.* São Paulo: Livraria Pioneira Editôra.
Caso, Alfonso
  1958   Ideals of an action program. National Indigenous Institute of Mexico:
          a report. *Human Organization* 17(1): 27–29.
Claessen, Henri J. M., and Skalník, Peter
  1978   The early state: theories and hypotheses. In *The early state,* H. J. M.
          Claessen and P. Skalník (eds.), 3–29. The Hague: Mouton.
Cohen, Abner
  1974   The lesson of ethnicity. In *Urban ethnicity,* A. Cohen (ed.), ix–xxiii.
          London: Tavistock.
Cohen, Ronald
  1978a   Ethnicity: problem and focus in anthropology. *Annual Review of
          Anthropology* 7: 379–403.
  1978b   State origins: a reappraisal. In *The early state,* H. J. M. Claessen and

P. Skalník (eds.), 31–75. The Hague: Mouton.
Cowell, Adrian
1984 *The decade of destruction.* (A series of films: *The search for the kidnappers, The blazing of the trail, In the ashes of the forest, The mechanics of the forest,* and *The storms of the Amazon*). Color videos. Nomad Films Ltd.: 46 Anson Rd., London N7 OAB, England.
Friedlander, Judith
1975 *Being Indian in Hueyapan: a study of forced identity in contemporary Mexico.* New York: St. Martin's Press.
Galvão, Eduardo
1961 Prefácio. In *Os índios Tenetehara: uma cultura em transição,* by Charles Wagley and Eduardo Galvão. Rio de Janeiro: Ministério da Educação e Cultura.
Giddens, Anthony
1987 *The nation-state and violence: volume two of a contemporary critique of historical materialism.* Berkeley: University of California Press.
Held, David
1989 *Political theory and the modern state: essays on state, power, and democracy.* Stanford: Stanford University Press.
Hill, Jonathan D., ed.
1988 *Rethinking history and myth: indigenous South American perspectives on the past.* Urbana: University of Illinois Press.
Hobsbawm, Eric
1983 Introduction: inventing traditions. In *The invention of tradition,* E. Hobsbawm and T. Ranger (eds.), 1–14. Cambridge: Cambridge University Press.
Lowie, Robert
1927 *The origin of the state.* New York: Harcourt, Brace and World.
Nash, June
1979 *We eat the mines and the mines eat us: dependency and exploitation in Bolivian tin mines.* New York: Columbia University Press.
Nolasco Armas, Margarita
1981 A antropologia aplicada no México e seu destino final: o indigenism. In *Antropologia e indigenism na América Latina,* C. Junqueira and E. de A.Carvalho (eds.), 67–85. São Paulo: Cortez Editora.
Ribeiro, Darcy
1970 *Os índios e a civilização brasileira: a integração das populações indígenas no Brasil moderno.* Rio de Janeiro: Editôra Civilização Brasileira S.A.
Service, Elman R.
1971 *Primitive social organizations: an evolutionary perspective.* New York: Random House.
1975 *Origins of the state and civilization: the process of cultural evolution.* New York: Norton.
Sherzer, Dina, and Sherzer, Joel
1976 *Mormaknamaloe: the Cuna mola.* In *Ritual and symbol in native Central America,* Philip Young and James Howe (eds.), 21–42. Uni-

versity of Oregon Anthropological Papers 9.
Smith, Raymond T.
  1984   Anthropology and the concept of social class. *Annual Review of Anthropology* 13: 467–494.
Stauffer, David Hall
  1955   The origin and establishment of Brazil's Indian Service, 1889–1910. PhD diss., University of Texas at Austin.
Stutzman, Ronald
  1981   *El mestizaje*: an all-inclusive ideology of exclusion. In *Cultural transformations and ethnicity in modern Ecuador*, N. E. Whitten (ed.), 45–94. Urbana: University of Illinois Press.
Taussig, Michael
  1980   *The devil and commodity fetishism in South America.* Chapel Hill: University of North Carolina Press.
  1987   *Shamans, colonialism and the wild man: a study in terror and healing.* Chicago: University of Chicago Press.
Urban, Greg
  1985   Developments in the situation of Brazilian tribal populations from 1976 to 1982. *Latin American Research Review* 20(1): 7–25.
Villa Rojas, Alfonso
  1971   Antropología aplicada y indigenismo en América Latina. *América Indígena* 31(1): 5–44.
Weber, Max
  1978   *Economy and society,* G. Roth and C. Wittich (eds.). Berkeley: University of California Press.
Whitten, Norman E., Jr., ed.
  1981   *Cultural transformations and ethnicity in modern Ecuador.* Urbana: University of Illinois Press.
Williams, Brackette F.
  1989   A class act: anthropology and the race to nation across ethnic terrain. *Annual Review of Anthropology* 18: 401–445.
Wright, Robin
  1988   Anthropological presuppositions of indigenous advocacy. *Annual Review of Anthropology* 17: 365–390.

1. An Ideological Triangle: The Struggle over San Blas Kuna Culture, 1915–1925

James Howe

Introduction: Ideology and Indian-State Relations

The vexed questions concerning ideology often take the form "What is the relationship between ideology and X?"—X most often being truth, reality, material conditions, interests, relations of production, or action. The last of these, action, most concerns me here. Defining ideology loosely as strongly held and strongly felt ideational aspects of culture, especially images, beliefs, and attitudes concerning collective selves, collective others, their social orders, and what to do about them, I am concerned with how ideology informs and shapes action.[1] This question has special relevance to the subject matter of this volume, relations between ethnicities and national or international powers, a field of study in which social images have in various ways been connected with action and practice (e.g., Whitten 1976; Said 1978; Todorov 1984; Sahlins 1985; Hawkins 1984; Comaroff 1985; Stoler 1985).

On one level, questions about the relationship between action and ideology, action and meaning, have only one answer: "No simple distinction between instrumental and symbolic practice makes sense . . . instrumental action is always simultaneously semantic, and vice-versa" (Comaroff 1985: 125). Orientations toward selves and others, moreover, are often embedded in forms and practices rather than openly articulated. At another level, however, it remains to be seen just how far and in what ways collective ideas shape action, and how much is fortuitous, random, or driven by other forces. In this chapter, I consider these issues in the light of an extended confrontation from 1915 to 1925 between the government of Panama and an indigenous people who resisted its authority. I argue that the actions taken by the actors in this struggle, though they obviously follow from their interests and material condition, make sense only if one takes into account their collective ideas and preoccupations, and, going one step further, the factors motivating those preoccupations.

Pacification and Civilization

In 1903, the year of Panamanian independence from Colombia, the San Blas Kuna were virtually independent. Living in several dozen island and mainland villages scattered along the eastern Caribbean coast of the Isthmus, the Kuna maintained a heavy commercial involvement with outsiders, and they formally acknowledged Colombian sovereignty, but they escaped effective national control almost entirely.

The new government of Panama, lacking the resources required to rule the San Blas coast, found itself powerless to change this situation, at least in the short run. Of necessity, it evolved a long-range policy of incorporating the region largely by changing indigenous culture. Also of necessity, it began with the two Kuna villages most open to the outside, Nargana and Nusatupu (the latter soon to be renamed Corazón de Jesús). These twin islands, located a few hundred yards apart in Western San Blas, soon became the cockpit of the region, the focus of controversy and struggle, where acculturative measures were first tried out. And the newly elected chief of Nargana, Charlie Robinson, a young man educated abroad in English, emerged as a principal actor in the struggles that followed.

Initially, the government worked through missionary intermediaries (Howe n.d.), first arranging for a contingent of Kuna boys to be enrolled in a Catholic school in the city, and then in 1907, sending a Jesuit missionary, Padre Leonardo Gassó, to Nargana (Gassó 1911–1914). Gassó worked intermittently in San Blas until 1911, his successors for a few years more. Provoking tremendous antagonism and turmoil, he ultimately failed to establish a permanent mission, but he did drive an opening wedge into Kuna separatism, and in 1909 the government established an outpost, Puerto Obaldía, on the Colombian border at the eastern end of San Blas.

In 1913 a British Protestant missionary, Anna Coope, was invited into Nargana by Robinson. Like Gassó, Coope inspired opposition and antagonism, but because she emphasized schooling more than he had, she also attracted adherents. Her success was short-lived, however. In 1915, President Belisario Porras toured San Blas, establishing a government headquarters, called El Porvenir, at the western end of the region, with a governor or *intendente*, and arranging to install police posts and schools on Nargana, Corazón, and two more progressive islands. As competition rapidly developed between government and mission schooling and several violent episodes ensued, Coope's schools were suppressed in 1919, and from about 1921 on, she and her co-workers were subjected to a form of house arrest.

From 1919 to 1925, the government imposed a policy of pacification and forced acculturation, first on Nargana and Corazón, and later on several other islands. Conservatives there resisted, as did the rest of San Blas. One confederacy, led by Cimral Colman of Ailigandi, moved from partial cooperation in 1915 to opposition, resistance, and finally rebellion. The other group, led by Inapakinya of Sasartii, although it moved in the opposite direction, from a tenacious pro-Colombian stance to cooperation with the Panamanian government against Colman, resisted intrusions and change within its own sphere just as stubbornly.

In 1925 Colman's confederacy, aided by an American explorer named Richard Marsh, revolted against Panama, killing a number of policemen and putting the rest to flight. With the assistance of the U.S. Minister, who arrived on a cruiser, the Kuna and the government negotiated a treaty that, to everyone's surprise, ended the conflict and led to further negotiations over the following years and decades.

In this chapter, I examine the period of secular acculturation, 1915 to 1925, in particular its ideological aspects. I am concerned with the images and ideas each party to the struggle had of its collective self, of the others involved, of what was at stake, and how those images and ideas informed action. This ideological emphasis is especially appropriate in this case, because to a surprising extent, what antagonists fought about was Kuna cultural practice. Material interests (trade in forest products, coconuts, and turtle shell; two banana plantations; possible future colonization and development; and not least, potential Kuna voters) mattered, of course, but the essence of the confrontation was cultural, both as a means to the end of political incorporation and for its own sake.

The struggle, never completely bilateral, involved third parties at almost every stage, among whom the most important were the North Americans, represented in this chapter by the explorer Marsh. In effect, one finds a triangle constituted by Panamanian acculturators, their Kuna opponents, and pro-Kuna North Americans.[2] I argue that although actors on the three sides agreed on the fundamentals at issue in San Blas (Kuna separatism, their rejection of outsiders, their leanings toward North American culture and power), each refracted the situation through a distinct ideological lens. Different factors, moreover, determined the shape of the lenses—for Panamanian functionaries, reaction against the U.S. presence on the Isthmus; for North American friends of the Kuna, immigration and race relations in the United States; and for the Kuna themselves, domestic organization and an identification of women with land, foreigners with spirits.[3]

The Kuna and the World

If the Kuna lack a monopoly on ethnocentrism, they have certainly developed it to a high degree. Then and now, they have struck observers as proud and aloof, sometimes to the point of xenophobia. They regard themselves as the *olotule*, "golden people," chosen by God, with whom they have a special relationship, and they call outsiders by the deprecatory term *waga*, a name well known to the *wagas* who dealt regularly with them. They could, in context, be quite amiable, even partially exempting English-speakers from their disdain, and the totality of their attitudes to change and foreigners was much more complex than public ideology suggested. Nonetheless, what struck outsiders, and what the Kuna projected, was insular pride.

Consonant with this attitude, they systematically equate non-Kuna with evil spirits (Howe 1986: 54, 61–63; Severi 1981,1988). A leader traveling to the city, for instance, may say that he is going to the stronghold of the illness spirits, and a person who dreams of a *waga* is actually encountering a malevolent devil called a *nia* (see Gassó 1911–1914, XI: 229). Kuna cosmology, moreover, externalizes supernatural danger (Howe 1986: 51–56), putting the blame for most illness and misfortune on spirits threatening from outside.

Many cultures, of course, equate foreigners and oppressors with evil spirits. Examples from Latin America include the ladino earth god of Mesoamerica (Vogt 1976: 16–17, 33) and the capitalist devils explicated by Taussig (1980). The Kuna, in fact, portray good spirits as well as evil in ways that echo their experience with European powers. Illness is vanquished through the mediation of helpful shaman-familiars (see Chapin 1983: 93–97, 309–368; Nordenskiold et al. 1938: 344–351; Sherzer 1983: 110–138); invisible allies who though in many ways stronger and more virtuous than humans (Howe 1986: 38–46) are obligated by Kuna verbal control to do their bidding. The carved wooden figures representing the shaman familiars often strikingly resemble eighteenth- and nineteenth-century Europeans in frock coats (Nordenskiold et al. 1938: 423–426), and some recent rituals have included large balsa statues of Douglas MacArthur and other powerful foreigners (Keeler 1969: 47–51).

Lévi-Strauss, in his famous analysis of a Kuna birth chant (1963), conveys the impression that the shaman-familiars conquer the evil spirits in invisible military campaigns culminating in pitched battles, an interpretation elaborated by Fritz Kramer (1970: 80–82). Chapin (1983: 329–330, 332–337), however, points out that except in a single chant-cure, the spirits are defeated through trickery and superior magic rather than force (see also Nordenskiold et al. 1938: 345–347). In the *nek apsoket* mass exorcism, for instance, which is the culminating contest with the invisible world (Howe 1976), spirits are overcome by throwing a party and liquoring them up with alcohol converted from smoke.

Oversimplification is a real danger here. The shaman-familiars are not just ethereal Europeans and North Americans, and the world of curing and spirit danger has its own logic and imperatives (comprehensively delineated by Chapin 1983; see also Severi 1981, 1988). Conversely, the inference that non-Kuna are completely dehumanized, that "the stranger is never a man for the Indians" (Severi 1981: 93), overstates the case. The relationship of foreigners to spirits is one of resemblance and partial equivalence, not identity. Nonetheless, the striking parallels between the realms of cosmology and foreign policy do reinforce a political stance of opposition to outsiders, while at the same time encouraging a flexible response combining diplomacy, trickery, force, and the manipulation of third-party allies. In previous centuries, third parties included colonists, pirates, and merchants, especially those who spoke English; in the twentieth, the obvious choices have been North Americans and Panamanian political parties.

In dealing with foreigners, Kuna men have been most concerned to protect their land and women, values whose commonplace nature can easily mask their cultural singularity and complexity. Since the early nineteenth century, outsiders have found Kuna men anxiously protective of their wives and daughters: Padre Gassó, with only moderate exaggeration, claimed that turn-of-the-century leaders were prepared to kill all their women rather than let them fall into foreign hands.[4] Significantly, the first non-Indians to establish themselves in San Blas were a priest, Gassó, who took pains to advertise his celibacy, and a female Protestant (Coope 1917).[5] The government teachers who arrived in 1916, all women, inspired distrust but not fear. With the male police, however, things were very different. They appear in Kuna oral tradition as a slavering horde, assaulting and appropriating women with impunity, just as they did in Kuna complaints to sympathetic outsiders during the 1920s.[6]

Reality was more complex—complex enough, in fact, to require detailed examination in a separate paper. Certainly, police ranks included a good many drunks and no-goods, whose boorishness could offend teachers as well as Kuna women, and in two cases from 1921 and 1923, a drunken policeman did indeed rape a woman in a jail cell. Both culprits were immediately removed from their posts, however; lesser miscreants were continually being weeded out; and veterans on the force, some of whom brought their wives and children with them, were less predatory. None of this cut much ice with the Kuna: concerning the rape cases, they focused on the crime and not the official response, and the most consensual or even symbolic relations outraged them. Thus, perceptions of sexual danger (which long antedated the police presence), however accurate or inaccurate, interpreted and shaped reality as much as they reflected it.

Not surprisingly, Kuna objected to mixed offspring as well as sexual contact, pointing with disdain to the mixture of races and ethnicities in the Panamanian melting pot. The equivalent in Kuna cosmology of Panama's human amalgam was the succession of "mixed" (*opuralet*) peoples, part-animal, part-human, part-spirit, who populated the world in the first eras of history, persisting as neighbors and threats to the earliest Kuna (see Howe 1986). "To mix" (*opure*) is also to confuse, to confound, to cause trouble, all of which the Kuna hoped to avoid by preserving their ethnic singularity.

Drawing boundaries in such terms is not, of course, limited to the Kuna: Indian castes (Mandelbaum 1988), American white Southerners (Dollard 1937; Williamson 1984), and colonial powers (Stoler 1989), among others, have represented and enforced racial and ethnic separation in terms of sexual nonaccess. But sexualized boundaries are not invariant or universal: Stoler (1989) shows, for instance, that the legitimacy of relations between colonizers and colonized and the ideology of sex and race changed as European empires in Asia evolved over time. Many ethnicities, similarly, give greater weight to other markers of difference. It is particularly interesting to find the Kuna placing the emphasis on sex, marriage, and physical difference as part of an ideology and structure, not of domination but of resistance.

In the Kuna case, this complex undoubtedly has roots in their history, notably the period in which they intermarried with French settlers (Stout 1947: 52–53; see also Severi's discussions, 1981,1988), which apparently ended when the Kuna turned against the settlers and killed them. I would also suggest, following an argument elaborated by Turner (1979; see also Rivière 1984: 87–100) that it is reproduced and anchored in, perhaps even generated by, the strategies and structures of domestic organization, which in the Kuna case means senior control of junior generations through matrilocal residence.

The Kuna matrilocal household, whose core consists of parents, daughters, and sons-in-law, depended in this era on an arrangement through which senior men and women exploited the labor of junior men by controlling access to their daughters (see Howe 1985; Howe and Hirschfeld 1981). Whereas young girls married soon after reaching puberty, boys generally had to wait until eighteen or twenty. In the intervening years, they worked with their father and other household males, as well as for themselves, demonstrating their industriousness to potential parents-in-law. Young women, meanwhile, were guarded and kept away from boys as much as possible. Eventually, a girl's parents asked a young man's for his arm, and in the marriage ceremony he was captured and dragged down the street, after which he worked for his wife's father until ready himself to succeed to headship of a household. Although the system could be subverted, to the extent that it worked it depended on control of access to marriageable young women.

In this respect, ethnic boundary-drawing replicated domestic strategy: in both, marriageable young women were protected on the inside, while men who might wish to have those women were kept on the outside. The crucial difference, of course, is that in the domestic sphere select young men would eventually be let in, while in the political, exclusion was permanent.

If Kuna women and the inviolability of their bodies signified ethnic difference and separation, by extension, their clothing did the same. Kuna male dress differed from that of Latins only in detail, but women's costume—which includes a gold nosering suspended from a hole in the septum, coin necklaces, huge gold earrings and chestplates, elaborate constricting bindings of wrapped beads on forearms and lower legs, printed skirt, red headcloth, and, as centerpiece, an elaborate sewn blouse, the mola—was strikingly different. This dress complex, which only appeared in the nineteenth century, developed partly as a response to culture contact. As numerous students of the mola have pointed out, the skirts and headclothes, the beads for leg bindings, the necklace coins, the gold jewelry, and even the cloth for sewing molas all come from external sources, and in recent decades foreign motifs have proliferated in mola design. Thus, one might regard women's dress either as a compromised symbol or as a symbolic mechanism mediating the oppositions and contradictions between inside and outside (Hirschfeld 1977; Sherzer and Sherzer 1976). Nonetheless, in its totality, women's dress was and is interpreted by both Kuna and outsiders as a fundamental sign of difference and separation.

After women, the value the Kuna were most intent on preserving was the land (see Howe 1986: 51–56). According to theology and cosmology, the land they occupied was a sacred trust from the deity, Great Father, which they were to care for (*akkwe*), watch over (*etarpe*), carry/maintain (*see*), and admonish (*unae*). The earth is itself one embodiment of God's wife, Great Mother, whom at the creation God put in place and admonished on her duties. Hunting, agriculture, and gathering of medicine plants, as forms of proper maintenance and respect, resemble filial obeisance, while mining, lumbering, and invasion by outsiders are violations, which the Kuna compare to cutting open a belly, rape, and incest (Howe 1986: 68). Thus, preservation of the land and protection of women, rather than distinct values, are in Kuna theory two aspects of the same thing, two enactments of the same coherent worldview.

The elements of the ideological complex sketched in here are important not only because they were embodied in Kuna dealings with others, but also because those others responded in turn. Later sections will show that each aspect of that complex—scorn for *wagas*, fear for women, opposition to intermarriage, and attachment to the land—provoked a strong reaction from the police who occupied San Blas and by the same token struck a chord with the North Americans to whom the Kuna turned for help.

Nationalism and Forced Acculturation

The Panamanian program in San Blas from 1915 to 1925 was notable for its cultural intolerance and for the extent to which the process and content of civilizing involved a tension between Latin and North American models, features that are best understood in the context of the problematic nature of Panamanian nationhood. I take it as axiomatic that all modern states foster national consciousness, new states most of all. Typically, the attempt is partly planned, even manipulative, partly unconscious and collective, partly a tool to facilitate control, partly a response to a felt need. And as Benedict Anderson (1983) argues, twentieth-century states have had to meet already established standards of authenticity: the task thus includes justification and self-explanation (Geertz 1973a,1973b,1973c,1973d) as well as integration.

In some respects, Panama's task was just normally difficult. A distinct if subordinate unit up through the nineteenth century, Panama had enjoyed considerable autonomy and periods of independence. True, foreign intervention had ultimately been needed to break free from Colombia, but other states have overcome compromised beginnings. Ethnically, Panama was fairly heterogeneous (Jaén Suarez 1979), but the majority of the population spoke the same primary language, and no significant primordial loyalties (Geertz 1973c) threatened national unity.

The continuing U.S. presence after 1903, however, which was much more pervasive and blatant than it has since become, cast everything into doubt. Worthy of only a U.S. "legation" and a "minister" rather than an embassy, Panama used the dollar as its currency, its government was kept afloat by lump payments for the Canal, and financial difficulties forced it to accept a U.S.-nominated fiscal controller. Its army was disbanded, its police disarmed, and the United States reserved the right to conduct maneuvers or expropriate lands anywhere in the country, even to intervene in civil disturbances (see McCain 1937; Conniff n.d.).

The Canal brought in another element perceived as a threat to national integration, forty to fifty thousand West Indian blacks, most with British citizenship, who were linked to the North American presence and who spoke Spanish as a second language or not at all. Today Antillean Panamanians have achieved considerable success integrating themselves into national society, but for several decades, perceived as a large intrusive foreign element in the body politic, they inspired at best, concern, and at worst, racist xenophobia (Conniff 1985: 64–66; Biesanz and Biesanz 1955: 213–231).

With the Antillean and North American presence, language and territory, both classic national symbols, gained special prominence. Anderson (1983) has noted that most Latin American countries share the same national language and thus, unlike many Asian and European states, do not differentiate themselves linguistically. In Panama, however, the most significant foreign others spoke a different tongue, highlighting Spanish as a nationalist symbol (Biesanz and Biesanz 1955: 224, 227). Territorial integrity, similarly, became doubly significant as the seemingly permanent North American enclave put that integrity out of reach.

If Panamanians reacted against the North American presence, they also identified with it, in a love-hate relationship. Panama's elites, like their counterparts throughout Latin America already proponents of modernity and progress (Burns 1980), could not help admiring and emulating the example of these virtues closest to hand, while at the same time taking note of the scorn and condescension with which North Americans viewed them and their country.

It is not surprising that the acculturative program in San Blas spanned the years 1915 to 1925, an era of assertive nation-building during the ascendancy of the Liberal party in Panama. A middle-class party, expansionist, commercial-minded, and anticlerical, with strong support among the lower classes and people of color, the Liberals were less closely tied to the North Americans than their conservative predecessors, and they increasingly resisted political domination while welcoming foreign investment (see Conniff n.d.). Their leader, Belisario Porras (President 1912–1916, 1918–1920, 1920–1924), appropriately memorialized for "the vocation of nationality" (Sisnett 1956), took a strong personal interest in acculturating the Kuna. And as Panama began to assert itself against the United States, a number of events further stirred up antagonism, notably the so-called Guerra de Coto with Costa Rica in 1921, which the United States foolishly attempted to mediate, and unsuccessful canal negotiations in the mid-1920s.

In this context, one can understand that the Kuna rubbed salt in the wounds of Panamanian pride. To its chagrin, the government found itself unable to effectively incorporate San Blas into the nation—a lack that threatened the country's territorial integrity as well as its sovereignty—or even to make a show of force in the region without borrowed North American vessels. Many Kuna villages continued to fly the Colombian flag up to 1920 (long after the Colombian government had lost interest). Unlike Panama's other two indigenous groups, who were unobtrusive *salvajes*, the *semi-salvajes* or *barbaros* Kuna arrogantly and loudly rejected civilization, and their contemptuous term for outsiders and their refusal to marry them were well known. All of this was publicly underscored during two successive presidential visits to San Blas (by Carlos Mendoza in 1910 and Belisario Porras in 1915), when several Kuna villages turned the official parties away, vehemently repudiating the president and Panamanian identity (*Diario de Panamá* 8/17–20/1910; *Excursión á la costa San Blas de Panamá* 1916: 7,11–13).

To make matters worse, the Kuna were strongly associated with just those forces that most compromised sovereignty. For several centuries falling within the British sphere of influence along the Central American littoral, the Kuna had allied themselves with pirates in the seventeenth and eighteenth centuries, and San Blas was the site of the brief Scots Colony in 1698–1700. The Kuna kept up commerce with English-speaking traders, many men shipped out as sailors, and English loan words dot their language.

In the twentieth century, the gringophile Kuna leader who initially played the largest role in external contacts, Charlie Robinson of Nargana, spoke almost no Spanish: his first interview with President Amador was conducted in English, the language in which he thereafter corresponded with the government. With the failure of the Catholic mission in San Blas, Robinson's alliance with the Protestant missionary Anna Coope further reinforced the apparent connection between Kuna intransigence and the Americans, an identification confirmed by two brief uprisings led by Robinson in 1919 against Panamanian impositions and in favor of the mission (see below). In an apologia published immediately after the 1925 revolution, the *intendente* or governor pointed to the fact that Coope received her mail direct from the Canal Zone postal service as evidence for a sinister American plot, and Castillero (1946: 27) alleges that the Indian leaders of the revolution were supported "most of all by a fanatic Protestant missionary woman who was instructing them in her religion." In fact, Coope, who was actually British, had little influence outside Nargana, and the real revolutionaries in 1925 perceived Robinson as an ally of the government (Erice 1975).

Thus, the intensity of the government's need to establish effective national control and to make Panamanians out of the Kuna is quite understandable. Just as San Blas, another uncontrollable enclave, resembled the Canal Zone, so the culturally and linguistically distinct and American-influenced Kuna were uncomfortably like the intrusive West Indians and Zonians. Today, Panama has to a considerable extent embraced cultural and ethnic pluralism as aspects of national identity, but in the 1920s it insisted on a single Latin cultural model, based on the Spanish language and traits from the country's mestizo interior. At the same time, however, since the acculturative program enacted modernity as well as national identity, it was inherently ambivalent, with some elements borrowed from North American culture, others opposed to it.

The Targets of Suppression

The process of forced change involved both the suppression of Kuna practice and the imposition of Panamanian alternatives, and, of course, in some instances, as when molas were taken off to put dresses on, the same action did both things simultaneously. But suppression and substitution were not always identical or synchronous, and for the purposes of this analysis, treating them separately facilitates understanding. I begin with the Kuna targets of police enmity.

At the highwater of their control in 1924, the police suppressed almost everything that seemed distinctively Kuna, from indigenous curing to gift exchange. In terms of both sequence and intensity, however, the police clearly had priorities, which, I suggest, were ideologically motivated. First, the occupying forces suppressed practices such as lice grooming or public nude bathing, which, because they offended their own sense of modesty or delicacy, were interpreted as tokens of barbarism. Second, they eliminated anything symbolizing ethnic separation or rejection of national sovereignty. And third, they opposed parallels to Latin institutions, things equivalent but different, such as Kuna village police. Within these categories, three cultural complexes inspired special antipathy—drinking and puberty ceremonies, women's dress, and territorial claims.

Conflict over land and coastal waters initially developed, not with the government, but with coastal black populations, who clashed with the Kuna as they came into San Blas after sea turtles and such forest products as ivory nuts and *níspero* latex. But the potential for difficulties with the government was soon apparent. A report from 1913 recorded with disapproval that "they believe themselves absolute masters of the forests and seas" and that the extractive activities the Kuna call theft were legitimate use of national resources.[7] An account of President Porras's 1915 tour of San Blas, similarly, noted ironically that Porras proposed "to visit *their lands*, as they call them" (*Excursión á la costa* 1916: 7).

The government, as it established control of the region, was sympathetic to Kuna economic needs, excluding non-Indians from farming inside San Blas, imposing penalties on thefts from Indian plantations (Decree #2, 3/05/20), and in the heated matter of turtle fishing, passing several measures that compromised between black and Indian interests.[8] But it adamantly opposed Kuna claims to control lands or waters outside their farms and villages, a position combining interest and ideology. Sales and leases of untitled and thus government-controlled lands called *tierras baldías* offered a source of revenue during this period (see Heckadon 1983): in San Blas, concessions were granted for a manganese mine, two banana plantations, and an abortive agricultural colony. Both government and private investors anticipated great things from the San Blas "gold coast" (*Panama Star and Herald* 8/27/24).

Even when economic interests were not immediately threatened, however, government functionaries took great offense at Kuna claims to control the territorial waters and *bosques nacionales*, because such control was the unique prerogative of a sovereign national government (something already lost, of course, in the Canal Zone). Efforts by Cimral Colman to secure legal title for San Blas using funds raised by levying coconut quotas on his villages, which suggested extralegal taxation, offended them even more. Since both sides saw control of the land as essential to their integrity, as a nation or as a people, conflict on this point was inevitable.[9]

Another key point of contention was *women's dress*. Secular authorities adamantly opposed "so horrible [a] manner of dressing" (Mojica: Castillo, 7/09/21), which they interpreted, correctly, as a fundamental symbol of cultural separation. They objected to tradecloth skirts on grounds of modesty, because they sometimes came untied in public (Mojica: Castillo 4/05/21), and they repeatedly fined men for cutting their wives' hair, but surprisingly, they paid little or no attention specifically to mola blouses.[10] What most revolted them were the "ugly and unhealthy" noserings (Vaglio: Colman 2/03/19) and bead leg bindings, which, because they deformed the flesh, became prime symbols of uncivilized and offensive crudity (Markham n.d. 1: 14, 24), much as foot-binding had for foreigners in China.

This issue, which had been a matter of relative indifference to both Catholic and Protestant missionaries, rapidly gained salience in the secular period.[11] After President Mendoza's visit to San Blas in 1910, a newspaper article asserted that Kuna women lived shorter lives than did men because of limb-binding (*Diario de Panamá* 8/17–20/10), and a reconnaissance report from 1913 noted with approval that Nargana appeared totally civilized, except for the women, with their "legs cinched up with cords and laces" (Hurtado: SecGJ 8/05/13). In April 1919, three years after public schools appeared on Nargana, President Porras decreed that female pupils could no longer attend wearing beads or noserings, which provoked a brief and unsuccessful uprising. By 1921, when police forced women on several pacified islands to give up Kuna dress altogether, many conservatives fled Nargana. In April of that year, when a woman from nearby Río Azúcar living in Nargana fled home after her nose ring was taken away, the police followed to bring her back, provoking the bloodiest encounter prior to the 1925 revolution itself, leaving six people dead (see Herrera 1984: 160–181).

A third focus of controversy was *alcohol,* and in particular drinking at Kuna puberty ceremonies, whose Spanish name, *chicha,* refers to the cane beer copiously consumed in them (Prestán 1975; Sherzer 1983: 139–153). A highly involved ritual complex, centering on a chant cycle performed for a pubescent girl, the *chicha* has two basic types, the shorter taking twenty-four hours or less, the longer three to five days. As with women's dress, the development of the *chicha* issue can best be understood as it developed over time, beginning in the missionary period.

Within a few months after his arrival in 1907, Father Gassó targeted both chichas and drinking parties thrown by black sailors (1911–1914, vol. 6: 88; vol. 9: 161–163, 183–184; vols. 12–15). Without moral objections to alcohol, he resented being kept awake by music and noise, and he associated drunkenness simultaneously with his conservative opponents, the defenders of *chichas,* and with modern decadence, represented by Protestant rum-drinking black sailors. After a series of confrontations, he had rum-selling prohibited on Nargana (vol. 17: 135), though by 1910 visitors noted the presence of several *cantinas (Diario de Panamá* 8/17–20/10).[12] Anna Coope, the Protestant who followed after Gassó, was an ardent prohibitionist who made suppression of drinking a keystone of her program. She persuaded Chief Robinson first to cut back on the number of *chichas* and then, in November 1914, to ban liquor altogether, moves that aroused heavy opposition (Coope 1917: 120–125,149–155).

Thus, by the arrival of the police in 1915, even though their outlook on modernism and temperance differed sharply from those of Gassó and Coope, alcohol had already emerged as a fundamental point of contention. The experience of teachers and police agents over the next few years only increased its salience. Drinking at *chichas*—public, enthusiastic, noisy, protracted, and with mass participation by both women and men—can easily shock outsiders, even those like the police who themselves drink. (Abstinence in the weeks or months between *chichas,* the norm except on Nargana, doesn't seem to have much impressed them.) Because the event begins when the brew is ready, regardless of day of week, drinking went on openly during school hours, and belligerent visitors or even local people sometimes spoke out while intoxicated. As a Kuna ally of the police recalled years later:

Those of the [unpacified] villages, who did not yet share with us the ideas of advancement, would give free rein to their unrestrained sentiments, loosing their tongues in mortifying words, face-to-face with the police, who armed as they were, and carried along by the current of the *fiesta*, at times did not know how to keep a clear head. One day an altercation of very bad tone took place, in which one of the disputants, a member of the outpost, let off various pistol discharges. In spite of having done them in the air, they caused annoyance and strong commentaries against the servants of the government. (Erice 1975: 287–288)

During these years, young modernist Nargana men who had been studying in the city began returning home, some of them to be recruited into the indigenous police. Oral tradition records that they made at least a few raids on nearby islands to smash pots full of brewing *chicha*. By 1919 the administration imposed prohibition on San Blas (Int: Garrido 4/ 02/19), prompting Kuna leaders to petition repeatedly in favor of *chichas*, which they justified as time-honored custom (e.g., SecGJ: Int #162, 2/04/ 21) but to no avail. When Indians on islands with police detachments pressed ahead with plans for *chichas*, confrontations sometimes ensued, most notably in 1920 on Ukkup Senni or Playón Chico, when the police, after shooting a pro-*chicha* Indian, ended up besieged in the schoolhouse until reinforcements arrived (see Herrera 1984: 149–160; Erice 1975: 286–287).

Thus, *chichas*, like women's dress, achieved their prominence through a truly dialectical process, in which one side's move provoked an equal or stronger countermove from the other, amplifying and focusing opposition. In each instance, the violence that eventually erupted only confirmed the conviction that compromise was impossible. This process, in addition to foregrounding *chichas* in a general way as exemplars of cultural difference, associated them more particularly with shame, disorder, and rebellion.[13] The indigenous policemen and other modernist Kuna felt impelled, by suppressing *chichas*, to deny the most blatantly crude feature of the Indian identity they wished to abandon, while Latin police and administrators focused, as both a practical and ideological matter, on disorder (e.g., Int.: SecGJ 2/22/21). Throughout the hemisphere, drinking by minorities and native peoples has for several centuries been blamed for excess, turmoil, and loss of personal and political control (Axtell 1985: 64–67; Taylor 1979: 28–72; Williamson 1984: 209–211). If police and bureaucrats brought with them into San Blas, as part of their ideological baggage, this assumption that alcohol and disorder went together, the association could only be confirmed by their experiences there with Kuna drinking.

The Program of Impositions

As with suppressions, the aspects of Panamanian national culture that the police forced on the Kuna form a distinct and ideologically consistent set, in which the five most important elements were schools, law and bureaucratic procedure, sanitation, streets, and dancing. In a different way, each asserted national sovereignty, the orderliness of *civilización*, and the dominance of Hispanic over North American culture.

Government schools enacted ideology on multiple levels. Most obviously, they "destroy[ed] the walls that separate the Indian from the white race" (*La Hora* 8/63), socializing children to patriotism, national values, and civilization. Even more important was the linguistic medium of instruction, which the North American presence gave special significance: in the struggles against the English language on Nargana, the Secretary of Education defended the suppression of Coope's schools on the "patriotic" grounds that Spanish was essential.[14] And on still another level, schooling itself was ideologically charged—it was the message as well as the medium. Padre Gassó, as astute as he was prejudiced, clearly recognized and loathed the liberal cult of schooling. He identified it too exclusively, however, with North America (1911–1914: vol. 15, 64), given the importance that "the secular equivalent of the church" had as a token of value, marker of social class, and source of individual and collective improvement in Europe and Latin America as well (Hobsbawm 1983: 271, 293–297, 1987: 174–179). As one *intendente* put it, "without schools there is no civilization" (Vaglio: Alfaro 11/14/20).

The Kuna response, which found them on both sides of the issue, was motivated by cultural values but in a more complex way. Traditional Kuna culture emphasizes apprenticeship in esoteric knowledge as a primary path to prestige and influence. This orientation obviously motivated those Kuna, including some moderates and conservatives, who enrolled their children in school; equally obviously, it inspired other Kuna, who perceived the threat to indigenous culture posed by schooling, to oppose it fiercely. As with *chichas*, agreement about what mattered underlay sharp disagreement about what should be done.

Along with schools, the administration imposed legal and bureaucratic forms of action—laws, decrees, resolutions, contracts, depositions, pay lists, vouchers, advances, and so forth—forms resonant with meaning for frustrated nationalists. The administration placed great emphasis on promulgating and at least seeming to implement rules and resolutions. Similarly, the civil register and the official census, the latter quite spurious as an enumeration of population, were taken very seriously as tokens of governance.[15] Essential features of the culture of bureaucracy, they were what functionaries unquestioningly did in any setting, but in a wider sense, as modes of action appropriate to full-fledged states, they were also tokens of sovereignty and true nationhood.

Emphasis in the administration's program also fell on sanitation and public health.[16] Whereas other observers have perceived Kuna islands as reasonably clean and exceedingly neat by most standards (e.g., Markham n.d.: 11), the police found sanitation appalling and insisted on massive cleanups: trees were chopped down, bushes and kitchen gardens cut out, stripping islands of all vegetation. Apparently quite genuinely horrified by the epidemics that swept through the islands, which included the influenza pandemic of 1919 and several waves of smallpox, the police and *intendente* lacked for the most part the means to genuinely improve Kuna health.[17] The measures they did impose are best seen as a symbolic reenactment of the public health program imposed only a few years before by the U.S. canal administration on Panama (Gorgas 1915; Isthmian Canal Commission 1917). This program, in which teams went house-to-house, forcing inhabitants to change householding practices and cut out vegetation, was the action that most interfered with the private lives of Panamanians and at the same time most obviously benefited them, bringing malaria, yellow fever, and other diseases under control throughout much of the country. In San Blas, the police in effect replicated that program by imposing on the Kuna what had been imposed on themselves, thus implicitly affirming their own advanced sanitary state as well as the existence of others less sanitary.

The cleanups formed part of a complex of physical changes imposed on each pacified island, of which a village park or plaza and houses rearranged in rows along streets were the crucial elements (see Foster 1960). The police and *intendente* could not abide the close-packed islands with small alleys between structures, and more generally they saw themselves as imposing order on a fractious and anarchic people. Their inability to perceive the control and order in Kuna life, although perhaps partially understandable in light of the confrontational nature of their relationship with the Indians, had to be willful—to cast themselves as the forces of order, and state control as the only appropriate kind of order, they *needed* the Kuna to be anarchic.

The most puzzling aspect of the police program is acculturation through social dancing. Earlier in the century, black sailors had occasionally brought gramophones and accordions with them (to Gassó's disgust), but the police dance policy really began in December 1918, when the teacher of the Nargana school, Ana Moreno de James, sponsored a student program of skits, recitations, and a *tamborito* dance entitled *La pollera*. The *tamborito* is a folkloric dance from the Panamanian interior, sometimes called the national dance (Cheville and Cheville 1977; Zarate 1962) and the *pollera* is the national costume (DeLeon 1980) worn by women on festive occasions. Both Coope and the more conservative Nargana Kuna were appalled, some adults objected vocally during the dance (others apparently approved), and the next day the police arrested a man who made remarks on the subject. These events led to a violent demonstration, in which opponents tried to free the prisoner, challenged police authority, and threatened the teachers, overwhelming the local detachment and forcing the *intendente* to put down the uprising personally. (The pro-nose-ring action mentioned above occurred a few months later.)

In the same period, the literate young turks returning from the city to Nargana began to organize themselves, in 1920 creating a club combining political and social functions, which soon began sponsoring dances. Also in 1920, Nargana held its first carnival, with an elected queen in her chariot, apparently supervised by the schoolteacher, who peers from one of the photographs of the event. Many Kuna men objected to letting their wives, sisters, and daughters dance, which they saw as an immoral act, but the police began enforcing attendance with confinement in jail or stocks, and as they extended their control to other islands, they established on each one a club with obligatory dancing to the music of a wind-up victrola.

Why dancing? Why recreation rather than faith or labor?[18] Here as elsewhere, multiple factors joined and interacted. In terms of an exterior, non-Indian model, urban political clubs sponsored by candidates and parties proliferated during this period. Fulfilling social as well as political functions, these clubs would have been quite familiar to police agents. As for Kuna equivalents, the police dances obviously replaced the *chicha* and its dancing, in a kind of secular version of the doctrine of superposition.[19] More fundamentally, I would argue that the dancing combined two somewhat disparate themes, Panamanian nationalism and modernity. In terms of the former, it is not merely that the *tamborito* and other *interiorano* dances are quintessentially Panamanian, but that carnival is arguably *the* key representation of national identity. The first carnival on Nargana was a nationalist beachhead in the conquest of Kuna culture, and each weekly dance prefigured and prepared for the main event.

The club dances, however, featured the fox-trot and jazz as well as folkloric forms.[20] This was, of course, the "jazz era," the time of "the dance craze" throughout Europe and the Americas, and almost everywhere both dancers and their appalled elders saw the new steps and music as embodiments of change and modernity. Padre Gassó (1911–1914: xiv, 18), among the appalled elders, saw this clearly, recognizing that to the extent that the craze had a national locus, it was the United States. Thus, I would argue, the dance clubs in San Blas simultaneously imposed the particularity of Panamanian national identity and the American-tinged generality of international modernism and progress.

Finally, the dancing was, in indirect form, quite sexual—Kuna preoc-cupations were in this context both prescient and self-fulfilling. Dancing under duress, with couples touching and holding each other as they never did in the *chicha*, offered an unmistakable sexual threat, a breach in the symbolic barrier between Kuna and *waga* to which parents and husbands vehemently objected.[21] The police, moreover, undoubtedly knew what they were doing: when they took Indian wives or (consen-sually) fathered mixed-race children, their superiors congratulated them for helping to make Panamanians out of the Kuna.[22]

The dances built up a deep reservoir of resentment, which burst its restraining dam during the revolution. In fact, just as each aspect of Kuna ideology provoked a Panamanian reaction, so the conclusion to this paper will show that key features of the government program produced their own antithesis in the actions of Kuna revolutionaries.

Vikings and Interlopers

The third side of the ideological triangle belongs, of course, to North Americans. With them we encounter a greater variety of actors, aims, interests, and viewpoints, and as a result, a polyphony of voices. I concentrate on a pivotal actor, Richard O. Marsh, the explorer and engineer who abetted and helped lead the Kuna Revolution, with some attention to his allies and associates. By the nature of events, Marsh was the only one to create a coherent, detailed depiction of the Kuna and the situation they faced. The elements he drew on, however, were all shared with other participants in events, and I would argue that his portrayal can be adequately understood only in terms of the culture and major social currents in the United States during the 1920s.

Marsh's involvement with the Kuna began in 1923 while traveling through the Darién region in search of land suitable for planting rubber. A chance encounter with several light-skinned Indians at Yaviza, inter-preted in the terms of folklore about white Indians, persuaded him to go back to the United States and organize an expedition to find the lost tribes he was sure were hiding in the forest. Returning to Panama in early 1924, Marsh and his party established a base camp below Yaviza, and then in late March they ascended the Chucunaque, eventually crossing the *cordillera* into San Blas on the Caribbean side, losing two members of the party to disease in the process. The San Blas Kuna soon gained Marsh's sympathy, and after interviews, first with Inapakinya, leader of one Kuna confederacy, and then Cimral Colman, leader of the other, he was shown some albinos—who are, as is now well known, not a distinct group but a genetic minority constituting less than 1 percent of the Kuna population. Marsh and Colman's confederacy put together a party of three albino children and five nonalbino adults to visit the United States, with the intention of lobbying the U.S. government on the Kuna's behalf under cover of studying "the White Indians."

Through the second half of 1924, the party attracted considerable publicity as it toured the American East, finishing up in Washington, D.C., where Smithsonian scientists conducted studies—Ales Hrdlička on Kuna physical anthropology, Francis Densmore on their music, J. P. Harrington and a colleague from the Post Office Department, Paul Vogenitz, on their language. Marsh spoke on behalf of the Kuna at scientific congresses, lined up supporters, and attempted to get the delegation a hearing at the State Department. A small committee was organized to supervise studies of Kuna albinism, consisting of Hrdlička, C. W. Stiles of the Public Health Department, and Charles Davenport of the Carnegie Foundation, the latter the leading eugenicist of the day (see Kevles 1985: 44–56; Rosenberg 1961: 89–97). The committee chose Davenport's son-in-law, Reginald Harris, as biologist for a second expedition.

In January 1925, Marsh, his party, and the Kuna delegation returned to Panama. In late February, after Marsh wrote and dispatched a declaration of independence to the city, the Kuna revolted. With the successful conclusion of the revolution and negotiations mediated by the U.S. Minister, Marsh managed to depart through the Canal Zone, escaping Panamanian retribution.

The principal sources for Marsh's portrayal of the Kuna and their situation are a book he later wrote (1934); passages from his field notes; various articles, manuscripts, and interviews; and, most important, the text of the "Declaration of Independence and Human Rights of the Tule [i.e., Kuna] People of San Blas and the Darien." This curious document, twenty-five handwritten pages in English, supposedly transcribed and translated from Kuna dictation by Marsh but very obviously composed by him, consists in large part of an extended history of the Kuna people, leading up to their recent oppression and decision to rebel.[23]

Throughout, Marsh insisted on the racial nature of threats to the Kuna. Panama he perceived as an essentially "negroid" country, with a thin stratum of white oligarchs on top,[24] and he insistently portrayed the policemen as blacks, though in fact mestizos predominated.[25] Playing up the notion of invasion and population movement, he made much of the different groups of turtlers, rubber-tappers, and plantation workers intruding into Kuna lands, in which light the policemen appear as merely the most dangerous of the dark-skinned populations threatening to overrun the Indians. And the pacification program itself he characterized as a form of "negro mongrelization."

Marsh's allies (at least those who left written records) saw things in similar terms. Reginald Harris's major work up to that point was a long article for the *Eugenical News* (1922) in which he explained the relative backwardness of various South American countries in terms of the extent in each of race crossing; his father-in-law Charles Davenport wrote President Coolidge and others during the Kuna revolution inveighing against the "licentious thieving negro police" in favor of a people "friendly to whites" rising up "to protect its property and the honor of its women."

Marsh's racial fixation can, to some extent, be seen as a product of his particular life history.[26] Except in his outspoken vehemence, however, he was typical rather than exceptional. Then and now, one of the facts about the Kuna to which outside observers most often point has been their refusal to marry non-Indians, interpreted as "a culture trying to keep itself racially pure and unassimilated."[27] And to an extent that people today find hard to grasp, open and unapologetic racism was the norm in the 1920s, not just in the South but throughout the United States (Perrett 1982).

In this context, the relevance of supposed Kuna whiteness is obvious. Marsh, who entitled his book *White Indians of Darien*, thought at first that the Kuna would unlock the secret of the origins of white races (1935), and he never gave up the idea that a white tribe or village lived at the headwaters of the Chucunaque and the Bayano, even after Harris's investigations in the second expedition strongly indicated otherwise (R. Harris 1925). During the Kuna visit to the United States, newspapers consistently referred to the party as "The White Indians" even when they noted that nonalbinos predominated. From start to finish, a patently racist fascination with white-skinned members of a normally nonwhite population impelled (in some cases even obsessed) explorers, reporters, newspaper readers, and almost everyone else touched by the episode.

Some of the individuals involved attributed this whiteness to Norse voyagers. The chatty memoirs of Major Johnson (1958), a member of both expeditions, reveal him as a Viking enthusiast, as was Harrington's collaborator Vogenitz: a newspaper article published during the Kuna visit lists the supposed parallels discovered by Vogenitz between Kuna and several European languages, notably Norse and German (*Washington Evening Star* 12/19/24).[28] In his book, Marsh only alludes in passing to Vogenitz's claims (1934: 220) and to the alleged "Sanskrit or Aryan structure, not *mongoloid* [original emphasis]" of the Kuna language, but in an unpublished paper written in the same period (1935) he develops at great length the idea that pre-Columbian Viking voyagers, among them such culture heroes as Quetzalcoatl, had left their genes behind with the Kuna.

It might be argued that in the heyday of diffusionism such speculation was fairly harmless. On the other hand, Teutonism, the glorification of supposedly Nordic peoples, began in the nineteenth century, and by the 1920s, in the form of assertions that "old Americans" derived from Nordic stocks (Grant 1916; K.Roberts 1920), it was a staple of nativist ideology (Higham 1955: 264–299; Chase 1977). Claims that Leif Erikson had discovered America, moreover, often constituted not-so-subtle propaganda against immigrants of the non-Nordic "Mediterranean" race (Higham 1955: 277). Thus, the choice of Norsemen as culture heroes, however innocent on the surface, resonates unpleasantly, as does Marsh's choice of a swastika for the Kuna revolutionary flag, even though that symbol was not yet identified with Nazism in particular as opposed to Aryanism in general. At the very least, the choice of Vikings was of a piece with fixation on white skins. Marsh, who had read a good deal of at least popular social theory, was a social Darwinist: he believed that races progressed or regressed, with collective choice and will strongly affecting the direction of social evolution, and that the Kuna were "the last remnant of a once great and highly developed people" (Declaration of Independence of the Tule, p.1).[29] Unable to portray contemporary Kuna society as civilized, he could do the next-best thing, claiming great intelligence for them, as well as high morals, a democratic polity, and general nobility.[30] In the words he put in their mouths, "Only in material and scientific development have we fallen behind." Leaning heavily on Hrdlička's investigations (1926), which found a close physical resemblance to the Maya, he linked the Kuna with the supposed "white-influenced" civilization that had built the great pre-Columbian monuments of the Americas. All this is in total contrast with "a questionable Panaman [sic] civilization, interpreted and administered by negro representatives of a race, who but a few years back were degenerate and degraded savages in Africa."

In sum, Marsh and his allies portrayed the Kuna as a plucky, noble, and long-established but also embattled people, descendants of an ancient civilization. If regrettably not white, they were strongly linked metonymically with the quality of whiteness, and they had Viking blood in their veins. Clinging to their racial purity, the Kuna were resisting a flood of dark-skinned interlopers who threatened to overwhelm them, take their land and women, and wipe out their distinctiveness.

Obviously, some elements in this depiction are objectively wrong: most policemen were not black, there are no pure white villages in the interior, the Kuna do not claim descent from pyramid-building high civilizations. But the errors matter less than the construction put on facts. And what is most striking about that construction is how much it resembles the understanding of their own situation held in that era by many "old-stock," white Anglo-Saxon "native Americans."

Questions of race are obviously relevant. White fears of blacks, especially unrealistic fears of black men preying on white women, were whipped into near-hysteria throughout much of the South in the period 1879–1915, provoking a wave of lynchings (Williamson 1984). Although lynchings subsided somewhat after 1915, in the South the separation of the races and the domination of one over the other continued to be symbolized in terms of a taboo on intermarriage, differential sexual access, and the purity of Southern white women (Williamson 1984; Dollard 1937). In this period, moreover, population movements became ominous, as many blacks migrated north, threatening to upset the southern political economy.

Anti-immigrant fears, which were at a peak in the early 1920s, also echo in Marsh's depiction of the Kuna predicament. After World War I, a strongly revived antagonism toward immigration was increasingly phrased in biological and racial terms. Eugenics and racist speculation, supported by the results from World War I intelligence testing, provided a rationale for exclusion of Southern and Eastern Europeans, envisioned as essentially dark-skinned peoples, with particular animus against Jews: "America is confronted by a perpetual emergency as long as her laws permit millions of non-Nordic aliens to pour through her sea-gates. When this inpouring ceases to be an emergency, America will have become thoroughly mongrelized" (K. Roberts 1920: 97). During the early 1920s, Davenport, Harry Laughlin, and other eugenicists played key roles in convincing Congress and President Coolidge of the need to restrict immigration, in a campaign that reached fruition only a few months before the arrival of the "White Indians," with the passage of exclusivist legislation in April 1924 (Higham 1955: 300–330; Kevles 1985: 96–97, 102–104; Chase 1977: 252–301).

The parallels between the depiction of the Kuna and the self-depictions of nativist Americans can hardly be laid to chance. Whether or not Marsh, Davenport, or anyone else explicitly voiced the parallels (I have not found any examples), their perceptions of their own selves strongly shaped their understanding of the Kuna alter. Consciously or unconsciously, Marsh tailored his descriptions of the Kuna plight to appeal to widely shared values and preoccupations, and the Indians aroused sympathy from himself as well as from others in considerable part because that plight could be understood in familiar and emotive terms.[31]

The nativist-immigrant opposition that informed understanding of the Kuna found its echo even among the social scientists studying them, surfacing in a ferociously anti-Semitic letter to Harrington from Vogenitz (1/14/25), in which the latter accused the Boasians ("that bunch of New York Jews") of sending spies to keep watch over and disrupt work on the

Kuna language, as part of a plot to preserve Middle American anthropology for themselves, to the exclusion of Gates, Morley, and Harrington. What Vogenitz had in mind was one theater in a more generalized competition between an establishment of Anglo-Saxon anthropologists, strongly represented in Washington, D.C., and Cambridge, and Boas's circle, in which Jews and immigrants were prominently represented. Harrington, in particular, felt an intense personal rivalry with Sapir.[32] Not merely a matter of ethnic representation, this opposition involved sharp differences on relevant political issues: Boas publicly attacked eugenics and nativist chauvinism, and his school's emphasis on culture challenged both the evolutionism and social Darwinism still espoused by some of the establishment anthropologists, as well as the hereditarian and racist theories then dominant in other social sciences (Cravens 1978).

In his collaboration with the Kuna, Marsh came to see them clearly as friends and comrades, but as a people, a significant category of others, they could be understood only in terms of the ideologically charged social oppositions of the United States in the 1920s. Ironically, for all that Marsh and the Panamanian police disagreed about everything else, they shared a perception of the Kuna colored by an affinity with white North Americans.

Ideology and Truth, Action, Third Parties

Throughout this chapter, I have used jarring discordant notes in actors' understandings of the situation in San Blas as indicators that ideology had come into play. The police were neither uniformly black, as Marsh insisted, nor all rapists, as the Kuna claimed. Among Panamanian misconceptions, Coope did not mastermind the 1925 rebellion, Charlie Robinson did not oppose *civilización*, and Kuna women did not die young from the effects of leg-binding. As a people, the Kuna are neither dirty and disorderly nor the descendants of Vikings and Mayan pyramid builders. As telling as these little sharps and flats are, however, I share Geertz's unwillingness to identify ideology in terms of its truth value or lack of it (Geertz 1973b; Giddens 1979: 185,192; Comaroff 1985: 4), to define it, in other words, as a systematic form of obfuscating false consciousness. The ideologies at work in San Blas were in part true, in part false, and in large part empirically untestable. Rather than telling lies or the truth, they put differing constructions on the facts and attached different values to them.

As Geertz argues strongly (1973b), the undesirable consequences of defining ideology in terms of truth value include a strong impetus to dichotomize between those with false views of the world and those who, in their fashion, see things as they are. This tendency appears, for instance, in otherwise admirable works by Michael Taussig (1980), Richard Price (1983), and Keith Basso (1979), which in different ways celebrate the clear-eyed realism of oppressed or embattled peoples, and at least in Taussig's case, contrast the fetishized delusions of their oppressors. All three obscure the point that even good guys see the world through ideological lenses, and that even when one side is in the right, its monopoly on virtue does not extend to the truth.

Ideology's presumed influence on events holds scholarly interest as strongly as its relationship to truth, though general pronouncements strongly outnumber intensive examinations of how ideologies inform and shape action, which is what I have attempted here. In the 1925 revolution, the decisive culmination of the Kuna-government struggle, rebels struck during carnival, a choice of moment and context with great ideological resonance. By attacking the police while they were dancing and drinking, they simultaneously turned the tables on the men who had suppressed *chichas* and imposed social dancing, violated a key Panamanian nationalist symbol, and as Alexander Moore (1983) has pointed out, they replicated the structure of the Kuna exorcism ritual, in which one gains control of evil spirits by liquoring them up (Howe 1976). Rebels killed children of mixed marriages, cut up policemen's bodies, and helped their own women put nose rings and molas back on, all expressions of outraged values concerning women, sexuality, and ethnic separation.

The effects of ideology can be seen, not just during the Kuna revolution, which might be interpreted as a brief moment of indeterminacy, the equivalent of Cortez's or Captain Cook's appearance from nowhere (Todorov 1984; Sahlins 1985), but over periods of years or decades. In San Blas, ideology guided actors to suppress one thing sooner and more insistently than another, to draw boundary lines through one domain and not another, and to yield or adamantly insist on one point but not another. Rival conceptions of the Kuna, their situation, and their links to others informed and guided action at every step.

The point is not that ideologies overpower material needs and interests (or vice versa), still less that events ever embody preexisting structures more than partially and imperfectly. The events and actions scrutinized in this paper show a great deal of contingency: undoubtedly, Kuna rebels also chose carnival because it made tactical sense and because it followed a few weeks after the return of Marsh's party to San Blas. Police opposition to the *chicha*, similarly, derived partly from liquor's ideological associations, partly from experience in the pacification process, and partly from historical accident—Padre Gassó, who first put drink on the acculturative agenda, opposed it not out of conviction but because his worst enemies (Protestant sailors and die-hard Kuna pagans) happened to drink, and for reasons even more personal and contingent, because carousers disturbed his sleep. Thus, in Sahlins's terms (1985), not only can events determine structure, but structure joins with other factors in influencing, not determining, events.

The process that yields events and outcomes, moreover, is thoroughly interactive: the plans, interests, perceptions, and values of one side work with or against those of the other. Kuna scorn for outsiders and their pejorative label, *waga*, grated on Panamanian sensibilities, and Indian concern with questions of race and endogamy struck a chord with both Panamanians and North Americans. The *chicha's* obvious equivalence with carnival, similarly, increased its prominence as a target, and the struggle for lands and waters heated up precisely because *both* sides saw an unbroken territory as a token of collective integrity. Above all, in the struggles over dress, drink, and dancing, one side's actions only increased the other's counteractions, progressively narrowing the scope of conflict—in effect, opponents developed a perverse consensus, an agreement that certain issues rather than others were worth fighting about, just as two opposed armies, through repeated skirmishes, settle on a place to do battle. When Geertz called for the serious examination of "ideologies as interacting symbols" (1973b: 207), he seems to have meant interaction within a single cultural system, but the phrase also sums up nicely what I am promoting here, which is taking seriously the articulation of contending cultural forms (Comaroff 1985: 6; Sahlins 1985).

Pushed one step further, my argument might seem to support the strongly interactive models of ethnic identity and boundary maintenance advanced by Barth (1969), who derives cultural differences between groups from interethnic relations, and by Hawkins (1984), who portrays Guatemalan Indian and ladino identities as "inverse images" generated by the pressure of Hispanic colonial ideology. In contrast, I find the Indian/Latin contrast in San Blas much less perfect and symmetrical than Hawkins's model, and Kuna culture less plastic than Barth's model would suggest. Even those Kuna traits taken as social diacritica responded as much to internal dynamics of Kuna social life as to external relations: though opponents fought much harder over *chichas* than singing gatherings, they did not reverse the relative importance of the two rituals. Similarly, for all that Panamanian disgust spotlighted nose rings and leg bindings, women's dress already functioned as an ethnic marker, and an item to which the police paid little attention, the mola blouse, has since become *the* prime symbol of Kunaité.

My emphasis on opposition and articulation, finally, should not obscure the point that third parties, third forces, third presences (sometimes distant or invisible) conditioned binary interaction. It is not that the Kuna were incapable of distinguishing policemen from spirits or prospective sons-in-law, that Panamanians could not tell Kuna from gringos, or North Americans tell Panamanians from European immigrants. But the experience of one social type influenced the perception of the other. Even a partial metaphor, an unrecognized equivalence, could structure their thinking and actions.

Complexes of this sort, I suggest, are the rule rather than the exception. It is not only that ethnic triangles (or quadrangles or pentangles) turn up throughout the world, not only that a state's relations with an ethnicity are often complicated by another state or ethnicity. More generally, it is that every binary social relationship is conditioned by elements external to the relationship itself, whether they derive from other contemporary relationships, past history, or an ideological preoccupation.[33] In perceptions of *the* other, which in most cases means the other immediately at hand, experiences with other others, however close or distant they may be in space and time, very often intrude.

Notes

Acknowledgments: For their thoughtful comments on this paper, I would like to thank Mac Chapin, Lawrence Hirschfeld, Jean Jackson, Ann Stoler, Paul Sullivan, and the participants in the conference on "Indians and the State in Latin America" at the University of Texas, Austin, April 29–May 1, 1988. A presentation by Francisco Herrera at the International Congress of Americanists, September 1982, first stimulated me to think seriously about nationalism and Panamanian indigenist policy 1903–1930, and his work since then has strongly influenced my thinking. I am grateful to Regna Darnell and Elaine Mills for advice and information.

1. This very general definition implies that ideology, far from being something distinct and separate, overlaps meaning, sentiment, cognition, and so forth. As Giddens (1979) argues, in studying ideology one is not looking at a distinct order of things, a closed symbolic system, but at an aspect of symbolic systems. The term *ideology* is useful here in focusing attention on the relationship between symbols and understanding on the one hand and political action on the other.

2. Among the documents cited here, communications between Panamanian functionaries derive from the archives of the Intendencia, Porvenir, unless noted otherwise. The abbreviations "Int" and "SecGJ" stand for Intendente and Secretaria de Gobierno y Justicia, respectively. Communications identified by the digits 819 come from Records of the Department of State relating to the Internal Affairs of Panama, 1910–1929, found in the U.S. National Archives. The numbers beginning with 819 identify file and document. The digits 80A–15 identify documents from the files of the Panama Canal Company, also in the National Archives.

3. Space limitations have forced me to overhomogenize the three sets of actors and their positions, neglecting, for instance, slightly more tolerant

members of the Panamanian government. Nonetheless, I believe that in general terms the positions sketched here do hold for each group.

4. Padre Gassó discussed their fears about women and outsiders at some length (Gassó 1911–1914: vol. 2, p.10; vol. 10, pp.185, 206–207, 227, 228). See also: O. Roberts (1827: 44); Coope (1917: 161); Misioneros Hijos del Corazón de Maria (1939); B. Perez: Pres. B. Porras 2/14/13, p. 67; Markham (n.d.: 6, 27).

5. Gassó (1911–1914): vol. 2, p. 12; vol. 5, pp. 57, 58; vol. 6, p. 20.

6. William Markham: Belisario Porras 2/01/24, Tioga Point Museum; Markham: Porras 2/08/24, Records of Department of State 819.00/1180); Marsh (1934: 222, 232); Decl. Independence; Marsh: Lassiter 2/02/25, 819.00/1163; interview of Reginald Harris, 819.00/1176; South: Sec.State 3/13/25, 819.00/1180; Markham (n.d.: 3).

7. E. Navas: B. Porras 5/10/13, Porras Archives, University of Panama.

8. Int: SecGJ #167, 4/16/21; SecGJ: Int #362b, 4/23/21; and numerous other documents in the archives of Porvenir.

9. In Kuna-government disagreements over land, the Kuna could sometimes stand on the side of private property, the government communal tenure: a report on a 1913 reconnaissance (Hurtado: SecGJ 8/15/13) noted that the government would have to convince the Indians that beaches (sites of disputes over turtling) were natural and do not belong to anyone in particular.

10. Table of punishments, 2d Detachment, March–June 1921.

11. Coope (1917: 170) objected to *piercing* infant septa for nose rings, but about women's costumes in general she was condescendingly tolerant (1917: 173–175); Gassó, for his part, cared so little about the issue that he had a Catholic Brother trained in goldsmithing to make nose rings and other jewelry in hopes of overcoming Indian opposition (1911–1914: vol. 22, pp. 110–112, 133–134).

12. Gassó (1911–1914: vol. 6, p. 88; vol. 9, pp. 161–163,183–184; vols.12–15, 22).

13. It may also be relevant that the Canal Zone imposed prohibition along with the United States in 1919, and that even traditional Kuna feel some ambivalence about alcohol. In a speech I heard at a 1985 meeting, when a Kuna leader needed a metaphor for something generally good but with numerous negative side effects, he chose the *chicha*.

14. The administration also insisted that Coope conduct Bible classes in Spanish, and that she cease giving babies anglophone names.

15. Revealingly, the *intendente* was incensed when he thought Coope was keeping a rival register of births.

16. Int: SecGJ #157, 9/14/20; Linares: SecGJ #165, 9/25/20; Linares: SecGJ #168, 10/06/20; SecGJ: Int #76, 1/13/21; General Order #1, 1/14/21; Perez: Int #198, no date; Linares: Perez #74, 2/12/21.

17. The government appointed a medical practicant for the region but gave him few supplies. Local authorities were generally unable to obtain vaccines for smallpox, until the explorer Marsh pressured President Porras in 1924.

18. In a provocative and at first glance plausible answer, Alexander Moore (1983) argues that the clubs reproduced a key institution, the weekly dance, characteristic of the black ethnic group of northern South America from which police were recruited. This interpretation, however, depends on Marsh's claim that the policemen were black, which Herrera has shown to be wrong (1984: 110–

115). Note also that after 1909 very few of the policemen were recruited from the blacks of Colombian origin in Puerto Obaldía, and that both the Hispanic *costeño* blacks and Antilleans living to the west of San Blas have cultural patterns distinct from those of northern Colombians.

19. Moore (1981: 275, n. 5) astutely points out that on contemporary Nargana, carnival and the competition among young girls to be named queen fill the same structural slot as traditional puberty ceremonies.

20. Several sources mention kinds of dances. A visitor to Nargana in 1923 writes that, watching in near-darkness, he couldn't tell whether it was "a waltz, two step or just plain hop" (Markham n.d.). A newspaper report on a visit to San Blas by the governor of the Province of Colón a few months after the revolution said that the Nargana youth danced el *"jazz"* to very modern music (*Star and Herald* 8/07/25). Garay, who visited San Blas in 1926, says they danced the fox-trot, *el danzón cubano*, and the *tamborito*; in a dialogue reproduced by Garay (1982: 13, 28), the postrevolution *intendente* alludes to Indian women having been forced to dance the fox-trot.

21. Markham (n.d.: 5); memorandum, Police and Fire Division, 3/02/25, 80A-15.

22. Castillo: Linares #14, 3/20/21; Linares: Castillo #126, 3/23/21. There are indications that higher level bureaucrats and the Liberal party explicitly promoted race mixing, a topic to be explored in another paper.

23. The available material from scientific congresses (e.g., the resolution of the AAAS in favor of the Kuna at its 1925–1926 meeting), covers much the same ground as the Declaration of Independence.

24. See the interview in enclosure 5, 819.00/1182, State Department records.

25. Marsh's claim that the policemen were blacks, which has been uncritically accepted by anthropologists and historians, and which forms the cornerstone of Alexander Moore's analysis (1983) of why the policemen imposed dances on the Kuna, was first challenged by Francisco Herrera (1984: 110–115). As far as Herrera and I can determine, there were a few black policemen, but the majority were mestizos from the city and the central provinces. Marsh's own photographs taken on Nargana show three men with light or medium-light skins and mestizo features.

26. Brought up in Washington D.C., and with a family home in southern Illinois (both places in that era bastions of segregation), from 1916 to 1922 Marsh ran a lumber company in St. Landry Parish, Louisiana, in the heartland of vigilantism and Jim Crow. For a few months in 1910 he served as First Secretary of the U.S. Legation in Panama, in a period when overt racism ruled in the Canal Zone (Franck 1913; Conniff 1985; McCullough 1977: 574–588); during this brief and decidedly undiplomatic foreign service career, Marsh managed to prevent the election as President of Panama of a distinguished mulatto leader, Carlos Mendoza (see Conniff 1985: 41–42, n.d.; Isaza Calderón 1982: 336–337). Politically and socially, however, he was more complex than his racial attitudes might suggest: after a trip to Nicaragua, he wrote the State Department in opposition to the Somozas and in support of Sandino.

27. *Orlando Sentinel Star* 4/10/73. Other typical remarks on Kuna racial purity can be found in: Panama Canal Company Records, 80-A-15, 1914–1925,

notes on "The San Blas Region."

28. See also a letter in Harrington's papers (Vogenitz: G.McL. Douglas 3/03/ 25).

29. Richard O. Marsh, Jr.: personal communication.

30. Ironically, one of Davenport's assistants administered tests to several members of the party, including one of the most learned ritualists in San Blas, concluding that their intelligence was very low (Allen 1926).

31. My claim that in some sense the Kuna were a metaphor for Anglo-Saxon America is reinforced by a parallel case from the same period. At the Second International Congress of Eugenics in 1921, a Scandinavian eugenicist named Mjöen presented a paper arguing that intermarriage between Lapps and Norwegians produced offspring that were physically, psychologically, and socially inferior. Mjöen's "evidence," which received such an enthusiastic reception that he toured the United States for the rest of the decade giving talks to sympathetic audiences, was telling and useful for American nativists precisely because, as an object lesson, it was simultaneously about and not about the United States (Chase 1977: 284–287).

32. Regna Darnell and Elaine Mills: personal communications.

33. Beidelman (1982) makes this point elegantly concerning missionaries, whose dealings with missionized peoples reflect their ambivalent relationship with the modern world that they both represent to their charges and try to exclude.

References

Allen, Grace
    1926   Reactions of eight San Blas Indians to performance tests. *American Journal of Physical Anthropology* 9: 81–85.
Anderson, Benedict
    1983   *Imagined communities: reflections on the origin and spread of nationalism.* London: Verso.
Axtell, James
    1985   *The invasion within: the contest of cultures in colonial North America.* New York: Oxford University Press.
Barth, Fredrik
    1969   *Ethnic groups and boundaries: the social organization of culture difference.* Boston: Little, Brown.
Basso, Keith
    1979   *Portraits of "the Whiteman": linguistic play and cultural symbols among the Western Apache.* Cambridge: Cambridge University Press.
Beidelman, T. O.
    1982   *Colonial evangelism: a socio-historical study of an East African mission at the grassroots.* Bloomington: Indiana University Press.
Biesanz, John, and Mavis Biesanz
    1955   *The people of Panama.* New York: Columbia University Press.
Burns, Bradford
    1980   *The poverty of progress: Latin America in the nineteenth century.*

Berkeley: University of California Press.

Castillero R., Ernesto J.
1946   Historia de la extraña república de Tule. *Biblioteca Selecta* 1(10): 17–
        36.

Chapin, Mac
1983   Curing among the San Blas Kuna of Panama. PhD diss., University of
        Arizona.

Chase, Allan
1977   *The legacy of Malthus: the social costs of the new scientific racism.*
        New York: Knopf.

Cheville, Lila R., and Richard A. Cheville
1977   *Festivals and dances of Panama.* Panama: n.p.

Comaroff, Jean
1985   *Body of power, spirit of resistance: the culture and history of a South
        African people.* Chicago: University of Chicago Press.

Conniff, Michael L.
1985   *Black labor on a white canal: Panama, 1904–1981.* Pittsburgh: Uni-
        versity of Pittsburgh Press.
n.d.   Panama since 1903. To appear in the *Cambridge history of Latin
        America,* forthcoming.

Coope, Anna
1917   *Anna Coope: sky pilot of the Kuna Indians.* New York: American
        Tract Society.

Cravens, Hamilton
1978   *The triumph of evolution: American scientists and the heredity-
        environment controversy 1900–1941.* Philadelphia: University of
        Pennsylvania Press.

DeLeon Madariaga, Edgardo A.
1980   *Presencia y simbolismo del traje nacional de Panamá, La pollera.*
        Panama: n.p.

Dollard, John
1937   *Caste and class in a southern town.* New York: Doubleday (Doubleday/
        Anchor edition, 1957).

Erice, P. Jesús, C. M. F.
1975   Historia de la revolución de los indios Kunas de San Blas. *Estudios
        Centroamericanos* 30 (319–320, 321): 283–304, 362–388.

Excursión á la costa de San Blas en Panamá
1916   *Excursión á la costa de San Blas en Panamá.* Madrid: Publicaciones del
        Boletin de la Real Sociedad Geográfica.

Foster, George
1960   *Culture and conquest: America's Spanish heritage.* New York: Viking
        Fund Publications in Anthropology, no. 27.

Franck, Harry A.
1913   *Zone policeman 88: a close range study of the Panama Canal and its
        workers.* New York: Century.

Garay, Narciso
1982 [1930] *Tradiciones y cantares de Panamá: ensayo folklórico.* Panama:
        n.p.

Gassó, P. Leonardo, S.J.
1911–1914 La Misión de San José de Nargana entre los Karibes (República de Panamá). *Las Misiones Católicas* 19–22, Barcelona (intermittent serial publication).

Geertz, Clifford
1973a After the revolution: the fate of nationalism on the new states. In *The interpretation of cultures*, 234–254. New York: Basic Books.
1973b Ideology as a cultural system. In *The interpretation of cultures*, 193–233. New York: Basic Books.
1973c The integrative revolution: primordial sentiments and civil politics in the new states. In *The interpretation of cultures*, 255–310. New York: Basic Books.
1973d The politics of meaning. In *The interpretation of cultures*, 311–326. New York: Basic Books.

Giddens, Anthony
1979 *Central problems in social theory: action, structure, and contradiction in social analysis.* Berkeley: University of California Press.

Gorgas, William
1915 *Sanitation in Panama.* New York: Appleton.

Grant, Madison
1916 *The passing of the great race, or the racial basis of European history.* New York: Scribner's.

Harris, Reginald G.
1922 Eugenics in South America. *Eugenical News* 7(3): 17–42.
1925 The white Indians of the San Blas and Darien. *Science* 61: 460–461.

Hawkins, John
1984 *Inverse images: the meaning of culture, ethnicity, and family in postcolonial Guatemala.* Albuquerque: University of New Mexico Press.

Heckadon Moreno, Stanley
1983 *Cuando se acaban los montes: los campesinos santeños y la colonización de Tonosí.* Panama: Editorial Universitária.

Herrera, Francisco
1984 La revolución de Tule: antecedentes y nuevos aportes. Thesis, Universidad de Panamá.

Higham, John
1955 *Strangers in the land: patterns of American nativism 1860–1925.* New York: Atheneum.

Hirschfeld, Lawrence
1977 Art in Cunaland: ideology and cultural adaptation. *Man* (new series) 12: 104–123.

Hobsbawm, Eric
1983 Mass-producing traditions: Europe, 1870–1914. In *The invention of tradition*, Eric Hobsbawm and Terence Ranger (eds.), 263–307. Cambridge: Cambridge University Press.
1987 *The age of empire: 1875–1914.* New York: Pantheon.

Howe, James
1976 Smoking out the spirits: a Cuna exorcism. In *Ritual and symbol in*

native Central America, Philip Young and James Howe (eds.), 69–76. Eugene: University of Oregon Anthropological Papers 9.

1985   Marriage and domestic organization among the San Blas Cuna. In *The botany and natural history of Panama*, William D'Arcy and Mireya Correa A. (eds.), 317–331. St. Louis: Missouri Botanical Garden.

1986   *The Kuna gathering: contemporary village politics in Panama*. Latin American Monographs, no. 67. Austin: University of Texas Press.

n.d.   Rival missions and conflict in San Blas, Panama, 1903–1925. In *The politics of popular religion*, Lynn Stephen and James Dow (eds.). American Anthropological Association, forthcoming.

Howe, James, and Lawrence Hirschfeld
1981   The star girls' descent: a myth about men, women, matrilocality, and singing. *Journal of American Folklore* 94: 292–322.

Hrdlička, Ales
1926   The Indians of Panama and their physical relation to the Mayas. *American Journal of Physical Anthropology* 9: 1–15.

Isaza Calderón, Baltasar
1982   *Carlos A. Mendoza y su generación*. Panama: Academia Panameña de la Historia.

Isthmian Canal Commission
1917   *Sanitary rules and regulations for the cities of Panama and Colón.*

Jaén Suarez, Omar
1979   *La población del istmo de Panamá del siglo XVI al siglo xx*. Panama: n.p.

Johnson, Harry
1958   *Heads and tales*. New York: Vantage Press.

Keeler, Clyde
1969   *Cuna Indian art*. Jericho, N.Y.: Exposition Press.

Kevles, Daniel J.
1985   *In the name of eugenics: genetics and the uses of human heredity*. New York: Knopf.

Kramer, Fritz W.
1970   *Literature among the Cuna Indians*. Etnologiska Studier 30. Göteborg: Etnografiska Museum.

Lévi-Strauss, Claude
1963   The effectiveness of symbols. In *Structural anthropology*, 186–205. New York: Basic Books.

McCain, William B.
1937   *The United States and the Republic of Panama*. Durham: Duke University Press.

McCullough, David
1977   *The path between the seas: the creation of the Panama Canal, 1870–1914*. New York: Simon & Schuster.

Mandelbaum, David
1988   *Women's seclusion and men's honor: sex roles in North India, Bangladesh, and Pakistan*. Tucson: University of Arizona Press.

Markham, William
n.d.   Untitled account of a visit to San Blas in May 1923. Athens, Pennsyl-

vania: Tioga Point Museum.
Marsh, Richard O.
1925   Blond Indians of the Darien jungle. *World's Work*, 483–490.
[1923] The primitive white people of eastern Panama. Anthropological
        Archives, Smithsonian Institution.
[1924] The Marsh-Darien expedition of 1924. Anthropological Archives,
        Smithsonian Institution.
1934   *White Indians of Darien.* New York: Putnam.
[1935] Lost colony of Greenland Norsemen: are they the white Indians of
        Darien? (privately held).
Misioneros Hijos del Corazón de Maria
1939   *Memoria del Vicariato Apostólico del Darién, Panamá, R. de P.*
        Panama: Imprenta Acción Católica.
Moore, Alexander
1981   Basilicas and king posts: a proxemic and symbolic event analysis of
        competing public architecture among the San Blas Cuna. *American
        Ethnologist* 8(2): 259–277.
1983   Lore and life: Cuna Indian pageants, exorcism, and diplomacy in the
        twentieth century. *Ethnohistory* 30: 93–106
Nordenskiold, Baron Erland, with Rubén Pérez Kantule; S. Henry Wassén, ed.
1938   *An historical and ethnological survey of the Cuna Indians.* Com-
        parative Ethnographical Studies 10. Göteborg: Etnografiska Museum.
Perrett, Geoffrey
1982   *America in the twenties: a history.* New York: Simon & Schuster.
Prestán S., Arnulfo
1975   *El uso de la chicha y la sociedad Kuna.* Mexico: Instituto Indigenista
        Interamericano, Ediciones Especiales 72.
Price, Richard
1983   *First-time: the historical vision of an Afro-American people.* Balti-
        more: Johns Hopkins University Press.
Rivière, Peter
1984   *Individual and society in Guiana: a comparative study of Amerindian
        social organization.* Cambridge: Cambridge University Press.
Roberts, Kenneth
1920   *Why Europe leaves home.* New York: Bobbs-Merrill.
Roberts, Orlando
1827 [1965] *Narrative of voyages and excursions on the east coast and in the
        interior of Central America.* Facsimile edition. Gainesville: Univer-
        sity of Florida Press.
Rosenberg, Charles E.
1961   *No other gods: on science and American social thought.* Baltimore:
        Johns Hopkins University Press.
Sahlins, Marshall
1985   *Islands of history.* Chicago: University of Chicago Press.
Said, Edward
1978   *Orientalism.* New York: Pantheon Books.
Severi, Carlo
1981   Image d'étranger. *Res* 1: 88–94.

1988   L'Etranger, l'envers de soi et l'échec du symbolisme: deux représentations du Blanc dans la tradition chamanique cuna. *L'Homme* 28: 174–183.

Sherzer, Dina, and Joel Sherzer
1976   *Mormaknamaloe*: the Cuna mola. In *Ritual and symbol in native Central America*, Philip Young and James Howe (eds.), 21–42. University of Oregon Anthropological Papers 9.

Sherzer, Joel
1983   *Kuna ways of speaking: an ethnographic perspective*. Austin: University of Texas Press.

Sisnett, Manuel Octavio
1956   *Belisario Porras, o la vocación de la nacionalidad*. Panama: Imprenta Universitária.

Stoler, Laura Ann
1985   Perceptions of protest: defining the dangerous in colonial Sumatra. *American Ethnologist* 12: 642–658.
1989   Making empire respectable: the politics of race and sexual morality in 20th-century colonial cultures. *American Ethnologist* 16: 634–660.

Stout, David
1947   *San Blas Cuna acculturation: an introduction*. New York: Viking Fund Publications in Anthropology No. 9.

Taussig, Michael T.
1980   *The devil and commodity fetishism in South America*. Chapel Hill: University of North Carolina Press.

Taylor, William B.
1979   *Drinking, homicide, and rebellion in colonial Mexican villages*. Stanford: Stanford University Press.

Todorov, Tzvetan
1984   *The conquest of America: the question of the other*. New York: Harper & Row.

Turner, Terence S.
1979   The Gê and Bororo societies as dialectical systems: a general model. In *Dialectical societies: the Gê and Bororo of central Brazil*, David Maybury-Lewis (ed.), 147–178. Cambridge: Harvard University Press.

Vogt, Evon Z.
1976   *Tortillas for the gods: a symbolic analysis of Zinacanteco rituals*. Cambridge: Harvard University Press.

Whitten, Norman
1976   *Sacha Runa: ethnicity and adaptation of Ecuadorian jungle Quichua*. Urbana: University of Illinois Press.

Williams, Raymond
1985   *Keywords: a vocabulary of culture and society*. New York: Oxford University Press.

Williamson, Joel
1984   *The crucible of race: black-white relations in the American South since emancipation*. New York: Oxford University Press.

Zarate, Manuel F.
1962   *Tambor y socavón*. Panama: n.p.

2. Symbolic Counterhegemony among the Ecuadorian Shuar

Janet Hendricks

In her article on recent theory in anthropology, Sherry Ortner (1984: 142–43) pointed out that one of the problems with the political economy approach in anthropology is the assumption that everything we see in the non-Western societies we study must be understood as having been shaped in response to the capitalist world system. While recognizing the immense impact of capitalist penetration on traditional societies, such a view often fails to acknowledge that societies necessarily interpret that penetration in terms of their own beliefs and practices. The impact of external forces indeed makes it necessary to permit a nation-state or even a world system context into the analysis. However, the articulation between nation-state and indigenous societies forms an interface in which indigenous responses are not merely reactions to external events, but rather are shaped by the internal dynamics of the indigenous culture as well as by the political and economic realities of the contact situation.

The rise of Indian movements as a form of resistance to the expansion of national frontiers is fast becoming the most important mechanism in national-indigenous relations in South America, and as such, highlights the need to analyze those relations from a more balanced perspective. Maybury-Lewis (1984: 132) states that South American nations will have to "revise their relationship with the Indians, who are no longer passive, but must be accepted as actors in the political process." The way indigenous populations, or at least their representatives, view themselves has changed. They are no longer naive exotic peoples with little knowledge of the world outside their own territorial boundaries, but rather see themselves as part of the world community. Yet, as these peoples take a more active role in the national political process, they bring with them different cultural meanings through which they make decisions, create political strategies, construct ideologies, and respond to the attitudes and beliefs of the dominant society.

The Federación de Centros Shuar, organized in 1964, is one of the oldest and most successful of the resistance organizations in South

America, and has become the model on which many recent attempts to organize are based. Historically, the Shuar were an Amazonian society economically based on horticulture and hunting, and politically based on a balance of power among autonomous groups engaged in constant warfare, feuding, shifting alliances, and trade. The Shuar Federation, however, has instituted major changes in Shuar political organization and modes of economic production. Most accounts of the Federation emphasize these changes, describing its interest in promoting cattle raising among the Shuar and its modern, Western-style organization, with a hierarchy of elected officials and a system of commissions designed to deal with the various ministries and agencies of the Ecuadorian government (Salazar 1977, 1981). However, resistance movements such as the Federation necessarily produce ideologies which retain elements of the native experience in which the social production of shared meanings is interpretable only from the perspective of native theory and practice. It is with this aspect of the articulation between the Ecuadorian state and the Shuar people that I will be concerned in this chapter.

The distinctly Shuar nature of the Federation is revealed in its leaders' critique of Ecuadorian cultural hegemony expressed in terms of a native theory of social agency manifested in metacommunicative speech acts. In recent years, there has been a growing interest in anthropology and other disciplines in the study of agency as a central problem in cultural analysis (Bourdieu 1977; Giddens 1979, 1984; Thompson 1978; Williams 1977). Among some anthropologists, agency itself is treated as a social product, created by people, and therefore subject to diverse cultural meanings (Basso 1985; Taussig 1980; Rosaldo 1980; Urton 1985; White and Kirkpatrick 1985). In most cases, authors have focused on native interpretations of events, as in Taussig's (1980) analysis of native interpretations of the colonial encounter and the capitalist economic system. However, the Shuar go further in that they not only interpret the encounter but set up a counterideology aimed at resisting the intrusion of nationalist ideas and practices.

Taking into account the native theory of agency is particularly important in the analysis of discursive social practices such as protests and counterhegemonic rhetoric, since forms of discourse are culturally and historically situated practices and are subject to the speaker's notions of the causes of the events in the world that constitute much of the subject matter of discourse. In the present example, the Shuar view the actions, including verbal actions, of white people in terms of a particular set of cultural presuppositions about the nature of social agency. To understand his critique, one must understand the notions of agency on which it is based as well as the nature of the actions and beliefs under attack.

As Ecuador extends its cultural hegemony into the Shuar territory through missionaries, schools, colonization, and development projects, it also spreads an ideology of Ecuadorian nationalism and a policy promoting ethnic assimilation that equates progress with whiteness and Christianity as well as economic development. For the Shuar, the values and practices of the national hegemony oppose some of their most fundamental beliefs about cause and effect relationships in the universe. Christianity, for example, lacks the essential ecstatic qualities of Shuar beliefs about humankind's relationship to the supernatural. Without direct contact with spiritual beings, there can be no harnessing of power for human use in goal-directed actions. Furthermore, Ecuador's notions of economic development are perceived by the Shuar, as well as other indigenous populations (Whitten 1976, 1978, 1985), as destructive of the very spiritual/natural elements (land, water, and air), represented as powerful beings in mythology, which are necessary in an ordered universe.

Thus, Shuar opposition to Ecuador's hegemonic expansion is more than a fear of losing cultural identity and autonomy, though that is an important motivation in the Shuar movement. Rather, it springs in part from a belief that whites have failed to understand the effects of their actions and, therefore, have fallen prey to destruction and greed that has culminated in the system of inequalities among people found in Ecuadorian society.

Sociopolitical Context of Counterhegemonic Rhetoric

The founding of organizations such as the Shuar Federation coincides with increased contact with national societies, placing indigenous populations in danger of progressive social, political, and economic marginalization. The Shuar have been lucky in many ways in that several factors allowed them to maintain their traditional culture longer and to organize sooner with a strong sense of identity still intact.[1] For many years the Shuar were isolated by their difficult terrain and by their well-deserved reputation as warriors. Colonization didn't begin in their territory to any great extent until about fifty years ago. At the same time, the increased need for trade goods led to more peaceful relationships among Shuar groups, and as the wars decreased, the population increased. The present population of about forty-five thousand is a significant factor in their survival as a group.

Two events led to the extensive acculturation of the Shuar west of the Cordillera de Cutucú and, ultimately, to the foundation of the Shuar Federation: the tremendous increase in colonization of the Shuar territory and the influence of the Salesian missionaries. The gold rush of the

1930s in eastern Ecuador brought many highland colonists into Shuar territory, but it was in the 1960s that the government became involved in colonization. Agrarian reform programs encouraged landless peasants from the Sierra to settle on *tierras baldías,* uncultivated and unused lands of the Ecuadorian Oriente. The government claims that its interest is in the economic potential of the Oriente, but the relatively small farms in the area are not being developed on a scale that would affect the national economy. At present, colonization is serving only political purposes, particularly as a substitute for true land reform in the highlands.

Salesian missionaries, who had established a permanent mission and boarding schools for Shuar children, saw the increase in colonization as a threat to their economic and religious interests. They feared that the hostilities generated by the influx of colonists would lead to the extermination of the Shuar or their retreat into the forest (Salazar 1977). In either case, the missionaries would lose converts and labor. The Salesian response was to try to protect the Shuar from the colonists by organizing the Federation. According to the Federation, by 1969 the Salesian's role in the organization was strictly religious (Federación de Centros Shuar 1976), and this seems to be largely true, though a few missionaries still have a strong influence in an advisory capacity.

Since its founding in 1964, the Shuar Federation has been relatively successful in comparison to indigenous organizations in other countries, raising the question of the extent to which the Ecuadorian government has allowed the Federation to succeed and why. Ecuador has never had a clearly articulated, comprehensive policy for dealing with its Amazonian Indians, nor has it had an Indian agency equivalent to Brazil's FUNAI (Vickers 1985). Until very recently, Ecuador has dealt with the question of indigenous peoples by ignoring their existence, a strategy which is, in effect, a policy of integration. The *mestizaje* ideology promoted in development programs claims that all Ecuadorians have an Indian heritage, thus eliminating the "Indian problem" and rejecting the possibility of a plural Ecuadorian society.[2]

Yet, Ecuador has recognized the Federation and has made some concessions to it. For example, IERAC (Instituto Ecuatoriano de Reforma Agraria y Colonización) has permitted Shuar communities to apply for global land titles, and the Ministry of Education helps support the Federation's bilingual radio schools. Certainly, there are still many unresolved problems, especially those concerning Shuar rights to their land and natural resources, but the concessions made suggest some degree of support, or at least acceptance.

Two motives come to mind that might explain Ecuador's acceptance of the Shuar Federation. First, the ultimate goal in the state's unofficial Indian policy is integration, and the Federation may be viewed as the most effective agent of change for the Shuar. For example, the Federation's activities in economic development programs such as cattle-raising demonstrate its potential for furthering the state's modernization programs (Chiriboga 1985). Furthermore, the Shuar reputation for ferocity is still an effective deterrent in preventing government forces from simply overrunning them. But the Federation, in its efforts to create a unified Shuar people, is doing the work of civilizing the Shuar by rejecting the more "savage" elements of Shuar culture. Of course, one of the Federation's goals is to see that the Shuar maintain a separate identity, but I doubt that most Ecuadorians see that as a very real possibility. After all, what they see is a people progressively more involved in the national political and economic system, that is, a people becoming more like them.

A second reason concerns Ecuador's fear of losing more territory to Peru.[3] While Shuar schools emphasize Shuar history, language and culture, they also promote patriotism and loyalty to Ecuador. The presence of federated Shuar on the border who are patriotic Ecuadorians with a reputation for protecting their territory is, at least temporarily, a safeguard against invasion.[4] Shuar centers on the border report the movements of Peruvian patrols to the army by radio. Also, many Shuar express their willingness to fight the Peruvians, as well as their intention of fighting Ecuadorian colonists, if their land is invaded. The Ecuadorian army would have a difficult time taking all of the Shuar territory in order to protect the border—it would be a bloody fight even if the Shuar ultimately lost—so allowing the Shuar to remain, and even giving legal titles to the border *centros* is a more effective measure until the Shuar are more fully integrated.[5]

Most of the Federation's success, however, must be attributed to the Shuar themselves. They are an intelligent and ambitious people, and take a pragmatic attitude toward incorporating new ideas into their economic and political strategies (Hendricks 1986). Also, the Shuar are described as arrogant and audacious, and as "indomitable warriors" (Bottasso 1982). "The exploits in which the Shuar have been the protagonists have created around them a true mythical halo, which has not disappeared" (ibid.: 12).

Perhaps the most important factor in the Federation's success is its role in reinforcing and recreating a sense of Shuar identity based on egalitarianism and hostility toward outsiders, and the belief system that supports these principles. Federation leaders make speeches that are broadcasted on *Radio Federación* or delivered in person as they travel to remote *centros*. The oratory of these leaders seems ambiguous at times in that it reinforces the hierarchical structure of the Federation while at the same time upholding values of egalitarianism. The Shuar are not unacquainted with forms of domination from within their own society. Differential possession of knowledge allowed some men to acquire enormous power and influence through careers as warriors, traders, shamans, and big men. Traditional Shuar society was egalitarian only in the sense that all men had equal access to the sources of knowledge through which one could obtain power, the acquisition and manipulation of which is a lifeong activity among Shuar men and is central to Shuar culture.

However, through Federation offices and involvement in the national market economy, an incipient stratification is emerging of which Federation officials are aware, but their antidevelopment attitude and their degree of acculturation (entrap them in contradictions) (Taylor 1981: 657). That is, Federation leaders, themselves at the top of the new hierarchical structure, still hold to the traditional Shuar values that reject domination except on the basis of individually acquired power as articulated in terms of native theory and discourse.

Of course, the domination that the Federation opposes is external rather than internal, and there is some historical precedence for Shuar resistance to external control. Stories of organized rebellion against foreign oppressors have a central place in the teachings of the Federation in its efforts to instill a sense of unity among the Shuar. Much of the ethnic pride of the Shuar today is the result of their view of themselves as a courageous people who have never been conquered militarily.

Shuar identity is firmly grounded in the practice of warfare, creating a climate in which an individual trusts only his or her closest kin. Clearly, the Federation has to restructure the traditional sense of identity among its people to include the notion of Shuar unity, so that they can effectively oppose external domination. However, the basic premises remain the same. The notion that close relatives are trusted allies survives in Federation ideology by defining all Shuar (and even Achuar) as one family, *"nuestra gran familia shuar."* The corresponding idea that everyone outside the immediate family is a potential enemy also survives in regarding all non-Shuar as a threat.

As the hostile "other" helped define the traditional sense of Shuar identity, the Federation had only to convince people that the common enemy was now the white colonist. In the western region where colonization increases daily and Shuar lands have been appropriated, seeing the colonist as the enemy is not difficult. However, for the Federation to increase its strength and become an effective political influence, it needed the membership of all the Shuar people. Much of the Federation's rhetoric is directed to the Shuar of the interior, where there has been little contact with whites and where there is still little threat from colonists. The contrast between the Shuar and the colonist is expressed in terms of the native theory of agency and speech.

In any discussion of Shuar beliefs or Federation ideology, one must keep in mind a regional context. Harner (1972) states that by the time of his fieldwork in 1956–1957, the western Shuar were in continuous contact with white Ecuadorians, missionaries, traders, and other agents of change, whereas the Shuar east of the Cordillera de Cutucú were not yet in direct contact with the white population. Even in 1982 when I began my fieldwork, many of the interior Shuar had had little contact with whites, though the Shuar Federation had become a major agent of change. There is, in fact, a continuum from west to east in which Shuar settlements become increasingly traditional, the Achuar east of the Macuma River being the most traditional group.

As a result of these regional differences, it is virtually impossible to talk about what the Shuar believe in terms of the whole population. Therefore, the theory of agency and speech and its role in Federation ideology that I describe in the following analysis is an ideal model, based on stated traditional values and discourse that reflects these values. Some speakers no doubt hold these beliefs, though others are more likely employing them pragmatically for the purpose of furthering the goals of the Federation, especially the goal of creating a sense of identity and unity among the people. In either case, the rhetoric produced by the Federation for its own people is effective in emphasizing the contrast between the Shuar and white Ecuadorians and encouraging a belief in the need to stand together as one people.

However, the public rhetoric of Federation leaders, that is, their press interviews and published documents, also suggests the influence of traditional values. Obviously, it would be counterproductive to openly express contempt for white Ecuadorians in terms of their lack of symbolic knowledge, since Federation officials must deal with the national society on its terms. Yet, even in discourse intended for white audiences, Federation leaders emphasize the importance of traditional Shuar knowledge, as for example in statements about forest management, bilingual/bicultural schools, and, especially, the necessity of maintaining the Shuar language. Furthermore, opposition to policies of integration and assimilation frequently take the form of programs designed to preserve and increase awareness of traditional knowledge systems.

Belzner (1981: 743) states that "the Shuar are able to clearly differentiate the values and behaviors appropriate to *blanco* culture from their traditional conceptual and behavioral system" and that they learned how to act out "new sets of roles while never losing their traditional values." My argument is similar in that the Shuar have been forced to adopt a Western form of political organization and its political roles to ensure their very survival, but Federation leaders challenge external domination symbolically through discourse based on the values embedded in the native theory of agency and speech.

Knowledge and a Theory of Agency and Speech

Investigation of an indigenous theory can reveal a great deal about a society's practices and the reasons behind them, because such theories are based on the reality they describe rather than the investigator's arbitrarily defined domains. Shuar reality is grounded in a belief in the equally powerful domains of the natural and supernatural worlds that influence every aspect of Shuar life from birth to death. Goal-directed action is achieved through practices that integrate practical and visionary knowledge, thereby mediating these domains.

Linguistically, the Shuar express the ideas of practical and visionary knowledge by distinct terms. *Unuímiamu* means "that which is learned," and refers to the technical knowledge consisting of all of the skills and facts learned from observation and instruction, including knowledge obtained in school. The verbs *nekástin* (to know) and *wainkiatin* (to see) are used in reference to visionary knowledge, that is, knowledge obtained through drug-induced visions and ordinary dreams.

While an understanding of practical or technical knowledge in human agency is easily accessible to the Western mind, the importance of visionary knowledge in day-to-day activities is less obvious. In the Western world, science, with its emphasis on observable and testable phenomena, constitutes the defining paradigm according to which we are accustomed to explaining reality. For the Shuar, however, the events that take place in daily life can be explained only by entering the supernatural world where truth about causality is found (Harner 1972). Furthermore, the role of visionary knowledge in social agency is linked to language and speech. Verbal images of the future in visionary experiences provide an individual with information concerning how to achieve his goals. In addition, visionary knowledge is necessary for "correct speech," verbal practices that lead to harmony and order in the social world.

Shuar subsistence practices provide evidence of the nature of causality as the Shuar perceive it and its relationship to notions of practical and symbolic knowledge. For example, in order to be successful, a Shuar hunter must have a great deal of practical knowledge of the jungle and its inhabitants, but he must also possess visionary knowledge that allows him to interpret dreams and sing magical songs. Without the technical knowledge, he would be unable to track and kill game, but without visionary knowledge, game would evade him, never allowing him to find the tracks or aim his weapons with accuracy. Similarly, a woman's control over nature in agriculture requires a technical mastery of gardening along with the symbolic observances that affect her relationship with Nuṇkui, the creator of all plants and animals.

Visionary knowledge is bound to verbal images of future events, images that tell the seer what he may expect or provide him with a means of directing those events. For example, magical songs manipulate events by expressing the desired effect verbally (Brown 1985). The garden songs sung by Shuar women always include the refrain, "I am a Nuṇkui woman," indicating the close personal affinity women feel toward the mythological being who represents the ideal woman, while at the same time producing an image of infallibility in gardening, since it is impossible for Nuṇkui's crops to fail.

Visionary knowledge is held in the heart, whereas the brain is the repository of practical knowledge. The Shuar say that learning occurs in the brain, and thinking (*enentáisatin*) occurs in the heart (*enentái*). The knowledge obtained through contact with the supernatural world in visionary experiences gives an individual a deeper understanding of the causes of events and the ability to use this knowledge in goal-directed action. Such knowledge is held in the heart and is necessary for thinking well (*péṇker anéntaimia*)).

An individual's speech reflects his or her ability to think well. As an externalization of one's thoughts, the words a speaker utters are said to come from the heart. Someone who lies or is constantly arguing with neighbors is said to think badly and have a bad heart. Incorrect speech occurs because the speaker's thoughts are not clear, not based on the truth found only in the visionary experience. If one has a good heart, one's words and thoughts will be good.

The relationship between speech and agency is expressed in statements about what constitutes "good" or correct speech. To say of someone *péṇker chichámai*, "he spoke well," signifies more than a display of verbal skill, but also includes the notion of speaking correctly. Because the effective use of language is a decisive factor in a man's success in social and economic activities, the Shuar are intensely interested in learning to speak well. To do so, however, means acquiring the knowledge that allows one to think clearly, particularly the visionary knowledge that gives the actor insight into the causes of events so that he is better able to control them.

The Shuar notion of correct speech is part of an implicit theory about language and speech, which is most concretely expressed in metacommunicative speech acts, that is, speech about speech. Shuar political oratory is filled with advice on how and when one should speak and what one should and should not say. When Federation leaders give audiences advice on how to speak correctly, they often do so in terms such as "you should live speaking thus." For example, a man should speak directly and forcefully, never joking or lying. He should speak with *paan' chicham*, "clear words." Open criticism or declarations of anger are interpreted as hostile actions, and lead to social disruptions, or even killing. Therefore, Federation leaders admonish their audiences to refrain from speaking angry words. Correct speech is believed to create harmony and order. Conversely, speaking incorrectly is directly associated with improper behavior and an absence of order.

Shuar Counterhegemonic Rhetoric

The critique of Ecuadorian cultural hegemony takes the form of speech about speech in which Shuar egalitarian and individual-centered values are opposed to the national ideology of domination. Discourse enters into the historical process of inevitable change, allowing speakers to reinforce collective values while demonstrating cultural resistance to subordination within the national power structure. Furthermore, the ideology of resistance expressed in Shuar discourse provides a foundation for many of the Federation's responses to the state's policies of hegemonic expansion.

Every culture contains some socially shared meaning associated with being human or having human capabilities. Among the Kalapalo, for example, the ability to speak illusively separates humans from other beings (Basso 1985). For the Shuar, the determining factor is the ability to speak correctly, that is, with a good heart. Shuar mythology tells us that incorrect speech, particularly lying, can have disastrous consequences. According to the myths, many of the animals of the forest were once able to speak as humans, but because of their deceptions in dealing with Etsa, Ayumpam, or other powerful beings, they were cursed, leaving them with only the animal calls they make today. Thus, it is not simply speech, but correct speech, that gives one a place in human society.

The Shuar also evaluate other human groups on the basis of speech. Seeger (1981: 82) suggests that "any society uses itself as a measure of others and is interested more in what another society lacks that they themselves have . . . than in what the other society has that they lack." The significance the Shuar place on language as a measure of other groups is indicated by their traditional warfare practices. Speakers of all languages other than Shuar are considered potential enemies. The Shuar say, "we only fight those who speak a different language." Moreover, it is explicitly forbidden to take the head of an enemy whose native language is Shuar. The most frequent enemies of the Shuar were the

Achuar, who speak a mutually intelligible Jivaroan language and possess a very similar culture. However, the Shuar insist that the Achuar language is entirely distinct from Shuar, and that the Achuar are animals.

Because Ecuadorians not only speak a foreign language, but are unsocialized in the proper ways of speaking, they are regarded as uncivilized, somewhat less than human, and therefore, dangerous. Even the ability to speak Spanish is looked upon with some skepticism among the less acculturated Shuar, leading some Federation officials to deny their knowledge of Spanish. In the following example from a speech, an official claims that he doesn't know the white man's language, emphasizing that he is no different from his audience. They know that he has had some formal education, but his denial is intended to tell them that his contact with whites has not affected him, that he still speaks as a Shuar.

Being thus, brothers, truly being Shuar myself,
and likewise, not being one who knows the white man's language,
being with all of you with total confidence,
I am here with you to collaborate well with you.
I, like you, do not know the white man's language.

In the modern context, suspicion of Spanish speakers occurs not only because of the association between human status and correct speech, but also because the Shuar language is under constant attack by the dominant society. For example, one commonly hears Ecuadorians say that "the Shuar speak the language of dogs," and before the Federation began its bilingual education program, Shuar children were forbidden to speak Shuar in schools. For many years, the state attempted to suppress even the use of Shuar names. The Office of Vital Statistics refused to recognize Shuar names when issuing identification cards. Claiming that Shuar names were "incorrect," they gave people Spanish names. The Federation's response was to demand to be allowed to run their own civil registration office so that Shuar names would be respected.

Miguel Puwáinchir (Federation president, 1987–1988) states that "language is the principal symbol of identity among ethnic groups in Ecuador" (1987: 8). In an interview, Puwáinchir said that policies that deny the Shuar the right to use their language and promote the expansion of Spanish are part of the domination by the state that the Shuar must resist if they are to survive.

However, the attempt to marginalize and repress the Shuar language is part of a larger national paradigm in which everything Indian is devalued. Whitten (1985: 223–224) views this paradigm as a series of "asymmetric contrasts implying a polarity of human capabilities." These contrasts include oppositions such as white/Indian, national/ indigenous, progressive/backward, hierarchical/egalitarian, civilized/ savage, educated/ignorant, and adultlike/childlike (Whitten 1985). Progress, in Ecuadorian ideology, is the transformation of the above opposites, ultimately from Indian to white.

In the Shuar view of nationalist ideology, these contrasts, which place some people above others and deny the rights of some groups primarily on the basis of their race, education, or wealth, are false oppositions stemming from the white man's lack of knowledge of causality. The Shuar see the white man as having a one-dimensional view of causation, focused on the use of technical knowledge. This limitation causes him to emphasize the material world, ignoring the spiritual and symbolic aspects of causation. His knowledge is limited to facts learned in school, since he lacks the symbolic knowledge acquired through visions.

This lack of knowledge causes a dehumanizing effect apparent in the speech and actions of Ecuadorians. For example, while the colonists perceive the Shuar as animals because of their intimate relationship with the forest, the Shuar say that the colonists treat one another as animals. The following statement by a Shuar man indicates an awareness of the colonist view of the Shuar and reveals what many Shuar see as the principal reason colonists cannot deal effectively with other people, their failure to seek and accept visionary knowledge.

"Look at them, the Shuar are ones who never work, living there in the montaña like wild pigs," that they tell us. But when my child is disobedient, I don't hit him with a stick to punish him, like an animal. I say, "you are not an animal." Then, I send him to the river after fasting, and have him drink *maikiua*. After drinking, the spirit will come and speak to him. The next day he will be healthy and well. Those who don't obey should be punished, but not like the colonists, with beatings, but with *maikiua*, in order to make them think well.

As noted in the last section, correct speech is linked to visionary knowledge by providing vital information and a good heart with which the speaker is able to control his speech in a manner leading to harmony and order in society. Ecuadorian nationals are frequently criticized for their manner of speaking, which reflects their lack of visionary knowledge and results in such undesirable consequences as the national ideology of subordination and dominance.

In pre-Federation Shuar society, dominance over others occurred only through the accumulation of personal power, especially that gained from visionary knowledge. Since such power is evident in the quality of a man's speech and in his behavior, it was not necessary for him to make overt references to his superior position over others. Ecuadorians, however, regularly use language to place themselves above others. This is evident in their tendency to rank people, as the series of oppositions noted above demonstrates. The Shuar criticize this tendency in Spanish and implore their people to avoid such uses of speech.

Well, this white man's language which we understand,
truly only in the white man's language
do we throw ourselves above others.

Leaders tell their people not to speak "carelessly" or "without cause," like the white man. Ecuadorians are said to say whatever comes into their minds, without thinking, seeing, or knowing. Such speech generates selfishness and is linked to the belief that progress to a more civilized state occurs as wealth increases. In the following excerpt from the speech of a local Shuar leader, the *teniente político*, the local Ecuadorian authority, is criticized because he is selfish and thinks only of his personal gain. The explanation given is his inability to see or know.

And the *teniente político*, that one,
that one doesn't hear anything concerning the Shuar,
not seeing anything, he only does thus.
They only say whatever,
talking only of the fines, only making fines,
they do thus, only ordering and ordering.
only taking money, that is the *teniente* now,
only taking money to smoke tobacco.

The inability to speak well, which is directly related to a lack of visionary knowledge, is marked in Shuar speech by the term *chichatsui* (doesn't speak). The same term is used for Ecuadorian nationals, and as in its use among the Shuar, its meaning refers to the inability to speak correctly and clearly. One context for using this term for a white man is in reference to his tendency to joke with or make fun of people. Correct speech among the Shuar is serious and does not show disrespect for others. White men, however, constantly make fun of one another and of other peoples. It is said that they don't know how to be serious and that their words are vague. The lack of seriousness in speech is associated with a general lack of care for correct speech. The following excerpt

suggests that the white man's words lead to distortions and misunderstandings, while Shuar speech allows clear expression of thoughts,
understandings, and knowledge.

Being thus, if I speak with the white man's words
I could allow mixing them into distortions.
But being thus, truly, it is better in the Shuar language,
what I know, what I understand, what I think,
I am here, brothers, to give to you all.

The careless use of speech among Ecuadorians is also reflected in their
continued use of the term "Jívaro" for the Shuar. Such derogatory labels
further emphasize the savage/civilized contrast in the national ideology
that serve as the rationale for domination over indigenous groups. In a
newspaper interview, Ampán Karákras criticized this practice, saying
that if Ecuadorians are so civilized, they should be able to correctly name
the components of the country's ethnic-national reality.[6]
    Lying is also regarded as careless speech, and the Shuar have had
considerable experience with the lies of Ecuadorian officials who claim
their support of the Shuar Federation, but fail to act. Responding to a
government official's promises, one Shuar said, "The Shuar don't need
pretty words filled with passion nor adorned with lies and deceptions;
that would demonstrate a lack of morality in our nature."
    The speech and actions of Ecuadorians are also said to center on
personal gain, without thought to their ultimate effects, not only on
other people, but also on the universe. Without the visionary knowledge
that gives the world its proper order, a man will speak only in his own
interests.

It is not that among the Shuar in the name of the assembly
he alone walks saying thus,
that in my opinion, in my own interest, mine alone,
he who is speaking, does not make that failing like the white men.

The proper order of the universe includes the notion of a harmonious
relationship between man and nature. Because Ecuadorian colonists do
not possess the necessary knowledge to understand the effects of their
actions, they disrupt this relationship, particularly through economic
strategies that destroy the forest. Veronica Naikiai (1987: 18), a Shuar
teacher, points out that an important factor in the Shuar adaptation to
the Amazonian environment is the belief that the forest is a living and
animated entity. All beings, including plants and animals, possess a

wakan, or soul. Mythology teaches the Shuar how to conserve the forest's resources, and contact with the other beings of the forest through magical songs (*anent*) ensures a harmonious relationship between man and nature. The Shuar laugh at the arguments of Western agronomists, knowing that the true source of agricultural abundance is Nuṇkui and that colonists fail in their agricultural pursuits because they do not know how to communicate with her (Naikiai 1987: 28).

Education is another sphere in which the Shuar perceive the lack of visionary knowledge as contributing to the ideology of domination, thereby disrupting the proper social order. The education of indigenous peoples in Ecuador is intended to promote integration: "The goal is technological and scientific development, affirming the interests of the predominant ethnic and socio-economic sector" (Puwáinchir 1987: 12). The Shuar perceive the Western form of education, with its emphasis on knowledge gained from books, as contributing to the belief in white superiority, represented in the national paradigm by the equation, white : Indian : : educated : ignorant. They hope that the education provided by Federation schools will not lead to the same kind of social stratification among the Shuar:

"We want them to be respected after studying,
behaving as others do, as good brothers,
let them live thus," one says.
We want to teach the children for that.
The youths, after studying in order to be teachers,
we do not want them to place themselves above everyone.

The basic technique of formal education is collective, in contrast to traditional individual teaching, based on observation and example, "and the personal transmission of techniques of symbolic control and supernatural powers" (Taylor 1981: 662). Only through the rigors and suffering necessary for obtaining visionary knowledge is a man recognized as more powerful than another, and even such men are not regarded as superior to others. The knowledge of a shaman or big man does not make him better than other men, only capable of influencing the world to a greater degree. The Shuar perceive Ecuadorian nationals as equating education (practical knowledge) with a man's value.

I, like you all, do not know the white man's language,
nor those who are educated, those who don't know,
nor those who are bad.
Everyone who doesn't know being equal,

I being one who doesn't know,
I want us to strengthen ourselves together, equally.
Being thus, I am not one to recognize those who don't know.

The Federation's response to public education in Ecuador is SERBISH (Sistema de Educación Radiofónica Bicultural Shuar). According to the Federation newspaper, *Chicham* (April 1986), the Federation wanted to create "an authentic Shuar education" through which Shuar children would learn what it means to be Shuar, what their culture means, and how to protect "the identity of a people who are in every way different from others." Shuar bilingual/bicultural education is intended to preserve the Shuar language and promote the development of the local culture, and to devise a curriculum that is relevant to the realities of Shuar life.

Ultimately, SERBISH's goal is the same as the Federation's, "the self-determination of the Shuar group within a concept of a pluralistic Ecuadorian state" (Puwáinchir 1987: 4). To this end, Shuar schools teach Shuar history and mythology, along with the traditional curriculum of Ecuadorian schools. As the teachers are Shuar, they reinforce Shuar rather than white values, and instruct students in the concerns and problems faced by the Shuar and other indigenous societies in Ecuador. Furthermore, the Federation still regards the individually oriented education of the family environment as as essential part of a Shuar child's education, particularly in the area of symbolic knowledge.

In conclusion, the Shuar interpret the values associated with Ecuadorian nationalism as resulting from the white man's ignorance of the nature of causality. This ignorance is exposed in the white man's manner of speaking, which demonstrates an inability to use language to create harmony and order. However, the Shuar not only interpret the spread of Ecuadorian national values in terms of their own theory and practice, but they also use that interpretation in constructing an ideology of resistance that is transmitted through the political oratory of Federation leaders at all levels of the organization. The interface between the Ecuadorian state and the Shuar is being formed, not solely by the impact of national/capitalist penetration of the indigenous culture, but also by the creative response of that culture in applying its own cultural meanings to the current situation in order to counteract the perceived dangers.

Notes

1. In referring to Shuar "traditional culture," I do not mean to imply that the Shuar were unaffected by direct and indirect contact with non-Shuar peoples.

The Shuar have a long history of contact with whites, though usually of a hostile nature, and they have had access to Western trade goods through extensive trading networks since the sixteenth century. However, until the fairly recent expansion of the national society into their territory, most of the Shuar could be considered "traditional" in the sense that they still possessed their essential economic, religious, and social systems.

2. Ecuador's policy toward its indigenous populations is, of course, far more complex than these brief statements suggest. Several comprehensive works are available that deal extensively with state policies toward Indians as well as indigenous responses to these policies (Ibarra 1987; Uquillas and Poveda 1987; Chiriboga 1985; Vickers 1985).

3. During World War II, Ecuador lost half of its Amazonian territory to Peru. The current boundary, designated by the Protocol of Río de Janiero of 1942, has never been fully accepted, as is suggested by Ecuadorian maps that still include all of the former territory. The territorial loss is a source of anger and shame among Ecuadorians, but it is also a potent political symbol used to justify development of the Amazon region.

4. The Federation newspaper, *Chicham* (April 1986), reported that during a visit to Shuar schools, the Director Nacional de Educación Compensatoria stated that it was known in Quito that Shuar schools produce true Ecuadorians who defend the Ecuadorian frontier, and that although problems exist, they should work together with other educational institutions to solve them. The Shuar response was that many government officials had come to Shuar centers, but had done nothing in Quito to help. Yamainch', the author of the article, stated, "Ecuadorians live here also and we make an authentic and legitimate defense of our Ecuadorian frontier . . . there are more Shuar centers than military posts on this frontier." Yamainch' continued, saying that although Quito recognizes our problems, we still have to fight "to defend our integrity, our culture, and our land."

5. Ecuador's colonization projects have also been described "as a means of asserting Ecuador's sovereignty in the lowlands" (Salazar 1977: 22).

6. For many years, Ampán Karákras has been a representative of the Shuar Federation in Quito and one of its principal spokesmen. The comment noted was published in the Quito newspaper, *Hoy,* July 25, 1987, and reprinted in KIPU: *El mundo indígena en la prensa Ecuatoriana,* vol. 9, published by Ediciones Abya-Yala.

References

Basso, Ellen
    1985   *A musical view of the universe: Kalapalo narrative and ritual performances.* Philadelphia: University of Pennsylvania Press.
Belzner, William
    1981   Music, modernization, and westernization among the Macuma Shuar. In *Cultural transformations in modern Ecuador,* N. E. Whitten, Jr. (ed.), 731–748. Urbana: University of Illinois Press.
Bottasso, Juan B.
    1982   *Los Shuar y las misiones: Entre la hostilidad y el dialogo.* Ecuador:

Mundo Shuar.

Bourdieu, Pierre
1977   *Outline of a theory of practice*. Trans. by R. Nice. Cambridge: Cambridge University Press.

Brown, Michael F.
1985   *Tsewa's gift: magic and meaning in an Amazonian society*. Washington, D.C.: Smithsonian Institution Press.

Chiriboga, Manuel
1985   Formas tradicionales de organización social y actividad economica en el medio indigena. In *Del indigenismo a las organizaciones indigenas*. Quito: Ediciones Abya-Yala.

Federación de Centros Shuar
1976   *Solución original a un problema actual*. Sucúa, Ecuador: Recopilación a cargo del Directorio de la Federación Shuar.

Giddens, Anthony
1979   *Central problems in social theory: action, structure and contradiction in social analysis*. Berkeley: University of California Press.
1984   *The constitution of society: outline of the theory of structuration*. Berkeley: University of California Press.

Harner, Michael J.
1972   *The Jívaro: people of the sacred waterfalls*. New York: Doubleday/ Natural History Press.

Hendricks, Janet Wall
1986   Images of tradition: ideological transformations among the Shuar. PhD diss., Department of Anthropology, University of Texas at Austin.

Ibarra, Alicia Illanez
1987   *Los indígenas y el estado en el Ecuador*. Quito: Ediciones Abya-Yala.

Maybury-Lewis, David
1984   Demystifying the second conquest. In *Frontier expansion in Amazonia*, M. Schmink and C. H. Wood (eds.), 127–134. Gainesville: University of Florida Press.

Naikiai, Verónica
1987   El uso del ecosistema en el antiguo pueblo shuar. In *Hombre y ambiente: El punto de vista indígena*, no. 1. Quito: Ediciones Abya-Yala.

Ortner, Sherry B.
1984   Theory in anthropology since the sixties. *Comparative Studies in Society and History* 26: 126–166.

Puwáinchir, Miguel
1987   La Federación de Centros Shuar y el problema educativo en la región Amazónica. Paper presented at the 46th International Congress of Americanists. Amsterdam.

Rosaldo, Michelle Z.
1980   *Knowledge and passion: Ilongot notions of self and social life*. Cambridge: Cambridge University Press.

Salazar, Ernesto
1977   *An Indian federation in lowland Ecuador*. Copenhagen: International Work Group for Indigenous Affairs, Document 28.

1981 The Federación Shuar and the colonization frontier. In *Cultural transformations in modern Ecuador*, N. E. Whitten, Jr. (ed.), 589–613. Urbana: University of Illinois Press.

Seeger, Anthony
1981 *Nature and society in central Brazil: the Suya Indians of Mato Grosso.* Cambridge, Mass.: Harvard University Press.

Taussig, Michael T.
1980 *The devil and commodity fetishism in South America.* Chapel Hill: University of North Carolina Press.

Taylor, Anne-Christine
1981 God-wealth: the Achuar and the missions. In *Cultural transformations in modern Ecuador*, N. E. Whitten, Jr. (ed.). Urbana: University of Illinois Press.

Thompson, E. P.
1978 *The poverty of theory and other essays.* New York: Monthly Review Press.

Uquillas, Jorge, and Juan Poveda
1987 Análisis institucional de las entidades con ingerencia en la Región Amazónica Ecuatoriana. In *Amazonia, presente y...?* Quito: Ediciones Abya-Yala.

Urton, Gary, ed.
1985 *Animal myths and metaphors in South America.* Salt Lake City: University of Utah Press.

Vickers, William T.
1985 Indian policy in Amazonian Ecuador. In *Frontier expansion in Amazonia*, M. Schmink and C. H. Wood (eds.). Gainesville: University of Florida Press.

White, Geoffrey M., and John Kirkpatrick, eds.
1985 *Person, self, and experience: exploring Pacific ethnopsychologies.* Berkeley: University of California Press.

Whitten, Norman E., Jr.
1976 *Sacha Runa: ethnicity and adaptation of Ecuadorian Jungle Quichua.* Urbana: University of Illinois Press.

1978 Ecological imagery and cultural adaptability: the Canelos Quichua of eastern Ecuador. *American Anthropologist* 80: 836–859.

1985 *Sicuanga Runa: the other side of development in Amazonian Ecuador.* Urbana: University of Illinois Press.

Williams, Raymond
1977 *Marxism and literature.* Oxford: Oxford University Press.

3. In Nēca Gobierno de Puebla: Mexicano Penetrations of the Mexican State

Jane H. Hill

The history of Indian-state relations in Mexico has been punctuated by civil war: the "Indian hordes" who followed Hidalgo, the Yaqui "rebels," the caste warriors of Yucatan, the Zapatista armies, and Primo Tapia's Tarascan militia exemplify the warrior-bandit tradition shared, as well, by the Mexicano-speaking people of the Malinche Volcano in Tlaxcala and Puebla. In the early days of the Mexican Revolution, Domingo and Cirilio Arenas, Mexicano-speaking brothers from San Bernardino Contla, led their barefoot troops fifty miles from their bases on the Malinche to burn the railroad station at Atlixco (Del Castillo 1953).[1] In 1968 Mexican troops killed ten men in the town of San Miguel Canoa after the murder of two "students" (a third had his hand cut off). Since 1970 a shooting war over land rights has erupted periodically between the Tlaxcalan towns of Muñoztla and Tetlanohca, triggering the deployment of troops into the area. Military convoys often pass through San Miguel Canoa, ostensibly to "repair roads." So the people of the volcano are thoroughly familiar with the most profound essence of the Mexican state—its armed might—and have occasionally dared to test it. This familiarity constitutes the dark background to any discussion of their relations with the state. But my concern here will be, not with the dramatic moments in which Malinche people provoke the revelation of the state in its full clarity, but with their everyday practices of the type that James Scott (1985) has called "the weapons of the weak"—especially talk, by which the people of the Malinche Volcano express their "penetration" of their situation and attempt to mount some small resistance. That such resistance, in the service of the maintenance of an autonomous indigenous sector, is a goal I take to be evident from the astonishing cultural persistence of the Mexican indigenous sector after nearly five hundred years of the most crushing domination.

"Penetration" is Willis's (1977) term for an interested understanding of its structural position by a group; such an understanding is a part of cultural knowledge. Willis differentiates penetration from "consciousness," which he takes to be a phenomenon of the individual level. He developed the concept in work with British working-class subjects, proposing that this proletariat as a *class* does not exhibit (nor is it able to develop) true "consciousness." Instead, proletarians construct cultural formations of "penetration," which, because of limitations on both the scope for proletarian action and on the possibility of full comprehension of their situation, may reproduce their situation with great precision.

Willis's idea of "penetration" captures the kind of sense constituted in talk about the state by Malinche people.[2] This talk is deployed in a rhetorical struggle for control of the material and symbolic resources that are cast up in the dialectic of the encounter between the Indian people of the Malinche and the sector that for them is exemplified by *in nēca gobierno de Puebla*, "the government of Puebla," the great city that lies at the base of the volcano. The terms of this talk are often borrowed from the rhetoric of the Mexican state, taken in turn (in a distorted and simplified form) from the language of profound political theoreticians. But the complex cultural filters constituted by the state and by local systems of thought have led to political understandings couched in strangely altered definitions of familiar terms, deployed within texts suffused with magic.[3] Yet this talk provides some foundation, however limited, for cultural resistance within the political-economic context in which Malinche people live. The goal of this chapter is thus to begin a careful exploration of its content and contexts. I argue that this system of "penetration" is adapted to periodic minima, when local resources are very scarce and domination by the state tends toward totality, yet permits flexible accommodation to periods when more resources become available.

The terms of interaction between the people of the Malinche and the Mexican state are dynamic. This is illustrated by the changing importance in the communities of government through the *municipio*, the lowest level in the hierarchy of state institutions. Hugo Nutini and his students, in a number of highly competent discussions of Malinche communities (e.g., Nutini and Bell 1980) claimed that the *municipio* organization was largely irrelevant to the local power structure. Important men in this structure, organized through religious hierarchies, saw municipal office as a minor assignment for low-ranking men. Frances Rothstein (1974), examining the budgets managed in the late 1960s and early 1970s by the municipal president of Mazatecochco, a Malinche-area *municipio* in Tlaxcala, showed that these were so minuscule that control of them was worthless. However, during the period in which I worked on the Malinche, in the last years of the Echeverría presidency and especially under López Portillo, massive infusions of petro-peso capital into the local infrastructure, administered through state and municipal offices controlled by PRI (Partido Revolucionario Institucional) functionaries, resulted in the leaders of the religious hierarchies giving more serious attention to municipal office and to the national political parties, especially the ruling party, the PRI. The flip side of the capital infusion was that land was needed for the new development. This meant that not only local leaders but also even the most retiring monolinguals had to seek good terms with the lords of the PRI to protect their land against seizure.[4]

This apparent shift in the relevance of the Mexican state for the people of the Malinche yields a central theoretical point of this chapter: from the point of view of such people, states are not stable monoliths, but may instead appear as a rather random system, driven by impenetrable and changing motives. This unpredictability constrains the range of options available to indigenous peoples as they try to maintain an autonomous sector.

Students of hunting and collecting populations find that long-term adaptations must have the flexibility to exploit the opportunities created by occasional plenty, but are constrained by periodic minima. We may draw an analogy to the situation of indigenous communities in Latin American states. Although the state can tend toward a total determination of the environment, as in the Guatemalan "development poles" (Manz 1988), generally it leaves interstices in which domestic and community life can be constituted in relative autonomy. But the structures that organize this life must be "adapted" to the possibility of such total determination in much the way that foraging societies are adapted to the minima of subsistence availability. And, just as foragers may try to influence their environment through devices ranging from the invocation of the spirit keepers of the game to the burning of brushland to encourage herbivore-attracting new grass, indigenous communities embedded in states will try to influence them as well. From time to time, circumstance elicits the full power of the state's potentials to organize, channel, and control resources—of violence, of material capital, of symbolic capital. Analysis of such circumstances permits refinement of our understanding of these constraints.

While there was some flow of resources into the Malinche communities during the late 1970s and early 1980s, the dominant trend of their relations with the capitalist sector organized by the state has been for the flow to go in the opposite direction. This occurs through several processes. Exemplifying what might be termed "primitive accumulation" by the capitalist sector of resources captured from the Malinche towns is the loss of their lands. This occurs through direct state seizure (as in the construction of roads) and through a variety of less obvious processes. These include bureaucratic collusion with private interests that want to claim Indian land, inattention to its continual alienation through private sale by desperate landholders or loss to illegal squatters, and the degradation of land quality through timber cutting and garbage dumping. Exemplifying processes that might be analyzed as the extraction of a "fund of rent" from a "peasant" sector is the very low price paid for corn, which indigenous cultivators feel a sacred duty to plant. Low prices to the cultivator result from a policy of price subsidies for basic foods, especially tortillas, for urban populations. But extremely low prices to the cultivator for food crops (the government is limited in its ability to prop up farm prices while simultaneously keeping basic foodstuffs cheap) makes cultivation a losing proposition.[5] This yields a continual supply of migrant labor to domestic service and the most marginal sectors of Mexican industry. The flood of migrants keeps wages low, feeding the need for price controls (Mexican wages are currently among the lowest in the world, well below those of traditionally low-wage Asian countries). Warman (1980:176) has argued that the Mexican industrial economy is "made of corn": the whole system is sustained by the capacity of the maize-cultivating sectors to develop strategies of involution in order to reproduce the labor force.[6]

Wolf (1982) suggests that in capitalist states the definition of the "political"—"who gets what when"—is entirely determined within the capitalist framework. Indigenous communities surely strive to be part of "the political," but they may use a set of "anticapitalist" strategies in their attempts to control resource strategy. The most important such strategy is the construction of a "sacred space."[7]

Each Malinche community is organized as a sacred space with a holy center. A remarkable proportion of community resources may be dedicated to the assertion of this definition. For instance, in a visit to San Miguel Canoa in 1988, I found that since my previous trip in 1985 during a period of acute national and local economic crisis, through repeated assessments of its citizens the town had raised thousands of dollars for a pair of architect-designed bell towers for its eighteenth-century church, a new bell for one tower, and a new hand-carved stone statue of Saint Michael the Archangel to crown the facade.

In addition to enhancement of the sacred center, communities attend to boundary maintenance through challenges to outsiders and sanctions against the alienation of lands, even though these are privately held. Resources are allocated within the sacred space of the community through a complex ritual system organized by ritual kinship and the religious hierarchy of *mayordomos*, stewards of the saints. Participation in this system takes about one-third of the time of adults over a lifetime, and up to as much as three-fifths of their income. The practice of reciprocity and the importance of selfless dedication to community service separate the people of the sacred space from the capitalist sector.

Worsley has suggested that a principal goal of the modern state is the proper classification of its citizens, to the end that: "there ... should be no groups, ethnic or otherwise, separating the citizen artificially from the political community as a whole and impeding the free exercise of the rational judgment of each individual citizen" (Worsley 1984: 252). The taxonomizing practices of the Mexican state are presumably directed toward such an end. Yet Malinche people have borrowed from this taxonomy to define an important part of the separating work of the sacred space, the high value placed there on cultivation.

The vision of the Mexican state proposed by the ruling party, the PRI, holds that its regime is an "institutionalized revolution" by "peasants (*campesinos*) and workers (*obreros*)." On the Malinche, nearly all men claim identity as *campesinos*, "cultivators" (and often reserve *obrero*, "worker," as a pejorative for men in enemy towns). Most men, though, work at wage labor. Some do this only during the slow periods of the agricultural season, but many men try to hold full-time work, cultivating only during their off hours. This is relatively easy to do, because the Malinche is bordered on the west and south by an important industrial zone. The city of Puebla, with a population of over a million, offers year-round employment in construction. Mexico City is less than two hours away by bus.[8]

The preferred identity of local men as *campesinos* endorses the tax-onomizing practice of the Mexican state. The Malinche, in spite of the importance of factory labor in its economy, is considered a "peasant" sector. This means that Malinche people are routed for political participation not into the national organizations for "workers" (very few of the Malinche factory workers belong to unions), but into the national peasant union, the CNC (Consejo Nacional de Campesinos).[9]

A second state taxonomic practice is the division of "Indians" (*indígenas*) from the remainder of its citizenry. Certain regions are recognized as "indigenous" zones. The Malinche region, inhabited though it is by thousands of people who speak Mexicano, an indigenous language of the Uto-Aztecan family (better known as Nahuatl or Aztec), is not considered to be such a zone, and there is no official recognition of the "Indian" identity of its people. No bilingual education was provided until 1988, when (I was told) a small program was to begin in San Bernardino Contla. The INI (Instituto Nacional Indigenista), the government agency dedicated to development of the indigenous sector, does not operate in the region (in contrast, INI is very active in the nearby indigenous zone of Zacapoaxtla, Puebla). The region has not attracted the attention of aficionados of the Nahuatl language, unlike the Nahuatl-speaking towns of Morelos, which are no closer to Mexico City and in fact exhibit lower percentages of Nahuatl speakers.[10]

It is interesting that a development of the late 1970s and early 1980s, the formation of "Grand Councils" of indigenous groups under the prodding of the PRI, entirely bypassed the Malinche and, indeed, the Nahua-speaking Indians of Mexico in general. Barre (1983) has chronicled this innovation in the taxonomizing practice of the "institutionalized revolution," which adds "Indians" behind "peasants" and "workers." By 1982 there were "Grand Councils" of the Otomis, the Matlatzincas, the Totonacs, and a variety of other groups, but no Gran Consejo of any Nahua-speaking region.

While Malinche people know that their colinguals are found widely in central Mexico, they do not consider themselves in any sense a part of a "tribe." While they have a strong sense of the unity of the Malinche region, the *pueblo*, the local community, is the principal site of loyalties, along with the República Mexicana itself. A system of "Grand Councils" might begin the unification of these local and regional entities. From the point of view of the Mexican government, a unified and mobilized Nahua-speaking population, over a million people localized in the heart of the republic, could constitute a genuine threat to national stability.

While the Mexican state recognizes that some of its citizens are "indigenous," it uses the strategy of incorporation of indigenous groups that Worsley (1984) calls "uniformity": "older ethnic identities are now *dépassés*, and ... a new synthesis ... has emerged in their place" (Worsley 1984: 252).[11] Ironically, the new synthesis around which Mexicans rally borrows heavily from the indigenous sector, and especially from the Aztecs, Nahuatl-speaking people like those of the Malinche, whose blood and world vision is said to have blended with that of the conquistadors to create the "cosmic race," the unique mestizo citizenry of modern Mexico. Theirs is a "new" civilization—the "pure" strain of Indianness is defined as part of the past.

Part of the state project of the forging of the cosmic race is the relentless "folklorization" of manifestations of Indian identity. These become "national traditions" that all citizens are encouraged to practice, so that they cannot constitute a gesture of separation in space or time that might make any group distinct. Especially important is the use of these "national traditions" in the state function that is among the most visible locally, primary education (public schools on the Malinche and throughout Mexico are run by a national bureaucracy). School festivals on the Malinche, as everywhere in Mexico, celebrate a canonical melange of *lo folklórico*, music and dancing in a variety of "regional" costumes. Thus, the elegantly controlled "deer dance," a principal symbol of modern

Yaqui identity, is transformed by the national dance theater, the Ballet Folklórico, into a spectacle of athletic contortion. On the Malinche, high-leaping young soccer players, descendants of the Tlaxcalan Nahuatl, compete to be chosen to perform the "Danza del Venado" (stripped of its Yaqui label) at graduation festivals. Just so, their own spectacle, the "Dance of the Moors and Christians," is danced in a denatured version throughout Mexico. Even the most dubious aspects of the Indian past are incorporated into these celebrations: in a graduation in San Miguel Canoa in 1982 I saw a twelve-year-old loincloth-clad "Aztec priest" simulate the sacrifice of a white-robed fifth-grade "virgin" on a pine table borrowed from some parental household.

These symbolic projects are not new. They appeared by the end of the seventeenth century, when the great Creole intellectual Sigüenza y Góngora arranged for a new viceroy a triumphal progress under arches crowned with the images of Aztec lords, who substituted for Greek gods as representatives of the governmental virtues. Today, they penetrate the relative symbolic isolation of Malinche people, who are exposed to a continual barrage of "folklore," especially through the state-run schools.[12]

The Nahuatl-speaking people of the Malinche attempt to struggle with the state's denial of their Indian identity and its recruitment of their most valued symbols for its own purposes by insisting that they are *mexicanos*, prototypical citizens of the Mexican state. They derive this identity from the fact that they "speak Mexicano," the Nahuatl language. This is a complex linguistic project that borrows, remodels (a term taken from Reisman 1970), and revalues tokens taken as "Spanish" and either contrasts these with "Mexicano" or reshapes them within its own terms. This adaptation is constrained by state policy that requires Spanish as the language of instruction in all local schools. Spanish is also a prerequisite for nearly all decently remunerative work. But the different ways to "speak Mexicano" construct symbolic distinctions between the complexly involuted levels of the community hierarchies, provide the rhetorical grounds for the struggle between "peasant" and (covert) "worker" elements in the communities, and permit linguistic flexibility by narrowing the structural distance between Spanish and Nahuatl. I have written in detail about the workings of this system elsewhere (Hill 1985, 1987; Hill and Coombs 1982; Hill and Hill 1986).

The term *mexicano* for what is known in the scholarly literature as "Nahuatl" is no mere localism. It was widely used both popularly and by elites until the late nineteenth century, when *nahuatl*, a neologism that I have been unable to find in classical or colonial-period texts, was introduced into scholarly usage by French authors. Malinche people (with one exception among the 126 subjects of a sociolinguistic survey) all assumed that the correct name was *mexicano*. Indeed, some people claimed to have never heard the term *náhuatl*, and thought that it referred to some other language. But Spanish-speaking people in Puebla universally insist that the "correct" name for the language is *náhuatl*.

Malinche people do not, of course, claim prototypical Mexican citizenship in so many words. Instead, their rhetoric is that of "partial penetration," and takes the form of a sort of etymologizing. The name of the language (and of the people of the Malinche, who call themselves *mexicanos*) is said to be the source of the names of certain symbols of the state, which are usually referred to in construction with the attributive *mexicano/a*. Some illustrations of local rhetoric are seen in the following examples:

1. Por eso ye n ōn nictoa, timexicanos, porque īca in mexicano titlahtoāh in to-República Mexicana. Es que legítimo mexicanos in tehhuān.

For that reason I say it now, we are Mexicans, because we speak Mexicano in our República Mexicana. It is that we are the real Mexicans.

2. Ah cómo no, para timodefenderōzqueh. Quēn ōmotehuih in Hernán Cortés? Quēn ōmotehuih in pueblo Hipoxopochtli [*sic*]? Quēnin? Puro mexicano! Por eso vino el himno nacional mexicano.

Ah, why not, in order for us to defend ourselves. How did Hernando Cortés fight? How did the people of Huitzilopochtli fight? How? With nothing but Mexicano! For that reason came the Mexican national anthem.

The latter remark was uttered in reply to a query about whether the Mexicano language was still needed. The discourse blends the Spanish conqueror, the Mexica Aztec (their patron was the war god Huitzilopochtli, who was not prominent in ancient Tlaxcala), and the Tlaxcalans ("us") into a single "Mexicano" tradition of "fighting" and "defense." The national anthem of Mexico is a martial affair—*Mexicanos, al grito de guerra* (Mexicans, rally to the cry of battle)—so to invoke it develops this theme. The slogan of "self-defense" is a centerpiece of the Malinche "idiom of resistance"—when asked to explain their economic and symbolic strategies, Malinche people say *Cē modefenderoa*, "One defends oneself."

This emphasis on the term *mexicano* is apparently unique to the Malinche,[13] and may reflect the extraordinary intensity there of exposure to the everyday life of Spanish-speaking Mexico, shared by no other

Nahua-speaking communities. The people of the Malinche are sur-
rounded by cities and industrial zones, their lands are criss-crossed by
superhighways, and they are heavily dependent on industrial wage labor.
This "permeability" of their situation makes for special problems in
maintaining the separation and coherence of their communities. The
claim of prototypical citizenship that their use of the term *mexicano*
proposes permits separation (through being "special" and "original")
and solidarity (through a shared unique identity), while simultaneously
asserting connection to a state that during the late 1970s and early 1980s
was an important source of resources, accessed through *política* conducted
in the rhetoric of citizenship.

This rhetorical strategy provides the flexibility essential to Indian
adaptations. When state resources vanish, the communities will have
not sacrificed their claim of internal coherence of identity, and so can
close and "defend" their members.[14] However, the usage permits their
members a symbolic ground on which to contemplate and develop the
meaning of citizenship in the state. This symbolic practice also addresses
the contradiction in which, on the one hand, the state fails to recognize
their uniqueness, but, on the other hand, constantly expropriates symbolic
goods that they feel to be their own to symbolize the national identity
(while, of course, their "Indian" identity, all too evident locally, guarantees that they will face discrimination in their everyday contacts with
the Spanish-speaking urban sector). Note that separation as an ethnic
subgroup under a "Great Council" would profoundly undermine the
claim of "prototypical citizenship" of *mexicano* people. Such a separation would not permit the same kind of symbolic flexibility, so the idea
of a "tribal grand council" is unlikely to find ready acceptance.

The rhetorical struggle for control of group identity and the meaning
of the term *mexicano* is accompanied by a struggle for the control of
time. Fabian (1983) has conducted an eloquent critique of the anthropological rhetoric that sees "the other"—the primitive, the peasant, the
underdeveloped world—as somehow also of another time, earlier than
our own. The Mexican state has joined enthusiastically in this virtually
universal Western symbolic practice, and views its contemporary indigenes as "survivors." Mexican anthropological rhetoric until very
recently saw Indians as a "backward" indigenous sector that would be
"developed" and "modernized" (although indigenist philosophy held
that this modernization should incorporate an indigenous worldview to
the greatest possible degree). Public presentations of the Indian component
of Mexican identity—the great murals on government buildings, the
national tourist sites, and international and internal tourist-oriented
advertising—focus on the heritage of the preconquest period. The
"folklorized" manifestations of Indianness that are a part of most state-

sponsored celebrations are also held to celebrate "tradition," the "colorful" (and static) living museum pieces that tame Mexican diversity.

Malinche people do use some of the temporalizing rhetoric that dominates Mexican discourse on ethnic differentiation. But their most important idiom of distinction, by all odds dominant in terms of sheer frequency of usage, is that of kinship. I have argued (Hill and Hill 1986) that this idiom constitutes a "rhetoric of continuity." While city people may be (perhaps) praised by being called *moderno* or *civilizado*, or disparaged by being called *coyotes*, far more commonly they are called *tohermanohtin*, "our brothers." This term borrows from the rhetoric of Christian fellowship to construct a clearly synchronic vision of structural differentiation. This rhetoric of continuity dominates Malinche discourse about the difference between two kinds of local people: those who prefer Mexicano language and "traditional" dress, and those who prefer Spanish and urban fashion. Such differences in practice have a clear disruptive potential. To use Spanish may implicate extreme social distance, or, worse, vulgar lack of respect. But unlike communities in Southern Mexico or in Chiapas and Guatemala, where to change one's mode of dress or to use Spanish to a fellow community member may lead to violent expulsion from the community, Malinche communities are very tolerant. For instance, use of the Mexicano language may be required in a ceremony, but it is entirely proper to hire elderly Mexicano-dominant assistants to utter the necessary blessings or prayers.

While urban clothing styles and the use of Spanish are found among all age groups in the communities, Malinche people generally speak of these as practices of *toconehhuān*, "our children." In contrast, Mexicano dominance and indigenous life-style are associated with *tētahmeh*, "people's fathers," or *tocohcoltiztzīn*, "our respected grandfathers." This generational idiom is, of course, temporalizing. But the "children" and "parents" referred to are not literal children and parents. Instead, the terms describe internal community differentiation in an idiom that emphasizes continuity through comembership in a "family." The contrast between "children" and "parents" or "grandparents" also emphasizes that the relationship between the two sectors should be one of *respeto*, "respect." *Respeto* is the most important quality by which relationships are evaluated, and its prototypical form is the deference of youth to the elderly.

Like the claim of prototypical identity, this rhetorical claim of synchronicity, "family" unity, and mutual respect serves complex functions. It exploits a nationally acceptable rhetoric of "Christian" and "family" values while constituting a resistance to the state's attempt to divide people by consigning some of them to the past, some to the future. This rhetorical practice facilitates the complex balancing act that preserves the indigenous family and community as intact units that will sustain their "children" when they are in need, but permit them to practice strategies that will enable them to capture resources from the urban, capitalist sector when these are available.

In spite of the fact that Malinche people appropriate (or attempt to recapture) some of the terms of citizenship in the Mexican state, calling themselves *campesinos* and *mexicanos*, prototypical citizens, few have much understanding of the organization of government beyond the most local level. The title of this chapter, *In nēca gobierno de Puebla*, "That government of Puebla," evokes the vague vision of the state in which their claims of citizenship are embedded. It comes from a narrative about the *Pillo* [píyo], a many-lived hero, which condenses several of the themes I have outlined above through which Malinche people assert their special identity and relative autonomy from the state. The text of this narrative, told by Don Otilio of San Miguel Canoa, is given below.[15]

In Cuento Den Pilloé

Machitia nicmolhuīlīz cē cuento den nēc antepasado, ōcmihtahuīliāyah in to-, tocohcoltzitzīhuān nēca tiempo ōmovivirhuiliāyah īpan Malintzīn cē, cē persona cē ītōcā ōcnombrarohqueh Pillo. Ōcnombrarohqueh Pillo nōn, nōn tēlpocatl pero āmo quimatiah, pero in īnacimiento nicān San Miguel Canoa.	It seems I will tell a story about that ancestor that our grandfathers who used to live in that time on the Malinche used to tell about, a, a person here that they called by the name "Pillo." They called him Pillo, that, that youth but they did not know, that his birthplace was here in San Miguel Canoa.
Huān tonces nōn angelito mozcaltia, āmo quimatia cōx, cōx Pillo, sino que ōcmachtiāya ōccalaquihqueh in escuela nīpapá, escuela, pero āmo ōcmatih tlen īvida in angelito, zan tres días de estudios ōquipix īnnahuācqueh in maestrohtin. Huān quihtoa, "Āmo melāhuac in ammaestrohtin, hasta ocachi nicmati, āmo namehhuān." Huān ōquihtohqueh, "Pero pues quēnin?" "Quēmah."	And then when that child was growing up, he did not know that he was really the Pillo, but he knew when his father put him in school, school, because he didn't know what kind of child he was, he had just three days of study with the teachers. And he says, "Surely you are not teachers, for I know more, not you all." And they said, "But how can it be then?" "Certainly."

Entonces quiliah, ōcōtzqueh
nītahtzīn īpapá nōn īpapá in
īmamá que "Xiquihto
moangelito yēcmati bastante,
melāhuac yōtēchtlān de maestro. Āxān, tlen ocachi mas
ticchīhuāzqueh, tlen ocachi
estudio timacāzqueh? Ocachi y
ōtēchpanāhui de maestro, pues
ocachi ye quimati." Tonces
ōquihtoh in nēca pipiltontzīn,
"Ya, tonz quīza de nicān toconēh."
Quihtohqueh, "Quēmah."

Entonces, ōqui-, ōquīncuiqueh
in ichcahuān ōyec pastor. Huān
de nōn ōmpa ōyah,
yōmotlaneloāyah nochi in
occequi īcompanero piltontztzīn.
Tonces ōquimilhuiāyah, "In tlā
de melāhuac
nannocompañerohhuān,
timotlālih, timotlānih īhtec in
nicānca cōcoy ōctzīn tcalaquih
de nicānca hormiga, cān
tiquīzatīhueh?"
Huān ōctohqueh, "Pero quēn
ticoneltocāzqueh?"
"Tlā nanquittāzqueh in
namēchittitīz, nitlayecanāz huān
xnēchchicahuīcān."
Huān entonces ye zan
ōmopitzāhuayah īhtec in, in, in
āzcacoyōctli de nīn hormiguita,
panōhtih hasta occē lado.
Quimiliah, "A ver, xtta cā y
ōniquīzāco." Toz in yehhuān
ōcmonehuīhqueh, cada quien
ītzontecon mopitzāhuac, pero
aīc queman āhueliti
ōmopitzāhqueh, porque tlēca ye,
calaquih, quīzatih occē punto,
pero occē vida nīvida. Occē,

Then they said, they called his
father, his father, his parents
thus, "Speak to your child who
really knows enough, for sure he
has finished with us teachers.
Now what more will we do,
what more studies will we give?
He has surpassed us as a teacher,
he already knows more." Then
he said to that child, "Now, then
our child is leaving here."

They said, "Yes."

Then, he went off with sheep as
a shepherd. And from there he
went, he used to mingle with all
the other boys, his comrades.

Then he told them, "If you are
truly my comrades, we will
arrange, we will go down, we
will enter this hole of these ants,
where will we come out?"

And they said, "But how will we
follow you?"
"If you see what I will show you,
I will guide and you all guard
me."
And then he just made himself
thin inside the tunnel of these
ants, he passed over to the other
side.
He told them, "Let's see, see
how I came out." Then they did
the same, each one made his
head thin, but they did not really
become thin, because then,
when they go in, they come out
at another place, but in another
life, his life. It was another,

melāhuac occē īvida Dios
ōcmomaquilih.
Tonces de nōn, yeca.

Entonces ōquimi-, ōquihtoh,
"Neh ācmo nitlapiāz.
Neh ye, neh, neh ācmo nitlapiāz.
In neh, ye nic-, ye ni-, ye
nireinarōz."
Tonces ōcquilih nīpapá in
īmamāhuān, "Huān tlen in teh
ticpiāz, in teh noconēh."
Ōquihtoh, "Neh, papá nīn
novida aīc quenman, āmo, mā
tētzīnōzqueh porque
neh niquiza, nipanoā huehca,
huehuēyi pueblos
niquīndefenderoa in nocnīhuān
de San Miguel Canoa."
"Pero quēn?"
"Pues quēmah."
Huān ihquīn quihtoa,
"Xiconmachīlicān nosombrero.
Neh nicmo-, nicpia in
nosombrero, pero āmo
nosombrero de, de zōyatl, neh
nicpia nosombrero de cāmpāna."
Huān ōctziliniāya nīsombrero,
ōtziliniāya de quēmeh in
cāmpāna. Nōn, nōn tlācatzīntli,
n ōn Pillo.
Tonces ōmochīhuāyah in Santa
Misa. Huān zan ītlan
ōcalaquiyah in tiōpantzīntli,
tlatzacuah mochīhtzinoticah in
Santa Misa, huān īc
memehtehuah in ti ōpantzīntli,
machilīzqueh hasta īpan in
Malīntzīn quipia nīn in
tiōpantzīntli huālquīzah in gente
tlahtlapolōh nochi cateh īpan in
Malīntzīn in gente.

truly God had given him another
life.
Then as for that, it was done.

Then he said, he said, "As for
me I will no longer be a shepherd. Now I, I will no longer be
a shepherd. As for me, I will
rule as king."
Then his father and his mother
said, "And what will you have,
you are my child." He said, "As
for me, father, never in this life
of mine, let us not do ill to
people because when I go out, I
pass far away to great towns
where I defend my brothers from
San Miguel Canoa."

"But how?"
"Well of course."
And thus he said,
"Recognize me by my hat. As
for me, I have my hat, but not
my hat of palm leaves, I have a
bell hat."

And when he rang his hat, it
rang like a bell. That, that is
that gentleman, that Pillo.

Then they were making the
Holy Mass. And he just entered
the church as they are making
expiation, performing the Mass,
and carrying images on their
shoulders in the church, they
would know that on the
Malinche she even has this
church where people come out
when a hole opens, all the
people that there are on the
Malinche.

Huān yōquīxmatiah tlen clase de
persona cē nōn, tēlpocatl
quiliah, ihcōn tlātlātiāya in
padre,
"Xquittā, hijo, tēchchīhuīlih in
favor, tēchhuica hasta tochān,
āmo xiyez malo, a ver quēn
tiāzqueh hasta nicān ticateh in
Malīntzīn."
Quihtoa, "Ayāmo xmoyolcoc
ōcān. Ahorita tiāzqueh,
xcalaquicān, nitlatzacuāz."
Tonces ōquitlatzacuāya den
tiōpantzīntli, huān occuel
cuālmemehtehuah in
tiōpantzīntli, huān de
ōtlahtlapoah occuēl de ōmpa
cah cān ōcatca ōmpa nicān San
Miguel Canoa.
Tonces yōquīxmatiah nōn
tlācatzīntli yōnemiah.
Tonces ōquihtoh in nēca, in
nēca tlācatzīntli, "In neh nochān
īpan in Malīntzīn, in ōmpa
nicpia nochān, neh notōcā in
īpillo." Huān ōctla-, ōctlāliayah
in arreata de, de orilla, orilla nōn
huēi ātlahtli, ītech
ōmohuiyoniāyah nōn tēlpocatl,
pero huehca para nōn ātlahtli
ītōcā "Huetziātl," zan
"Cuānhuetziātl," ōmpa cah nōn
in ōn, inōn, nōn ātlahtli, ītech
nōn huēi ātlahtli
ōmohuiyoniāyah nōn, nōn Pillo
ōctōcāyōtiāyah. Huān tonces
ōncan, ō-, ōmonāmictīh,
ōquipix cē īfamilia, huān tonces
nōn īfamilia, ō-, ōyec zan ihcōn
ōquīzah yōpanoāyah huān tonces
ōqui-, ōcahcico nīfamilia ye
quipia nīpiltzīntli, ye
cocōxcācuiticah.

And when they realized what
kind of person that youth was
they say, thus the priest asks,

"Look, my son, do us a favor,
take us to your home, do not be
mean, let's see how we will go
to here where we are in the
Malinche." He says, "Don't
worry any more. Now we will
go, go in, I will close it up."

Then he was closing up the
church, and again they were
coming carrying the church, and
when it opened again there it
was in the place where San
Miguel Canoa is here.

Then they realized that that
gentleman was alive.
Then that gentleman said, "As
for me my home is on the
Malinche, there I have my
home, as for me my name is her
Pillo." And she is setting down a
lasso of the banks, the banks of
that great barranca, for that
young man to swing in it, but it
is a long way away to that
barranca named "Falling Water,"
just "Head Falling Water," there
where the barranca is, in that
great barranca where that one
who used to be called Pillo was
swinging. And then there he got
married, he had a wife, and then
when his wife was there, he just
went out, he passed over,
and then when he arrived when
his wife has his child, then she
is becoming sick.

Huān toz ōquilih, "Xnēchili in pura verdad, ta quēmeh āquin ōmichihqueh, cōx in nēca nocnīhuān de Canoa, unos ōyah en ciudad de Puebla, in āquin ōmichīhuāltihqueh. Tlā tinēchilīz de nicān, de nicān Canoa, nozo nimitzmictīz, huān tlā tinēchilīz de ciudad de Puebla, toz āmo nimitzmictīz." Pues in yeh ōctoayah in nēca zoātzīntli xamo mosalvarōz. Ōquilih, "Tlā de Puebla in āquin ōnēchchīhuāltihqueh nicpiāz nopiltzīntli." Tonces ōccocolih bastante chicahuac in nēca gobierno, de Puebla.
Tonces ōyāyahqueh in, ōyāyahqueh ye riarohtih in Puebla.
Ōquīntlachichinaltiāyah nōnqueh cuānmeh, para con eso quītzquiāyah, yecah guerra in gobierno. Ōquīmictiāyah miec tropa, miec fuerza ōc ōltihtlāniliāyah in nēca gobierno para que ōquīmictīzqueh nōnqueh personas ītōcā Pillo.
Pero aīc quēnman ōquīmictihqueh, porque ye occē īvida. Zan yeh in cuānmeh ōquīntlachichinaltiāyah, huān ōtlatōtōponiāyah in cuānmeh ōmocuepayah como personas de nōnqueh, nōnqueh cuānmeh de īca mismo īvoluntar, porque nōn Pillo, tlahco pe-, ītlahco gente, huān tlahco de mono, ōcatca nōn personas ītōcā Pillo.
Tonces cuando cualāni, cuando mococoh nīfamilia, ōquipix in īpiltzīntli, ōquihtoh, "Neh nicmictīz in angelito." Ōhuāllah,

And then he said, "Tell me the simple truth, who bewitched you, is it perhaps some of my brothers from Canoa, some who went to the city of Puebla, who bewitched you. If you will tell me here, someone from Canoa, I will kill you, and if you will tell me someone from the city of Puebla, then I will not kill you." Well, that lady said something, perhaps to save herself. She said, "Surely the ones who bewitched me to have a child are from Puebla." Then he very strongly hated that government of Puebla.
Then they went, those who went then whipped Puebla.
They made those heads burn up, the government did, in order to in that way seize the advantage in the war.
They killed many troops, that government sent many forces in order to kill those people called Pillo.

But they never killed him, because he had another life. They just made those heads burn, and when they shot the heads they turned into people with those, those heads by means of his very will, because that Pillo was half, half of him was a person, and half was a doll, he was that person named Pillo.
Then when he gets angry, when his wife was sick, she had his little son, he said, "As for me I will kill the baby." He came,

huān ōcalaquilih in espada in
angel de la guardia, huān
ōmotlalih īpan īcaballo, ihcōn
ōcuicatinēnca in angelito
chōcatinēnca. Ōmpa tlāmi in
cuento, de Señor Pillo de la
Malīnchī.

Tonces cuando, cuando nōn oc,
quemeh ōquihtoh, "In neh
nimomiquilīz ītech in ciudad in
nēchmictīzqueh pero miec, cada
pueblo, solamente in nēch-,
nēchtōcāzqueh in nocuerpo para
nimomiquilīz, pero cōza de
quihtōzqueh, in neh
nimomiquilīz de zan cē bala
nēchmacāzqueh huān īhtec
nocuācaxōn nēchtlalīzqueh, aīc
quēnman nimomiquilīz miec
yōmonehuīhqueh nēchmictia īc
San Luis Teolocholco, īc
Tetlanōhca, īc La Resurrección,
īc San Pablo del Monte, pero zan
nēchmaca cē balazo. Quihtoa,
"Yōnimomiquilih como Pillo,
pero āic quēnman nimomiquilih
in neh, momiquilīz. Pero
cuando ahcīz in hora huān
nicmictlāmīz, huān hasta
nētōcāzqueh pero por pedazo,
nēchchīhuāzqueh cada pedazo
de, de nīnacayō, para con eso
nochi mortaja en cada pueblo,
que tōcāzqueh īc San Pablo del
Monte, La Resurrección īc San
Luis Teolocholco īc Tetlanōhcoa
īc Huamantla, nochi in nōnqueh
pueblohtin que in tōcāzqueh
nīnacayō cada īpedazo de
īnacayō ye mortaja, huān cada
pueblo ōmpa quēmah tlāmīz in
último vida de Señor Pillo de la
Malīnchī."

and when he put the sword into
the guardian angel then he
mounted upon his horse, thus he
went carrying the baby who
went along weeping. There the
story ends, of the Lord Pillo of
the Malinche.

Then when, when regarding that
he said thus, "As for me I will
die in the city where they will
kill me, but many, each town,
they will just bury my body in
order for me to die, but they will
say often that I will die of just
one bullet which they will put
into my head
but I will never die even though
many equally kill me in San
Luis Teolocholco,
in Tetlanohca, in La
Resurrección, in San Pablo del
Monte, but they only give me
one bullet. He says, "I died as
Pillo, but I will never die as
myself, he will die.

But when the hour comes when
I will die at last, and they will
even bury me but piece by piece,
they will wrap each piece of, of
his flesh and this with its shroud
in each town, that they will bury
it in San Pablo del Monte, La
Resurrección, in San Luis
Teolocholco, in Tetlanohca, in
Huamantla, in all of those towns
when they will bury his flesh
each piece of his flesh in its
shroud, and each town there
certainly will end the last life of
the Lord Pillo of the Malinche."

The Pillo, like other legendary peasant heros, stands for a long tradition of violent resistance. While Don Otilio's narrative was not the moving performance of a master storyteller, the rhetoric of this resistance is obvious in it. The "sacred space" of San Miguel Canoa and the Malinche is distinguished from "the government of Puebla," with the potency and independence of the former asserted. The space is mapped, with the church at its center; the Pillo, like a church tower, wears a bell instead of a palm-leaf hat. The unity of the Malinche region is expressed in the listing of the towns and in the Pillo's instructions that a piece of his flesh be buried in each one. The equivalence of earth and flesh is expressed thereby, and the equivalence of the people of San Miguel Canoa with the earth of the volcano is asserted when they emerge from the earth in their church.

The Pillo is master of his world, using the great barrancas as his lariat; he belongs to the Malinche, female spirit of the mountain, and moves freely within her realm, under the volcano, through ant tunnels. The Pillo disdains school, where he can learn nothing, and devotes himself to a valued rural *oficio*, shepherding.[16] The guns of the troops of the government of Puebla cannot kill him, for he has many lives. Thus, his biography constitutes an assertion not only of the separateness of his space, but of the "control of time." Of most interest in the story of the Pillo, however, is his fight against *in nēca gobierno de Puebla*, "that government of Puebla." The designation of this entity as a primordial enemy reflects both the history and the contemporary situation of the Malinche region vis-à-vis the city.

In return for Tlaxcalan assistance in the conquest of the Aztecs, Charles V and Philip II of Spain restricted land ownership in the province to Indians. But immediately to the south, the city of Puebla was founded to organize Spanish occupation of the region.[17] Pressure from this new center was intense; in spite of royal restrictions on Spanish land ownership in Tlaxcala, even in the sixteenth century hundreds of Spaniards moved into the province. By the beginning of the seventeenth century, Tlaxcala was split into two sectors, one of "Indian continuities, population decline, and corporate action" and the other "a bustling European subsociety . . . connected with the rest of New Spain and increasingly rooted in general provincial life" (Szewczyk 1976). Gibson (1967) believed that by this date the uniquely "Indian" identity of the province was very much a thing of the past. But since the official policy of the government of New Spain continued to hold that Tlaxcala was "Indian," but Puebla was "Spanish," the notion of *in nēca gobierno de Puebla* captures beautifully the Indian's partial penetration of the historical situation. The fact that the enemy of the Pillo was not simply "Puebla," but its "government," indexes Indian attention to the state as a particularly Spanish sector.

The designation of *in nēca gobierno de Puebla* as the enemy of the people of the Malinche captures a contemporary concern as well. The story of the Pillo was told by Don Otilio, who lives in San Miguel Canoa, a town located barely in the state of Puebla, artificially separated from its own western ward of San Isidro Buensuceso by the ruler-straight line of the Puebla-Tlaxcala boundary shown on map 1.

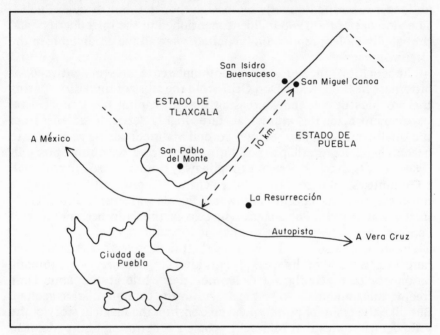

Map 1. The Puebla-Tlaxcala boundary

Canoa is one of the most "indigenous" communities on the Malinche, with virtually 100 percent of its population of about 15,000 speaking Mexicano. Many women, children, and elderly men are monolingual. From 1920 until 1960 its ethnic distinctiveness was accompanied by political autonomy; Canoa was the *cabecera* "seat" of its own *municipio*. By the late 1950s an important industrial corridor had developed along the Mexico City–Veracruz highway on the northern edge of the city (the Puebla Volkswagen plant, in the 1970s the largest industrial facility in Latin America, is the cornerstone of this district) and needed space for expansion and worker housing. The Tlaxcalan state line blocked expansion to the north and northwest, so such space was available only in the indigenous *municipios* of Canoa and La Resurrección. In 1960, these were merged into the larger *municipio* of Puebla, and given the status of *junta auxiliar*.

This reorganization, demoting Canoa and La Resurrección to "auxiliary" status, enabled the city of Puebla to control new water sources high on the volcano and to develop residential subdivisions, industrial parks, and garbage dumps on the lands of the formerly independent towns. Canoa could no longer deal with the state and national government directly; every petition had to go through the Puebla municipal authorities. Applications for development or regulation in the community were no longer submitted directly by local authorities, but through Puebla. The violence of the 1968 incident mentioned in the introduction, and the equally violent repression it elicited, were all too predictable in the circumstances.

The people of Canoa must have contemplated this history with special bitterness in 1983, when Don Otilio told the story of the Pillo. During the previous decade, an increasing flow of capital from the federal government made full municipal status highly desirable, at least from the small-time local perspective. Several Malinche towns petitioned to become separate municipalities during this period, with some possibility of success, since they strove to split away from other relatively small communities. But to successfully separate Canoa, with its valuable resources, from the enormous power of Puebla was simply unthinkable in the real world. The magical success of the Pillo became, in this context, especially pleasant to imagine.

The story of the Pillo, like the other rhetorical projects I have reviewed here, is a "weapon of the weak." This kind of talk asserts the symbolic autonomy of the indigenous communities while at the same time freeing their members to "forage" within the capitalist, state sectors. But, like the claim of prototypical citizenship, the magical story of the Pillo demonstrates that Malinche people's penetration of the Mexican system is, to borrow Willis's (1977) usage, "limited." It serves the ends of resistance and the construction of relative autonomy, but it tends to reproduce a structural position in which continual expropriation of the resources of the communities by the state can continue. For the intact and coherent indigenous community is not merely a source of symbolic strength and material succor to its citizens. Its capacity to involute in response to "superexploitation," and thereby to continue to reproduce almost entirely with its own resources an important component of the Mexican labor force, is a fundamental component in the "balancing act" of the Mexican state itself, which has displayed a remarkable political stability in the context of economic dependency. The degree to which this balancing act can continue in the face of today's hyperinflation and capital drain may be largely dependent on the ingenuity of citizens in the indigenous peasant sector.

Notes

1. Domingo Arenas was probably killed by Zapatista officers (León-Portilla 1978).

2. In an earlier paper (Hill 1985), I used the term "consciousness" to discuss the ideological foundations of language use among the people of the Malinche. Having discovered Willis's work, I believe that his notion of "penetration" is a more accurate term for the sort of understanding of their situation that Malinche people have.

3. I have explored some of these redefinitions in an earlier paper, where David Coombs and I examined the use of *humilde* in Quechua-speaking communities in Peru (Hill and Coombs 1982). There we argued that the redefinitions are often ambiguous, matching the process that Reisman (1970) called "masking".

4. The Partido Revolucionario Institucional, "the Party of the Institutional Revolution," has controlled Mexico since the 1930s.

5. While corn cultivation on the Malinche is mainly for domestic consumption, nearly all cultivators hope to make money by the sale of surpluses. Warman (1980) has shown that in Morelos such sales have a clearly negative impact on the household economy, and no longer constitute a viable strategy for acquiring cash.

6. While Warman (1980) emphasizes the ingenuity of the peasant sector, recent work by Lomnitz, Vélez Ibañez, and others draws our attention to equivalent ingenuity among urban people. The elaborate family networks and mutual aid societies of urbanites may be a comparable involution, which keeps the work of reproduction largely within the domestic sector.

7. Other important strategies are mobility, secrecy, and hierarchy. Detailed discussion of these is beyond the scope of the present chapter, so I sketch them only briefly here. The strategy of mobility is clearly evidenced in labor migration but is most important during periods such as the 1910 revolution, when local systems are especially stressed. On the Malinche I have met elderly women who were *adelitas*: women (often with little children) who abandoned their devastated homes and fields to follow their men in the revolutionary armies. On the Malinche secrecy is seen in the reluctance to discuss local magical practices, such as the techniques by which the *tlaciuhqueh*, "hail bringers," manipulate the weather. Secrecy amplifies community solidarity and coherence by providing a set of symbols that are inaccessible to penetration by outsiders. Hierarchy is seen in the training for leadership that people receive in the ritual system. Thus, if senior men are assassinated, people in lower-level careers will be ready to step into their place. These strategies work. The towns of the Malinche date from *congregación* in the late sixteenth and early seventeenth centuries (some may date to the preconquest period). Most recently, the 1910 revolution and the influenza epidemic of 1918 virtually depopulated many of them (even given probable miscounting, the figures from the 1920 census are horrifying), but they have re-formed with surprising vigor.

8. Women are viewed locally as marginal to the ritual system, to the task of making a living, and even to the major local symbolic adaptation, the "syncretic

project" of "speaking Mexicano, with its complex dialectic of purism and hispanization" (Hill 1987). Very few women have regular wage labor. While women may own land and do much field labor, they are not treated as the first-line cultivators. The work of women is endlessly opportunistic, involving, in addition to a full range of household tasks, the scut work of agriculture, small trade (which may contribute a very large proportion of cash income to a household), and a few crafts. Women support men in the stewardship of the saints. While some types of ritual kinship involve single-sex dyads, the major types require two couples. While men tend to be ideologues, women are often cynical or negative about local institutions.

9. Among the CNC activists I have met are a man who works as a policeman in Puebla and a man who has held a steady full-time job for many years in a factory that makes ammunition. In April of 1988, during a hotly contested national election, the CNC announced that it would be legal for members of the union to purchase used pick-up trucks (made before 1983) in the United States and import them into Mexico without the usual fees. Bakers, schoolteachers, and small industrialists scurried to join the CNC so that they, too, could rush to Ciudad Juárez to buy a Texas *troca* (a border-Spanish neologism that Malinche people were amused to learn was synonymous with their *camioneta*).

10. The impact of attention by urban intellectuals seeking their "roots" by learning Nahuatl is brilliantly treated in Judith Friedlander's study of the Morelos town of Hueyapan (Friedlander 1975). Only in 1988 did we finally encounter such an enthusiast in San Miguel Canoa. The neglect of the Malinche region may be due to the fact that it lies largely within the state of Tlaxcala. The Tlaxcaltecans fought on the Spanish side in the conquest, and are often considered "traitors" to the Indian component of Mexican identity. The fact that the volcano on which they live bears the name of La Malinche, Doña Marina, mistress of Cortés (who stands prototypically for the subjugation of the Indian) may also render the locale problematic. For local people, though, the female spirit of the volcano is no pliant victim, but a dangerous patroness of illicit love, who lures men to their deaths in her treasure-filled caves.

Note that I am here using "Nahuatl" to refer to the Nahua speech of the Central region (the states of México, Morelos, Tlaxcala, and the Cholula-Huejotzingo area of Puebla). "Nahua" is a more general term that includes varieties of the language spoken in other regions such as the Sierra de Puebla, Vera Cruz, Michoacán, and so on.

11. Note how Worsley seems to "presuppose" the idea that the ethnic identities merged in the synthesis are "older," and that the synthesis itself is "new." I will return to this point.

12. While "folklore" appears on the Malinche, it has not yet invaded the sacred sphere. For instance, in San Miguel Canoa the "Dance of the Moors and Christians," a favorite part of the national "folklore," is performed at school graduations. But a very different, unsanitized, version surfaces on the day of the festival of the patron saint: real machetes are used, not the schoolboy wooden swords, and clowns joke obscenely among the dancers. School graduations are for some purposes treated like sacred occasions (graduates have ritual sponsors, called *padrinos*), but they are still marginal to the construction of the sacred space.

13. I conducted an informal survey on this point through the *Nahua News-letter*. Several investigators answered my question about *mexicano*, and none had seen the same usage in their field areas.

14. In August 1988, with Mexico in full-blown economic *crisis* and the fifty-year PRI domination clearly eroded, Mexicano was more in evidence than ever in San Miguel Canoa. The language clearly posed no special barrier to making a living—the *crisis* meant that Nahuatl-speaking women who sold corn-on-the-cob and homemade tortillas on street corners made more money than school-teachers. But the young Spanish speaker living in the town in hopes of learning the language reported to us that his efforts to speak were rejected: "When I speak Mexicano, the people don't respect me."

15. In sad anticipation of a time (that I hope will never come) when it may be dangerous to be known as an assistant of anthropologists from the United States, I have given Don Otilio a pseudonym. While this denies him rightful credit for his knowledge and friendship, it may protect his life and property. For those who wish more information about him, he is S5 in Hill and Hill (1986).

16. The narrator of the story, Don Otilio, took up goatherding, in addition to corn cultivation, as his main occupation only a year or so after telling the story, when he was in his early fifties. The herding largely replaced construction work as his source of cash income.

17. Puebla has drained its hinterlands of resources; a case study is provided in Bonfil Batalla's (1973) study of the underdevelopment of the ancient city of Cholula.

References

Barre, Marie-Chantal
  1983   *Ideologías indigenistas y movimientos indios*. Mexico: Siglo Veintiuno.
Bonfil Batalla, Guillermo
  1973   *Cholula: la ciudad sagrada en la era industrial*. Mexico: UNAM/INAH.
Del Castillo, Porfirio
  1953   *Puebla y Tlaxcala en los días de la revolución*. Mexico.
Fabian, Johannes
  1983   *Time and the other*. New York: Columbia University Press.
Friedlander, Judith
  1975   *Being Indian in Hueyapan: a study of forced identity in contemporary Mexico*. New York: St. Martin's Press
Gibson, Charles
  1967   *Tlaxcala under Spanish rule*. Stanford: Stanford University Press.
Hill, Jane H.
  1985   The grammar of consciousness and the consciousness of grammar. *American Ethnologist* 12: 725–737.
  1987   Women's speech in modern Mexicano. In *Language, gender, and sex in comparative perspective*, S. U. Philips, S. Steele, and C. Tanz (eds.), 121–160. Cambridge: Cambridge University Press.
Hill, Jane H., and David W. Coombs
  1982   The vernacular remodelling of international languages. *Applied Linguistics* 3: 224–234.

Hill, Jane H., and Kenneth C. Hill.
  1986   *Speaking Mexicano*. Tucson: University of Arizona Press.
León-Portilla, Miguel
  1978   *Los manifiestos en Náhuatl del Emiliano Zapata*. Mexico: UNAM/
           INAH.
Manz, Beatrice
  1988   *Refugees of a hidden war: the aftermath of counterinsurgency in
           Guatemala*. Albany: SUNY Press.
Nutini, Hugo G., and Betty Bell
  1980   *Ritual kinship: the structure and historical development of the
           compadrazgo system in rural Tlaxcala*. Princeton: Princeton Uni-
           versity Press.
Reisman, Karl
  1970   Cultural and linguistic homogeneity in a West Indian village. In *Afro-
           American anthropology*, Norman E. Whitten, Jr. and John F. Szwed
           (eds.), 29–144. New York: Free Press.
Rothstein, Frances
  1974   Factions in a rural community in Mexico. PhD diss., Department of
           Anthropology, University of Pittsburgh.
Scott, James
  1985   *Weapons of the weak*. New Haven: Yale University Press.
Szewczyk, David M.
  1976   New elements in the society of Tlaxcala, 1519–1618. In *Provinces of
           early Mexico*, I. Altman and J. Lockhart (eds.), 137–154. Los Angeles:
           UCLA Latin American Center.
Warman, Arturo
  1980   *"We come to object": the peasants of Morelos and the national state*.
           Baltimore: Johns Hopkins University Press.
Willis, Paul
  1977   *Learning to labor*. New York: Columbia University Press.
Wolf, Eric R.
  1982   *Europe and the people without history*. Berkeley: University of Cali-
           fornia Press.
Worsley, Peter
  1984   *The three worlds*. Chicago: University of Chicago Press.

4. To Be Indian, to Be Bolivian: "Ethnic" and "National" Discourses of Identity

Thomas Abercrombie

Introduction

Indians and Colonial Discourse

Many of the authors in this book share the goal of "decolonizing" anthropological approaches to the cultures of Latin America. This necessitates consideration of the colonizing cultures and the colonial situation, along with the colonized, as objects of study. Decolonization requires abandoning the assumption that indigenous societies are autonomous cultural isolates and recognizing that, faced with colonial and state domination, they are inevitably altered by their relationship to dominating forces. This new approach recognizes as well how colonizing cultures, and their "states," are shaped by their relationship to those they dominate (Stoler 1989). It is this interface, this asymmetrical, rigged, power-infused discourse, that is the focus of investigation here.

Such an approach highlights the old problem of defining the unit of study. It certainly does not solve the problem, since we must still analytically "bound" the sociocultural "voices" discernible in intercultural discourse. How we do so must simultaneously offer a viable alternative to the methodological assumptions—involving closed "Saussurean systems"—of a structural-functional or structural/semiotic approach. One option is to focus on the particular situations, institutions, and processes in which colonial interlocutors apprehend one another, recognizing that for the actors, it is this *interface* that determines the cultural whole, even when the interface is *experienced* as a defensive wall, insulating their world from that of their Other. Instead of a "whole-cloth," we must see, then, a plurality of partially and asymmetrically interpenetrating meaning systems, and we must ask how these systems form and interact.

In the Andean case, centuries of colonial domination (and resistance to it) have produced many hundreds of small, community-sized "ethnic groups," centered on the "county seats," towns into which pre-Columbian populations were forced to settle. Within these rural towns, "Indians" (as they are called, deceptively, by city folks) generally define themselves as members of a local group, coterminous with town-territory, and beyond it, as citizens of the province and department defined by the nation-state to which they also pertain. Among such towns, even closely neighboring ones, the indices of shared culture may reduce to speaking an "Indian" language (Quechua and/or Aymara), and to a similarity of cultural practices, many of which (like saints' fiestas, town council governments, etc.) have been elaborated from the impositions of "state culture."

In some cases, these community-based cultural units have common pre-Columbian origins as territorial fragments of larger past polities, and have drifted apart due to colony-imposed isolation from one another. In most cases, the clearest index of cultural similarity among even neighboring towns—indeed, within Spanish America in general—is the analogous means used to resist the dominant culture. The colonizers, too, have adapted to their changing prey: urban "non-Indians" continue to make the relationship of their culture to that of "Indians" fundamental to their own identities, if usually via "ostensive self-identification by negation" (White 1978: 151).

More than four-and-a-half centuries have passed in the Andes since the first interpretive clash between utterly distinct cultural Others. Colonialism has been much tardier in coming to some of the lowland areas of the Amazon basin, perhaps accounting for the relative ease with which lowland specialists seem to know when they have found Indians (that is, truly "Native" South Americans). In the highland region, however, the intercultural discourse of colonialism has matured to the point that its interlocutors have already internalized their respective images of one another to a considerable degree. Given their advantage in force, it is not surprising that aspects of the colonizers' value systems have become hegemonic, so that the stigma attached long ago by Europeans to "Indianness" has worked its way into "Indian" self-consciousness as well. Consequently, self-proclaimed Indians are exceedingly scarce, apart from urban representations of "Indian" types in folkoric pageantry: they persist in this discourse only as romanticized or stigmatized alters.[1]

Ethnic Categories and Ethnic Groups

In the early nineteenth century, postindependence politicians sought to ban the term "Indian," and to replace it with "Bolivian" or "Peruvian." But that, and allied policies that aimed to privatize land and create the climate in which an agro-industry might ripen, did nothing to stop rural peoples from insisting, sometimes through revolt, on a degree of self-determination, including the retention of collective land tenure and the continued reproduction of cultural difference (see Platt 1982, 1984; Rivera 1984). In this century, postrevolutionary governments legislated the replacement of the resilient "Indian" and "indigenous" by *campesino* ("peasant"), insisting again on aiding in rural peoples' "self-improvement." Nonetheless, the sorts of "Indian" practices that such regimes have decried (though for certain circumscribed purposes, admired as well) continue to persist. Multiple and diverse, the "differences" of rural cultural formations can be appreciated in their particulars through an ever-growing body of ethnographies (Abercrombie 1986; Albó 1975, 1976a, 1976b,1979, 1987; Bastian 1978; Godoy 1981; Harris 1982; Platt 1978; Rasnake 1988a, 1988b).

In the pages that follow, the reader will note that I slip between analysis of a particular rural cultural formation, "K'ulta culture" (itself internally divisible), and references to a generalized rural cultural type to which K'ulta belongs. This slippage, typical of Andeanist ethnography, accedes to the colonial situation itself, which continues to posit itself in the form of a relationship between two opposed cultural poles, "Indian" and "European," glossable as "rural" and "urban." But to suggest the existence of *a* rural/indigenous culture in the Andes, what is often called, in the literature, "the Andean," is usually to fall victim to "non-Indians'" essentializing stereotype of "the Indian." In other words, "the Andean" is only rightly studied as a (usually utopian) image projected by various urban groups (Flores Galindo 1986). This intellectual tradition also defines cultural boundaries "etymologically," assuming that trait continuities from a pre-Columbian past are adequate to analytically constitute contemporary cultures. We must avoid, too, essentializing *a* Hispanic urban culture. In spite of George Foster's (1960) early warnings, we still fail to appreciate the implications of the cultural multiplicity of the colonizers, who, after all, came from "The Spains," a variety of culturally distinct "nations" within an absolutist empire. In the Andes an "urban," "Hispanic" or "European" culture exists, like an "Indian" one, only when we are studying stereotypes. I do not therefore dismiss such stereotypes as "mere" images, since, as they are produced in, and produce, systems of inequality, they are often invested with terrible power.

Although such power is experienced as symbolic as well as physical coercion, we must beware of psychological reductions that collapse long-term discursive relationships into the minds of individuals. A recent analysis of miners' "popular religion," for instance, suggests that we see such beliefs and practices as a folk-theory or critique of capitalism made through the subtle transformation (or deformation) of Indians' cosmologies as they become proletarianized (Taussig 1980, based largely on Nash 1979; see also Platt 1983). This analysis may work as a literary allegory of the colonial experience, a reading of the colonial context in the subjective transformation of a single generation. But rural-to-urban migration and proletarianization is a well-studied reality; it has been going on now since the conquest (and before), and it has produced some permanently interstitial cultural formations. There is enough evidence already to suggest that a specialized urban/mining "cosmology" has existed for a few hundred years. The "urban Indian" fashioners of such cosmologies (the distinct cultural type known in the eighteenth century as *indios criollos,* now called *cholos/cholas*) have been around for yet a longer time, as a dominant force in mining, in petty marketing, and as rural elites. Consigning such complex and long-lived cultural forms to the status of an ephemeral subjective acculturation that rural "Indians" pass through on their way to becoming urban "nationals" misses the larger point, since even when it is "true" in an individual case, the cultural order thereby taken up has a life and history of its own.

We can begin to characterize some regional "types" of rural group, the varying histories of which owe to combinations of pre- and postconquest sources and effects. For example, the small scale of most social groups in Bolivia's Department of Oruro contrasts with the size of Macha, in the neighboring Department of Potosí, which has a population in excess of ten thousand individuals. While Macha more or less conforms in territory and internal social divisions to a single preconquest dual-organized kingdom (see Platt 1982, 1986, 1987), K'ulta, an Oruro group, is a fragment of what had been a larger kingdom. Yet this process of fragmentation has advanced still further in the vicinity of Lake Titicaca, near La Paz. I have documented the colonial and republican dynamics of this process of fragmentation—which is also a process of cultural genesis—elsewhere (Abercrombie 1986).

The highly fragmented and factionalized rural region near La Paz (Albó 1975, 1976a) has recently become the principal hotbed of a different sort of cultural genesis, one that uses language as a key index. Indigenous nationalist movements like the Movimiento Revolucionario Tupac Katari foster an equation of language and culture (and class) to self-consciously generate ethnic awareness. This foment is centered in the major urban areas of La Paz (for Aymara) and Cochabamba (for Quechua). The relative success of these movements in their respective zones of influence may be tied to both the relative fragmentation of solidary rural groupings in these regions (subject to the greatest incursions of hacienda expansion and to the deformations introduced by the Agrarian Reform when haciendas were expropriated) and the reaggregative possibilities arising especially in these city-influenced areas via city-based indigenous language broadcasting (Albó 1987).

We must carefully differentiate these essentially political formulations from the analytic use of the Aymara and Quechua labels in the anthropological literature. When authors of ethnographies of small-scale communities have sought to characterize a more-inclusive "type" to which their community pertains as a "token," they often turn to these language categories or to the more-embracing "Andean." Perhaps it is because language seems misleadingly the clearest index of cultural difference (but see Urban and Sherzer 1988; Boas 1940), but it certainly also results from the previous existence of these language-equals-culture labels in the literature (as in, for instance, the HRAF).

For the fact is, in Bolivia, use of the language name to characterize cultural pertinence makes no sense at all. As Albó (1976b) has shown, based on the language data of recent census reports, the boundary between the two languages is continually shifting in the Bolivian highlands, with Aymara, in most cases, rapidly giving way to Quechua. Moreover, some degree of bi- and multilingualism is the norm. Language here is an index of the relative influence of a linguistic hierarchy propagated by historically specific forces, not of "indigenous" cultural boundaries.

Having rejected pan-Andean, language-based, and historically derived "ethnic regions" as characterizers for more general "cultural groupings," it behooves us here to limit ourselves to a particularist orientation. Whatever meanings might adhere to a certain form of kinship system, or moiety organization, or ritual battle, or whatever other "pre-Columbian" trait one might highlight, are today produced and interpreted within the (semi-open) semiotic systems produced at locally or situationally specific intercultural loci (or "town groups"), which intersect with national and international systems as significantly as with neighboring town groups. And it is to such a particular example that I now turn.

Ayllu K'ulta, where I have carried out fieldwork, corresponds closely to the district recognized by the Bolivian state as Canton Cruce-Culta. It is a good example for a variety of reasons other than my knowledge of it: because it is of intermediate scale (about six thousand inhabitants); because it emerged ex nihilo during the colonial period as a fragment of a documented pre-Columbian polity; and because it contains internal *ayllu* segments in the process of fissioning into yet smaller "cultural groups," as are most such polities in Bolivia and Peru. That is, K'ulta's existence as a unit is as contested and contestable as the majority of rural groups in the area, and midway in the process of fragmentation or "micro-ethnogenesis," between the Macha and Lake Titicaca extremes.

In the following section of the chapter I will show how K'ulta emerged as a recognizably distinct voice, with a long history of internalizing its

Other (that is, the "states" that have dominated it). This quest for—and analysis of—a particularly *rural* cultural identity, suffers the disadvantage of creating a hypostatization, making a *whole* entity out of what is but *part* of a relationship. To counterbalance this effect, I will turn in the final section of the paper to K'ulta's *urban* complement, the modern cosmopole and state, also a hypostatization, with its own internalized Other. I hope to show that rural/"Indian" and urban/"non-Indian" cultural formations are coimplicated as parts of a single "colonial situation," while remaining distinct analytic arenas, as experientially "real" mutual hypostatizations constituted by each Other's gaze in a discourse of power and identity. But to demonstrate this we must turn to specifics.

The State within the Indian

Identity and Sociocultural Unit Definition: The Case of K'ulta
Self-labeling in the countryside generally reflects the "segmentary" nature of the region's groups. Each is composed of a hierarchy of *ayllus* (intratown groups), with numerous patrilines and hamlets, the lower organizational levels within each *ayllu*.[2] In the K'ulta case about six thousand people are divided into five territorially bounded and mostly endogamous named *ayllus*. These *ayllus* subdivide a 1,000 sq/km territory, across which more than 120 hamlets are scattered. These constitute landholding exogamous patrilines. Group identity also takes a segmentary form: hamlet/patriline membership (the lowest "corporate" level) is of great significance in terms of everyday practice, while *ayllu* solidarity involves cross-cutting alliances among patrilines/hamlets, the defense of common *ayllu* lands, and by the election of *ayllu*-level authorities through fiesta sponsorship.[3] The moiety level (*ayllus* are grouped into "upper" and "lower" divisions) then intervenes between *ayllu* and the maximal local unit, "Ayllu (and Canton) K'ulta." At the center of this Canton-Ayllu there is an empty ritual-center town with church, offices of the *ayllu* authorities, civil registry, and so on. When repeatedly asked where he or she is from, a K'ulta inhabitant will recite a litany working inward from most inclusive (Bolivia) to least inclusive (hamlet or lineage name), pausing at length on "Ayllu K'ulta" as the clearest but least compromising or "private" of group memberships.

One certainly will not hear reference to terms like *Andean*, *Indian*, or *Aymara*, nor will one hear any reference to a group called Asanaqi, a conquest-period "kingdom" into which the *ayllus* and territory of K'ulta were once woven.[4] Asanaqi, like the more embracing federation of kingdoms it belonged to (the Killaka federation), has been effectively erased from local memory, except for a trace persisting now only in the ranking of mountain deities. And yet, if one could have crossed today's K'ulta territory with the conquistadors in the 1530s, there would have been no trace of K'ulta.

Indeed, if one travels across "K'ulta territory" today, one might well, in the northern and western parts of the area pertaining to "its" *ayllus* Ala-Kawalli and Qollana, find that many people there reject the notion of belonging to Ayllu K'ulta. This is because K'ulta is midway along the process of fission along its segmentary seams, as constituent *ayllus* seek autonomy, which is to say, cantonal status and a direct association with the Bolivian state.

This process of fragmentation characterizes most of Bolivia's rural polities today, and can be accounted for as in part a product of the expansion and improvement of the road system and transportation, increasing participation in the cash economy and marketing activity, and the erosion of the perceived benefits of continued participation in larger segmentary entities like K'ulta. Nonetheless, the groups hiving-off of K'ulta share in common the effort to reproduce, in a microcosmic form, precisely the sort of administrative/ritual structure that character-izes K'ulta: All are planning or building a capital town, dividing into subsections among which authority posts may rotate, and developing some form of *fiesta-cargo* system by which to create the authorities whose mediating roles will define the new group and its components vis-à-vis the state. The reproduction of this institutional framework can only in part be accounted for as a product of state exigencies. For state recognition, a canton must have a platted capital town, situated on a road. However, the *fiesta-cargo* systems and internal segmentation re-produced in the new towns in K'ulta territory respond to no state requirements, past or present, though at one time both *fiestas* (saints' day celebrations) and *cargos* (offices in town councils) were required by church and state. But to understand the significance of these *locally* produced sociocultural forms, and to see how they simultaneously meet and subvert interventions of church and state, we must consider how they were produced and what meaning system they engender.

Encomienda, Reducción, Cabildo, and Buena Policía

Until the mid-seventeenth-century foundation of the town of Santa Barbara de K'ulta, "K'ulta territory" was no more than a herding district divided up among several of the *ayllus* of the former Asanaqi kingdom, who held the lands against the expansive pressure of what had been the kingdoms of neighboring Charka federation. Between "first contact" and the end of the sixteenth century, Asanaqi was turned into a rent-producing property for conquistadores, divided into town districts, and meddled with in a variety of ways. In 1599, after the first few waves of epidemics, the area of K'ulta was so sparsely populated that Crown representatives were able to declare it uninhabited and, claiming it as Crown territory, put it up for auction. This was not just a revenue-producing measure, of course, but a means of providing lands to those Spaniards without the influence to receive a grant in Indians (an *encomienda*). In the case of these lands, however, the predominant Asanaqi lord was able, because of his people's ready supply of cash-convertible llamas and alpacas, to purchase the land back for the *ayllus* that claimed it.[5] Sometime thereafter (by the mid-seventeenth century), the town of Santa Barbara de Culta was founded, and the population of a large territory around it grouped together, as a political and ecclesiastical annex of the capital of the Asanaqi, Condo Condo (see Abercrombie 1986).

In part, the "emptiness" of K'ulta territory, a broken high-altitude region unsuitable for most agriculture but with numerous small, grass-rich "plains" between its jagged mountains, was a product of colonial policy as well as European-borne disease. Before the conquest, the kingdoms and federations of the region were in no sense urbanized; "capitals" like Condo Condo were but small settlements, perhaps no larger than many other such settlements clinging to hillsides through-out the territory. Aggregation into "civilized" towns was achieved through the imposition of a colonial resettlement policy, creating a few "concentration" towns in place of a multitude of difficult-to-subjugate hamlets.

In the first wave of Spanish colonial impositions, huge federations like the Killaka, comprising the Killaka, Asanaqi, Awllaka-Urukilla, and Siwaruyu-Arakapi kingdoms, were divided along social-structural lines as spoils of conquest. Thus, hereditary kingdom lords, and the "subjects" they controlled, became "natural lords" under the protection of the Spanish monarch. Under this system they owed rents to conquistadors who had temporary rights over them. At this early date, the Spanish understood little about indigenous social organization, so many king-doms, as well as federations, were fractured. However, the Killaka and Asanaqi kingdoms were treated in the opposite manner: they were lumped together as a single Crown-supervised grant of Indians (an *encomienda*, or *repartimiento*—a distribution and districting unit). The Crown gave a *conquistador-encomendero* rights to labor and tribute, but demanded in return that the grantee give the Indians civilization and Christianity. Thus, each grantee was to "resettle" the Indians, supervise the building of a church, and hire a priest to convert them.

Initial policies were, however, relatively vague and laxly enforced, making census, tribute collection, and evangelization difficult. Only with Viceroy Francisco de Toledo was the whole Indian population of Spanish Peru (which then included the area that is today Bolivia) subjected to a sweeping and planned transformation (Málaga Medina 1975). It was in 1574 that Toledo decreed the resettlement of the two kingdoms' population (then 11,526 individuals) from numerous smaller settlements into but four towns. Only two of these early colonial towns, San Pedro de Condo and San Juan del Pedroso (modern Challapata) correspond to the highland extension of Asanaqi (AGNA 9.17.2.5.; Cook 1975). The policy of "resettling" populations into concentrated *reducción* towns was to prove impractical to enforce, since Indians needed to reach distant fields and pastures to sustain themselves as tributaries. The result over time as people filtered back to remote corners and the population grew again (after an initial plummet) was the recognition of many more *reducción* towns, rather than abandonment of the policy.

Each *reducción* town was created in the image of a model Spanish town, with a plaza at the center of a tick-tack-toe style grid of streets (Foster 1960: 34–49). Around the plaza were placed a church, city council offices (*cabildo*), and jail. Living in them was to inculcate *"buena policia,"* the mark of civilization that Indians, by definition, lacked (Lechner 1981). The *cabildo* system as instituted by Toledo was modeled upon Spain's "democratic" communities. It included yearly rotating elective authorities, specifically *alcaldes* and *alguaciles*, posts inherited by the Spaniards from the Moors. But Toledo was not interested only in a change of forms, or necessarily in the promotion of democracy. Instead, such authorities were to carry out, under the guidance of the *encomendero* and local priest, the desired cultural transformation. They were to gather their people into the church for Spanish instruction and frequent catechism sessions, help to keep the nightly curfew (to stem adultery and fornication), to act as the jailors of refractory citizens, to do the rounds of their towns at specified hours—now rung out by newly forged church bells, and in general to locally instantiate the European gaze. But in some ways the system was adapted to extant Andean traditions. First and foremost, in the building of new towns and in the collection of tribute, tacit recognition was given to Andean *ayllus*, which were, at this point, smaller territorial fragments of kingdom-level *ayllus* that found themselves under a town's jurisdiction. A number of these fragment *ayllus* constituted the population and territory of each new town. Second, each political unit above the *ayllu* was to be divided into moieties, and town authorities established in moiety pairs. Finally, to ensure that the hereditary elite (whom Toledo and the chroniclers he commissioned branded as "illegitimate tyrants") did not undermine the supposed democracy of the towns, he excluded native nobility from full participation in the councils.

These steps were allied to some *truly* repressive measures that sought to extinguish idolatry in all its guises, so that a rational Christianity (and the submission to the divinely sanctioned authority of the absolutist monarch) could take hold. Only when cults devoted to idols, mummies, ancestral mountains, and sky beings were abolished could Andeans be wooed to the advantages of civitas and "good order."

The former semipriestly local nobility were at this time converted into purely secular "administrators" of royal subjects, who, like the landed gentry of the European dominions of Spain, were allowed to reign as "natural lords" (if only through the sufferance of the king). In pre-Columbian times, the hereditary elite were the patrons of the *wak'a*-ancestor cults (as representatives of "senior lines" in closer proximity to the gods than their subjects) through which their authority was legitimated at the same time as their subject communities were defined as collective descendants of ancestor deities. Such rites provided a positively laden value and conceptual framework that, by motivating a voluntary subjection of commoners to rulers, linked local kinship-residential units to *ayllus, ayllus* to kingdoms, and kingdoms to larger political units including, for a short time, the Inca state. The destruction and replacement of such complex ritual-economic-political cults by Christian practices within *reducción* towns, and the displacement of noble authority by elective town councils, might therefore have represented a truly radical transformation of Andean cultures.

But while this organized effort at sociocultural reform might seem guaranteed to have eliminated the differentia of "Indianness," forces from both above and below mitigated against it: the Spanish semifeudal colony could not do without a labor force culturally constituted as such, and found that they could not make "Indians" work for them through direct rule, without the mediation of native nobles and resultant partial autonomy; the colonized, too, no matter how effective their tactics of appropriation and reinterpretation of colonial impositions, found that retaining limited autonomy under colonial conditions was only possible by reproducing their (stigmatized) Indianness.

On the one hand, Indians, as a category of person with limited rights, subject to the benevolent paternalism of the colonizers, could not be done away with without losing the prerogative of levying forced labor, and without threatening the basis of aristocratic privilege (*no hay Indias sin Indios,* "there is no Indies without Indians," went the popular refrain—invoked to curb both ethnocidal and genocidal excesses). Besides, these policies were undermined by both expedience and the very same legal arguments that justified the assertion of the *king's* authority. For this reason, and because, as many attested, the Spaniards could not make the *naturales* ("naturals," as Indians were sometimes called) do their bidding without the supplication of their hereditary lords, the latter were left in place, although their territories and *ayllus* were fractured and many of their ritual duties and prerogatives outlawed (see Murra 1968).

Conversely, the "reduced" Indians appropriated the institutions of *doctrina* (rural parish) and *cabildo* (town council), and their lessons, in a novel way. Christ was equated with the sun; the Virgin, with the moon; saints, with atmospheric mediating powers (such as lightning) capable of carrying Christian potencies to men (Gisbert 1980; Cock and Doyle 1979; Silverblatt 1988); while the Spaniards' almost Manichean Christianity (Platt 1987) turned the ancestral deities "of below"—*manxapacha*, the Aymara term for underworld chosen as a gloss for the Spanish hell—into the diabolical opponents of the heavenly host. The Christian concepts also articulated, in the cultural synthesis that took place in these towns, with the pastoral and sacrificial idioms of socialization and authority of preconquest days. "Indians" came, at least by the mid-seventeenth century, to regard themselves as civilized sons of (a solarized) Christ; their pre-Columbian ancestors as the defeated satanic race of a prehuman age; and the underworld place-deities that they continued to ritually celebrate as the sources of necessary chthonic potencies that, domesticated by Christian powers, could still sustain them (Abercrombie 1986). These anti- or pre-Christian underworld beings and powers are portrayed (by today's "Indians") in the likeness of the Spaniards' image of Indians as Others (un-Christian and without *buena policía* regardless of Spanish efforts, as many colonial Spanish and contemporary urban accounts paint them). The asymmetrical power of the colonial gaze ensured the alienation of the Indian self (pushing it into the nearby and well-remembered past), but guaranteed its retention, in the shape of the transformed Indians' Other's Other.

Fiesta-Cargo Systems and the Demise of Kingdoms and Hereditary Lords

It is ironic that the tactics of resistance should have been developed through the very institutions and doctrines that the colonizers had strategically imposed to erase the past and to destroy resistance, but that is precisely what happened. It was the priests' responsibility to teach the ritual and doctrine of Christianity in the church during mass and catechism, but the Indians themselves were saddled with the *cofradías*, lay "confraternities" in the Spanish style, organized for the celebration of Christian feasts and transmission of the faith. In Spain and in colonial cities, these were formed along guild lines, with all of their mutual aid functions (Christian 1981; Celestino and Meyers 1981). But in the *reducción* towns, they became an essential structure for the articulation of *ayllus*. In some cases, each *ayllu* may have become a separate *cofradía* and specialized in a particular saint cult (Celestino and Meyers 1981; Platt n.d.; Varon 1981). In the Bolivian area, all Indians in the district of the *reducción* town seem to have become automatic members of all *cofradías* of the *reducción*. That is, elaborate intra- and inter-*ayllu* turn systems developed to spread the weight and honors of the responsibility equitably around. I have already noted that elective town council (*cabildo*) posts were instituted as moiety-level rotational posts. Sometime during the seventeenth century, probably, but certainly by the mid-eighteenth, these systems of civil and ecclesiastical obligations merged into a single system throughout the region, becoming what is called, in the literature, the *fiesta-cargo* system, a "prestige" ladder or fixed individual career of ritual and civil obligations. Individuals also belonged to patrilines and *ayllus*, however, and individual careers were intercalated (through patriline and *ayllu* rotational systems), to (re)produce town-level *ayllus*. Data from the late eighteenth century make it clear that such rotational systems were also extended beyond town boundaries to create complex intertown and interregional rotative systems through which the kingdom links among town-*ayllus* and federation links among different kingdoms were sometimes reaffirmed (see AGNA 9.6.5.6, F39v-40r). Thus, it seems that while colonial impositions of this sort conspired against the hereditary nobility and their (pre-Columbian-shaped) polities, they could also be made to work for them.

Indeed, although they were in large measure prevented from participating in the *cofradías* and *cabildos*, the hereditary elites aimed to become the heads of these organizations (sometimes via end-run maneuvers). For example, in Asanaqi, individuals who had reached the post of *jilaqata* in the rotative career system traveled to San Pedro de Condo, which had been the old capital. There they presented their staffs of office to Saint Peter, who is identified with the mountain Tata Asanaqi, and (most probably) were formally endorsed by the hereditary lord.

The hereditary elites' legitimacy was undermined, too, when they were forced by the Spanish to act as the henchmen who exacted the pound of flesh from their loyal subjects. Early on, in part through their efforts as legal advocates, some of these native aristocrats managed to buffer the impact of Spanish extractions of tribute and personal service (Rivera 1978; Stern 1982). A few, the "captains of the *mita*" who directed the labor levy to the great mining machine of Potosí, even tried to re-create lost glories through their organizational roles there (Saignes 1987). But by the eighteenth century, Indians had deserted the labor draft and abandoned their origin towns in massive numbers, settling in other areas or even becoming permanent wage-workers in the mines to avoid the combined weight of *mita* levy, tribute, personal service to priest and *mallku* (the Aymara term for a hereditary lord), and that most-hated of eighteenth-century obligations, the requirement to purchase unneeded goods from profit-gouging Spanish provincial administrators (*corregidores*) at exorbitant prices (Golte 1980; O'Phelan 1985).

Leadership, Legitimacy, and Rural Rebellions

A third blow to the native lords' authority came from the priests. Whether out of greed, hunger for power, or humane concern for their flocks, priests often sided against the lords. The Llanquipacha brothers, lords of Asanaqi in the town of San Pedro de Condo, apparently sent their priest, who had helped Indians in a suit against them, packing. In the latter case, when Indians from a nearby annex heard a rumor of the priest's exile, they stormed the town and murdered their kingdom lords (ANB EC 1781, no. 83).

From 1780 to 1783, rebellions extended throughout the Peruvian vice royalty, but the balance sheet of victims and alliances demonstrates that it was not a millenarian effort to displace all things Spanish and return to pre-Columbian forms. This was no longer possible. By the 1780s Hispanic and Catholic institutions and practices (and some Spaniards— at least, priests) had become necessary for "indigenous" societies. We can see this both in the nature of rebel fighting strategies and in the importance for rebels of colonial religion and administrative forms. In 1780 in the mining center of Aullagas, for example, local officials learned that town moieties (from the adjacent groups Macha and Pocoata) were preparing to descend on the town for their traditional (postconquest) ritual battle (*tinku*) in order to jointly murder all the town's Hispanic residents. But they were going to do this during the September feast of the powerful, devil-slaying Saint Michael, which now provided the ritual matrix within which such battles were fought (AGNA 9.5.2.1).

Rebel leaders of the 1780s like Tupac Amaru, Tomas Catari, and Tupac Catari did not simply take advantage of the priests' hostility to *corregidores* for strategic purposes; they needed the priests to celebrate the mass. All of these rebel leaders, in fact, dragged priests (at least, those who were not active collaborators) about with them on their campaigns, along with saint images, because Christianity, or aspects of it, like the town and its *cabildo* and *cofradía* system, had become an integral part of "being Indian." Although some priests were killed, especially when they tried to give refuge to other Hispanic officials, no rebel leader proposed throwing Christianity or the priests aside in favor of solar idols and *wak'as*. Similarly, though Tupac Amaru designated himself Inka Rey del Peru, he also called himself Viceroy; Tupac Catari, acting in such a role, appointed Oidores (colonial judges) within his rebel camp (Diez de

Medina 1981 [1781]: 180). The king, and most of the authority positions (if not their occupants) and administrative units of the colonial order were to be respected subsequent to the rebellions. During the first drawn-out rebel siege of La Paz, Tupac Catari, often cited as the most savage and bloodthirsty of rebel leaders, paused to have his priests lead processions and say mass during holy days of obligation (Diez de Medina 1981 [1781]: 127, 198–202). His starving adversaries had earlier watched from within the city walls as Catari's troops apparently looted the churches of the Indian peripheral parishes. In reality, he had saved precious relics and images from the flames of the siege, and built both a battlefield tent-church overlooking the town and a more permanent church out of reach of counterattacks, in which his Indians could be ministered to by captured and collaborationist priests.

As Szeminski (1987) has argued, missives from the rebels reinforce these impressions: their correspondence makes it clear that they expected both God and king to reward them for what they regarded as a kind of housecleaning, ridding the realm of a bad element who, through unbridled greed had become outlaw apostates. Spaniards became enemies because they failed to live up to the precepts of the religion and law that they had foisted on Indians. "Long live the King and death to the bad government" was the battle cry of Indians in their holy war, their mission from God, just as it was in the urban revolts of the same period.

Rebels clearly distinguished between the bad government that they sought to topple and the institutional structures of the colony that they sought to occupy for themselves. Rebel leaders sought, that is, to forge a link between the "nations" over which they ruled and the colonial state apparatus. Rebels sometimes discriminated finely between the "American-born" mestizos and Creoles, with whom they were willing, perhaps, to make amends, and the Peninsula-born Spaniards (*Chapetones*) against whom the mestizos and Creoles also held a grudge. We will see below that some mestizos and Creoles during this period also briefly harbored notions of an alliance of *all* "Americans" against the *Chapetones*. These hopes were soon dashed, in part because the "foot soldiers" among the indigenous rebels seem not to have drawn the fine distinction between "Spanish-Spanish" and "American-Spanish." By the time independence was achieved, and Creoles had made *themselves* into the "native-born" of their own nation-state (see Anderson 1983), substate distinctions among Indian nations had become anathema to them.

At the time of the eighteenth-century rebellions, colonial domination had become inextricably imbedded in the fabric of "indigenous" culture and society, and the efforts of later republican-period liberalism to dislodge "Indianness" met fierce, and largely successful, resistance. Such resistance, which has persisted to this day, often appeared—and appears—"revisionist" and procolonial against the enlightened-individualism with which it struggles. So the synthesis of old colonial institutions of *cabildo* and *cofradía* tends still to be reproduced today, even in the midst of social change and fragmentation. This does not mean, however, that the "civilizing" project that accompanied conquest was a complete success, and Christianity and *buena policía* integrally transplanted. As I will show, its assimilation by the occupants of *reducción* towns was quite selective, and their interpretation different from what the colonizers might have liked.

Christian Hegemony in K'ulta Political Theory

To appreciate the nature of the "local" perspective on the colonial conjuncture, it is helpful to turn to a short example that illustrates the virtual interdependence of "Christian" and "indigenous" deities, and of the state and ethnic group. Elsewhere I have analyzed this in various of its manifestations. Here I will focus on the public fiesta rites by which local authorities are invested with power.

In K'ulta political thought, the power of locally produced authorities is conceived via a metaphor linking productive practice to that of social practice: authorities are respectfully addressed by their "subjects" as *Tata Llantiru*, "Father Herd-Leader," applying to them the "leaderly" qualities possessed in nonhuman "wild" form by the *llantiru* (Spanish *delantero* = leader), the strong male llamas that lead the herd to and from pasture and to and from the maize-producing valleys to which K'ultas travel yearly with llama caravans. So authorities as ritual sponsors have been equated with the lead llamas, who are the sacrificial victims in *fiesta*-associated rites. This correspondence encapsulates the authorities' rise in status. They become leaders of the human herd, of which Christ is the herder, and, like Christ, herders of men.

The main events of all K'ulta *fiestas*—always involving a saint or Christian devotion—involve the acts of sacrifice and consumption of llamas. Events begin with an initial sacrifice in the llama corral in the sponsor's hamlet, accompanied by complex sequences of libation dedications. The llamas to be killed are then "made to flower," colored yarn being sewn into their ears as they are given *chicha* to drink and *coca* to chew. After the llamas' blood is dedicated to Tatala (the sun, Jesus Christ), and while the meat of sacrificed llamas is still being butchered within the corral, the sponsor's wife-takers (his *tullkas*) don the beasts' pelts and dance in a humorously lascivious way, as *jañachu* (literally, nonproducer; figuratively, male alpaca), just at the moment when the sponsor is addressed, like the real sacrificed animals, *llantiru* (herd-leader). Then the sponsor's entourage undertakes a mini-pilgrimage to his "*fiesta* house" in the town of Santa Barbara de K'ulta.

On the way, the lead llamas are dressed in the sponsor's ritual clothes (*ponçho*, scarf, and *montera* [cowhide battle helmet]). Once there, there is a second sacrifice—of more *llantiru* males—and while the followers consume the llama meat during the obligatory banquet that follows, the sponsor is draped with gifts of locally woven woolen cloth in a rite parallel to that through which the sacrificial llamas have gone. He is then addressed as *Tata Awatiri* (Father Shepherd). On the last day of the feast, it is the turn of the saint image to pass through this process, being first stripped of its layers of woolen textiles and then passed on to the next year's sponsor to be clothed again. The sponsor then distributes the carrying cloths worn by the saint to his followers, who wear them triumphantly back to the sponsor's hamlet. Here the appropriation of qualities possessed by the saint, as a fragment of the primary celestial power, is clearly expressed.

As a result of these rites, sponsors take on a title otherwise reserved for Christ, "Father Herder," and respond to their followers with the term *t"ama*, "herd." In effect, the sacrificial sequences performed by sponsors as part of all saints' feasts, and those performed as part of tribute collection, carnival rites, and national holiday sacrifices by *cabildo* authorities, establish the metaphorical transmutation of "herding" from the plane of "economic" production to that of social production, via the metaphorical equation of human ritual sponsor with their domesticated animal sacrificial victims. Here "interiorization" and "exteriorization" of leadership qualities among animal, human, and divine genera are accomplished with the particular aid of locally pro- duced woolen clothing, produced from the "natural" form "worn" by the llama before it is given human clothing and its pelt converted into humans' "cultural" skin (see also Turner 1980).

The sequence of events in the metacommunicative process of sacrifice and fiesta performance—and a founding myth describing the celestial origin of this process (analyzed in Dillon and Abercrombie 1988; see also Rasnake 1988b)—make it clear that the model for the appropriation of "natural" powers for social purposes is, precisely, the *Tata Awatiri* who lives on high: Jesus Christ, the Lamb of God and Shepherd of Men. In the myth, it is the Solar-Christ's conquest of "wild" pre-Columbian beings (the Supay-Chullpas) that creates the conditions required for "civilized" life. In this story, in which the Chullpas (the mummified corpses within pre-Columbian tombs) are portrayed as essentially prehuman, living in an age when animals and humans formed a single, "natural" community without cultigens or domesticates, seasons or death, the figures of the founding time—the Spanish conquest—achieve apotheosis, and colo- nial discourse is made into a first principle. The gods of the oppressors,

residing prototypically in *alax pacha* (heaven) are required for the reproduction of K'ulta society; and not only of its authorities (who preside in
the Spanish-founded *reducción* town), but of the very processes of food
production.

Modern day "indigenous ethnic groups" and "indigenous cosmologies"
are unintelligible apart from their struggle with the state: they are
founded upon its existence, and they are recreated only insofar as they
can maintain, and mold to their own purposes, a "state within." They
are also, however, founded upon a vision (shared by rural people, in their
images of wild, pre-Columbian *Chullpas*, and urban ones, in their images of rural people) of pre-Hispanic Indianness, now pushed back into
not only a preconquest past, but a precultural one.

City people, however, have constituted themselves in complementary
fashion, always via a discourse of mutual incomprehension carried out
with "Indians" through a sort of cultural pidgin. Prevailing urban
notions romanticize Indians, stripping them of their complex understandings of history and power relations and projecting them as living
fossils into the *Chullpa* past, thus taking a version of one-half of the
rural-dwellers' own ambivalent identity sources for the whole. Urban
"non-Indians" also enjoy "playing" Indians, as well as appropriating for
themselves (and for their nationalist projects) a generalized indigenous
ancestry. In addition, city-dwellers, and especially those most interested in "folklore" and anthropology, have adopted for themselves a very
partial reading of "indigenous" cosmology, thereby creating for themselves an "original" and "chthonic" anticosmos that serves as diabolical
foil to their "civilized" selves in the tragicomedy played out every day
in urban class struggles and exteriorized each year in dance-drama such
as those of Oruro's carnival rites. There, we will find an "Indian" within
the "non-Indian," analogous to the "*Chullpa* within," and the complement of "the state within," K'ulta culture.

The Indian Within: Ethnicity and Urban Identities

As tumultuous change was in progress in the countryside, the cities
experienced transformations as well. A series of revolts (some real,
others merely feared and imagined; some led "from below," some by
"Creole" elites) jarred the cities and mining centers during the fractious
eighteenth century. At stake, fundamentally, was the replacement of a
relatively clear-cut two-class system whereby Spanish impresarios gained
fortunes administering productive enterprises operated by levied Indian
labor (an activity from which the interstitial *castas* were essentially
excluded), by a more complex system in which most city dwellers no
longer fit neatly into either category. Increasingly important were the

interstitial kinds of people such as the mass of *indios criollos* (Creole—
city-born—Indians), mestizos, freed slaves, and a wide variety of inter-
mixtures, demarcated by a baroque system of racial categories in eighteenth-century censuses. But a simpler, two-category system of ethnic
ascription remained operative nonetheless. This bipolar order hinged, of
course, on the transmutation to the colonial situation of the *ancién
regime* distinction between plebeians who labored (Indians) and aristocrats who did not (Spaniards). But the existence, first, of a native
aristocracy, second, of categorically ambiguous racial-cultural mixes,
and, third, of a host of intermediary occupational strata, as Indians
moved permanently into the cities and thus lost the rural-ethnic "nationality" that made them clearly Indians, served to challenge the
Indian/Spaniard opposition, and consequently the colonial order itself.
This expansion of ambiguous or interstitial roles led to an increase in the
complexity of "ethnic" categories, on the one hand produced by those
who sought to index, via clothing, speech, and occupation, their departure
from some stigmatized—more "Indian"—previous identity, and on the
other by the continual effort from above to chill such movement by
expanding the reach of the stigma to cover the new categories.

The city of Oruro began as a *reducción* named San Miguel de Oruro,
but when silver was discovered on a nearby hillside in 1609, a Spanish
settlement, San Felipe de Austria de Oruro (after Philip II), was established adjacent to the Indian town, which came to be known, like the
Indian parishes of Potosí, as *la ranchería* (Cajías 1983, 1987; Crespo 1967;
Mesa and Gisbert 1970). As in many of the early colonial towns meant
for Spaniards, firm parish boundaries insulated the Spaniards both from
the Indians, and from common labor and the manual trades (*oficios*). The
latter had become the *metiér* of mestizos as well as an ever-increasing
number of *indios ausentes* who had fled their homelands.

Although there was no forced levy in Oruro, as in Potosí, Spanish mine
owners attracted Indian labor through a variety of means, some coercive.
But the necessity, after Viceroy Toledo, to pay tribute in coined silver
obligated Indians to seek wages in any case. In the first century after its
foundation, Oruro's single Indian parish (the *ranchería* of San Miguel)
filled up with Indians from the southern part of the viceroyalty of Peru.
On arrival, they were grouped with others from the same "home"
provinces into newly created *ayllus*, now named after these provinces of
origin. Thus, Indians were to be constrained within their *naciones* even
as they fled them. To complete the reproduction of rural *reducción*
structures, *cabildo*-type authorities were established within the new
ayllus, and a new "lordship" was created to rule over all of these: thus,
over the (urban) *ayllu* Indians of Oruro, the Spanish appointed a hereditary *cacique gobernador* (governor chief) analogous to the native lord of

rural kingdoms, but corresponding to no pre-Columbian polity. Made into a replica of a rural *reducción*, Oruro's *ranchería* became, like Potosí, a microcosm of the region from which it drew its labor force.

This "organic," if invented, urban Indian society was integrated into a whole dominated by the Spanish parish, later the seat of the *matriz* (matrix or womb), the cathedral of the bishopric established there. Expressed through an asymmetry of power in a system of production, the colonial whole, at the level of the Spanish city, was also dramatized during the sixteenth and seventeenth centuries in certain orderly religious processions. In Corpus Christi, the body politic paraded in its aggregate parts, divided neatly into its component guilds (brotherhoods of Spaniards and craftsmen) and *naciones* (urban *ayllus*). These marched in hierarchical order, led by the *Alferez Real* (royal standard-bearer), behind the host, ensconced in its solar-disk monstrance, in an allegory of submission to God and divinely appointed king. Reproduced in the *fiestas reales* (feasts of the royal *rites-de-passage*) and for special rogations when epidemics or ruinous weather threatened, such rituals also included dramatic presentations weaving sacramental plays (like Saint Michael's conquest of Satan and the seven deadly sins) into allegories of divine conquest (like the battle of Moors and Christians), just as in the processions of Spain at the time (Arías 1980; Bayle 1951; Wardropper 1953). Such scenes in the New World differed from those of the Old in their insistence on redoubling the hierarchy of estates and offices with that of native nations. Ambiguities in the determination of nationhood, inherent in the colonial situation itself, were to produce the most disfiguring blemishes on this body politic.

From Indians to Creole Indians

On the one hand, among the inhabitants of the *ranchería*, *ayllu* Indians were held (conceptually at least) apart from the guilds, which were dominated initially by the mixed-blood *castas* (castes, like mestizos, mulattoes, etc.). But as Indian workers settled into urban life, they progressively lost their ties to home "nations," and turned to the craft guilds (and to guilds of specialist mining labors) for their group affiliations. This produced a category known as "Creole Indians," analogous to today's mumbled and insulting *cholo*), urban folk without clear indices of rural ethnic pertinence but "Indians" just the same, in the Spanish and mestizo purview. In the 1680s when that century's most elaborate census disclosed the extent of the problem for the royal fisc, the Viceroy Duque de la Palata tried to rectify the situation by ordering the return of all such Indians to their home provinces (Sanchez-Albornóz 1978). This and similar efforts sought not only to buttress the flagging Indian levy pool and the higher tributes paid by Indians who remained in their "original" homes, but also to reestablish the clear lines between Spanish owners and (levied) Indian workers. Likewise, royal officials entertained ideas about repatriating mestizos (or at least the "illegitimate" ones, without ties to admitted Spanish progenitors) to the provinces of their Indian mothers. But the urban economy now required these skilled workers and craftsmen. In the mining sector, it was the *castas* and the Creole Indians who served now, rather than rural native lords, as the link between Spanish owners and raw Indian-labor recruits. They performed the roles of work-gang leaders (the whip-wielding *caporales*) and filled the need for skilled labor in the increasingly technical mining sphere (Bakewell 1984; Buechler 1981).

Economic necessity or not, this "nonethnic," and to a large degree, "non-Indian" mass proved a thorn in the side of the Spanish elite, especially insofar as their unofficial activities, well organized within the guild associations they had formed, produced a burgeoning entrepreneurial system. Replete with a multitude of clandestine ore mills and foundries, guilds of allied mestizos, mulattoes, and Creole Indians, drew disaffected mita-Indian recruits and even an ambiguous class of Spaniards into their ranks, making up an "underground economy" that diverted silver from the official mills and foundries of the elite (Tandeter 1981; Martiré 1975–1977). Empowered by surreptitiously wresting the means of production from Spanish hands, this was, indeed, an unusually capitalist protoproletariat.

Identified as a threat, not only economically but to the whole colonial order, this sector was stigmatized as a plebe, precursor to the "popular class" of today. From the Spanish perspective, they formed a particularly pernicious form of debased Indianhood, a wild and unruly lot. The Spanish governor of Potosí, characterized one such group, known as *Q'aqchas*, in the following terms: "These Caglcha [Q'aqcha] people live like barbarians, without living up to the precepts of religion, since when the Church calls its faithful during Holidays, those who are employed in theft attend neither mass nor Doctrina [catechism], nor any of the other exercises of obligation" (AGI Charcas 481: 3v–4r).

Owners of "official" mills thus argued that these "fallen" Indians could be saved (along with the Spanish monopoly on power) by sending them back to their rural parishes, where they might yet acquire *buena policía* and become proper Indians. By the eighteenth century, the body politic had been drawn and quartered, and religious processions like sixteenth-century Corpus rites had given rise to devotions divided according to stations, independently organized via guilds and brotherhoods, but also calendrically dispersed and with distinct objects of devotion. The guild rites of the emergent plebe were denigrated by the "decent folk," who stayed indoors during such processions. Although it proved impossible to return this plebe to their presumed rural roots, their guild rites were constrained to the sphere of wildness, itself relegated precisely, as are those of today's miners and the "ideal typical" religious practice of today's *populacho*, to that semitolerated moment of pre-Lenten excess that is carnival.

From Spaniards to Creole-Spaniards to Bolivians

Even as the Spanish elite struggled against the emergence of an empowered urban proletariat, which threatened the fundamental category distinctions between colonizers of European origin and *nación*-based Indian colonized, problematic nationality became increasingly salient—and divisive—*within* the category of "Spaniard." Like the Creole Indians whose Indianness—and subjugability—was suspect, because of their birth within the Spanish urban sphere, the loyalty and civilization of those whom the accident of birth in the colonies made into Creole Spaniards were suspect as far as "metropolitans" were concerned (Lafaye 1976). Thus, the best administrative posts, and the possibility of parlaying power in the colonies into power within the metropole (in Spain itself), were limited by the Council of the Indies to "real" Spaniards (Anderson 1983; Pagden 1987). Creoles like Bolívar (who got his comeuppance in a failed social-climbing effort in Madrid), were understandably frustrated, even if they had for the most part managed to achieve positions of "aristocratic" power in the colonies. Erupting finally into a war of independence in the first quarter of the nineteenth century, the frustrations were given an early airing in the city of Oruro during the general rural rebellion of the 1780s.

As rural fighting spread to the *Audiencia* capital to the west and to the commercial power of La Paz to the north, some of the most powerful Creoles of Oruro decided to seize the moment (the early days of February 1781, near the time of carnival) to achieve independence from Chapetón domination. After grabbing control of the local militia, Oruro's Creoles, joined by mestizos and urbanites of all sorts, seem to have taken it into their heads to respond to the earlier appeals by Indian rebel leaders (the Amarus and Cataris) to form a common front. The revolution was quashed by royalist troops within ten short days. But in the meantime, Creole idealists lived to regret their actions.

In the opening bouts, Creoles called upon the rural Indians of the region to support them by invading the city, which they did, in the thousands. But how to tell Creole Spaniard from Chapetón from mestizo? The answer was for all of the Europe-affiliated to dress in Indian garb to greet their newfound "countrymen" and lead them to their proper targets, which resulted in the almost complete elimination of the Spanish-born competition in the space of hours. But within days, Oruro's Creole rebels found that these Indian allies had their own ends in mind, such as the redistribution of recently collected tribute, and were far from unanimous in their support of Creole and mestizo goals. Subsequently, the Creoles found themselves under attack by the rural Indians (Cajías de la Vega 1982).

After such experiences, Creoles were warier of Indians (and vice versa) in their subsequent struggle for independence against a crippled Spain in the early nineteenth century. "Oppressed" Creoles, which is to say Spaniards-turned-oligarch-Bolivians, did not choose to identify Indians as their spiritual elder brothers in national identity until much later. During the nineteenth and early twentieth centuries, Liberal policies forged an alliance between Creoles and rural land-holding mestizos, by recognizing mestizos' private claims to (usually usurped) lands. The object of such alliances was, ultimately, Indian ethnocide (Platt 1984; Rivera 1984). Creoles may have thought they were drawing a firmer boundary between savagery and civilization, more effective in combatting the Indian threat. But as Platt (1987: 320) argues, they had taken in a "Trojan Horse," putting mestizos in position for their ultimately successful drive to national hegemony after the 1952 revolution. Already in the 1940s, in the wake of the disastrous Chaco War, a burst of growth in the cities fueled a rise in the economic, political, and intellectual stature of the mestizo sector of the population, many of whom had served as officers in the war. With their rise to economic and political power came the indigenism that has marked Bolivian political rhetoric increasingly since the 1952 revolution.

But even before the victory of the 1950s revolution, proindigenists had begun to discover and promote folk culture: they joined the ranks of the urban dance groups, swelling with pride in the Indian origins of such groups as they did so. The new Creole elite, made up, now, of former mestizos and their more European brethren within a now-wider class of *gente decente* (decent folk), has once again put on Indian clothing, as they did in self-protection in 1781. But this time they seek to become proud, if temporary, faux Indians in dance, rather than in humiliating flight. The carnival representation of Indians in Oruro may be a joyous celebration of (reinvented) roots, but it involves another equally important aspect. For they dance as a personal sacrifice to the city's patroness, the Virgin of the Mineshaft. We should not be surprised to learn that this Virgin's fame rebounds to *her* alleged conquest—in the days *before* the Spanish conquest—of evil Indian antigods, a feat capable of giving even the preconquest fatherland the caché of civilization.

Carnival and the Representation of Identity

Carnival might be largely about Indians, but when more than forty dance groups, comprising over five thousand individuals, take to the streets during the now-officialized folkoric festival that is carnival in Oruro, nary an Indian (permanent and self-professed, that is) can be found. Carnival in the rural context is a universal "holy day of obligation," a time to consecrate germinating fields and growing herds (see Harris 1982; Rasnake 1986), and rural people would have no time to travel to the city, even if there were a place for them there. It may be that "Indian" miners danced these figures well into the eighteenth century, but since the mid-twentieth, by which time they had become, for Creole society, an Indian-identified, proletarianized "plebe," they have been displaced by the urban elites in these roles. Now elevated to the stature of a nationalist event, its dance styles spreading rapidly into similar urban festivals in Bolivia as well as in Chile and Peru, carnival is Oruro's proudest possession, attracting thousands of (mostly well-to-do, urban-Bolivian) tourists. What makes such dances so attractive, apparently, is their frequently mentioned mixture of Christian and chthonic rites and images, the presence of the god Momo, who in Oruro wears Indian dress.

As in the copycat performances (much lamented by Orureños) of Gran Poder (in La Paz), Candelaria (in Peru's Puno), Copacabana (in the homonymous lakeside town), and Urqupiña (in the suburbs of Cochabamba), the most oft-cited motive for dancing is not, however, the revivification of ancient underworld gods, but rather the fulfillment of an individual promise to the Virgin (Albó and Preiswerk 1986). In Oruro, this partly painted and partly sculpted image, like that of Copacabana of the type known as Candelaria, is endowed with special ties to the pre-Columbian indigenous past (MacCormack 1985). She is capable of providing access to boons originating in the diabolical Indian sphere, but also capable of defending one against the dangers emanating from it, and indeed, of emerging victorious after her confrontation with such forces.

In Oruro's modern origin myth (learned by most people directly or indirectly from published sources, such as the tourist guides and comic-book histories that circulate during carnival) the Virgin of the Mineshaft (in the form of an Inka *ñusta* or as the Pachamama) is said to have saved Oruro's preconquest Uru inhabitants from destructive monsters sent by their god, Wari. According to the story, the Urus had become too "good" for Wari's tastes, and he sent giant ants, a snake, toad, condor, and lizard to punish them for their apostasy (which was a itself a form of precocious Christianity). The Virgin (in the form of an Inka *ñusta*, "princess") or as the *Pachamama* (Earth Mother), brought out her sword and, cutting off the offending creatures' heads, turned them to stone in the same act. The monsters became the toads, now fossilized in the city's several stone *genius loci* (Guerra Gutierrez 1970; Nash 1979).

While the "toads" may have been killed by the Virgin in her earlier incarnation as *ñusta*, they are still held to be very powerful places, spots where telluric or chthonic forces from the Indian past—held by city folks to be the same as those of the religion thought to be still practiced in secret by contemporary Indians—can be mobilized by the faithful. These places receive special devotions on the first Friday of each month, but with much greater intensity on carnival Friday, the day before the forces of wildness emerge onto the streets. Nash (1979) describes these rites in some detail (analyzed also in Taussig 1980), focusing on those of the miners.

On the Friday of carnival, miners pour libations to the *Tios* (anthropomorphic figurines with large and erect phalluses, found in significant tunnels in each mine), then offer a white llama in sacrifice. Afterward, the mines are closed up for a week while these beings eat and reinvigorate the veins of ore. The sacrifice is performed in conjunction with special devotions to an image of the Virgin of the Mineshaft located at the entrance to each mine. Then, while the mines are closed, miners engage in devotions to the Virgin of the Mineshaft (whose main image is located in a special chapel above the center of the city), along with most of the rest of Oruro's population. The choice of Friday for the sacrifice is not arbitrary: in the countryside, Friday is especially maleficent, *not* good for sacrifice. But in the mines and cities, every Friday (and to a lesser extent, Tuesday) the toads and the *Tio-Supay* are thought to be receptive to sacrifices, especially on the first Fridays of every month and carnival Friday, days when in official Catholicism stations of the cross are performed in memory of Christ's sacrifice.

But it is not only good Catholics, performing the stations of the cross, and Oruro's miners who perform first Friday rites, but the bulk of Oruro's population as well. The majority stick with the burning of incense-offering bundles within their businesses or homes, often presided over by hired shamans (*curanderos* [Sp.]/*yatiris* [Ay.]/*yachaq* [Qu.]). The object is to increase well-being, especially of the economic sort. In some cases, businessmen have shamans "consecrate" a special amulet, to draw customers and increase sales. The offering bundles, or *mesas* as they are called, are sold in quantity at special stands in all of Oruro's markets, and business is brisk on first-Friday evenings.

A fraction of devotees, especially petty street merchants and truck drivers, burn their *mesas* at one of the stone relics of the "toads" conquered by the Virgin. Like the miners' *Tio-Supay*, the everyday citizens' toads and the chthonic Wari/Pachamama conjunct reached through them are especially efficacious in connection with lucre. Their efficacy, at least in generating an identity that satisfactorily taps the wild powers apparently unattainable for nonbelieving, civilized folk, depends in great part, like the K'ulta sacrificial scheme, on the recreation of a particular uptake of history. This history superposes the powers of Christian beings over those defeated but still-powerful forces left over from the previous, chthonic "Indian" age. Consequently, most practitioners assume that their rites are authentically "Indian," and take the deities addressed, the toads and Pachamama and the Tios, for "Indian" gods. The Indians whose cosmos corresponds to these urban beings, however, may only be found a few days each year, dancing in the streets.

Over five thousand Orureños, mostly from the urban bourgeoisie, dance through the streets each year during carnival. Organized into *cofradía*-like troupes dedicated to the Virgin of the mineshaft, the vast majority of dancers are costumed as wild Indians and pre-Columbian devils. In carnival's climax, all of these teluric beings—associated with pre-Columbian *Chullpas* and mine *tio-supays*, shed their wildness, their proud links to the past, and hear mass before the Virgin. The variety of motives for joining groups and meanings attached to dancing within Oruro today makes interpretation of the whole a difficult endeavor. A whole social history and morphology, too complex to analyze in the present context, parades through the streets during carnival nowadays, in which membership in a specific group often indexes neighborhood of residence, class background, ideological stance, and social aspirations of those who join.

The imagined Indian who is briefly lionized in carnival costume is not the contemporary professed-Christian type who lives in places like K'ulta, but an Indian from the past, one whose religion is dedicated entirely to underworld beings like those that Oruro's Virgin conquered, in myth, and domesticates, in pantomime, at carnival's end. Orureños' creation of their "masqued" images of suppressed past identities, forms but a prelude to the resuppression of such identities in the abnegations of Lent (as of Ash Wednesday) that presage renewed submission to the Christ of Easter and of official church doctrine. Regardless of the diverse origins and orientations of Oruro's dance groups, and the brevity of their masques, all represent, in some form, an "Indian within," elevated to a high and powerful rank within urban "folk" religion, as it is within a nationalism in sore need of an anti-imperialist and legitimating identity. There may have been no Indians before Columbus, and there may be extremely few self-identified Indians in Bolivia today, but in this nation founded by the "illegitimate" American-born among America's European conquerors, there is no legitimate citizen without Indian alters to be represented.

Conclusion: Cultures in Colonial Discourses

Like rural dwellers who call upon the dead and *Chullpa* forces to aid
them in production, only to exile them once again, city people do
likewise with the Indian within them, externalized in dance as a form of
personal sacrifice, and then dutifully "re-repressed." The *Chullpas* and
"Indians" thus brought into being are, however, very different entities,
even if the general shape of the colonial discourse in which both are
engaged seems to remain constant. It would be as foolhardy to lump
them together as some generalized Andean culture as it would be to treat
them as the still-separate products of entirely discrete cultures. In the
Andes, serious distortion results when we seek to portray indigenous
cultures in an allochronic (Fabian 1983) ethnographic present. Even if
our goal is to represent a clandestine culture of resistance, cleaned up by
expeditiously "air-brushing" out (in Clifford's 1986 metaphor), all the
"our cultural" impurities that mar our vision of a fully "Other" Other,
we end up only with another abstract semantic schema, a virtual *langue
dureé* (as a hard-bitten Braudelian Saussure might have expressed it),
which exists not across time, but at no time. When we excise the
Hispanic and Christian from our accounts of rural Andean cultures and
paint them as purely chthonic, insular indigenous cosmoses, we deny
the counterhegemonic effect achieved by rural peoples when they
subject their own representations of an uncivilized, antiworld past to the
enculturing transformations of their brand of Christianity. To peg them
to this vision of a pre-Columbian past, even if the *Chullpa* age is in some
sense a past that has been alienated from them, is to reproduce the urban/
Hispanic stereotype of rural Indians, and make ourselves into colonial
coconspirators.

These related images of Indians and *Chullpas*, distinct in the meanings
they engender within the action contexts in which they are brought into
being, both describe, within their respective forms of historical consciousness, a remembered past that must be transformed by heavenly
Christian powers in order to become fully human. As Taussig (1987:377)
has put it:

> these "memories" [are] hegemonic fictions read into the past as an
> outcome of the ideological struggles of the present—an invented
> tradition, fictions held by both Christianized Indians, such as those
> of the Sibundoy Valley [and we might add, the Andes in general],
> and the Church, as well as by the colonists as a group.

Both forms of historical consciousness repress and then resurrect wild
pasts, which might be ultimately transcended within their social narra-

tives but are at the same time ineradicable, converted into needed sources of power and generation within their respective systems of social production. I am not suggesting that Oruro's carnival and K'ulta's fiesta enact the same narrative. On the contrary, their narrative structures are quite different, and "formulate different narrative meanings, and they constitute those meanings in different modalities of social time and space. These in turn are correlated with different forms of social agency and different patterns of relationship between social actors and processes" (Turner 1988: 276). It is true that such symbolic orders are the means by which political economies, structured systems of inequality, reproduce themselves. This fact leads some (such as Friedlander 1975) to suggest that we should contribute to the future genesis of a redemptive class consciousness by refusing to credit such ideologies, turning instead to class analysis (and so the ritual systems by which rural ethnic groups produce themselves are instead to be considered the ideological instruments by which they are oppressed as a peasantry). But this is to miss the point that "the way in which relations in any system are signified is an irreducible part of its reality" (Comaroff 1987: 312), and, consequently, may become instrumental in challenging and changing that reality. Redemption is possible, in the discursive narratives of conquest in which "Indians" and "Chullpas" persist, not because such schemas create an ideological smokescreen to conceal the origin of the structured system of inequality to which they give form, but precisely because these images, referring always to concrete social groups, make it "virtually impossible to ignore the dependence of meaning on politics—in this case colonial, racist, and class oppression" (Taussig 1987: 391).

Colonials may have tried to extirpate Indians' "memories" of the power of their precolonial past, but:

> the Church and its culture of conquest were in fact strengthening them as a new social force, ensuring the transmission of myth into reality and of memory into the future. Yet while a mystique was thus built into the past to haunt the living as *mal aire* [the "evil wind" that blows up from *chullpa* tombs], this same invented past could be seized for magical power to thwart not only *mal aire* but the vast range of distressful conditions ascribable to sorcery. (Taussig 1987: 377)

Taussig describes some forms of intercultural shamanism—specific to the Sibundoy valley in Colombia—by which, he suggests, it may be possible to rework or undo "the history of sorcery with its memory," perhaps disordering the structures "whereby history has put memory at the service of colonization" (Taussig 1987: 391–392). While the specific

forms of shamanism evoked by Taussig—involving the use of hallucino-
gens—may not be characteristic of the Bolivian Andes (where hallucino-
gens are generally not employed), shamans devoted to the cure of non-
Indians through the invocation of Indian wildness do excellent business
in Bolivia's cities and pilgrimage centers. Yet, these shamans, whose
commercial success hinges excessively, perhaps, on the embodiment
and commoditization of the urban image of Indian wildness, do not, I
would argue, constitute the most effective forms of rural counter-
hegemony. This can be found, instead, in the appropriation of hegemonic
powers in meaning orders such as K'ulta's sacrificial fiestas and libation
"memory paths." The specialized shamanic forms of city and pilgrimage
centers—which accompany and give expression to rural-urban linkages
through petty marketing and labor migration—contribute their share to
the effect. They do so, however, through the structured miscommuni-
cation that they engender, as a pidginized and personal contact point
between discourses that may be historically linked, but continue (as long
as each other's image of its alter is affirmed through such links) to be
shielded from one another as interpretive contexts, as distinct foci of
cultural production.

I have here used the term *discourse*, qualified as *colonial* to highlight
its asymmetrical power dimension, as an aid in conceptualizing the
mutually internalizing relationship between rural and urban poles in a
more embracing sociocultural order. The term is, however, problematic. On the one hand, it reinforces a tendency to latch onto easy
oppositions (like rural/urban, Indian/state, etc.) as hypostatized speakers engaged in discourse. But cultures and the groups they constitute do
not speak to one another; it is their members who formulate and share
images of cultural alters, and interact with individuals from other milieu
(as in urban shamanism, pilgrimage rites, marketing). From the
essentialized group perspective, one might imagine two partially intersecting discourses, but each involves an imaginary, self-constructed
alter, even if both assume it to be embodied in "real" Others.

Another difficulty with *discourse* ensues from imagining it in the
singular, when in reality members of multiple contexts of cultural
communication evoke, for distinct ends, varying images of cultural
alters. Cultural orders are not closed systems; they assume and interpret
cultural others with whom they, periodically, engage in more overt
forms of contact and struggle. But there is a degree of insulation between
the K'ulta fiesta-sacrifice and the Oruro carnival, an insulation born of
prejudice and exclusion (which we call, in the rural context, clandestinity).
And this insulation creates a degree of interpretive closure that the
systemic and individual links between rural and urban contexts do not
penetrate. It is, of course, an extreme oversimplification to reduce the

many sorts of communicative contexts that do generate such partially closed interpretive systems to two, as I have done by privileging urban carnival and rural fiesta.

Examining the full range of "sub-" and "intercultural" meaning contexts within the rural and urban areas and between them is a task beyond the scope of this chapter. I must nevertheless suggest that shifting from a "semantic-grid" to a "pragmatic interaction context" framework for cultural analysis opens an analytical Pandora's box, one in which we must imagine a great multiplicity of "cultures" overlapping in a great many ways; sometimes intersecting outright, along a border, but more often segmentally embedded or cross-cutting one another through individuals' plural "memberships" in them. Not all are of the same type or scale or significance. For the purposes of my own argument I have privileged two sorts, and have downplayed some of the cross-cutting contexts/foci that make these less distinct (shamanism, pilgrimage rites, urban migrants' clubs, marketing, etc.). I have done so in part because these latter have, of late, received so much attention (as in Taussig 1987) that they threaten to overshadow the degree to which frontier sorceries *fail* to create a single discourse, a fully shared interpretive field, out of the conjunction of Spaniard and Indian, and of city and countryside. This continuing failure contributes to the continued success of cultural resistance to colonial hegemonies, even as it thereby helps to reproduce the system of domination.

Bolivian "Indians" and their "cultures" may be, as successive national regimes have had it, either the salvation of the nation or the principal obstacle to its development, but the images of them entertained in rites such as Oruro's carnival (like images of state-Christian power internalized in rural cultural contexts) will be at the heart of national development—and the development of a national identity as well as a multitude of "ethnic" identities within the nation—for many years to come, especially as the "Indians" they purport to represent come increasingly to adopt the Other's Other as their own internal demon. It seems to me that the challenge to culture theory that confronts us as we face up to the complexities and ambiguities of partially intersecting urban and rural (and intermediary) spheres of colonial discourse in places like Bolivia will be anthropology's internal demon for many years to come as well.

Notes

The fieldwork from which the ethnohistorical and ethnographic cases of K'ulta and Asanaqi have been drawn was carried out between 1979 and 1982, and was supported by doctoral research fellowships from Fulbright-Hays, Sigma Xi, the Center for Latin American Studies and Division of Social Sciences at the University of Chicago, the Whatcomb Museum, and Fulbright IIE, and is presented in Abercrombie (1986). Research on colonial ethnogenesis in eigh-teenth-century rebellions (in the AGI, Seville, during 1987), was supported by a postdoctoral fellowship from the U.S.-Spanish Joint Committee for Cultural and Educational Cooperation. Research during 1988 on carnival in Oruro was made possible by postdoctoral grants from the Joint Committee on Latin American Studies of the ACLS and SSRC, from Fulbright, and from the Wenner Gren Foundation for Anthropological Research. Revisions on this chapter were carried out while I was a Mellon Fellow at the Stanford Humanities Center during the 1988–1989 academic year. I thank all of these institutions for their support. Discussions with Rafael Sanchez were instrumental in formulating, in an earlier version of this chapter, some of the ideas developed here. Mary Dillon, who accompanied me as co-worker in most of the above research endeavors, made extensive comments and criticism that have led to substantive changes. I have also made free use of comments and criticism offered by Nancy Farriss, Ruth Mazo Karras, and other participants in the Ethnohistory Seminar at the University of Pennsylvania, where I presented (in November 1988) some of the arguments developed here. Finally, I must acknowledge the criticism of Greg Urban and the participants of the Austin conference that gave rise to this book, which has also had an impact on revisions. As always, I alone bear the responsibility for the shortcomings of the final product.

1. The main exception in Bolivia is the recent appropriation of the term by *Katarismo*, the La Paz–based Indian nationalist movement, which tries to revalue "Indian" in a way comparable to North America's "black pride" (see Albó 1987).

2. *Ayllu* is a name for a unit of social organization about which there is much confusion in the Andean literature, in part owing to the wide variability among the sorts of units to which it is applied in different regions. In the K'ulta and Macha case, an *ayllu* is a political and territorial unit, composed of many exogamous patrilines/hamlets among which the *ayllu* lands are divided (except for certain lands held in common among all the patrilines), and in defense of which the often feuding lineages will fuse in land wars known as *ch'axwas* (see Platt 1987).

3. Hamlets and patrilines are often, but not always, identical. Some hamlets are divided into more than one patriline, while some patrilines include more than one hamlet.

4. I use the term *kingdom* here with some trepidation, since it implies monarchy, whereas the Andean norm was dual organization. No unambiguous native terms for these units have emerged from the documents. Platt (1987) chooses *ethnic group* for such units, while Sallnow (1988) uses *naciones*.

5. This particular land title, copied into a 1940s K'ulta petition to the Villaroel government, is in the possession of J.C., an elder leader of the area. Yuspagarpan.

References

Abercrombie, Thomas
    1986   The politics of sacrifice: an Aymara cosmology in action. PhD diss.,
           Department of Anthropology, University of Chicago.
AGI (Archivo General de Indias, Sevilla)

Charcas 481, "Informe de San Just, Governador de Potosí, sobre la decadencia a que esta reducido el gremio de Azogueros por los . . . Caglchas . . .," Potosí,1762.

Charcas 481, no. 19 2º, "Gremio de Azogueros al Superintendente," 1762.

Lima 807, "Potosí 1751. Testimonio de la Causa contra varios yndios por querer seguir la costumbre del robo de metales." 2 piezas, 138 +112 folios.

AGNA (Archivo General de la Nación de Argentina)
9.5.2.1. Intendencia de La Plata 1780–81, Copiador de cartas. "15 de Nov., 1780, Carta de Don Manuel Alvaraz Villaroel . . . Coronel del Batallon de Milicias en el Asiento de Minas de Aullagas . . .[Escrito en 24 de Sept., 1780]."
9.6.5.6. Mita de Potosí 1797. "Testimonio del Quaderno 3º de los Autos obrados sobre la mita de Potosí (duplicado)."
9.17.2.5., "Retasa de Francisco de Toledo" [1575, copia anonymo de 1785].

Albó, Xavier
1975   La paradoja aymara: solidaridad y faccionalismo. *Estudios Andinos* 11: 67–109.
1976a   ¿Khitipxtansa? ¿Quiénes somos? Identidad localista, étnica y clasista en los aymaras de hoy. *América Indígena* 39(3): 477–528.
1976b   *Lengua y sociedad en Bolivia, 1976*. La Paz: Instituto Nacional de Estadística.
1979   The future of oppressed languages in the Andes. In *Language and society*, W. McCormack and S. A. Wurm (eds.), 309–331. The Hague: Mouton.
1987   From MNRistas to Kataristas to Katari. In *Resistance, rebellion, and consciousness in the Andean peasant world: 18th to 20th centuries*, Steve J. Stern (ed.), 379–419. Madison: University of Wisconsin Press.

Albó, Xavier, and Matías Preiswerk
1986   *Los señores del gran poder*. La Paz: Centro de Teología Popular, Taller de Observaciones Culturales.

ANB (Archivo Nacional de Bolivia)
EC 1781 no. 83, "Autos formados sobre el tumulto que acahecio en el pueblo de Condo Condo; y muertes que executaron en los Llanquipachas."

Anderson, Benedict
1983   *Imagined communities: reflections on the origin and spread of nationalism*. London: Verso Editions.

Arías, Ricardo
1980   *The Spanish sacramental plays*. Boston: Twayne.

Bakewell, Peter
1984   *Miners of the red mountain*. Albuquerque: University of New Mexico Press.

Bastian, Joseph
1978   *Mountain of the condor: metaphor and ritual in an Andean ayllu*. St. Paul, Minn.: West.

Bayle, Constantino, S.J.
1951   *El culto del Santisimo en Indias.* Madrid: Consejo Superior de Investigaciones Científicas, Instituto Santo Toribio de Mogrovejo.
Boas, Franz
1940   *Race, language and culture.* New York: Macmillan.
Buechler, Rose Marie
1981   *The mining society of Potosí 1776–1810.* Ann Arbor: University Microfilms, published for the Maxwell School, Syracuse University.
Cajías de la Vega, Fernando
1982   Repercusiones de la rebelión tupacamarista en la villa de Oruro y comarcas aledañas. In *Actas del coloquio internacional 'Tupac Amaru y su tiempo' (Lima y Cuzco, 11–16 noviembre 1980).* Lima: Comisión Nacional del Bicentenario de la Revolución Emancipadora de Tupac Amaru.
1983   Los objetivos de la revolución indígena de 1781. El caso de Oruro. *Revista Andina* 1 (2): 407–428
1987   La sublevación Tupacamarista de 1781 en Oruro y las provincias aledañas: sublevación de indios y revuelta criolla. PhD diss., Sevilla.
Celestino, Olinda, and Albert Meyers
1981   *Las cofradías en el Perú: región central.* Frankfurt am Main: Verlag Klaus Dieter Vervuert (Editionen der Iberoamericana: Reihe 3, Monographien u. Aufsätze; 6).
Christian, William A., Jr.
1981   *Local religion in sixteenth-century Spain.* Princeton: Princeton University Press.
Clifford, James
1986   On ethnographic allegory. In *Writing culture: the poetics and politics of ethnography*, James Clifford and George E. Marcus (eds.), 98–121. Berkeley: University of California Press.
Cock C., Guillermo, and Mary Eileen Doyle
1979   Del culto solar a la clandestinidad de Inti y Punchao. *Historia y Cultura* 12. Lima: Museo Nacional de Historia.
Comaroff, John L.
1987   Of totemism and ethnicity: consciousness, practice and the signs of inequality. *Ethnos* 52(3–4): 301–323.
Cook, Noble David, ed.
1975   *Tasa de la visita general de Francisco de Toledo.* Lima: Universidad Nacional Mayor de San Marcos.
Crespo, Alberto
1967   La fundación de la villa de San Felipe de Austria y asiento de minas de Oruro. *Revista Histórica* (Lima) 29: 3–25.
Diez de Medina, Francisco Tadeo
1981 [1781]   *Diario del alzamiento de indios conjurados contra la ciudad de Nuestra Señora de La Paz, 1781.* Transcription, introduction, notes, study by Maria Eugenia del Valle de Siles. La Paz: Don Bosco/Banco Boliviano Americano.
Dillon, Mary F., and Thomas Abercrombie
1988   The destroying Christ: an Aymara myth of conquest. In *Rethinking*

history and myth: indigenous South American perspectives on the past, Jonathan D. Hill (ed.), 50–77. Urbana: University of Illinois Press.

Fabian, Johannes
1983   *Time and the other: how anthropology makes its object.* New York: Columbia University Press.

Flores Galindo, Alberto
1986   *Europa y el país de los Incas: la utopía Andina.* Lima: Instituto de Apoyo Agrario.

Foster, George M.
1960   *Culture and conquest: America's Spanish heritage.* New York: Wenner-Gren Foundation for Anthropological Research, Inc.

Friedlander, Judith
1975   *Being Indian in Hueyapan: a study of forced identity in contemporary Mexico.* New York: St. Martin's Press.

Gisbert, Theresa
1980   *Iconografía y mitos indígenas en el arte.* La Paz: Gisbert y Cía.

Godoy, Ricardo
1981   From peasant to miner and back again. PhD diss., Columbia University.

Golte, Jürgen
1980   *Repartos y rebeliones. Túpac Amaru y las contradicciones de la economía colonial.* Lima: Insituto de Estudios Peruanos.

Guerra Gutierrez, Alberto
1970   *Antología del carnaval de Oruro.* 3 vols. Oruro: Imprenta Quelco.

Harris, Olivia
1982   The dead and the devils among the Bolivian Laymi. In *Death and the regeneration of life,* Maurice Bloch and Jonathan Parry (eds.),45–73. Cambridge: Cambridge University Press.

Lafaye, Jacques
1976 (1974) *Quetzalcóatl and Guadalupe: the formation of Mexican national consciousness, 1531–1813.* Trans. by Benjamin Keen. Chicago: University of Chicago Press.

Lechner, J.
1981   El concepto de "policía" y su presencia en la obra de los primeros historiadores de Indias. *Revista de Indias* (41) 9165–166: 395–409.

MacCormack, Sabine
1985   The heart has its reasons: predicaments of missionary Christianity in early colonial Perú. *Hispanic American Historical Review* 65(3): 466–493.

Málaga Medina, Alejandro
1975   Las reducciones en el Virreinato del Perú, 1532–1580. *Revista de Historia de América* (México) 80: 9–42.

Martiré, Eduardo
1975–1977 Tolerancias, prevenciones y regulación participadora de los indios capchas de Potosí en la explotación del cerro. In *Estudios de política indigenista española en América* 3: 291–303. Valladolid: Seminario Americanista.

Mesa, José de, and Theresa Gisbert
  1970   Oruro: origen de una villa minera. In *La minería hispana e ibero-americana. Contribución a su investigación histórica.* 8 vols. (1970–1974). Vol. 1: *Ponencias del I Coloquio Internacional sobre Historia de la Minería* (1970): 559–590. León: Cátedra San Isidoro.
Murra, John V.
  1968   An Aymara kingdom in 1567. *Ethnohistory* 15(2): 115–151.
Nash, June
  1979   *We eat the mines and the mines eat us.* New York: Columbia University Press.
O'Phelan Godoy, Scarlett
  1985   *Rebellions and revolts in 18th century Peru and Upper Peru.* Cologne: Böhlau Verlag.
Pagden, Anthony
  1987   Identity formation in Spanish America. In *Colonial identity in the Atlantic world, 1500–1800,* Nicholas Canny and Anthony Pagden (eds.). Princeton: Princeton University Press.
Platt, Tristan
  1978   Symétries en miroir: Le concept de yanantin chez les Macha de Bolivie. *Annales, E.S.C.* (Paris), 33(5–6): 1081–1107.
  1982   *Estado boliviano y ayllu andino.* Lima: Instituto de Estudios Peruanos.
  1983   Identidad andina y conciencia proletaria: Qhuyaruna y ayllu en el norte de Potosi. *HISLA Revista Latinoamericana de Historia Economica y Social* (Lima) 2: 47–73.
  1984   Liberalism and ethnocide in the southern Andes. *History Workshop Journal,* 17.
  1986   Mirrors and maize: the concept of yanantin among the Macha of Bolivia. In *Anthropological history of Andean polities,* John V. Murra, N. Wachtel and Jacques Revel (eds.), 228–259. Cambridge and Paris: Cambridge University Press and Editions de la Maison des Sciences de l'Homme.
  1987   Entre ch'axwa y muxsa. Para una historia del pensamiento político Aymara. In *Tres reflexiones sobre el pensamiento Aymara,* Thérèse Bouysse-Cassagne, Olivia Harris, Tristan Platt, and Verónica Cereda, 61–132. La Paz: HISBOL.
  n.d.   Ayllu and cofradía in a Macha parish. Paper delivered at 1985 meetings of the American Society for Ethnohistory, Chicago.
Rasnake, Roger N.
  1986   Carnaval in Yura: ritual reflections on ayllu and state relations. *American Ethnologist* 13(4): 662–680.
  1988a   *Domination and cultural resistance.* Durham, N.C.: Duke University Press.
  1988b   Images of resistance to colonial domination. In *Rethinking history and myth: indigenous South American perspectives on the past,* Jonathan D. Hill (ed.), 136–156. Urbana: University of Illinois Press.
Rivera C., Silvia
  1978   El mallku y la sociedad colonial en el siglo XVII: el caso de Jesus de

Machaca. *Avances* (La Paz) 1.
1984   *Oprimidos pero no vencidos. Luchas del campesinado aymara y qhechwa 1900–1980.* La Paz: HISBOL/CSUTCB.
Saignes, Thierry
1987   De la borrachera al retrato: los caciques andinos entre dos legitimidades (Charcas). *Revista Andina* 5(1): 139–170. Cusco.
Sallnow, Michael J.
1988   *Pilgrims of the Andes.* Washington, D.C.: Smithsonian Institution Press.
Sanchez-Albornóz, Nicolás
1978   *Indios y tributos en el Alto Perú.* Lima: Instituto de Estudios Peruanos.
Silverblatt, Irene
1988   Political memories and colonizing symbols: Santiago and the mountain gods of colonial Peru. In *Rethinking history and myth: indigenous South American perspectives on the past,* Jonathan D. Hill (ed.), 174–194. Urbana: University of Illinois Press.
Stern, Steve J.
1982   *Peru's Indian peoples and the challenge of Spanish conquest.* Madison: University of Wisconsin Press.
Stoler, Ann Laura
1989   Rethinking colonial categories: European communities and the boundaries of rule. *Comparative Studies of Society and History* 31(1): 134–161.
Szemiski, Jan
1987   Why kill the Spaniard? New perspectives on Andean insurrectionary ideology in the eighteenth century. In *Resistance, rebellion, and consciousness in the Andean peasant world, 18th to 20th centuries,* Steve J. Stern (ed.), 166–192. Madison: University of Wisconsin Press.
Tandeter, Enrique
1981   La producción como actividad popular: "ladrones de minas" en Potosí. *Nova Americana* (Turin) 4: 43–65.
Taussig, Michael T.
1980   *The devil and commodity fetishism in South America.* Chapel Hill: University of North Carolina Press.
1987   *Shamanism, colonialism and the wild man: a study in terror and healing.* Chicago: University of Chicago Press.
Turner, Terence S.
1980   The social skin. In *Not work alone,* J. Cherfas and R. Lewin (eds.), 112–140. London: Temple Smith. (Abridged version of longer ms.)
1988   Commentary: ethno-ethnohistory: myth and history in native South American representations of contact with western society. In *Rethinking history and myth: indigenous South American perspectives on the past,* Jonathan D. Hill (ed.), 235–281. Urbana: University of Illinois Press.
Urban, Greg, and Joel Sherzer
1988   The linguistic anthropology of native South America. *Annual Review*

of Anthropology 17: 283–307.

Varon, Rafael
  1982   Cofradías de indios y poder local en el Perú colonial: Huaraz, siglo
          XVII. *Allpanchis* 17(20): 127–166.

Wardropper, Bruce W.
  1953   *Introducción al teatro religioso del siglo de oro.* Madrid: Revista del
          Occidente.

White, Hayden
  1978   The forms of wildness: archaeology of an idea. In *Tropics of discourse:
          essays in cultural criticism.* Baltimore: Johns Hopkins University
          Press.

5. Being and Becoming an Indian in the Vaupés

Jean E. Jackson

Introduction

Tukanoans, the indigenous inhabitants of the Vaupés region of south-eastern Colombia, are being introduced to a new form of Indian consciousness as a consequence of their increasing incorporation into the Colombian nation-state.[1] This chapter argues that the nascent self-awareness Tukanoans are acquiring represents a significant shift from their traditional notions of themselves as tropical forest Indians and as Tukanoans to one more akin to ethnic group consciousness. An ethnic group is here conceived of as a recognizably distinct group of people substantially embedded in a larger society (see Barth 1969). Rather than a separate culture, an ethnic group is to be thought of as a subculture, its inventory of culturally distinct traits having been produced to a significant extent by interaction with other sectors of the society. Traditional tribal cultures are usually conceptualized as having been formed by factors such as isolation and adaptation to a specific ecological niche, with any extratribal contact generally limited to interaction with neighbors. While Tukanoan culture differs in some significant respects from this ideal type, as present-day Tukanoans evolve into an ethnic group, we can say that traditional Tukanoan culture fits the tribal schema more than the newer one.

This chapter examines an indigenous rights organization in the Vaupés, using it as a springboard for understanding how Tukanoans' concept of themselves is beginning to change in its essential nature. In a sense, then, this chapter is not so much about *being* Indian as *becoming* Indian.[2]

What is particularly valuable in an analysis of the Tukanoan case is that we can see the *beginnings* of a "tribal" group becoming incorporated into the dominant society to such an extent that virtually all of the cultural forms comprising their legacy from the past are being redefined, reevaluated, and assigned new functions. Of course, in a region so vast, some Tukanoans (a minority) have traveled along this road quite a bit;

most, however, are just starting on this journey.[3] The beginnings of this process occurred in the United States and Canada long before there were anthropologists around. Similarly, with some exceptions, Central American and highland South American groups have already been incorporated into the dominant society in many crucial respects. Hence, parts of lowland South America afford the only opportunity to observe the initial stages of this process.[4]

This chapter is to be seen as an initial report on an ongoing research project. Sources include twenty-two formal interviews conducted in Colombia during March 1987. I also engaged in a number of informal conversations with native leaders, change agents, and residents (both Tukanoan and white) of Mitú, the capital of the Vaupés, and with individuals in Bogotá who are knowledgeable about Colombian indigenous rights organizing and development efforts among Colombian Indian groups. All interviewees characterized themselves as concerned about Colombian Indian autonomy and Indians' overall well-being. Continuing archival work in the Vaupés and Bogotá, and dissertation fieldwork in 1968–1970, have provided other sources of information.

For reasons of space, this chapter can only introduce the topic and highlight the actors and institutions playing a role in changing Tukanoan identity. A comprehensive treatment would contextualize the Vaupés case by discussing the history of land reform and indigenist organizing throughout Colombia. It would also examine the role of various change agents in the region, such as personnel from the numerous governmental development agencies, missionaries, guerrillas, *colonos* (homesteaders), local coca paste traffickers,[5] anthropologists, and representatives of national and international indigenist organizations. It should also be noted that Tukanoans have responded to the extensive and stressful intrusions from the dominant society in ways not discussed here—for example, some have been drawn to a messianic option.[6]

This paper explores a secular option some Tukanoans have been attracted to—the Regional Council of Vaupés Indians—CRIVA. CRIVA is actually a federation[7] representing a number of local indigenous rights groups.[8] It should be noted that the vast majority of Tukanoans are less self-consciously indigenist than are active members of CRIVA, and many Tukanoans are indifferent or hostile to the organization. A discussion of the origins and evolution of CRIVA, thus, while useful as a springboard to begin a discussion of the topic of emerging politicized, self-conscious Vaupés Indian identity, in no way can claim to exhaust it.

The Vaupés

The Vaupés is in the Colombian sector of the Central Northwest

Amazon, a region including both Colombian and Brazilian territory, roughly the size of New England, on the Equator. Tukanoans number about twenty thousand. Tukanoans have traditionally lived in multi-family longhouses, one per settlement, on or near rivers. Longhouses, as well as the more recent settlement pattern of nucleated villages, are separated from each other by two to ten hours' canoe travel. During this century four to eight nuclear families inhabited a longhouse, and present village size ranges anywhere from 15 to 180—one or two mission towns are larger. Population density is quite low, at most .3 inhabitants per km^2. The men of a settlement hunt, fish, and clear swidden fields in which the women grow bitter manioc and other crops.

The units of traditional Vaupés social structure, in ascending order of inclusion, are the local descent group, the sib or clan, the (ideally) exogamous language group, and the poorly understood phratry.[9] The language group is a named patrilineal descent unit composed of from six to more than thirty clans (see Sorensen 1967). Distinguishing features are (1) the language and name; (2) separate founding ancestors and distinct roles in the origin myth cycle; (3) the right to ancestral power through the use of certain linguistic property such as sacred chants; (4) the right to manufacture and use certain kinds of ritual property; and (5) a traditional association with certain ceremonial or near-ceremonial objects. Membership is permanent and public; the one fact known about an individual before anything else is his or her language group.

Although varying internally in some traditional customs, ecology, and degree of acculturation, the Vaupés is a single society in many respects. This homogeneity derives from the similarity of observable phenomena, ecological and social, and from the similarities in Tukanoans' "models for perceiving, relating and interpreting" (Goodenough 1964: 36) their world. Furthermore, Tukanoans see themselves as parts of an interacting whole. Many apparent examples of cultural diversity in the Vaupés are actually mechanisms helping unify the settlements of the region. Multilingualism is an example: the various languages, somewhat like different uniforms in a football game, facilitate the interaction by serving as emblems of the participating groups.[10]

Background to the Current Situation in the Vaupés

Many kinds of change agents have participated in transforming Tukanoan life. At present the most important ones are Catholic and Protestant missionaries; personnel from a variety of government agencies; and whites residing in the region, in particular *colonos* (homesteaders), retired rubber gatherers, and coca paste traffickers. Protestant missionaries belong to various evangelical nondenominational groups, such as

New Tribes Mission, and the North American–based Summer Institute of Linguistics/Wycliffe Bible Translators, or SIL. Catholic missionaries are all Colombian nationals.

In the 1970s the Colombian government instituted wide-ranging legislation affecting Indians that included regularization of Indian land claims into reserves (*reservas*) and preserves (*resguardos*). A *resguardo* is collective ownership of land by the Indian group. A reserve is land owned by the state with usufruct rights given to the inhabitants. This legislation led to establishing a *resguardo* in the Vaupés of some three million hectares. That so much territory has been ceded to so few Indians, with so very little pressure coming from them, is indeed remarkable, and merits much greater attention than can be paid in this chapter. It reflects an extremely unstable national political situation (see Riding 1987) and a policy implemented by a fundamentally weak national government that attempts to win hearts and minds in the countryside and thus prevent leftist guerrilla groups from gaining more converts.[11] Some of the more militant highland Indian groups doubtless played a role in these developments as well, in addition to some well-publicized scandals involving Indian atrocities.[12] During this time, Indian organizing, with the participation of international indigenous rights organizations, led to the establishment in 1982 of the National Colombian Indian Organization (ONIC), and a great deal of discussion about Colombian Indian groups, their current status and probable future, in the national press.

Although space does not permit a comprehensive discussion, it is essential to understand some of the fundamental differences between Andean Indians and their counterparts in the Colombian forests and plains. Vastly different situations obtain in white-Indian relations depending on what region one is talking about, and this is sometimes obscured by pan-Indian rhetoric. First, with few exceptions, Andean conflicts have most often been over land itself, whereas in lower latitudes the problems have been with small-scale (and more recently large-scale) extractive industries, *colonos* (homesteaders), and mission-aries. Actual land pressures appeared only later—although these are currently very real in some lowland areas of the country. In the Vaupés there is virtually no land pressure; population density, as we have seen, is quite low. And Tukanoans now have three million hectares of *resguardo*.

Intensive white-Indian interaction has been occurring in the Andean sector for some four-hundred-plus years. This history in itself forms part of what groups such as the Paez consider their legacy: as one interviewee put it, these bitter memories bind them as much as their language. Furthermore, Andean peasants had been part of a state system for centuries before the arrival of the Spanish. In contrast, nonviolent white-Indian interaction in the lowlands most often was on the basis of Indian attraction to white trade goods, offered by missionaries or individuals involved in extractive industries.[13]

Another contrast is found in the legislation creating Indian reserves and *resguardos*. The native community that oversees the communal property and deals with the state, and in several ways functions as an autonomous political unit is the *cabildo* (municipal council). In Andean areas, *cabildos* evolved from a traditional form of communal leadership, but, contrary to what is sometimes stated in the Colombian indigenist press, no such council traditionally existed for regions like the Vaupés. One interviewee from an Andean Indian community, a very knowledgeable Indian rights organizer, did comment on this as a failing of ONIC's policy-making, saying that ONIC has assumptions about priorities, such as defense of land, language, tradition, and how to struggle against large landholders. However, since these are not the conditions found in the Vaupés, ONIC ought to do a study to discover the conditions there and what the Indians there think.

Also, for the most part, highland Indians tend to be more suspicious and hostile to white intrusion than are lowland Indians—after any initial periods of violence have ceased. In addition, culture change usually takes place at a slower pace in Andean areas, if the local communities have any say-so in the matter at all. The examples of the Colombian Paez and Kogui are quite instructive. In contrast, lowland Amazonian Indians and most plains Indians, to the degree they are able, more readily participate in the intrusive economy and are far more willing to adopt its values.[14] Why this is so is complex, having to do with land tenure systems, history, degree of aggregation of population, overall population size, the nature of the exchanges taking place, and so forth. What is important to note is that often Andean Indian communities' and indigenist organizations' cultural assumptions can have more in common with non-Indian Colombia than with the worldview of their fellow Indians in the plains and tropical forests. However, this is a position most Indians involved in Indian rights organizing would reject out of hand, for understandable political reasons.

Because of the long-term struggles experienced by Colombian Indians in Tolima, Cauca, Antioquia, and other highland areas, these people are much more self-conscious of their cultural distinctiveness; they are ethnic groups, as defined in the beginning of this chapter. Andean groups are far more politicized, and their organizing and publications reflect this. As we shall see below, this can lead to misunderstandings and conflicts in a national movement that, while trying to be a pluralist movement, still needs unifying symbols and ideology. Sometimes the symbols adopted are not, as thought, pan-Indian.

Another factor that must be mentioned but cannot be comprehensively explored here is the interaction between the national Indian rights movement and the various national political fronts who seek to use popular movements as a springboard toward an insurrectional, revolutionary movement. Great tension at times exists between ONIC and the left, particularly in cases of violence between guerrillas in rural areas and Indian communities.[15] True, some local sectors of Indian rights groups have referred to themselves as guerrillas and promoted violent solutions, and in some cases such confrontations occurred long before the non-Indian guerrilla movement became established in Colombia. But knowledgeable Colombians are aware of the different objectives of these various organizations and the struggles over who is to have hegemony in Andean Indian areas. In fact, the left no longer talks in terms of how best to incorporate the Indian movement into the popular movement.

Andean Indian responses to the radical left, for example, Sierra Indians' responses to the M-19[16] faction, are often simply along the lines of "leave us alone, we have different problems." But often open confrontation exists, as when Cauca valley *campesinos* (peasants) requested help from demobilized guerrillas to stop Paez Indian cattle rustling. The Paez stated that the rustling was a form of political resistance.

Thus, despite some similarities between Andean Indian communities and Indian communities elsewhere in Colombia, one should not lose sight of the very significant differences, especially given that lowland areas are so poorly understood in the rest of the country and the direction of Indian-to-Indian communication and political pressure is, for the most part, from highland to lowland. This is a crucial difference in itself, for whereas Andean groups have experienced pressure only from external *non*-Indian sources (e.g., leftist and populist movements, the state, the Church—although this is changing somewhat as Colombian Indian leaders confer with indigenous leaders from other nations), the impact of external *Indian* influence on Tukanoans in organizations like CRIVA has been significant.

Space does not permit a thorough discussion of the roles missionaries have played in the Vaupés. Suffice it to say that until recently, apart from the rubber trade, practically all relations between Tukanoans south of the Vaupés River and the non-Indian world have involved Catholic missionaries acting as intermediaries, on both sides of the border. Although today the priests have less clearly coercive means of enforcing their authority than in the past, the Church is still very powerful: it is virtually impossible to ignore or bypass them in the parts of the region controlled by the Prefecture.

Members of SIL or Protestant evangelical organizations such as New

Tribes Mission can today point to many Protestant settlements, particularly among the Cubeo (see Goldman 1981; Wright 1981a). Some earlier estimates assign as much as a third of the inhabitants of the combined *comisarías* (comissariats) of the Vaupés and Guainía to Protestant sects (Reichel-Dolmatoff 1971: 7). Due to the more than sixteen languages in the area, SIL has had more bases in the Vaupés than anywhere else in Colombia of comparable area and population numbers.

With few exceptions, missionaries are the only non-Indians who are permanent residents in the eastern Vaupés outside of the administrative center of Mitú (two-thirds of the Vaupés is *resguardo*). Catholic missionaries have traditionally conducted trade, established shops, bought surplus products (especially food for their boarding schools), and occasionally hired Tukanoans. In some of these activities, despite their religious goals, missionaries have clearly been "agents of secularization" like missionaries among the Toba (Miller 1970). Local nonmissionary representatives of the Colombian government had until recently been so few that the missions had much de facto and in some respects de jure governmental authority. A recent example is the missions' informal regulation of coca paste trade south of the Vaupés River.[17] Powerless to stop the trade, Catholic clergy were successful in some areas at prohibiting dealers from making payments with firearms and alcohol for a period of time.

While one cannot say that missionaries are in the region to promote cultural autonomy and self-sufficiency, at times they *have* served as buffers between Tukanoans and highly exploitative change agents, such as most rubber gatherers. An especially interesting chapter in the recent history of the Vaupés is the role missionaries have played in the emerging indigenist movement. At times they have seen expressions of "Red Power" as threatening to their own enterprises, but at other times they apparently concluded that encouraging the growth of such movements and forming alliances with leaders was a way of giving discomfort to enemies (i.e., some of the other change agents in the region).

Some of the Catholic priests in the Vaupés, members of the Javerian order, became very radicalized during the mid to late 1960s; this trend continues today. Many were involved in the progressive Golconda movement (Stoll 1982: 175), and some continue to write about Liberation theology topics in mission publications. The anticommunist and progovernment stance assumed by foreign Protestant organizations has undoubtedly been an element in the assumption by many Catholic clergy of a left, traditionalist, and nationalist (e.g., anti-*gringo*) stance.

Today some publications by Catholic priests are still quite radical in tone, praising socialism and favorably comparing Indian communities with other sectors of Colombian society. However, when confronting

socialism as constructed by other leftists in the country, especially
social scientists, the authors can become quite conservative. For
example, in one instance, Msgr. Belarmino Correa Yepes of the Vaupés
Prefecture addresses the readers of *Unidad Indígena*, the official publication of ONIC, speaking favorably of socialism: "During the time
when we cannot count on living in a socialist state that respects and
makes others respect culturally distinct groups with their own traditions,
I find it very difficult to do something within the context of the present
structures" (*Unidad Indígena* 1975b: 8). However, an editorial in a
missionary journal states: "In contrast to the barking of the Marxist
anthropologists, our missionaries offer works and reality" (*Revista de
Misiones* 1976: 57).

Part of this shift in consciousness has been the result of missionary
personnel listening to anthropologists working in the Vaupés and elsewhere and adopting language and concepts that are convenient to their
purposes.[18] The alliances and conflicts between Catholic missionaries
and anthropologists (mostly Colombian) are complicated and fascinat-
ing. For example, the Church states that studying anthropology without
humanistic bases creates an anthropologist who is irreligious and indifferent, and a compromised anthropology (*Revista de Misiones* 1983: 118).
An earlier article in this magazine chides Vaupés anthropologists for
having helped create the "complex" Tukanoans have today (*Revista de
Misiones* 1974: 224). The Church formed its own Missionary Colombian
Anthropological Center, began a publication, *Etnia*, in 1965, and opened
an Ethnographic Museum in Bogotá in 1973. Clearly, the presence of
anthropologists in the Vaupés and exposure to activist anthropology
(e.g., the Declaration of Barbados) have had an effect on the Church's
mission policies—and have also nourished continuing ambivalence and
sometimes hostility toward what missionaries understand to be
anthropology's objectives.

The same can be said for indigenism: while CRIVA is the Prefecture's
inspiration and to some extent its creation, in other instances indigenism
is attacked in Church publications.[19] Thus, part of this assumption of
the indigenist mantle has been the result of the radicalization of some of
Colombia's Catholic missionaries, and part has been the result of the
effects anthropologists, Colombian and foreign, had simply by their
presence in lowland Indian territories. In addition, SIL, which has *not*
been involved in indigenism in Colombia, has nonetheless presented an
image of people dedicated to studying indigenous language and culture,
and has published various collections on Colombian indigenous culture
and linguistics.[20] These events threatened the Prefecture's image of
itself and its justifications for its activities. Furthermore, SIL actively
promoted bilingual education, various secular development projects,

and the creation of a corps of indigenous leaders to take over religious proselytization when the linguist teams left their communities.

Hence, during the last twenty years some priests became aware that several high-status and knowledgeable outsiders saw traditional Tukanoan culture as valuable, worth preserving, and even superior to Colombian culture in some respects, and this has had an impact on their outlook and programs. Part of the Catholic response was to appropriate these notions, with the resulting sponsorship of, for example, "Indian weeks" in which ceremonies and dances are performed. Such activities were anathema to Catholic missionaries twenty-five years ago.

When SIL/WBT's contract was up for renewal in 1975–1976, young Colombian linguists and anthropologists entered the campaign to have the organization removed (*Micronoticias* 1978: M-54). In the Vaupés itself, from 1969 to 1975, six SIL/WBT teams were dislocated, and the conflicts came to national attention in the press (Stoll 1982: 175). Here the Church, Colombian anthropologists, and national Indian rights leaders found it advisable to be temporary (and mutually suspicious) bedfellows, an alliance SIL bitterly complained about (see Cass 1981).

Both SIL/WBT and New Tribes Mission oppose certain traditional practices that Catholics are increasingly willing to overlook, which further takes them into the relativist anthropological camp. Dancing, drinking manioc beer, and taking the hallucinogen *banisteriopsis* are examples. Goldman (1981: 8) noted a Cubeo revival in 1970, encouraged by the Church, that included "the resumption of previously forbidden mourning rites and the reconstruction of the communal *malocas* (longhouses) that earlier missionaries had put to the torch."

Another response to SIL/WBT's presence was the Catholics' altering their educational policies. In 1965 they instituted a project whereby Tukanoan catechists would teach religion and the rudiments of Spanish spelling. They subsequently came to speak favorably of bilingual education and later on promoted hiring Tukanoan secondary school graduates to teach primary school in outlying communities. Today they promote bicultural education.[21]

The Church has unquestionably made substantial changes over the past fifteen years, but the picture that emerges is confused. Sometimes it seems as though a total about-face has occurred; rather than espousing a "now we civilize them" policy, priests apparently sometimes conclude that today's position should refer to how well-off Tukanoans are in their "element," and that one should try to better their lives, yes, but not if it deprives them of their traditions. One priest, disillusioned, commented that Tukanoans are "by nature made to live in the longhouse seated on their stools. They had the possibility of changing and didn't do it." He mentioned that whereas the Church is now in favor of bilingual and bicultural education, this upsets the parents, who say that their children already know how to speak their languages, do not see any reason to learn to write in them, and want to learn Spanish.

CRIVA

CRIVA began in 1973 with the backing of the Prefecture; its leaders were and have continued to be selected from the graduates of the Prefecture's María Reina *Internado* secondary school (which became a government school in 1975). Today approximately 80 percent of teachers in the Vaupés are Indian and bilingual.

CRIVA claims members from thirty-five different ethnic groups, although it should be noted that the vast majority of Tukanoans are significantly less politicized than active CRIVA members, and many Tukanoans are indifferent or hostile to CRIVA. The Tukanoans who live far from Mitú are for the most part not actively involved in the movement, and many apparently do not respect the leaders or the positions they espouse.[22] Traditionally, the Vaupés had no federated regional organizations, or political corporate groups or leaders above the level of the settlement. This is not to say that Tukanoans are not adept at making collective decisions, but that the structure and purpose of a pan-Vaupés organization like CRIVA is foreign to them.

Although perceived pressure from nonmissionary whites such as anthropologists doubtless played a role, certainly the main reason behind the Prefecture's encouraging the founding of CRIVA, in 1973, was its rivalry with SIL, which dates back to the 1940s. As Stoll (1982: 66) aptly notes, "[indigenous rights] organizing . . . was sometimes difficult to distinguish from patronage battles between rival brokers." Clearly, from the beginning the Vaupés Indian rights movement was an endeavor greatly influenced by non-Indians and continually linked to larger disputes occurring in all government agencies concerned with indigenous affairs, the struggle between SIL and Catholic church leaders, and debates occurring within the national anthropology establishment.[23] For some time the Vaupés has been a battleground in a "War of the Gods," as a film made by Brian Moser characterized it, and the entry of organizations such as CRIVA into the fray added a new interest group and level of intrigue.[24] An SIL veteran maintained that organizations like CRIVA would destroy Indian culture faster than anything else, and that mutual "blackmail" between rival outsiders (which permits each to go about its plans, scrutinized by the others) was a superior alternative (David Stoll, personal communication).

CRIVA soon began to change, affected by the coca paste traffic and by outside organizations such as CRIC (Regional Council of Cauca Indians) and ONIC. CRIC's attempt to reproduce itself elsewhere in Colombia has not met with success in the Vaupés. Difficulties with ONIC, difficulties within itself, difficulties with local state representatives, difficulties with the Church, difficulties with other Vaupés Indians sum up my impressions about CRIVA.

Virtually all interviewees, Indian and white, in Mitú and in Bogotá agreed that at present CRIVA has very little influence. The one area in which CRIVA was successful, from the Prefecture's point of view, was in its pressuring SIL and New Tribes missionaries to leave the region, especially in 1974.

As we have seen, some of CRIVA's problems—structurally and in image-management—definitely stem from its close association with the Prefecture. All non-CRIVA members interviewed agreed that in part CRIVA was a white creation. The Church maintains that it facilitated the founding of CRIVA to speed up the death throes of the debt-peonage system from the rubber period. A Mitú priest commented that Father Valencia Cano founded CRIVA because of the rubber exploitation of the Indians, to take the yoke from their necks, to show them they were not subject to anyone. While this surely was a major motivation, the role of the Church vis-à-vis CRIVA is more complicated. One interviewee in Bogotá, very much involved in indigenous grass-roots projects and knowledgeable about the Vaupés, commented:

> The priests say "you have to organize." And they organize, but the priests said that in order to continue managing the people. Thus although they [CRIVA leaders] are artificial officials, this corresponds to the interests of the mission. And with these Indians taking on state jobs comes individualism [e.g., a tendency to self-interest rather than commitment to one's constituency].

In a letter from CRIVA to *Unidad Indígena*, CRIVA disputes a reporter's attributing to a CRIVA member a statement that CRIVA encounters problems "because the leadership has not had the sufficient force, but has supported the dependency on Msgr. Belarmino Correa, who does not value indigenous culture" (*Unidad Indígena* 1984: 5). The writers of the letter denounce the article, saying it was not legally authorized by CRIVA, and that they demand the name of the author in order to: "take very drastic measures against this individual, because we know that he is trying to divide the good relations that we have always had with our Prefecture" (ibid.). In another letter in *Unidad Indígena*, the "Comrades of the Vaupés from Santa Rosa" strongly criticize the "mediocre" education provided by the Javerian clergy, because it is "given in a capitalist style, and they don't know the reality of our necessities." This letter appears on the same page as a message from CRIVA, but, perhaps significantly, is not directly linked to it (*Unidad Indígena* 1975a: 5).

An example of the problem of paternalism is the extremely interesting comment by Monsignor Belarmino in ONIC's official organ:

> what if we leave the Vaupés (not a difficult thing to do), do you have a half-human solution for this people? Can the Indians defend themselves alone today? Would you be capable of controlling the avalanche of irresponsible people who are interested only in their personal advance?. . . You have the word and hopefully in the direction you're going you don't place the Indian in worse conditions than he was formerly. (*Unidad Indígena* 1975b: 8)

However, when talking about other kinds of outsiders being able to help Tukanoans, he states: "Indians of the Vaupés: In congresses and reunions of 'Whites' one thinks . . . that the Whites want to help you leave your marginalized position. But they . . . won't resolve your problems, you must find the solution" (October 1973, quoted in *Un Pastor en la Selva*: 39). One priest I interviewed did comment that the Church should change its position regarding CRIVA: "The Church has to leave CRIVA alone, so that it can mature, not be dependent. When a child falls down, you have to give him a hand up, but sometimes they have to pick themselves up."

Some interviewees commented that CRIVA is too linked to whites in general. A government functionary in Mitú stated that "CRIVA's leaders have more fear of whites than they do of their constituency, so they accomplish nothing." According to a lawyer involved in Colombian Indian land claims cases: "they are waiting for those in power to do something—now it's waiting for a response from the government, tomorrow waiting for an investigator to give them money. It's not an *Indian* organization at all. Like most Indian organizations, it is conceived and made rational with the rationality of the white."

Another activist located in Bogotá indicated that CRIVA was too involved with the politics of the national Indian movement and this led to their being manipulated by other Indians with different interests. He criticized these outsider Indians, saying that they say: "'we're going to work with the *gente de base* [the people of the communities],' but they're bureaucrats, they speak Spanish, they manage the white world. Now, it's true the local people may have to learn to manage the white world, but they must do so for their *own* interests." The theme of paternalism and unwillingness to let CRIVA mature and find its own identity came up several times. CRIVA leaders are still in some ways playing the role of students—both in terms of traditional Indian authority, in that all the leaders are young, and in terms of their ability to define and obtain what they want. Fostering leadership under these circumstances is difficult. One Bogotá interviewee remarked: "these groups would have been better *without* help from outsiders, it's another example of paternalism, they don't let them mature . . . the last thing CRIVA needs is another group of assessors making recommendations."

CRIVA also has a problem with internal divisions. One indication of this is the number of times CRIVA calls for unity in its own publications, for example: "[During the third congress] a great interest was seen for the necessity for UNITY without distinguishing tribes, nor clans, nor religious beliefs, in order to study the most urgent problems" (from a report by CRIVA in *Unidad Indígena* 1976b: 8). In the same issue, Tukanoans are criticized for their "lack of great interest on the part of the distinct communities and surroundings."

The Church undoubtedly sees its promotion of CRIVA as an answer to the many critics who have accused missionaries of creating divisions and exacerbating previously existing factions in Tukanoan society. It is clear to all who know the Vaupés that the Prefecture has indeed employed a range of divide and conquer tactics over the years for winning Tukanoans away from rival enterprises. One of the most worrisome features of the strife among missionaries pertains to potential consequences in Bogotá: the specter of increased legalized repression of Indian civil rights movements justifying itself with claims of being necessary to solve disputes among evangelical, Catholic, indigenist, and traditionalist interests.[25]

However, the question of factionalism in the Vaupés is more complicated. Traditional Tukanoan society was hardly a utopia in this regard, and what may initially appear as new divisions probably build on already existing fault lines. The splits between old and young, proacculturation versus traditionalist, Mitú-oriented versus backwoods, are lines of cleavage that combine with the newer rivalries connected with allegiances to different non-Indian patrons. Furthermore, indigenous institutions of leadership are a complicated matter in the Vaupés, where a general dislike of individuals who assume superior airs is coupled with unmistakable indicators of hierarchy. Certainly, the Catholics exacerbated this with their policy of bypassing traditional headmen and appointing as settlement *capitanes* younger men who looked more favorably on the Church. The Church's catechist program in the early 1970s is another example; the local community's complaints about sullenness were fully merited in the case of one Desana catechist I visited with in a Tuyuka community on the Tiquié in 1970. And in the use of Tukanoan school teachers, the priests must contend with gripes from the host communities about arrogance (again, often fully warranted, especially if the teachers are Tukanos in a non-Tukano community). Thus, CRIVA and its problems of representation and leadership are to some extent continuations of already well-established patterns of conflict.

Part of CRIVA's problems stem from the fact that the more one becomes effective in a nontraditional form of leadership, especially if it involves brokering with outsiders, the less accepted one is as a traditional, authentic member of the culture. The one exception to this seems to be messianic leaders, but this is really an instance of the culture itself changing its ideas of leadership and what it means to be "traditional."

It also appears to be the case that CRIVA members who are from distant settlements and spend a lot of time in Mitú are becoming alienated from their communities. While Mitú has a substantial Indian population, politically and culturally Mitú is a white settlement, the only one in the entire Vaupés. An Indian activist from outside the Vaupés commented:

> very weak . . . these Indians don't have representation in the communities, they are in the hands of the *mestizos* and don't have direct contact with the communities. They were formed in the mission and have interests unsuited to the communities' interests . . . they are more interested in their own personal development. When the *resguardo* of the Vaupés was being created, it was all due to pressure from outsiders, there was no Tukanoan pressure.

CRIVA leaders seem to see a solution in being bicultural. One commented to me:

> Earlier they thought that to speak Spanish was superior, but it's the opposite. We are Indians. We don't reject the other culture but accept what is useful to us. It's biculturalism: you learn to dance and become a *payé* [shaman] but also you learn how to dress differently when you're with *doctores* [high-status whites]. But when you're with the people, you paint yourself and are with the people.

This interviewee maintained that CRIVA does attempt to find out what the communities want; for example, attempting to enlist older, traditional Tukanoans for teaching history classes in the schools became something CRIVA promoted after finding out that this was what people in the communities wanted. But other Tukanoans I spoke with stated that there is little communication between most communities and CRIVA. With few exceptions, CRIVA leaders appear to limit their travels south of the Vaupés River to mission villages, and when CRIVA sends delegations, the delegates do the talking.

In fact, policies about bilingualism and biculturalism can be found in the publications of the Prefecture, in government documents concerned with developing indigenous communities, and in CRIC and ONIC organs. We really do not know what the majority of Tukanoans think in this regard.

Many of the interviewees most knowledgeable about indigenous organizing stressed that indigenist organizations are most successful when they are most threatened. CRIVA lacks a strong identification with an issue: founded in terms of the struggle against the remaining traces of rubber debt-patronage and some incursions from *colonos* (homesteaders), its response to a new threat, coca paste trafficking, was hardly one of a unified stance against a white-introduced plague. One interviewee, for example, described one of CRIVA's branch organizations as little more than a coca-growers' guild, regulating prices and organizing payoffs. Currently, there is nothing that is both visibly and urgently menacing to fight for. Tukanoans indisputably face many dangers—inroads into Tukanoan traditions are perceived as threats to cultural integrity, and everyone in Mitú can come up with a long list of how Tukanoans could be better off. But it is hard to adopt the militant rhetoric one reads in publications from Indian groups elsewhere in the country (whose members are being assassinated, evicted, imprisoned, etc.), to "fight for" something like higher employment rates or for less of the discrimination Tukanoans experience. As Stephen Hugh-Jones notes, when discussing threats to Tukanoan identity, CRIVA represents a set of solutions looking for a problem (personal communication).

The national political situation and resulting policies make it now possible to speak of the *advantages* of being Indian in Colombia, or at least in the Vaupés. I am not referring to the familiar resentment expressed by some whites about *any* pro-Indian legislation, but analyses by knowledgeable people of the potentially negative consequences of pro-Indian government policies for groups like CRIVA. As one interviewee, a consultant in a number of pro-Indian projects, put it:

Indians constitute only 3 to 4% of Colombia's population. It's good if the government knows you are an Indian, you can guilt-trip them into coming to study your community, talk to you, offer you things. Compared to the *campesinos* [peasants], they're pampered. Some groups like the Arhuacos are sophisticated and win battles against the *colonos* [homesteaders—usually peasants] by manipulating journalists.

Or, as another put it: "to have access to these services you must *be* an

Indian. Not perhaps a real Indian, but the appearance is important."

One government agent involved in Indian rights legislation commented that: "[Mitú Tukanoans] . . . they are molded by Colombian law
now, they participate in the national system, *resguardos, cabildos . . .*
they don't pay taxes, they receive public health. To be an Indian is an
advantage in this sense." He noted that the above-mentioned advantages
may not prove to be so in the long run because Tukanoans have not had
the conditions under which to develop a strong enough sense of ethnic
identity, or perhaps even a notion of being superior to white society, as
have some Indians elsewhere in Colombia: "CRIVA says Indians have
been discriminated against and now you must treat them well because
they have been so badly treated. But whereas the Koguis say 'the whites
are our younger brothers' [i.e., of lower status], they [Tukanoans] don't
think like this in Mitú." Of course, "advantage" is only relative. *Why*
certain policies and edicts are advantageous has to be spelled out,
especially if one is speaking of long-term advantages.[26] And these knowledgeable people warn that groups like CRIVA risk co-optation and
increasing dependency on the government.

Co-optation can also occur in interactions with other Indians. Some
of CRIVA's characterizations of itself and the Tukanoan communities it
represents do not fit with most Tukanoans' views of themselves and
their culture. For example, a CRIVA member told me: "the people
wanted to end with the sense of isolated groups, such as Desana, Cubeo,
and move towards unity, so that all the groups could reunite like
brothers. To look for unity." This individual made a specific comparison between CRIVA and CRIC, saying that more respect comes if groups
unify themselves. While more traditional Tukanoans are probably not
upset with the idea of forming federations for the purposes of promoting
Tukanoan well-being, they probably would be upset with the idea of
ending with the distinctions between Desana and Cubeo, and so on. I
cannot imagine Tukanoans in the near future coming to agree that all the
riverine Indians of the Vaupés should see one another as brothers.[27] In
promoting this, CRIVA would probably be seen not as a bulwark against
the end of Tukanoan culture but as speeding it up.

Some basic characteristics of Tukanoan society are distorted or not
mentioned in Colombian Indian rights publications. For example,
Unidad Indígena describes Vaupés language groups thus: "to each tribe
corresponds a territory whose limits are clearly recognized and respected; in keeping with tradition and mythology, this territory is
communal property of the entire tribe" (1976c: 6–7). Whatever traditional
Tukanoan notions are of land ownership, an association between land
and language group exists in a symbolic, mythological sense only.
Furthermore, local communities are intermingled with respect to lan-

guage group affiliation; often a community's closest neighbors all belong to other language groups. In the same article, language groups are described in the following terms: "each culture conserves almost all of its own characteristics; each tribe speaks its own language, and owing to the contact between the different tribes, it results that in general each person speaks three, four or more different languages" (ibid.). No mention is made here of the basis for so much contact: language exogamy. In this quotation, language is viewed in the conventional sense as a marker of a distinct cultural entity, a "tribe."

Furthermore, the article also states that the presence of missionaries is the reason Vaupés communities are divided and have problems among themselves. While it is true missionaries have produced much divisiveness, especially with regard to patronage battles among different missionary organizations, such a statement ignores the traditional raiding and feuding characteristic of lowland Amazonian groups, traditions still very much alive in Tukanoan mythology and ethnohistory (see, for example, Goldman 1981)—as well as other traditional causes of factionalism. Such a picture does not only appear in the national indigenist press; a book written by a CRIVA leader, Jesús Santacruz, *Fundamental Principles of CRIVA*, is full of ethnographic errors showing the same type of bias.

In another issue of the national newspaper, we find the romantic assertion that the land is worked communally: "the communities . . . conserve, each one, its territory, which is communal property of all the tribe, and they work it communally. They live from the abundant fruits that the jungle gives them spontaneously and from hunting" (*Unidad Indígena* 1976a: 11). Other examples can be offered of what I consider to be a systematic bias toward describing Tukanoans in terms of a general image of tropical forest Indians—an image that is simplified, romantic, and idealized. Incomprehensible arrangements, such as language exogamy, though fundamental to Tukanoan social structure, are glossed over or not mentioned at all. Insofar as Tukanoans are coming to describe themselves in these terms, as is evidenced by the Santacruz book, we have the beginnings of a process of cultural co-optation: Tukanoans are learning how to be proper Indians from non-Tukanoan Indian images and values. Many examples of this process can be found among Native Americans in the United States and Canada; what is interesting in the Vaupés is that we are seeing the beginnings of it.

Despite its unique characteristics, understanding the Tukanoan case helps our general comprehension of how ethnically diverse and relatively powerless peoples can maintain their cultural and political autonomy within a highly bureaucratized and centralized state, be it capitalist or socialist. Tukanoans' traditional culture provides only a few empowering mechanisms in the current situation of extensive and rapid intrusion by the larger society. In societies like this one, as yet without a perceived threat to land base or to physical survival,[28] how to get to the point of being able to choose which aspects of modernization would be beneficial and which too costly may require traveling far on the road to incorporation. Interesting counterexamples (e.g., Maybury-Lewis 1983; Chapin 1985; Bonfil Batalla 1981) can be offered, but for many groups the battles won for cultural authenticity and autonomy have been somewhat pyrrhic victories, for the cost in terms of factionalization and acceptance of foreign mentalities and increased economic and cultural dependency has been high.

Nonetheless, barring catastrophe, Tukanoan culture *will* continue in the foreseeable future, albeit a culture evolving into a subculture—an ethnic group—as it increasingly participates in the dominant society. Whether Tukanoans respond to changing conditions by retaining, revamping, or rejecting traditional cultural forms is a matter of empirical observation and analysis. But it is certain that the meaning of any forms retained will be altered. Increasingly, Tukanoans' casting aside, altering, or preserving various traditions will be in part a matter of strategy in political engagements with non-Tukanoans—government agents, other Colombian Indians, the Church, and so forth. In this regard, understanding the history and current position of CRIVA is extremely instructive. Understanding the considerable differences separating Andean Indians from Indians of the forests and plains of Colombia has also been important.

The examples offered above of such strategies' influencing Tukanoans' presentation of themselves to others and, perhaps, ultimately to themselves, are enlightening. The example given of indigenist publications' emphasizing the coterminality of Tukanoan language groups and clearly defined territories is congruent with the most effective pro-Indian position to take in the struggle for a secure land base. The absence of descriptions of Tukanoan language exogamy fits with general notions about face-to-face communities and cultural homogeneity in small-scale tropical forest Amerindian societies.

However, what we are seeing is not a black-and-white situation of Tukanoans' *either* resisting *or* accepting white society, or even "Indian" society as experienced and imparted by non-Tukanoan Indians. To some extent, Tukanoans will resist hegemonic attempts, yes, but the content of Tukanoan representations of their culture and identity will be gradually transformed as a result of Tukanoans' encounters with non-Tukanoan ideologies, be they about modernization, religion, or indigenism.

The Vaupés is instructive as a case study because it illustrates many of the factors impeding, or at least complicating, the establishment of genuine self-sufficiency, increased autonomy and empowerment of native groups vis-à-vis the state, and maintenance of cultural authenticity. The most significant factors are: (1) bureaucratization, co-optation, and marginalization of leaders in indigenist organizations vis-à-vis traditional sectors, (2) lack of a sense of threat to land or other natural resources, (3) the siren coca, which promised the ultimately false promises bonanzas always offer, and (4) paternalism and divergent interests in institutions promoting change, even if they see themselves as promoting indigenous well-being. The role of outsiders working with local Tukanoan leaders—priests, government agents, anthropologists, representatives of national and international Indian rights organizations, lawyers promoting civil and human rights legislation, and so forth—is extremely complex.

This chapter has suggested that Tukanoan conceptualizations of themselves as "Indian" are in a process of evolving into a form quite different from the traditional consciousness. The new consciousness is far more self-conscious and politicized. It derives from Tukanoans' increasing embeddedness in the Colombian nation-state, a process turning them into an ethnic group, as opposed to a distinct culture. It also stems from Tukanoans' being instructed by non-Tukanoans—both whites and Indians from elsewhere in Colombia and the world—on what it means to be an Indian, and, in some instances, what it means to be a Tukanoan. The problems CRIVA faces, both in terms of its own identity and its ability to represent all Tukanoans, vividly illustrate many of the general problems faced by any indigenist organization (see Smith 1985). In particular, a notable number of factors, internal and external to the organization, mitigate against CRIVA's achieving true grass-roots representativeness. In particular, certain factors that can be characterized as advantages to being an Indian in Colombia, which particularly apply to the Vaupés case, can still produce obstacles to achieving autonomy and group cohesion.

Notes

This chapter is part of an ongoing research project concerned with changing identity among Tukanoans of Colombia. I am grateful to the MIT Provost's Fund for funding the trip to Colombia in March 1987, and for continuing support for archival research. My thanks to all in Colombia who so willingly gave of their time and energy, in particular: Javier Saenz, Jaime Arocha, Elizabeth de Reichel, Elsa Gómez-Imbert, Juanita Saenz, Martín von Hildebrand, Elías Sevilla-Casas, Enrique Sánchez, Raúl Arango, Roque Roldán, Clemencia Plazas, Tito Vargas,

Francisco Escobar, Samuel Valencia, Juan Baylón, Mario Gonzalez, Milciades Rodriguez, Alberto Betancur, M.X.Y., Dario Cardona, M.X.Y., Janet Barnes, Simeon Timoté, Martha Lucía Peña Vázquez, Carlos Morales, Adolfo Triana, Myriam Jimeno, Leonor Herrera, Marianne Cardale de Schrimpff, François Correa. My appreciation also to the Anthropology Department of the National University, the Anthropology Department of the University of Los Andes, the Office of Indian Affairs, and the Colombian Anthropology Institute. Also thanks to the participants at the 1987 Bennington South American Indian Conference who commented on an earlier oral version. A related paper was given at the symposium on "Anthropological Discourses and the Expression of Personhood in South American Interethnic Relations" at the Chicago 1987 AAA meetings (also see Jackson 1989). Readers of previous drafts who kindly offered suggestions include Darna Dufour, Amitai Etzioni, Christian Gros, James Howe, Stephen Hugh-Jones, Theodore Macdonald, David Stoll, and Robin Wright.

1. "Tukanoan" refers to all riverine indigenous inhabitants of the Vaupés. Makú, forest-dwellers who also differ in other respects, are not included (see Silverwood-Cope 1975). Although many Tukanoans live on the Brazilian side of the border, this chapter considers only those in Colombian territory.

2. See Jackson (n.d.) for a discussion of how conventional notions of culture fail to characterize this change. Also see Wolf (1982); Cowlishaw (1987); S. Hugh-Jones (1987).

3. Bear in mind that we are not talking about *contact*—even extensive and with radical consequences—between whites and Indians, which has been occurring for centuries.

4. Groups such as present-day Wampanoag, Sioux, Navaho, Miskito, and Kuna, however, have much to teach us about later stages of this process.

5. Coca paste is an intermediate stage between coca leaf harvesting and processing, and the production of cocaine per se, which, to my knowledge, does not occur in the Vaupés. For information on coca in tropical forest areas of Colombia, see Arango and Child (1984) and Jaramillo, Mora, and Cubides (1986).

6. Messianic-type movements among Arawakans are analyzed by Wright and Hill (1986) and Wright (1981b), and among Tukanoans by S. Hugh-Jones (1981).

7. CRIVA would be termed an ethnic federation in Smith's (1985) typology.

8. A list of acronyms: ONIC—Organización Nacional de Indígenas de Colombia; CRIVA—Consejo Regional de Indígenas del Vaupés; UNIP—Unión de Indígenas del Papurí; UDIC—Unión de Indígenas Cubeos; UNIZAC—Unión de Indígenas de la Zona de Acaricuara; ORIVAM—Organización de Indígenas del Vaupés Medio; UNIQ—Organización de Indígenas del Querarí; ORIT—Organización de Indígenas del Tiquié; ALUBVA—Alianza y Lucha del Bajo Vaupés.

9. This is a simplified description; in particular the Cubeo and Makuna are exceptions in some crucial respects.

10. For more comprehensive treatments of Tukanoan ethnography, see Århem (1981); Goldman (1963); C. Hugh-Jones (1979); S. Hugh-Jones (1979); Jackson (1983); Reichel-Dolmatoff (1971). Also consult Chernela (1982, n.d.).

11. See "Programa Nacional de Desarrollo de las Poblaciones Indígenas" (National Program for the Development of Indian Populations), and former

president Belisario Betancur's *El Indígena: raíz de nuestra identidad nacional* (The Indian: root of our national identity).

12. See Stoll (1982), on the Planas Affair, a series of tortures and killings in the Columbian eastern plains perpetrated by homesteaders on Guahibo Indians.

13. Violent interactions have characterized Tukanoan-white relations well into the twentieth century. Stephen Hugh-Jones notes that one could say that [in the Vaupés] the economies of Indians and whites are *complementary*—Indians want goods, whites want rubber, coca, and so on, while in the highlands the two economies are antagonistic—both want the same land (personal communication). Also see Jackson (1984a).

14. This is not to say that highland Indians do not change over time (the Otavaleños of Ecuador are a good example) nor that lowland groups do not seek to preserve their lifeways and reject certain elements of white culture. The Colombian Arhuacos are an example.

15. Reports of such clashes between the FARC (Revolutionary Armed Forces of Colombia, the oldest, largest, and best organized of the several guerrilla organizations) and Indians appear regularly in the Colombian press. See, for example, *Unidad Indígena* (1985) regarding the assassination of a local Indian leader.

16. A radical urban guerrilla faction that until recently tried to launch a national movement from various rural areas, which is alleged to have kidnapped and assassinated the SIL linguist Chester Bitterman in 1981. The Brazilian *Jornal da Tarde* of Oct. 17, 1985, reported a base of 500 M-19 in the Colombian Vaupés (as reported in *Aconteçeu* 1987: 97). However, Stephen Hugh-Jones is of the opinion that such claims are flimsy and basically serve the purpose of justifying a strong military presence in the Brazilian Vaupés.

17. This has been remarked on by so many people knowledgeable about the Vaupés that I have no doubts about its accuracy; for understandable reasons I am not attributing this information to any named persons.

18. Five Vaupés anthropologists, myself included, participated in a constructive-criticism session with Catholic clergy in Bogotá in early 1969.

19. See, for example, "¿Problema indígena o indigenista?" (Indian problem or indigenist problem?), *Revista de Misiones* (March–April 1974: 57–58).

20. The SIL publications dealing with Tukanoan nonlinguistic culture (e.g., a book on material culture) are superficial and not very useful; nonetheless, such activities were a prod to the Catholics to engage in similar enterprises.

21. Not all of the wrinkles have been ironed out of this one: when I asked a priest in Mitú how the Church could reconcile having elder Tukanoan men teach about myths, given the mission of the Church to preach the gospel, he replied, "this is what is waiting for us to deal with."

22. I am grateful to Darna Dufour for information on this matter.

23. See Friedemann and Arocha (1982); Arocha and Friedemann (1984); Friedemann (1984); Arocha (1984).

24. See also Stoll (1981, 1982); van Emst (1966); Reichel-Dolmatoff (1972); Hvalkof and Aaby (1981); Jackson (1984b).

25. *Cultural Survival Newsletter* (1979); Urbina (1979a, 1979b); Martinez (1979); *Unidad Indígena* (1979: 10).

26. An example is the Akwesasne Nation's policy about not utilizing federal

assistance, especially welfare programs, described in the film *Akwesasne: Another View*. Similarly, Morris (1985) has argued that legislation favoring Australian Aborigines has only succeeded in creating a welfare-dependent minority.

27. See Jackson (1983) for a discussion of the scandal that erupted in 1970 when it was found out that a priest was promoting a marriage between two Tukanos—who of course called each other "brother" and "sister."

28. In this, the Tukanoan communities of the Colombian Vaupés differ markedly from their Brazilian neighbors.

References

Aconteceu
   1987   General confirma: M-19 na fronteira. *Centro Ecumênico de Documentação e Informação*, Especial 17, São Paulo.
Arango, M., and J. Child
   1984   *Narcotráfico imperio de la Cocaina*. Medellín: Editorial Percepción.
Århem, K.
   1981   Makuna social organization: a study in descent, alliance and the formation of corporate groups in the north-western Amazon. Uppsala: Acta Universitatis Upsaliensis, Uppsala Studies in Cultural Anthropology 4.
Arocha, Jaime
   1984   Ejercicio de la antropología en grupos indígenas Colombianos. In *Un siglo de investigación social: antropología en Colombia*, J. Arocha and N. S. de Friedemann (eds.), 301–380. Bogotá: Etno.
Arocha, Jaime, and N. S. de Friedemann, eds.
   1984   *Un siglo de investigación social: antropología en Colombia*. Bogotá: Etno.
Barth, Fredrik, ed.
   1969   *Ethnic groups and boundaries*. Boston: Little, Brown.
Betancur, B.
   1984   *El indígena: raíz de nuestra identidad nacional*. Colombia: Dirección General de Integración y Desarrollo de la Comunidad, División Asuntos Indígenas, Ministerio de Gobierno.
Bonfil Batalla, G., comp.
   1981   Introduction to *Utopía y revolución: el pensamiento político contemporáneo de los Indios en América Latina*. Mexico: Editorial Nueva Imagen.
Cass, J.
   1981   Just Bible translators? Colombians have doubts. *Boston Sunday Globe*, March 8, p. 16.
Chapin, Mac
   1985   UDIRBI: an indigenous project in environmental conservation. In *Native peoples and economic development: six case studies from Latin America*, T. Macdonald (ed.), 39–54. Cambridge, Mass.: Cultural Survival.
Chernela, Janet
   1982   An indigenous system of forest and fisheries management in the Uaupés basin of Brasil. *Cultural Survival Quarterly* 6: 2.

n.d.   Why one culture stays put: a case of resistance to change in authority and economic structure in an indigenous community in the Northwest Amazon. In *Change in Amazonia*, J. Hemming (ed.). Manchester: Manchester University Press, forthcoming.

Cowlishaw, G.
1987   Colour, culture and the aboriginalists. *Man* 22(2): 221–237.

Cultural Survival Newsletter
1979   Colombia's "Proyecto de Ley." 3: 2–3.

Friedemann, N. S. de
1984   Etica y política del antropólogo: Compromiso profesional. In *Un siglo de investigación social: antropología en Colombia*, J. Arocha and N. S. de Friedemann (eds.), 381–428. Bogotá: Etno.

Friedemann, N. S. de, and J. Arocha
1982   *Herederos del jaguar y la anaconda*. Bogotá: Carlos Valencia.

Goldman, Irving
1963   *The Cubeo: Indians of the Northwest Amazon*. Illinois Studies in Anthropology, no. 2. Urbana: University of Illinois Press.
1981   The New Tribes Mission among the Cubeo. In *ARC Bulletin 9*, Wright and Swenson (eds.), 7–8. Boston: Anthropology Resource Center.

Goodenough, Ward H.
1964   Cultural anthropology and linguistics. In *Language in culture and society*, Dell Hymes (ed.), 36–39. New York: Harper and Row.

Hugh-Jones, Christine
1979   *From the milk river: spatial and temporal processes in Northwest Amazonia*. Cambridge: Cambridge University Press.

Hugh-Jones, Stephen
1979   *The palm and the pleiades: initiation and cosmology in Northwest Amazonia*. Cambridge: Cambridge University Press.
1981   Historia del Vaupés. *Maguaré: Revista del Departamento de Antropología* 1. Universidad Nacional de Colombia, June, pp. 29–51.
1987   Yesterday's luxuries, tomorrow's necessities; business and barter in Northwest Amazonia. Ms.

Hvalkof, S., and P. Aaby, eds.
1981   *Is God an American?: an anthropological perspective on the missionary work of the Summer Institute of Linguistics*. Copenhagen: IWGIA (International Group for Indigenous Affairs) and Survival International.

Jackson, Jean E.
1983   *The fish people: linguistic exogamy and Tukanoan identity in Northwest Amazonia*. Cambridge: Cambridge University. Press.
1984a   The impact of the state on small-scale societies. *Studies in Comparative International Development* 19(2): 3–32.
1984b   Traducciones competitivas del evangelio en el Vaupés, Colombia. *América Indígena* 44(1): 49–94.
1989   Is there a way to talk about making culture without making enemies? *Dialectical Anthropology* 14(2): 127–144.
n.d.   Changing Tukanoan ethnicity and the concept of culture. In *Amazonian synthesis: an integration of disciplines, paradigms, and methodolo-*

gies, Anna Roosevelt (ed.), forthcoming.

Jaramillo, J., L. Mora, and F. Cubides
  1986   *Colonización, coca y guerrilla.* Bogotá: Universidad Nacional de Co-
          lombia.

Martínez, H.
  1979   Nuevas denuncias indígenas. *El Espectador,* Nov. 4.

Maybury-Lewis, David
  1983   Contrasts in Brazilian Indian development. Paper given at the Latin
          American Studies Association Meetings, Mexico City.

Micronoticias
  1978   Declaración del comité de profesores del departamento de antropología
          de la Universidad Nacional sobre el Instituto Lingüístico de Verano.
          Julio–Agosto, M-54, pp. 2–4.

Miller, Elmer
  1970   The Christian missionary, agent of secularization. *Anthropological
          Quarterly* 43(1): 14–22.

Morris, B.
  1985   Cultural domination and domestic dependency: the Dhan-Gadi of
          New South Wales and the protection of the state. *Canberra Anthro-
          pology* 8(1, 2): 87–115.

Pastor en la Selva, Un
  1982   Monseñor Belarmino Correa Yepes: bodas de plata sacerdotales 1957–
          1982. Bogotá: Impresos Beper Ltda.

Reichel-Dolmatoff, Gerardo
  1971   *Amazonian cosmos: the sexual and religious symbolism of the Tukano
          Indians.* Chicago: University of Chicago Press.
  1972   El misionero ante las culturas indígenas. *América Indígena* 32(4): 1138–
          1149.

Revista de Misiones
  1971   March, no. 539, pp. 38–43.
  1974   Sept.–Oct., no. 561, pp. 254–255.
  1976   March, no. 570, pp. 57–62.
  1983   May, no. 613, p. 118.

Riding, Alan
  1987   Truce between Colombia and rebels is unravelling. *New York Times,*
          Aug. 10, p. A-11.

Santacruz, J.
  1985   *Princípios fundamentales del Consejo Regional Indígena del Vaupés.*
          Comisaría Especial del Vaupés.

Silverwood-Cope, Peter
  1975   Relatório a propósitas sobre a situaçao dos indígenas do Uaupés—Alto
          Rio Negro. Brasília.

Smith, R.
  1985   A search for unity within diversity: peasant unions, ethnic federations,
          and Indianist movements in the Andean republics. In *Native peoples
          and economic development: six case studies from Latin America,* T.
          Macdonald (ed.), 5–38. Cambridge, Mass.: Cultural Survival.

Sorensen, Arthur P., Jr.
  1967   Multilingualism in the Northwest Amazon. *American Anthropologist* 69: 670–682.
Stoll, David
  1981   Higher power: Wycliffe's Colombian advance. In *Is God an American? An anthropological perspective on the missionary work of the summer institute of linguistics*, S. Hvalkof and P. Aaby (eds.), 63–76. Copenhagen: IWGIA (International Group for Indigenous Affairs) and Survival International.
  1982   *Fishers of men or founders of empire? The Wycliffe Bible translators in Latin America*. London: Zed/Cultural Survival.
Unidad Indígena
  1975a   Carta de los compañeros del Vaupés. Aug. 1975, no. 7, p. 5.
  1975b   Misioneros del Vaupés nos escriben. May 1975, no. 5, p. 8
  1976a   Las comunidades indígenas en Colombia: comunidades de la selva. June, no. 14, p. 11.
  1976b   Conclusiones del tercer congreso del consejo regional indígena del Vaupés. April, no. 12, p. 8.
  1976c   El Vaupés: Geografía. Nov., no. 17, pp. 6–7.
  1979   Los derechos de la población indígena. Oct., pp. 6–11.
  1984   Letter from CRIVA and reply of editorial board. April, no. 67, p. 5.
  1985   Asesinada Rosa Elena Toconás. Aug., no. 74 , p. 3.
Urbina, A. M.
  1979a   Lucha contra abandono de la tierra: el problema de los indígenas. *El Espectador*, Sept. 25.
  1979b   No más leyes para archivar y confundir: El estatuto indígena. *El Espectador*, Oct. 13.
van Emst, P.
  1966   Indians and missionaries on the River Tiquié, Brazil-Colombia. *Institute Archives of Ethnography* 50, pt. 2, pp. 145–197.
Wolf, Eric
  1982   *Europe and the people without history*. Berkeley: University of California Press.
Wright, Robin
  1981a   Demons with no heads: NMT and the Baniwa of Brazil. *ARC Bulletin* 9: 9–13. Boston: Anthropology Resource Center.
  1981b   History and religion of the Baniwa peoples of the upper Rio Negro valley. PhD diss., Stanford University.
Wright, Robin, and Jonathan D. Hill
  1986   History, ritual, and myth: nineteenth century millenarian movements in the Northwest Amazon. *Ethnohistory* 33 (1): 31–54.

6. Ethnic Discourse and the Challenge to Anthropology: The Nicaraguan Case

Martin Diskin

Throughout the Americas, Indians are representing themselves through their own organizations and spokespeople.[1] Threats to group survival, heightened political awareness, and support from international organizations have all encouraged Indian people to tell their own story. During the eleven years of Sandinista government, the people of the Atlantic Coast of Nicaragua, Costeños, have developed local leadership that now speaks for them. In that period, much of it in conflict with the Nicaraguan (Sandinista) state, they have made their case to an international audience. In this chapter, I examine this new voice, this ethnic discourse.

Under what political and historic conditions has it arisen? How does it represent or alter the nature of Costeño ethnic groups? At precisely whom are these statements aimed? How may this particular kind of public discourse be analyzed by anthropology? Finally, what does it teach us about the nature of ethnicity, on the one hand, and the anthropological enterprise, on the other?

Anthropology has traditionally served as the voice of indigenous people and ethnic minorities. Anthropological descriptions and analyses are today joined by descriptions and analyses produced by those studied. The "native" voice is distinct from anthropological convention and sometimes in conflict with it.[2] By insisting on self-representation, Indians implicitly challenge anthropology to broaden its goals and enlarge its circle of discussion.

Some anthropological work has moved in this direction. The use of a dialogic style (Rabinow 1977; Sullivan 1989) in anthropological writing facilitates an indigenous presence. Another step is the encouragement by anthropologists of direct native self-expression in print, through such technical support as the adaptation of computer keyboards to non-Western languages (Bernard and Salinas 1989). The inclusion of indigenous voices in ethnographic representation will stimulate anthropology to reevaluate its proprietary claim to tribal and peasant groups and enrich the discussion about advocacy and the political nature of much of anthropology (Hastrup and Elsass 1990; Wright 1988).

Ethnicity and the Ethnic Discourse

Native self-representation is a demonstration of ethnicity in action.[3] Ethnicity is manifest through self-referential statements by people in ordinary conversation or in public by their leaders, in what I call here the ethnic discourse. Ethnic discourse expresses the creation or reinforcement of group identity, among or between groups, where it establishes "the vessel of meaning and emblem of contrast" as De Vos and Romanucci-Ross (1982: 363–390) call it.

In multiethnic societies, each ethnic group appears to negotiate its position vis-à-vis dominant or subordinate groups. Ethnic discourse may be part of a hostile exchange, used by dominant groups to retain their privilege or gain further advantage over others. When dominant groups use invidious ethnic stereotypes to reinforce inequitable treatment of minorities, it has been described as "conjugated oppression" by Bourgois (1988; cf. also Cabarrus 1982). Ethnic discourse can be an indicator of social tension and strain. Sometimes dominated groups "learn to labor" (Willis 1977) or develop "leveled aspirations" (MacLeod 1987), that is, accommodate, albeit unwillingly, to a harsh stratification system. Others fight against "imposed ethnicity" if only to contest denigrating and injurious treatment (Nagengast and Kearney 1990: 61). Ethnic discourse marks each of these different kinds of engagement between social sectors. In the example of Nicaraguan Costeños, ethnic discourse is employed to alter the historic image of coastal peoples and argue for specific guaranteed rights from the central government.

The ethnic discourse, a tool in ongoing social negotiation, is therefore eminently situational, with strategic and tactical aspects. For this reason, the ethnic voice may assume a variety of identities. Nicaragua's Costeños refer to themselves on different occasions as tribal members, Indians (in a pan-Indian sense), as part of the Fourth World, and as citizens of a nation-state. The identities chosen may shift depending on the group's allies and adversaries of the moment, the resources they seek, and, of course, timing.[4]

The formation of ethnic identity takes place on two levels. One involves changes among group members and the other the public image. Elements for the elaboration of ethnic identity may exist in group traditions and be expressed, as for some highland Guatemalan Indians, through a blend of myths and local Catholic practice. New ideas introduced by Catholic social action were assimilated to this traditional base to help form, in Kay Warren's term, a "reinterpreted orthodoxy"

(1978:114) that explained Indian identity within a repressive society. For
Mixtec migrants to the United States, the dislocations caused by migration gave rise to political activism to combat the conjugated oppression
of negative stereotyping and discrimination. This activism has produced an "emergence of a self-conscious and deliberate elaboration of
ethnicity by Mixtecs themselves as they migrate north from Oaxaca"
(Nagengast and Kearney 1990: 62).

In Hale's (1989) study of group consciousness and worldview of the
Miskitu on the Atlantic Coast of Nicaragua, he found that both traditional elements and new activism contributed to the sharpening and use
of an ethnic discourse. Through the seventies and eighties, militant
consciousness developed that coupled an awareness of Indianness with
demands for group rights, especially to land. At the same time, at the
community level, people Hale talked to exhibited no resentment of the
role of multinational corporations on the Atlantic Coast. Rather, they
displayed what he calls "anglo affinity," nostalgia and fond memories of
the North American company foremen, managers, commissaries, and
salaries that were common several decades ago. Those two elements
taken together, ethnic militancy and Anglo affinity, constitute "contradictory consciousness," that is, illogically coexistent worldviews. His
full analysis however, points out how these two elements interacted to
aid in ethnic mobilization. That is, the Anglo affinity maintained an
edge to their anti-Sandinista views and also did nothing to discourage
U.S. support for their military and public relations efforts.

When the ethnic struggle for rights and power seizes center stage, it
momentarily displaces other structural patterns such as internal class
stratification, regional group hierarchies, and historic enmities.[5] Ethnic
or "communal" organizations, those based on kinship and other primary
relationships, become interest groups. The shapes they take range from
highly "associative" forms, that is, "manipulative, utilitarian, nonmoral,
in which one person uses another person as a means to an end" or
communal, that is, "moral, nonutilitarian, in which persons use one
another as ends in themselves" (Cohen 1981: 324–325). Cohen's analysis of the Sierra Leone Creoles points out that their organizations
represented themselves with varying degrees of emphasis on ethnicity
(1981: 316) according to group goals and external pressures. He also
shows that success in this political struggle may create a clear ethnic
identity where none existed before. Sierra Leone Creole ethnic identity
only developed recently through threats to their social and economic
position.

Ethnic discourse often uses the language of cultural traits. Cohen
judges this a tactical option to be manipulated. My preference is to
discuss it as a discourse to indicate that the cultural elements are

assembled into a whole by the actors themselves rather than by outside analysts. The goals of ethnic politics, whether to conjugate oppression or to mobilize for liberation, are often achieved by the appropriation of cultural symbols. For the Pacific part of Nicaragua, national leaders do not regard the Atlantic Coast as Indian territory.[6] Rather, its difference from the rest of the country is perceived as racial. Costeños were (and are) often referred to and regarded as black, while the Miskitu were routinely referred to as *zambos*.[7] A significant goal of Costeño ethnic organizations, dominated by Miskitus, was to change the public perception that coastal people were culturally undifferentiated and largely black (permitting racism to add to the conjugation of oppression). The use of the category "Indian nations" evoked entities that held certain inalienable rights that were the object of debate and conflict all over the world.

The ethnic discourse increasingly prefers the nation as the unit of advocacy. A nation, in Anderson's (1986) phrase, is an "imagined community," but the "imagined" does not mean fictitious, rather, a widely used ideology among group members or leaders. The imagined condition of the nation is no different from the imagined condition of the pueblo, tribe, lineage, or band, that is, it is part of the group's shared identity. One significant difference between the nation and the tribe, band, or lineage is that the latter three categories are often the product of anthropological or state imaginings, whereas the nation is usually preferred by ethnic group members themselves.[8]

The strength of the nation image lies in its ancient validity. As Anderson says, "If nation-states are widely conceded to be 'new' and 'historical,' the nations to which they give political expression always loom out of an immemorial past, and, still more important, glide into a limitless future" (1986:19). This process, as Anderson's insightful treatment explains, is not spontaneous but depends on stringent conditions such as the existence of a religious community, official writing system, a specific, shared notion of time, and control of the media (Anderson 1986: chaps. 2, 3; cf. also Wylie 1982 for an example concerning the Faroe Islands).

Events in the Soviet Union, the Middle East, India, South Asia, Africa, and Latin and North America attest to the power of the ethnic discourse and the idiom of nationality in instances of conflict with the state. In spite of that power, the claims for separatist autonomy, self-determination or statehood, based on cultural and historical arguments, normally stimulate little sympathy within modern states (Hannum and Lillich 1980).

The state and national stratification systems are perhaps the most important environmental features for the analysis of ethnicity. The state's impact in shaping the community has been neglected by anthropology perhaps because of its complexity, perhaps because small communities are the preferred fieldwork sites for anthropologists. But the study of ethnicity entails a consideration of conflict and domination, between different ethnic groups and between ethnic groups and the state.[9]

The ethnic discourse, because of its cultural content and its instrumental character, both parallels and contrasts with anthropological description. It resembles anthropology in its explicit use of descriptive and analytical cultural categories. However, ethnic self-representation is part of an effort to change the general image of a people, to combat oppression, and to change the on-the-ground functioning of the systems described, through the very act of description. Thus, while both the anthropological and the ethnic point of view seek to represent indigenous and other groups to a wider public, ethnic discourse is explicitly geared toward changing a situation for the better for its members. The instrumental goals of anthropology are less obvious and would require a separate analysis.[10]

The similarities and differences between the anthropological and the ethnic approach should be explicitly recognized. By clarifying and situating each endeavor, conversation is facilitated between them. Anthropology has focused on the description and analysis of culture. That task builds on the century-old accretion of theory and data about non-Western peoples. Culture has been the intellectual product of anthropology; ethnicity is the product of its practitioners. Ethnic discourse, the expression of groups seeking change, is more than another cultural product. It may invigorate groups and it may constitute a plan for internal change. The transformative power of the ethnic discourse means that it may transcend mere analysis. It dramatizes a situation where those anthropologists and others, who comment on ethnic activism, should recognize their own activist tendencies. In the next section, I examine this phenomenon for Nicaraguan Costeños.

Miskitu Nation–Sandinista State

The Atlantic Coast of Nicaragua has historically been a culturally distinct zone from the politically dominant mestizo Pacific. Costeño groups include the Amerindian Miskitu, Sumu, and Rama; Afro-American English-speaking Creoles; and the Garífuna, another Afro-American group whose culture reflects long residence and intermarriage with indigenous groups of the Atlantic Coast of Honduras and Belize. While these groups constitute the indigenous and ethnic populations of the Atlantic Coast, mestizos, Hispanic peasant migrants from the Pacific side of the country, have grown to become the largest group on the coast during the past three decades (Hale and Gordon 1987).

In the 1980s, MISURASATA (Miskito Sumo Rama Sandinista Asla Takanka—"Miskito Sumo Rama Together With the Sandinistas") assumed the role of organizational spokesperson for all Costeños.[11] This discourse began in the sixties during the dictatorial Somoza regime, and reached its most intense point during the eleven years of Sandinista rule. It remains to be seen, in early 1990, after the Sandinista defeat at the polls, how state-ethnic relations will unfold under the new UNO government.

Background

The humid tropical "Mosquito Coast" region contains approximately 55 percent of national territory, and about 10 percent of the national population. From the time of the Spanish Conquest, its hostile environment obstructed the effort to incorporate it into the nation-states of the region. During the nineteenth century, England and Spain competed for hegemony of the Atlantic Coast (Floyd 1967). From the 1860 Treaty of Managua through the Reincorporation (1906), the Atlantic Coast formally fell under national jurisdiction but effectively remained independent and remote from national influence. The various treaties recognized rights for the Miskitu population concerning taxes and land. The de jure sovereignty of Nicaragua over the entire territory did not provide a satisfactory balance, from a coastal perspective, between indigenous interests and national rights (Rossbach and Wunderich 1985). That remains one of the sore points for coastal sensibilities today.

The withdrawal of British influence marked the beginning of another form of foreign domination, by U.S.-based multinational corporations. Operating within a cordial developmentalist atmosphere, and buttressed by a U.S. diplomatic (and occasionally military) presence, they assumed significant control over the region into the 1950s (Vilas 1989: 13–59, 60–95; Bourgois and Hale n.d.).

Nicaraguan government plans, such as the UNESCO-supported "pilot Project for Basic Education on the Coco River," carried out between 1955 and 1965 by the Ministry of Education, saw economic integration and cultural assimilation as the solution to the coastal problem (Vilas 1989: 81–83).

Atlantic Coast Indigenous Activism

During the sixties and seventies, the two principal indigenous advocacy organizations were SUKAWALA, National Association of Sumo Villages, and ALPROMISU, Alliance for the Progress of Miskitos and Sumos (Vilas 1989: 89–92). A Central America–wide organization that acquired UN consultative status, CORPI, Regional Council of Central American, Mexican, and Panamanian Indian Peoples, was also active in the seventies (Diskin 1989: 12). These groups, indigenous in membership and staff, made links with other indigenous organizations, many of them United States Native American groups. There were tactical and theoretical differences among them in regard to their views about the best way to press for rights. Within the growing international indigenous rights movement, there were also advocacy groups and nongovernmental organizations that, while not staffed by indigenous people, included indigenous rights into their funding and support plans. This movement focused on international human rights law, particularly the extension of individual human rights principles to whole peoples (Bonfil 1981; Bonfil, Ibarra, et al. 1982; Centro Antropológico de Documentación de América Latina, or CADAL, 1983, 1985; Documentos de la Segunda Reunión de Barbados 1979; Stavenhagen and Nolasco 1988). This international movement made significant strides in developing the idea of Indian rights. It sponsored conferences on ethno-development, issued declarations (Barbados), and became integrated into the United Nations human rights structure. As a result of this worldwide effort, indigenous peoples began describing indigenous culture themselves, developing challenges to international law and arguing for a new charter for indigenous rights.

The 1979 Sandinista Revolution

With the Sandinista triumph of July 1979, the coastal context changed for two reasons. First, the Sandinista government's determination to bring the revolution to the coast quickened the pace of Costeño activism. Second, the U.S. assault on Nicaraguan sovereignty accelerated the conflictive aspect of this interaction.

Sandinista receptivity to dialogue and support for MISURASATA facilitated a more direct and militant ethnic discourse. But coastal leaders perceived Sandinista ideas as uncomfortably close to the assimilationist tone of the previous regime (Hale 1989: chap. 1). In the first public encounter in Puerto Cabezas in November 1979, it became clear that the great future obstacle to be overcome was the almost nonoverlapping visions held by each party (Adams 1979).

The creation of MISURASATA was compatible with Sandinista notions of organizing. MISURASATA could serve as the vehicle for Sandinizing the coast. But the Pacific-oriented Sandinistas were not aware that MISURASATA's agenda of coastal issues were distinct from the anti-imperialist, nonaligned, socialist principles of the Sandinista revolution. MISURASATA, using its new public status and heightened access to the population, became an ethnic opposition organization par excellence.

Differences between coast and government sharpened in the 1980 literacy crusade. For Costeños, the promotion of literacy in Spanish meant a policy of national integration and assimilation. MISURASATA actively worked to add coastal languages (Miskitu, Sumu, and English) to Spanish. This effort was successful and MISURASATA staffed the campaign with literacy instructors. Thus, they won an important point and, in the process, greatly expanded their organizational structure on the coast. Some members of MISURASATA saw this as a vehicle for achieving an even more ambitious set of goals, far beyond literacy. Speaking of that period, an important Miskitu military leader said recently: "we put literacy within the framework of the indigenous struggle, and our main objective was to deepen the sense of indigenous autonomy" (*Envío* 1988: 23).

The U.S. effort to militarily overthrow the Sandinistas, beginning about 1981, capitalized on the growing tensions between Miskitu populations and the Sandinista army. The United States supplied arms and training to Costeño fighters. Although it downplayed its direct military input, it used its media access to describe the coastal situation as an assault on the Miskitu (Diskin 1987: 85–88). The United States' public position (endorsed by Miskitu leaders) was that the Sandinistas obstructed the Miskitu right to self-determination (U.S. Department of State 1986: 1). As military conflict escalated, the ethnic discourse became more bellicose, stressing the military history of Miskitu warriors (Nietschmann 1986:12–14).

During this period, the two most prominent leaders of MISURASATA, Brooklyn Rivera and Steadman Fagoth, achieved considerable international recognition. They both went into exile in Honduras in 1981, but soon became bitter enemies and expressed differences in handling the antigovernment campaign. After their rift, Rivera went to Costa Rica, where he led MISURASATA and YATAMA until his return to Nicaragua in the fall of 1989. Fagoth founded MISURA in Honduras; that changed into KISAN and finally blended into YATAMA. Still, they successfully promulgated an ethnic discourse concerning the Atlantic Coast, at least outside of Nicaragua. In testimony given before the U.S. Senate, Fagoth described the Miskitu as a "communitarian tribe," with a "national" structure composed of councils of elders that held a "magna" council meeting once a year (Fagoth 1980: 1–3). Fagoth (n.d.), in a later publication, listed as the "philosophical elements of the indigenous nation," inalienable land rights, a developed legal system, and self-government.

The arena for defining Indian-state relations in Nicaragua now shifted to an international one, with opinion lining up for or against the Sandinistas in general, and the underlying issues of indigenous rights sometimes forgotten. The pro-Sandinista position regarded indigenous claims to be counterrevolutionary, while the anti-Sandinista position was supportive of all Indian rights. For anti-Sandinistas, Indian rights were invoked as a way to sharpen the attack (e.g., then UN Ambassador Kirkpatrick's exaggerated and unfounded claims[12]) and for supporters of the Nicaraguan Revolution the Atlantic Coast was a side action that diverted energy from the more important Pacific side. However, for indigenous rights activists, Native American groups, and international organizations, the outbreak of hostilities on the Atlantic Coast was a wrenching experience that caused sharp disagreements among activist Native American organizations. Fierce debates took place between such groups as the World Council of Indigenous Peoples, the American Indian Treaty Council, the American Indian Movement, and the National Indian Youth Council in the pages of *Akwesasne Notes*. Many of these groups were critical of the Sandinistas but, especially after 1984, judged that the costeño-Sandinista exchange held more promise for Indian self-determination than similar situations in other countries, including the United States.

Autonomy

In the fall of 1984, the government announced the formation of a national autonomy commission whose mandate was to develop a plan for Atlantic Coast autonomy. During that fall, meetings were arranged between MISURASATA (led by Brooklyn Rivera, from Costa Rica) and the government to discuss a solution to the conflict. Four meetings were held, three in Bogotá and the last one in Mexico City in May 1985 (Diskin, Bossert, Nahmad, and Varese 1986). In May 1985, shortly after talks broke off with MISURASATA, a cease-fire agreement was reached with a Miskitu military commander in the community of Yulu. That coincided with the announcement that Miskitus who had fled their villages during the fighting could return, with government help. A policy decision was also taken at that time to distinguish between Costeño insurgents and contras (Diskin et al. 1986).

MISURASATA's differences with the government are reflected in the language each side used in draft agreements. MISURASATA wanted government recognition of the Miskitus, Sumus, and Ramas as "indigenous sovereign peoples . . . possessed of the natural right to freely determine their own political, economic, social and cultural development in accord with their values and traditions" (MISURASATA 1984). The government's view was that the "ethnic groups of the Atlantic Coast must enjoy special rights of autonomy that guarantee their ethnic identity and that must be consigned in the laws of the republic with constitutional rank" (Government draft agreement, Bogotá, Dec. 8, 1984). In response to this, Rivera expressed his displeasure with the denomination "ethnic groups," rather than nations, by quipping that ethnic groups "run restaurants." Rather than claiming that the government's interest in autonomy was the fruit of the ethnic struggle and seeking to reduce the area of disagreement, MISURASATA took a bellicose stance, encour-aged by its mostly foreign advisers. That stance was supported by the U. S. military that provided training and equipment, such as the speedboats (*piranhas*) that attacked coastal communities from Costa Rican sanctuaries.

Although the negotiations with MISURASATA broke down in April 1985, the autonomy process continued, through regional autonomy commissions. A *consulta popular* was conducted in village assemblies in the northern region and door-to-door surveys in the south, to discuss the details of the draft autonomy statute. In April 1987, a multiethnic assembly in Puerto Cabezas ratified the draft statute, and with the final ratification by the National Assembly in September 1987, Atlantic Coast autonomy became part of the constitution. The government and MISURASATA continued to hold opposing views concerning the autonomy statute. For the government, this was a step ahead of all Latin American countries in its recognition of multiethnicity, protection of cultural practices, and use of natural resource exploitation to benefit local communities. The Sandinista government kept the autonomy law as the centerpiece of their Atlantic Coast policy. The statute was used to seek community support and to invite Miskitu *alzados* (rebels) to return without disarming to sustain discussions about modifications of regional autonomy. A system of regional and zonal organizations was begun to organize community projects within an autonomous framework. The law granted political autonomy for the entire coastal population, divided into two autonomous regions, one in the northern part of the coast and the other in the south. In each autonomous region, there would be an election to pick a regional assembly that would legislate regional matters. The Sandinista plan left the ethnic character of the assemblies an open question. The voters could elect people strictly on ethnic or any other grounds.

For MISURASATA, this was an imposed, top-down effort that did not involve adequate participation. It skirted the land issue, the recognition of Indian country as demanded in 1981, and the granting of self-determination. MISURASATA, after its metamorphosis into YATAMA (Mother Land Indian Communities) wanted an ethnic territory, Yapti Tasba (Mother Land), as homeland for the Miskitu, Sumu, and Rama. The elected assembly provision of the law clashed with MISURASATA's long-standing demand that it be the sole representative of all Costeños.

YATAMA was founded in April or May 1987, with support from the U.S. government and the Honduran army. YATAMA represented the unification of Indian leadership (Steadman Fagoth, Brooklyn Rivera, and Wycliffe Diego, long associated with Fagoth). These three leaders were flown to the major coastal refugee camps in Honduras, where they told the people not to participate in the repatriations that were planned by the UN High Commissioner for Refugees and the Sandinista government. They advocated an intensification of the fighting to pressure the Sandinistas to negotiate a draft treaty they had written (Diskin and Peplinsky 1987: 9–10). YATAMA failed to engage in significant military action and did not succeed in holding back the large-scale return of Miskitu refugees. YATAMA's guiding document was the MISURASATA treaty of April 1987. That treaty drew clear distinctions between indigenous peoples (Miskitu, Sumu, and Rama) and ethnic groups (Creoles, Garífuna, and ladinos, i.e., mestizos) (MISURASATA 1987).

In spite of YATAMA'S militant position, there was declining enthusiasm for fighting among Miskitus in Nicaragua as well as in Honduras and Costa Rica. The attitude of Honduran and North American military authorities in Honduras was not supportive of dialogue with the Sandinistas (Anaya 1987). Colonel Eric Sánchez of the Fifth Battalion, the Honduran military commander of the Mosquitia, where most Miskitu refugees lived, said that "the only good Indians are fighting Sandinistas in Nicaragua" and threatened those who were not good Indians with jail (ibid.: 4–6). In mid-1987, the ethnic cause and Rivera's personal popularity seemed to be stagnating. Within Nicaragua, a growing group of ex-*alzados*, based in Yulu, were moving toward satisfactory implementation of the autonomy statutes. What looked like a shift in the Miskitu position on the land issue was expressed by Uriel Vanegas, a returned Miskitu military leader, who said:

Let there be no mistake, we don't want to be the owners of all the land of the Atlantic Coast. That's simply not true. There are lands which should belong to the Indians, and there are other lands which should stay in the hands of the state, the way it is now. But we don't want to see maneuvering, to see the government taking economic advantage of the best lands. The Indian communities need good land for their development. (*Envío* 1988: 25)

The MISURASATA treaty was the operative position of the organization. Rivera indicated real willingness to return to the country and negotiate. On February 2, 1988, Rivera signed an accord, agreeing to a truce and pledging further negotiation.

Several features of the larger political environment were also influential. Although the Central American Peace Plan (Esquipulas II), signed on August 7, 1987, made no mention of Indian-state relations or conflicts, it nevertheless created a regionwide conciliatory tone.[13] Various Indian leaders link Esquipulas II with the achievement of their goals (Envío 1988: 26). On February 3, 1988, the day after the Sandinista-YATAMA accord, Congress denied the Reagan administration further funding for the contras and, after another negative vote in March, passed a contra "humanitarian" aid bill that contained $1.4 million for YATAMA. The approval of those funds signaled that the United States would support efforts for a negotiated solution.

The 1990 Elections

YATAMA and its leadership were active in discussions that led to their return to Nicaragua and participation in the 1990 Nicaraguan elections. Rivera, Fagoth, and other leaders entered the country under an agreement brokered by ex-President Jimmy Carter in his capacity as election observer (LASA 1990: 38–39). Although it was not an official party, YATAMA ran candidates in the regional council elections. YATAMA's candidates did extremely well in the RAAN (North Atlantic Autonomous Region).

Thus, it appears that the constitutional mechanisms installed by the Sandinistas functioned well enough to permit YATAMA to become the predominant voice for Atlantic Coast peoples to continue the ethnic struggle. YATAMA's bid for hegemonic status will now have to be carried out through multiethnic assemblies. It is likely to encounter different problems than it had with the Sandinistas. It remains to be seen whether UNO, with its developmentalist policies, will show greater comprehension than the Sandinistas for Costeño points of view. Also, since ethnic politics are now much closer in nature to national party politics, there will be pressures to make deals and compromises with other national interests in order to accomplish ethnic goals. It is certainly less likely that clashes with the central government, over land, for example, will receive attention or support from the United States. In May 1990, the UNO government created a cabinet-level Institute for the Development of the Autonomous Regions (INDERA), and named Brooklyn Rivera as its first minister.

The Ethnic Discourse

Throughout the conflicts of the eighties, MISURASATA and its successor, YATAMA, heightened contacts with both the Sandinista state and their external allies. That process produced a body of statements, the ethnic discourse.[14] The schematic structure of this discourse begins at the most general level, with definitions of the nature of ethnic identity and nationhood, then proceeds to the cultural specifics of Costeño populations, and then with cultural details about the Miskitu people. It ends with the specific rights that derive from the prior discussion. One clear difference from anthropological representation is that cultural description occupies a rather small, subordinate role in the discourse. The entire discourse builds toward the demands for rights from the state:

A. General Premises

1. "ethnic identity is historically prior to the formation and consolidation of national social classes and survives beyond their dissolution" (MISURASATA 1981: 1 [translation mine]).

2. "the creation of the nation-state is historically later than the creation of indigenous nations" (ibid.).

B. Costeño Character

1. The Miskitu, Sumu, and Rama people are Indians. Each is a culturally unitary people (that is, with its own languages, music, rituals, etc.), descended from the original inhabitants of the region, prior to the "immigrants who have violated Indian rights" (MISURASATA 1981: 2–3). "The Creole, Carib (Garífuna), and Ladinos are ethnic communities who live in harmony with the Indian Peoples in the autonomous territory of Yapti Tasba" (MISURASATA 1987: Art. 1, b).

2. Indians are nations, culturally homogeneous within defined territorial limits with original possession of the land (MISURASATA 1981:1).

3. Indians are attached to the earth in a spiritual sense. "Our land is our mother" (Nuestra tierra es nuestra madre) (Fagoth n.d.: 154).

C. Group Constitution

1. "Miskitus are a communitarian, democratic tribe" (Fagoth 1980:1).

2. A system of governance is in effect over the entire territory. For the Miskitu this alludes, historically, to the Rey Mosco monarchy as well as to the Councils of Elders (Fagoth n.d.: 156).

D. Rights That Derive From the Above

1. Self-determination—"All people have the right to self-determination. By virtue of this right they freely determine their political
status and freely pursue their economic, social and cultural development" (MISURASATA 1981: 3; MISURASATA 1987: 19, Art. 1, c).

2. Prior inalienable rights to possession of territory, definition of
boundaries, and manner of land use (MISURASATA 1981: 4;
MISURASATA 1987: Art. 1). The territory defined in the 1981
document is the same geographical area later referred to as Yapti
Tasba (MISURASATA 1987: 19–20).

3. Absolute right to define group membership (MISURASATA
1981: 3).

In its entirety, the ethnic discourse is a political document, that is, its
purpose is to alter the relationship between ethnic groups and the state.
It seeks to accomplish this by reformulating the accepted notions of the
composition of ethnic groups. One way is to draw on similar situations
elsewhere (in January 1990, a Miskitu told me that the Miskitu people
were like the Lithuanians). It also describes the culture of the ethnic
groups in terms that have universal legitimacy.

The ethnic discourse may be analyzed into various components. First,
group character derives from a "fourth-world" perspective that emphasizes the aboriginal purity of the group: they are "tribal stewards of the
earth." Inherent harmony is attributed to such groups—they are
"communitarian." Second, familiar political terms are used—these
groups are "democratic." Third, the groups are described by terms that
have universal legitimacy—they are nations. These groups are presented
as moral entities whose needs and goals are distinct from those of the
state (Nietschmann 1986; esp. MacDonald 1988, who uses Scott's
"moral economy" argument; Hale 1990: 15–21).

The group description is both logical (primacy of ethnicity over social
class) and contestable. The land rights demanded, framed as ownership
of an Indian territory, involve about one-third of the country. The right
to determine territorial and group membership (and, presumably, to
exclude others from group membership) is an effective definition of self-
determination.

At some critical points, the ethnic discourse contradicts other accounts. For example, in the scholarly literature there is disagreement
concerning the authenticity of the Miskitu monarchy (Dennis and
Ohlien 1984; Helms 1986). The monarchy is certainly important to
Miskitu people, even though it may well have served historically as
another instance of British indirect rule. Further, statements about

councils of elders, as group decision makers, are simply not recorded in the literature. However, during the conflicts, both MISURASATA and MISURA claimed to take decisions based on the guidance or veto power of their respective councils of elders. Beyond that, however, is the notion that, given the dispersed community pattern, and the variety of production forms and environmental niches, it seems improbable that a centralized form of governance was possible. The ubiquitous presence of the Moravian church could have functioned as a form of social control in most Miskitu communities. But that is hardly an aboriginal pattern of governance. In more recent times, native regional government was even less feasible, given the operation of the Nicaraguan state and the multinational corporations.

Community land tenure forms are less well understood. In a slash-burn regime, the generalized use right to land is effectively communal in that community membership is the threshold requirement for working land. Hale has presented data to show that after the reincorporation, in 1914, when land titles were issued, the British agent began receiving individual petitions for land titles from the communities of the mouth of the Río Grande. Instead of the individual petitions he was receiving, he asked for group title petitions to facilitate his work, and the community responded by making one large request for land, creating a precedent for the argument supporting communal tenure (Hale 1990:18). At that time, the land not titled (4,000 hectares were titled) was considered "national land." Hale clarifies two points here. First, the Sandy Bay people probably had individual tenure forms based on household production prior to asking for a community land grant. Second, the records Hale examined show that multinational corporations, in this case North American banana companies, had effectively taken land within "Indian country." Neither of these points is present in the Costeño arguments concerning communal land use patterns or in the notion of Indians as "stewards of the earth." However, by framing the demand for territory, rather than community land rights, the ethnic discourse undercuts the government argument embodied in the autonomy law. It also explains the underlying intensity of the disagreement between the two sides.

Helms shows that, in Asang, cash-producing land, such as that used for cacao production, is individually owned. Communal subsistence activities are not as widespread as the ethnic discourse insists (Helms 1971). In general, Miskitu communities were well integrated into a cash economy. Rather than a subsistence economy, it was very common to work for cash in multinational extractive industries (lumber, fishing, mining, bananas). This appears to contradict the claims regarding communal subsistence patterns.

The historical truth value of the elements of the ethnic discourse is not the immediate tangible issue. While the terms *Indian* and *nation* have content, the final judge of whether Costeños are Indian nations is not the scholarly community but the society at large. And while autonomy and self-determination are important for international law, they are strongly influenced by the ethnic struggles of the moment (Hannum and Lillich 1980). That makes this debate an openly political one. The disagreement and conflict over these issues are really about the balance of power between ethnic groups and the state. To enter into the debate, anthropologists legitimately bring data collected by themselves and others. But the positions taken stem fundamentally from political views. In this context, anthropology and activism intersect.

Reflections and Conclusions

In Nicaragua, the process that led to the constitutional autonomy statute still remains to be implemented under a new government, and has not yet conclusively defined the nature of coastal ethnic groups. The negotiated autonomy solution was shaped in part by arguments contained within the ethnic discourse, fortified, to be sure, by military means. At the same time, the autonomy statute has not ratified the ethnic discourse, particularly with respect to these demands for regional territorial control. In territorial administrative terms, the present autonomy statute refers not to nations, but rather to the administrative divisions created by the statute ("autonomous regions").

While, in a scholarly context, these issues may be analyzed in the anthropological literature, the challenge they offer should not be conceived of as a contest for the truth. Rather, it should be understood as an opportunity for reflection on the anthropological enterprise itself. As the field struggles with the issue of ethnographic representation (cf. Rosaldo 1980:105–106; Geertz 1983; Marcus and Fischer 1986; Bernard and Salinas 1989: see especially introduction; Said 1979; Clifford 1988; Prakash 1990; Jackson 1989), it becomes clearer that the ethnographic endeavor in general is strongly political. Knowledge of the other arises from a grid of understandings of the world, composed of the assumptions that anthropologists as citizens and political actors carry with them. These assumptions guide scholarship, and, beyond this, they inform opinion in the anthropologist's society.

Part of the political dimension of anthropological work is advocacy. Fieldwork in coastal Nicaragua has dramatized the encounter of anthropological advocacy with that of the ethnic discourse. Hale expresses this very well in the introduction to his thesis, where he discusses the implications of "politically positioned" anthropological research in a highly charged atmosphere (1989: xix). His research makes it clear that anthropology is taking seriously the injunction to locate itself in the system that connects scholars and those studied. Not doing so leads to erroneous analyses, like that by scholars who helped in the internment of Japanese-Americans during WWII (Starn 1986) or in "missing the revolution" in the Andes because of "Andeanist" bias (Starn n.d.).

Hale's analysis of Miskitu "contradictory consciousness" is possible only by seeing the political context in which this consciousness makes itself known. Further, the identification of worldview at the community level, in combination with the ethnic discourse produced by the leadership, makes sense precisely because Hale is himself politically positioned, that is, he openly accepts his political analysis of this fluid and rapidly changing moment. Hale's sense of contradiction is the product of his frankly engaged sense of the situation. His work has little of the essentialist quality of many anthropological studies, but it leaves a well-reasoned argument that will be of use to future ethnic leaders and students of ethnic politics.

Ethnic discourse may abundantly contradict accrued knowledge of a group and may be seen as the manipulation or rewriting of group history. But, at the same time, it may well be the mechanism for sociocultural change. Just as ethnic identity can be the product of the ethnic discourse, other group aspects, such as land tenure, may be changed by the ethnic discourse. Communal land tenure may become an operative reality. The discourse may also have the effect of instituting genuine community councils of elders, perhaps blended with the ubiquitous role of Moravian pastors in each community.

Less directly, the act and ideology of resistance, appeal to warrior traditions, and claims of military superiority over the Sandinistas have had an effect on the 1990 election that helped produce a YATAMA victory. Now, the new ethnic leadership must cope with autonomous regional councils, links to national parties, and contacts with other governments or nongovernmental organizations and international agencies (UN, OAS). Perhaps the discourse of leaders (the bellicosity of Fagoth, the politicking of Rivera) will be internally reconciled and modified in order to lead.[15]

Although anthropology may seek to appropriate ethnicity by defining it within the canon (i.e., as the intellectual property of the profession), it would be a mistake to deal with it so narrowly. The differences concerning the content of terms like *nation* and *Indian* are debatable among politically active people with or without professional credentials. Because of the unique subject matter of anthropology, anthropological participation in political debate will be more substantive. And given the conjunctural, rapidly changing nature of ethnic politics, anthropology's dual character, as observer and engaged participant, is appropriate. Therefore, frontal engagement and open debate by anthropologists is the way the ethnic discourse may be taken seriously.

What differentiates ethnicity from other kinds of group behaviors and cultural manifestations is that ethnic reality is larger than the consensus of the professional fraternity; ethnicity operates in the political world and the criteria for its success are political. Organized for achievement, not universal to all humans, ethnicity must be judged on its own terms and in relation to its expressed goals.

In grappling with the concept of ethnicity, anthropology opens a door to new colleagues, those previously the "objects of study." All participants in situations of rapid change, be they combatants, bystanders, or analysts, have a stake in the outcome. The challenge for anthropology is not to shrink from this fact or coyly ignore it, nor to worry about making enemies. Rather, we must harness our interests to the real, humane insights that anthropology has produced over the years and try to create an engaged science of liberation.

Notes

Acknowledgments: I gratefully acknowledge the critical attention offered in previous drafts by Neils Braroe, Jean Jackson, and Lisa Rofel. I am, of course, solely responsible for the content of this chapter.

1. Indian populations are rarely recognized or mentioned in the political constitutions of Latin American countries. Exceptions to this are the recent constitutions of Nicaragua, Brazil and Colombia. At present, there is an effort to amend Article 4 of the Mexican constitution, to include mention of the multiethnic nature of the country and to establish a legal basis for further rights for Indians. Its outcome in the national congress is uncertain (INI 1989).

2. Among indigenist anthropologists, the preferred term of reference is *Indian* at this moment. The term *indigenous* is also widely used. In specific contexts, terms like "ethno-national problem" (Centro Antropológico de Documentación de América Latina 1985: 5) are used, or "etnias indígenas, or grupos étnicos" (Varese 1979: 357–359).

3. See Williams (1990) for a survey of recent thinking concerning ethnicity.

4. Jackson's (1989) analogy between pidgin-Creole languages and their different modalities, or registers, and the ethnic discourse nicely captures the intention and goal-directed quality of ethnic discourse.

5. Varese points out that ethnic mobilization always involves reference to class at least within the greater society: "en el momento en que una etnía necesita movilizarse políticamente es precisamente porque su posición en el contexto social mayor (regional o nacional) es una posición de clase" (1979: 363).

6. For many Nicaraguans, the community rituals of Monimbo, Masaya, and Subtiava, Matagalpa, are Indian. The populations of the Atlantic Coast, in spite of their distinctive culture, have not been seen as Indian.

7. The Miskitu have intermarried with Afro-American populations for a considerable time and, as a community, present an enormous phenotypic

spectrum, from blond, even albino, to obviously African types. The blending of phenotype and culture, as in the phrase Zambo-Miskitu, is not restricted to lay Nicaraguans. Adams (1988:16), in discussing biological reproduction and expansion, refers to Miskitus as "Africanized." Mary Helms, calling them "so-called Indians," notes that, in spite of their "miscegenation" they seem to have preserved much of their indigenous culture (Helms 1976: 9–10; cf. also Helms 1977). This suggests that the analysis of the "anthropological discourse" might be a useful endeavor.

8. Moore argues that the Cheyenne were designated a tribe by outsiders, whites, administrators, and anthropologists. But he asserts that they were a "tribal nation" and, as such, had clearly "crystallized in history long before its members were buffeted by a nation-state" (1987: 321). Moore's interest in challenging the notion of Cheyennes as a tribe suggests that, as in the case of other Native American groups, national status will be a better launching point for acquiring any rights than that of tribe.

9. For some scholars, the state is the leading and determining element in shaping social life (Skocpol 1979). Charles Tilly (1987: 169–191) identifies state activities, especially in war-making and state-making, as "organized crime." He thus credits the state with great, although not necessarily licit, power. In the same volume, Laitin introduces the useful notion of a *hierarchy of cleavage bases*, that is, the ordering of region, language, class, or ethnicity as factors producing polarization or alliance formation and "what consequences these constellations of forces have had for consensus-building within the nation-state" (1987: 285). Central to Laitin's analysis is that circumstantial and situational factors must be given great credit in understanding state-local group interactions. Here, from a state point of view, local culture and ethnicity figure strongly for the purpose of governing.

10. See Starn for examples of anthropological involvement in the internment of Japanese-Americans (1986) and the failure of anthropology to understand the importance of the Shining Path movement in Peru (n.d.).

11. The Miskitu ethnic discourse has always claimed to speak for all the Costeño populations, but there is little evidence that Creole, Garífuna, and mestizo populations felt themselves included. For these three groups, ethnic identity is not bound up with Indian status. Further, although the Miskitu discourse claims to include all, their explicit distinction between Indians and "ethnic groups" effectively excludes the Creole, Garífuna, and mestizos.

12. Kirkpatrick said, in the *Washington Post*, March 2, 1982, that the "assault" on Miskitu Indians by the Sandinista government is "more massive than any other human-rights violation that I'm aware of in Central America today."

13. Yatama's major support group in the United States, the Indian Law Resource Center, argued that the 1987 Esquipulas II accord should include the resolution of the Atlantic Coast problem in addition to that of the contras (Indian Law Resource Center 1988).

14. The Costeño ethnic discourse appears in a series of documents presented publicly as statements of position, draft treaties, articles, and books written by Miskitu leaders or their sympathizers. Miskitu leaders, especially Rivera, had a group of advisers, mostly North American, that helped orient them during the 1984 negotiations and subsequently. While at the rhetorical level all Miskitu

leaders were in agreement, tactically there were some strong disagreements. Fagoth represented the more bellicose U.S.-supported military path to achieving self-determination, while Rivera spent much time intensifying his relations to the indigenist Fourth World movement. Rivera refined the means of group representation, both to the Sandinistas and to a larger audience, as well as the negotiating skills to implement policy. Fagoth and Rivera broke over these issues and were enemies for about five years, because, according to Rivera, Fagoth was trying to kill him (personal communication 1982).

15. The naming of Rivera as head of the new ministerial-level Institute for the Development of the Autonomous Regions (INDERA) has caused an open rift with Steadman Fagoth. Fagoth accuses Rivera of siding with the central government and frustrating regional autonomy. Rivera says that Fagoth "is allying with the Sandinistas for his own interests" (Gasperini 1990: 4; Barricada 1990). A variety of discourses may be developing through the rivalry of leaders and the offices they have access to after the election (*Envío* 1990:16–19). One holds that coastal interests are better obtained through cooperation with the central government (Rivera). The other (Fagoth) wishes to maintain organizational strength on the coast, even through the apparently contradictory method of making common cause with the Sandinistas, the enemy for the past decade.

References

Adams, Richard N.
  1979   Transcript of an interview with the leaders of MISURASATA, October 1979. Puerto Cabezas. 24 pp.
  1988   Strategies of ethnic survival in Central America. Texas Papers on Latin America (Prepublication Working Papers of the Institute of Latin American Studies), no. 88-10. Austin: University of Texas. 24 pp.
Anaya, James S.
  1987   The CIA with the Honduran army in the Mosquitia: taking the freedom out of the fight in the name of accountability. Report on a visit to the Honduran Mosquitia during April 1987. Albuquerque: National Indian Youth Council, Inc. 32 pp.
Anderson, Benedict
  1986   *Imagined communities: reflections on the origin and spread of nationalism.* London: Verso Editions.
Barricada
  1990   Instalan Consejos Regionales Autónomos. May 6, Managua.
Bernard, Russell, and Jesús Salinas Pedraza
  1989   *Native ethnography: a Mexican Indian describes his culture.* London: Sage.
Bonfil, Guillermo, ed.
  1981   *Utopía y revolución: el pensamiento político contemporáneo de los indios en América Latina.* Mexico: Editorial Nueva Imágen.
Bonfil, Guillermo, Mario Ibarra, Stefano Varese, Domingos Verissimo, and Julio Tumiri
  1982   *América Latina: etnodesarrollo y etnocidio.* San José, Costa Rica: Ediciones FLACSO.

Bourgois, Phillipe
1988   Conjugated oppression: class and ethnicity among Guaymí and Kuna banana workers. *American Ethnologist* 15(2): 328–348.
Bourgois, Phillipe, and Charles Hale
n.d.   The Atlantic Coast of Nicaragua. In *Annotated bibliography of Nicaragua*, N. Snorr (ed.). Ann Arbor: Pierian Press. Forthcoming.
Cabarrús, Carlos Rafael
1982   El auge de los grupos étnicos; un resultado de capitalismo. *Polémica* 3: 6–17. Costa Rica.
Centro Antropológico de Documentación de América Latina (CADAL)
1983   Civilización: configuraciones de la diversidad. Mexico: CADAL and Centro de Estudios del Tercer Mundo (CEESTEM).
1985   Civilización: configuraciones de la diversidad. Mexico: CADAL.
Clifford, James
1988   *The predicament of culture: twentieth-century ethnography, literature, and art.* Cambridge, Mass.: Harvard University Press.
Cohen, Abner
1981   Variables in ethnicity. In *Ethnic change*, C. F. Keyes (ed.), 307–331. Seattle: University of Washington Press.
Dennis, Philip S. and Michael D. Olien
1984   Kingship among the Miskito. *American Ethnologist* 11(4): 718–737.
De Vos, George, and Lola Romanucci-Ross, eds.
1982   *Ethnic identity: cultural continuities and change.* Chicago: University of Chicago Press.
Diskin, Martin
1987   The manipulation of indigenous struggles. In *Reagan versus the Sandinistas: the undeclared war on Nicaragua*, T. W. Walker (ed.), 80–96. Boulder, Colo.: Westview Press.
1989   Revolution and ethnic identity: the Nicaraguan case. In *Conflict, migration, and the expression of ethnicity*, N. L. González and C. S. McCommon (eds.), 11–27. Boulder, Colo.: Westview Press.
Diskin, Martin, Tom Bossert, Salomón S. Nahmad, and Stéfano Varese
1986   *Peace and autonomy on the Atlantic Coast of Nicaragua.* A Report of the LASA [Latin American Studies Association] Task Force on Human Rights and Academic Freedom. Pittsburgh: LASA Secretariat.
Diskin, Martin, and Hansruedi Peplinsky
1987   Report of the ICVA (International Council of Voluntary Associations) Mosquitia Mission. June 9, 1987. 18 pp.
Documentos de la Segunda Reunión de Barbados
1979   *Indianidad y descolonización en América Latina.* Mexico: Editorial Nueva Imágen.
Envío
1988   The Atlantic Coast: two leaders' paths rejoin. Interviews with Uriel Vanegas and Hazel Law conducted by Douglas Carcache. *Envío* 7: 19–33. Managua, Nicaragua: Instituto Histórico Centroamericano, Apartado A-194.
1990   Update, Atlantic Coast. *Envío* 9(107): 16–19. June. Managua, Nica-

ragua: Instituto Histórico Centroamericano, Apartado A-194.

Fagoth, Steadman
1980   A witness to genocide. *AFL-CIO Free Trade Union News* 7(3): 1–3. March. Department of International Affairs, AFL-CIO.
n.d.   La Moskitia: autonomía regional. N.p.

Floyd, Troy S.
1967   *The Anglo-Spanish struggle for the Mosquitia.* Albuquerque: University of New Mexico Press.

Frente Sandinista de Liberación Nacional (FSLN)
1981   Declaración de principios de la revolución popular sandinista sobre las comunidades indígenas de la costa atlántica. August 11. Managua, Nicaragua.

Gasperini, William
1990   Miskito Indians confront Chamorro. *Christian Science Monitor*, June 19, p. 4.

Geertz, Clifford
1983   Thick description: toward an interpretive theory of culture. In *The interpretation of cultures*, 3–30. New York: Basic Books.

Government of Nicaragua
1984   Draft Agreement. December 8. Bogotá, Colombia.

Hale, Charles R.
1989   Contradictory consciousness: Miskitu Indians and the Nicaraguan state in conflict and reconciliation (1860–1987). PhD diss., Department of Anthropology, Stanford University.
1990   Land, power, and identity: from ethnic conflict to autonomy in revolutionary Nicaragua. Paper given at the MIT symposium on ethnic groups and states, May 1990.

Hale, Charles R., and Edmund T. Gordon
1987   Costeño demography: historical and contemporary demography of Nicaragua's Atlantic Coast. In *Ethnic groups and the nation state*, CIDCA/Development Study Unit (ed.), 7–32. Stockholm: University of Stockholm.

Hannum, Hurst, and Richard B. Lillich
1980   The concept of autonomy in international law. In *Models of autonomy*, Y. Dinstein (ed.). New Brunswick, N.J.: Transaction Books.

Hastrup, Kirsten, and Peter Elsass
1990   Anthropological advocacy: a contradiction in terms? *Current Anthropology* 31(3): 301–311.

Helms, Mary W.
1971   *Asang: adaptation to culture contact in a Miskito community.* Gainesville: University of Florida Press.
1976   Introduction. In *Frontier adaptations in lower Central America*, M. W. Helms and F. O. Loveland (eds.), 1–22. Philadelphia: ISHI Publications.
1977   Negro or Indian?: the changing identity of a frontier population. In *Old roots in new lands*, A. M. Pascatello (ed.), 157–172. Westport, Conn.: Greenwood Press.

1986 Of kings and contexts: ethnohistorical interpretations of Miskito political structures and functions. *American Ethnologist* 13(3): 506–523.

Indian Law Resource Center
1988 Report on the Nicaraguan Indian peace initiative: a search for Indian rights within the Arias Peace Plan. Washington, D.C.

INI (Instituto Nacional Indigenista)
1989 Propuesta de reforma constitucional para reconocer los derechos culturales de los pueblos indígenas de México. August. Mexico: INI, Comisión Nacional de Justicia Para los Pueblos Indígenas de México.

Jackson, Jean
1989 Is there a way to talk about making culture without making enemies? *Dialectical Anthropology* 14(2): 127–143.

Kirkpatrick, Jeane
1982 *Washington Post*, March 2.

Laitin, David
1987 Hegemony and religious conflict: British imperial control and political cleavages in Yorubaland. In *Bringing the state back in*, P. R. Evans, D. Rueschmeyer, and T. Skocpol (eds.), 285–316. Cambridge: Cambridge University Press.

LASA (Latin American Studies Association)
1990 Electoral democracy under international pressure: the report of the Latin American Studies Association Commission to Observe the 1990 Nicaraguan Election. March 15, 1990. Pittsburgh: Latin American Studies Association.

MacDonald, Theodore
1988 The moral economy of the Miskito Indians: local roots of a geopolitical conflict. In *Ethnicities and nations: processes of interethnic relations in Latin America, Southeast Asia, and the Pacific*, R. Guidieri, F. Pellizzi, and S. J. Tambiah (eds.), 107–153. Houston: Rothko Chapel; Austin: Distributed by University of Texas Press.

MacLeod, Jay
1987 *Ain't no makin' it: leveled aspirations in a low-income neighborhood*. Boulder, Colo.: Westview Press.

Marcus, George, and Michael M. J. Fischer
1986 *Anthropology as cultural critique*. Chicago: University of Chicago Press.

MISURASATA
1981 Propuesta de la tenencia de la tierra de las comunidades indígenas y criollas de la Costa Atlántica. July 28. Managua: photocopy.
1984 Draft agreement. December 8. Bogotá, Colombia.
1987 Treaty of peace between the Republic of Nicaragua and the Indian Nations of Yapti Tasba. Reprinted in *Akwesasne Notes*, Late Spring, 19–20.

Moore, John H.
1987 *The Cheyenne nation: a social and demographic history*. Lincoln: University of Nebraska Press.

Nagengast, Carole, and Michael Kearney
  1990   Mixtec ethnicity: social identity, political consciousness, and politi-
         cal activism. *Latin American Research Review* 25(2): 61–91.
Nietschmann, Bernard
  1986   Third-side geopolitics in Central America: the Miskito revolution and
         the Nicaragua conflict. Mimeo. 18 pp.
Prakash, Gyan
  1990   Writing post-orientalist histories of the Third World: perspectives
         from Indian historiography. *Comparative Studies in Society and
         History* 32(2): 383–408.
Rabinow, Paul
  1977   *Reflections on fieldwork in Morocco.* Berkeley: University of Cali-
         fornia Press.
Rosaldo, Renato
  1980   Where objectivity lies: the rhetoric of the anthropology. In *Rhetoric
         of the human sciences,* D. McKloskey (ed.), 87–110. Madison: Uni-
         versity of Wisconsin Press.
Rossbach, Lioba, and Volker Wunderich
  1985   Derechos indígenas y estado nacional en Nicaragua: La Convención
         Mosquita de 1894. *Encuentro* Nos. 24–25. Managua: Publication of
         the Universidad Centroamericana en Nicaragua.
Said, Edward
  1979   *Orientalism.* New York: Random House.
Skocpol, Theda
  1979   *States and social revolutions: a comparative analysis of France,
         Russia, and China.* Cambridge: Cambridge University Press.
Starn, Orin
  1986   Engineering internment: anthropologists and the War Relocation
         Authority. *American Ethnologist* 13(4): 700–720.
  n.d.   Missing the revolution: anthropologists and the war in Peru. Ms.
Stavenhagen, R., and M. Nolasco, eds.
  1988   *Política cultural para un país multiétnico: coloquio sobre problemas
         educativos y culturales en una sociedad multiétnica.* Mexico: SEP, El
         Colegio de México, Universidad de las Naciones Unidas.
Sullivan, Paul
  1989   *Unfinished conversations: Mayas and foreigners between two wars.*
         New York: Knopf.
Tilly, Charles
  1987   War making and state making as organized crime. In *Bringing the state
         back in,* P. B. Evans, D. Rueschneyer, and T. Skocpol (eds.), 169–191.
         Cambridge: Cambridge University Press.
United States Department of State
  1986   *Dispossessed.* Washington, D.C.: Office of Public Diplomacy, U.S.
         Department of State.
Varese, Stéfano
  1979   Estrategia étnica o estrategia de clase? In *Indianidad y descolonización
         en América Latina: documentos de la segunda reunión de Barbados,*

357–372. Mexico: Editorial Nueva Imágen.

Vilas, Carlos M
   1989   *Class, state, and ethnicity in Nicaragua: capitalist modernization and revolutionary change on the Atlantic Coast.* New York: Lynne Rienner.

Warren, Kay
   1978   *The symbolism of subordination: Indian identity in a Guatemalan town.* Austin: University of Texas Press.

Williams, Brackette F.
   1990   A class act: anthropology and the race to nation across ethnic terrain. *Annual Review of Anthropology* 18: 401–444.

Willis, Paul E.
   1977   *Learning to labor.* New York: Gower Press.

Wright, Robin M.
   1988   Anthropological presuppositions of indigenous advocacy. *Annual Review of Anthropology* 17: 365–390.

Wylie, Jonathan
   1982   The sense of time, the social construction of reality, and the foundations of nationhood in Dominica and the Faroe Islands. *Comparative Studies in Society and History* 24(3): 438–466.

7. Strategies of Ethnic Survival in Central America

Richard N. Adams

The State and Ethnic Relations

This chapter will consider the state, in Weberian terms, to be a government-centered network of public power relations that makes decisions and administers for the benefit, the welfare, and the survival of all its members. Ethnicities are subgroups within the purview of the state whose members use the subgroup to promote their collective interests. In the ideal world, the state would seek to negotiate the conflicting interests of the various ethnicities for the benefit of all. There is a basic conflict, however, between the state and all ethnicities housed therein except that which rules the state. The best interests of the whole (the perspective of the state) can rarely be congruent with the best interests of a single ethnicity. Most states are "ethnocratic," that is, they are controlled by a particular ethnicity.[1] In ethnocracies, the interests of all other ethnicities tend to be subordinated, thus creating conflicts that cannot always be readily distinguished from the structural conflicts inherent in the operation of the state.

The ladinos, who have long dominated the Mesoamerican states, are divided between those who, on the one hand, favor a rigorous liberal policy to achieve labor control through forced, but always strategic, deculturation and social control based directly on threat of force (as exemplified by the Barrios regime of the 1870s), and those who, on the other hand, favor an *indigenista* policy, also liberal-inspired, but designed to obtain the conformance of Indians to labor controls through "civilizing" and "educating" them.[2] What is common to both policies is the wish to get Indians to conform to the interests of the dominant ladinos. All Central American states except Belize are clearly ethnocratically controlled by mestizo sectors. They differ in the extent to which the interests of subordinate ethnicities are ignored or marginalized.

If the ideally neutral state cannot exist, something like it may be found where the central government's interests differ from those of a regionally dominant ethnicity. Two cases will illustrate: Mayan-ladino relations in Chiapas, Mexico, and Kuna-mestizo relations in Panama.

The regional ethnic situation in Chiapas, Mexico, is a historical continuation of the ladino-Indian relational system of the western highlands of Guatemala. The Mexican Revolution, however, changed the priorities of the Mexican national state. The sometimes violent ethnic conflicts historically characteristic of Mexico, Guatemala, and El Salvador were seen to be counter to the development of the national-state. The national government's priorities, therefore, sought to lessen regional ethnic conflicts throughout Mexico, including those generated by ethnic problems in Chiapas, by advocating an almost aggressive *indigenista* policy (for overall history, see Wasserstrom 1983; for national *indigenista* policy activity, see the numerous reports and monographs of Mexico's Instituto Nacional Indigenista). The Mexican state, thereby, appeared in a somewhat neutral role, trying to balance the interests of the two major ethnicities of the region.

The Kuna of Panama have for over fifty years enjoyed a negotiated autonomous relationship with the government of Panama (Moore 1983; Howe 1985). This has given them considerable control over the Comarca granted them by the government as well as access to the government in Panama City. They have been able to defend much of their land from the incursions of the expanding campesino population. This autonomy has been accompanied by a level of ethnic solidarity that is not enjoyed by any other indigenous ethnicity in Panama. Bourgois (1989) has provided a useful comparison of the ethnic relations of the Guaymí, on the one hand, and the Kuna, on the other, with the administration of the banana plantations in Bocos del Toro. The Kuna work on the plantation as temporary migrants but have consistently been under the control of Kuna leaders. They have enjoyed occupational benefits in terms of jobs held and living conditions that the Guaymí have uniformly failed to achieve. The reasons are complex, but clearly the advantages enjoyed by the Kuna derive in part from their initial and continuing negotiated relationship with the central government.

The ethnic state relations just cited are cases in which the ethnicity lies within the territorial bounds of the state. Since ethnicities are separate and somewhat autonomous entities, they can, and not infrequently do, have relations with other states. The United States has entered the scene in this capacity in a number of instances that will be discussed later in terms of "third-party derivative power."

Ecological Factors in Ethnic Survival

Central America presents widely divergent ecologies within which ethnicities and the state contend for their respective survival. These are conditions that need to be examined first because the strategies for survival must operate within the constraints they impose.

Demographic Variables

Population size is, in the long run, perhaps the most important single factor that determines the Darwinian process. Large populations can afford large losses and still survive. Small populations obviously cannot.

The very size of the indigenous population of Guatemala—three to five million, depending on who is counting—is a long-run advantage unmatched anywhere else in the hemisphere. There is a great discrepancy in the estimates of the size of this twentieth-century population. Pro-indigenous advocates have claimed that as much as 85 percent of the population is "Indian," and they would surely be right if everyone with an indigenous ancestor were included. If, however, we are referring to people who identify themselves as members of an indigenous ethnicity, then the figure could not hold.

The censuses give some figures that suggest a decelerating decline in the total population. While the basis of census judgments is notorious, nevertheless I suspect that their figures are closer to some kind of social truth than claims based on ancestry. What is of much greater importance, however, is that four of the five departments with the highest percentage of Indian population manifested an increase in the proportion of Indians over the last intercensus period. This means that in the western highlands there is a core area where the Indian population is becoming stronger. It seems likely that the northern part of Quetzaltenango and San Marcos, and southern Huehuetenango, are part of this area, were it possible to separate out the figures. It is here that Carol Smith locates her commercial core of Indian development, and in two of these departments (El Quiché and Chimaltenango) the greatest loss of Indian life was sustained in the 1979–1984 period.

While in the overall picture there may be a slow decline in the Indian proportion of the national population, it is overbalanced by two facts: the rate of decline is decreasing and may level off, and the rate of absolute growth is accelerating markedly. This picture suggests that the future of Guatemala may well see a consolidation of the ethnic identity based on a more stable population.[3]

While no one has any real idea how many indigenous peoples remain in El Salvador, Baron Castro estimated a total of 375,000 in 1940 (cited in Marroquin 1975: 755), Adams (1957) possibly as high as 400,000 in the early 1950s, and Maxwell (1982) possibly 367,500 Nahuat-Pipil speakers in the early 1980s. A report, prepared by the Ministerio de Cultura y

Table 1. Guatemalan Indian Population in Five Departments over Time

Department	1950 Total Pop.	1950 Percent Indian	1964 Total Pop.	1964 Percent Indian	1981 Total Pop.	1981 Percent Indian
Totonicapan	99,434	96.6	142,873	94.2	204,419	97.1
Sololá	82,869	93.8	107,429	93.1	154,249	94.2
Alta Verapaz	188,758	93.4	263,160	92.0	322,008	89.4
El Quiché	174,882	83.7	255,280	84.9	328,175	85.2
Chimaltenango	122,310	77.5	161,760	76.1	230,059	79.8

Table 2. Total Guatemalan Indian Population over Time

Census Year	Total Population	Indian Population	Percent Indian
1950	2,788,122	1,491,725	53.5
1964	4,245,176	1,842,802	43.3
1981	6,054,227	2,536,523	41.9

Table 3. Changes in Guatemalan Indian Population over Time

	1950–1964	1964–1981
Guatemalan intercensus interval	14 yrs.	17 yrs.
Change in Indian percentage of total	53.5 to 43.3 (10.2 pts.)	43.3 to 41.9 (1.4 pts.)
Percentage increase in absolute numbers	27	73

Comunicaciones (1985: 2), asserted that 9 percent of the national population, or approximately 450,000 people, were Indian. Adrián Esquino, a Nahuat from El Salvador interviewed in 1987, claimed that 36 percent of the population was Indian (Esquino 1987: 14). The issue is, as always, complicated by the question of how they ultimately identify and define themselves. That so many Indians can remain in a clandestine state, where much of the Salvadoran population seems unaware of their presence, is possible in part because they are a marked minority in the population at large—probably not more than 20 percent, and likely less. In comparison, the Guatemalan Indians constitute easily one-half of the national population.

The importance of the Guatemalan Indian expansion, however, can be seen when we compare figures with neighboring Honduras, where between 1778 and 1980, the Indian population increased from only 88,000 to 178,500, dropping from 67.4 percent to 4.6 percent of the total population. Quite clearly, the Guatemalan Indians' economic and agrarian plight poses an infinitely greater threat to the state than is the case in Honduras.

The very small numbers involved in Costa Rica clearly make the Indians of that country totally subordinate to the decisions of the state; serious overt opposition can be little more than symbolic. In contrast, any suggestion of serious political activity by Indians in Guatemala or El Salvador instantly causes anxiety in the ladino ethnocratic state. The Miskitu on the Nicaraguan Atlantic Coast posed a threat to the emerging Sandinista state only in part because of their absolute numbers—upward of eighty thousand. They are a major part of the Atlantic regional population. The neighboring Sumu—perhaps four thousand—take on political importance only in company with the Miskitu. And the Rama are more important to the Sandinistas for their symbolic worth than because of any serious threat they pose to the state. Indeed, the Atlantic coastal indigenous population constitutes only a small part of the total population. In relative terms, however, it is very important, since it composes a quarter of the total population in a region of effectively no roads and poor communication.

Environmental Variables

The Spanish colonial aversion for the tropics was important in Central American history. Although the Mexican tropical Caribbean coast was dominated early, the first settlements in Central America were in the highlands and on the Pacific Coast. After this they slowed down and occupied the Atlantic lowlands gradually or not at all. Efforts to extend military and evangelical hegemony over the (now) Nicaraguan and

Honduran Atlantic coasts produced dreary results. Conquerors entered and departed, leaving disease and genes, but no colonies; missions were established, experienced short lives, and then were driven out or abandoned. The Spanish conquerors seemed to prefer a somewhat arid climate, the Guatemalan Oriente and neighboring Sonsonate, the "colonial core" area delineated by Lutz and Lovell (1988). The highlands were difficult and cold, the Atlantic Coast damp and hot.

In the annals of Western colonial expansion, the notion that a region is "empty" usually has meant that Westerners simply have not found it attractive enough to enter, exploit, or colonize. It has also meant that the colonizers did not think the resident aboriginal inhabitants were worthy of mention.

While obviously varying with the topography and the technology of transport, geographical distance is a major factor in the degree to which an ethnicity is accessible to state control. It is difficult to be much concerned about a group that is distant in a region that is of no particular economic or political value to the state.

Through the nineteenth century, the Atlantic Coast and its human inhabitants were of little interest to the Hispanophone populations of the Central American highlands and west coast. So slight was the interest that the standing dispute between Guatemala and the United Kingdom over Belize was left unresolved, and the national boundary between Nicaragua and Honduras was not finally settled until early 1960. Indeed, travel in Central America was generally difficult until after World War II; in the mid-nineteenth century, it still required more than a week to travel from Puerto Barrios to Guatemala City, and to travel through Central America usually warranted a book (e.g., Stephens 1969 [1841]; Morellet 1861; von Tempsky 1858).

Indeed, until World War II, one of the few times the Nicaraguan state had shown interest in the Atlantic Coast was when Sandino tried to obtain the cooperation of the Miskitu in his cause in the 1930s (Brooks 1989). After British interest subsided in the nineteenth century, Honduras tended to ignore all but the banana-growing regions. When, in the mid-1950s, the boundary dispute with Nicaragua heated up again, the only regional response was for both governments to rush public health programs into the region, apparently to show that they had really cared all along (Adams 1957).

While the Atlantic Coast has been the major area of Central America to have benefited from this "distance" in recent years, it should be recalled that the aboriginal peoples of northwestern and northern Guatemala also benefited from delayed Spanish conquest. It is only in recent decades that serious entries have been made into the Darien.

For isolated groups, ethnic identity is a relatively marginal concern. It becomes important when contact with other societies—ethnicities—poses some kind of threat to one's identity or survival. Therefore, the expansion of, first, indigenous, then colonial, and, most recently, nation-states has constantly reduced the time and space between societies. Maintaining self-identity has emerged as a central problem as marginal peoples have been swept up by expanding state interests and demo-economic pressures. In a sense, the Miskitu perceived no threat to their ethnic identity until successful revolutionary leaders tried to win them to the cause.

State Strategies in Dealing with Ethnicities

Superior Military Force and Strategy
Every state has resources that provide overwhelming advantages over the individuals and groupings that make up its domain. First among these is the control of force. While Weber argued that the state had the sole legitimate use of force, history has demonstrated that the definition of what is accepted as legitimate often varies with who controls the force. Weberian legitimacy, therefore, is one result of the fact of the state's superior force.

Since the end of World War II, the major use of armed force—military, police, state, and private terrorist groups—in Central America has been to obtain conforming behavior in the national population. There have been no Central American wars in spite of external attempts to create them. Rather, the armies of Guatemala, El Salvador, Nicaragua, and, briefly, Honduras have been used to fight insurgency and, in some instances, to terrorize the civilian population.

Both Guatemala and El Salvador have a constant fear of political opposition among Indians and have thus periodically resorted to the use of force to scare them into quiescence. The extent and intensity of the use of force has varied. In El Salvador, certainly with the 1932 slaughter but perhaps before (Anderson 1971; Davis 1988), *ethnocide* has been the effective and overt (although perhaps not stated) policy. Labor was needed, but Salvadoran coffee labor has for years been effectively worked by mobilizing individuals apart from family units.

While the killing of Indians in Guatemala and El Salvador has always been accepted by the state as an appropriate way to deal with their opposition, it is my impression that the wholesale slaughter of the 1979–1984 era marked a turn toward genocide. It is difficult to interpret such a holocaust as merely an attempt to kill political subversives. It has been argued that a desire to eliminate Indians from agricultural lands was involved, as the slaughter also succeeded in driving people into refuge in Mexico, separating many of them from their land. An urban ladino engaged in agricultural production reflected this view by saying: "We will not have peace or progress in this country until we reduce them from four million to two" (personal conversation).

The effect on the Indians of Guatemala has been a superficial retreat into political conformance. The events of the past decades are, however, immediate and fresh in the memories of certainly hundreds of thousands, if not millions, of Indians, and they are aware of the role of the state in perpetrating the violence.

Setting a National Agenda

While the recourse to force is the ultimate and always potential basis of state control, it is not the one to which most people usually respond, since the constant use of force is, ultimately, self-destructive. The intelligent state (always supposing there is one) seeks to control the wider environment so that people find it convenient to make decisions that conform to desired policies. This is achieved through all sorts of laws, regulations, and practices that may be summed up as the setting of the national agenda.[4]

Since liberal interests first prevailed in Central America with independence, the national agendas have consistently been oriented toward greater or lesser national development. In no country of the Isthmus have the specific interests of indigenous ethnicities been explicitly defended in the enunciation of these national agendas. Indians, if included, have always been categorized as part of the national labor force, and state language concerning them is usually in terms that hide the ethnic issue behind some nonethnic usage such as *mano de obra*, *campesinos*, or *jornaleros*. This was as true of the Guatemalan revolutionary governments of 1944–1954 as of their predecessors and successors.

In the post–World War II era, it was the magic of "development" that provided the context for promoting the state's interests instead of those of the Indian populations. This continues today, although in many respects the intervening years have modulated efforts to give apparent recognition to indigenous interests. Planning and policies are always in accord with the perceived interests of the larger state.

The role of emerging Mayan bourgeois, educated, and professionally trained individuals of Indian extraction is unquestionably important in the emergence of the national-level consciousness of the Indian population. It has, however, yet to make much of a mark on the setting of the national agenda. Indian politicians are having some influence within the national Congress, but there are few of them, and their efforts are constricted to limited areas. To date, unfortunately, the most obvious effect of Indian political action has been to contribute to the insurgency that brought about the 1979–1984 holocaust. Indians are, therefore, very apprehensive about being too politically visible.

Control of the Economy

An important source of state power is the ability to manipulate the flow and distribution of goods, money, and services needed by the population and by the agencies of the state itself. While in the world at large this varies greatly between socialist and capitalist nation-states, in Central America only Nicaragua has made any attempt to institute an overtly socialist regime. Even there, however, the capitalist agenda still operates.

Subordinate ethnicities generally suffer from the free operation of capitalist economies. Since non-Indians are usually most strategically located in the national field, they usually gain at the expense of the others. Nondominant ethnicities are rarely in a favorable strategic position and seldom are powerful enough to be favored by the operation of the market. There are some major counteractions under way, however, and they will be taken up below, in the discussion of economic expansion.

State Integration

In their dealings with nondominant ethnicities, states usually favor one of three rather different strategies of control: encapsulation, assimilation, or extermination. In spite of recent events in Guatemala, genocide is rarely an overt policy, and is seldom even the favored policy. It may be resorted to when nondominant ethnicities not only seem to hold no promise of being harnessed into the state agenda, but pose a real obstacle to those goals. Such was the case, for example, in the extermination of Indians in the western expansion of the United States, and in the Argentine *conquista del desierto*. It is arguable whether at some point such a goal was involved in the Guatemalan military policy in the northwest highlands in the 1979–1984 period.

Overt policies and efforts to deculturate and assimilate are milder, and more common, responses to the same perspective that can lead to extermination. Reference has already been made to the case of El Salvador, and similar efforts have taken place from time to time in Guatemala. Often, however, integration takes place less in response to specific governmental intent than as a result of ongoing state-supported

capitalist activity. Thus, indigenous communities that were characterized as "ladinoized" in the early 1950s (barrios in Guazacapán and
Chilquimulilla, Acasaguastlán in Guatemala, Panchimalco and Izalco
in El Salvador, Subtiaba and Monimbó in Nicaragua, and Matambú in
Costa Rica) have been losing their Indian basis of identity through being
forced to compete under unfavorable conditions with expanding ladino/
mestizo sectors of the national society (Adams 1957). Ethnic reawakening
has occurred where a political opening presented itself (i.e., in Subtiaba
and Monimbó).

The *indigenista* policies that emerged at the end of the nineteenth
century were, among other things, a way of achieving liberal goals
without such violent side effects. These policies became the hallmark
of progressive thinking on the part of liberal and revolutionary government well into the second half of the present century. They have so
dominated the thinking of citizens and politicians alike in Guatemala
that even after the terrifying massacre in Patzicia in 1944, newspapers
avoided the economic and political problems confronted by the indigenous
population in favor of editorials calling for greater *indigenista* measures—
more education, health, literacy, and, in general, civilization of the
Indian (Adams 1990).

The only mode of integration that permits cultural autonomy also
involves the geographical encapsulation of the ethnicity, or some significant portion of it, by the state. The Comarca system of the Kuna, or the
reservations set up in Costa Rica and, apparently less effectively, in
Honduras, are of this kind and, whether meeting the approval of outsiders or not, are usually welcomed by the indigenous population as the best
of the poor alternatives that exist. The most favored alternative from the
Indian perspective—complete autonomy—is not likely to be allowed
under the general conduct of nation-states.

Rather, the setting aside of a territory in which the indigenous group
has certain rights not enjoyed by others and is provided with some degree
of autonomy is probably the most that such ethnicities can hope to gain
within the modern nation-state system. Honduras, Costa Rica, and
Panama have all set land aside for Indian groups. Their success varies,
of course. Honduran Indians have suffered encroachments on their lands
even with legal protection (Cruz Sandoval 1984). In Costa Rica the status
of indigenous reserves varies. In general they are probably better off than
elsewhere, but they also suffer from encroachments and crowding
caused by the growing indigenous population.[5] In Panama, we have
already alluded to the Kuna. Much more vulnerable are the Guaymí,
who have not succeeded in finding a legal relationship of autonomy with
the state, and the Chocó, themselves often intruders into new lands
(Young 1971; Torres y Arauz 1980; Comité Patrocinador 1982).

Indigenous Ethnic Strategies for Survival

Given the overwhelming advantages that states enjoy over unfavored ethnicities, it is surprising not only that the latter have continued to exercise a decisive role historically, but that they have been emerging into ever greater prominence in recent decades. They do exist, however, and they repeatedly come into being because they are one of the very few kinds of large human organizations that can exert a strong psychological claim on individuals. In order to do this, they must maintain solidarity. That in turn requires that they retain active control over the cultural and symbolic elements that constitute the external signals or markers of their self-identification.

The process of ethnic identity is so complex that the tools of a single discipline cannot begin to penetrate it. Social anthropology is particularly interested in the external markers and symbolic vehicles that provide the focus of an individual's and, therefore, of the collectivity's, identification.[6] A great variety of things serve this purpose. History, however, is a naturally selective process that has ascertained that certain of these are particularly effective in keeping ethnicities together. A common language, control over territory, some degree of endogamy, and selected rituals seem to have been especially effective.

Control of Language

Perhaps the most commonly cited ethnic marker is language, and there is no question that the loss of language signals not only the loss of basic tools of self-expression, but also much of the cognitive framework that depends on the persistence of those forms. For almost all Central American ethnicities, language is a major concern. For many Guatemalan Indians, diverse in their Mayan languages and dialects, the indigenous language remains *the* language. While there is a great deal of bilingualism, especially among males, linguistic chauvinism is also developing among some of the more urbanized components. The Academia Maya Quiché has come into being specifically to defend the purity of Quiché. Similar groups for other languages are also active.

In the Nicaraguan government's efforts to strengthen the central symbolic core of the Atlantic Coastal Indians, considerable work has been directed to writing in Miskitu, Sumu, and Rama. The case of the Rama—perhaps 650 people—a fragile surviving ethnicity located on the southern Atlantic Coast, is particularly instructive. They have split into at least two components, one composed of town dwellers, the other those who live in the bush. Recent work by Colette Craig suggests that these two groups split in terms of adaptation to the more complex coastal scene. The townspeople almost totally lost the Rama language and, indeed, assumed in general that it was all but lost except possibly among those in the bush. Craig not only succeeded in recording and analyzing the Rama language but, with the firm support of the Nicaraguan authorities, is currently involved in attempting to reacquaint the town dwellers with their linguistic inheritance. This is certainly one of the few (if not the only) cases of a state taking such pains to reconfirm the ethnicity of a language that is on the verge of extinction (notes from a verbal presentation at a meeting of the Latin American Studies Association, New Orleans, March 1988).

Control of Territory

If language is perhaps the most central symbolic feature among possible foci of ethnic identity, control of basic resources certainly is the feature of greatest importance from the point of view of material selection. A great deal has been written about the special meaning that many indigenous groups attach to the land, and there is no question but that it has a special place within the symbolic repertory. Stephen Gudeman (1986) has described in a most imaginative way how the country people of Panama have undergone extreme changes in their model of the world as their relative control over their land has changed.

The sustaining issue in controlling territory is that it is also an economic resource. In addition, however, the common dependence of a group of people on a territorial resource is a strong basis for solidarity. Generational ties are tightened when the inheritance of land is at stake.

Control over territory has successfully replaced language in some cases of solidarity. In the Montañas de Jalapa in eastern Guatemala there is a population that firmly asserts that it is indigenous, but it has not retained an Indian language. The people of the indigenous barrio of Subtiaba in León, Nicaragua, firmly assert their claim over shrimp-producing waters along the coast as their common property. Monimbo, the barrio of Masaya that was so active in the revolution, retains its indigenous identification principally on the basis of common territory.

Territory may play a number of roles for an ethnicity, but that crucially concerned with identity need not play an economic role. The identification with a lost or future homeland, for example, may have had, and might in the future have, some economic significance, but for the moment is purely a feature of identity.

Control over Community

While ethnic groups often find common residential areas, it is also the case that the emergence of an ethnicity and its continued saliency is very commonly marked by using residence as a mechanism to retain exclusive control over people and property. Residence also, therefore, becomes an important component of the identity system. The range of importance and intensity of identification with a community varies broadly, but in Middle America perhaps the most famous theoretical argument is Eric Wolf's (1956) concerning corporate (or "closed corporate") community. Wolf argued, in brief, that Mesoamerican Indians had used the community organization as a way of protecting ethnic identity by tying control over communal land, and religious and political activity, into a single social organization and ritual program. "Community," of course, implies much more than merely an organized aggregate of coresidents. It involves daily interactions and familiar patterned behavior, internal factions and alliances, love and hatred, but with all, it also involved a recognition of common good and, if necessary, common defense against outsiders. In a generic sense, it is the minimal self-reproducing organization of the human species.[7]

Control of Selected Rituals

Social organization is constructed by standardizing certain behaviors, ordering conduct and expectations so that one may predict the actions of another. Some of these orderly behaviors act as critical symbols of the ethnicity itself. Since most human behavior is fairly sloppy, it is important that some things be done with particular care and be kept inviolate and protected from entropy. Thus, some performances are explicitly ritualistic and are retained specifically as devices to keep the system in order.

Besides (and in rare cases, possibly in place of) the critical issues of language, territory, and reproduction, ethnicities will ritualize certain social organizational forms that then symbolize their distinctiveness. The use of such forms necessarily implies social relations; their use affects not only the members of the collectivity, but equally marks those who are thereby excluded.

Guatemala provides two classic cases of ritual differentiation of indigenes and ladinos, the religious organizations and *compadrazgo*. The *compadrazgo*, or ritual co-godparenthood, is a common Catholic-sponsored fictive kin relationship that is well known over the Spanish world. By 1950, this had become integrated within the indigenes-ladinos ethnic relations system in a fairly ritualized way. Ladinos could serve as godfathers of indigenous children, but not the reverse. When the former was instituted, it usually reflected a relation of dependency and subordination on the part of the indigenous compadre enabling him to draw on the economic and political favors of the ladino. In turn, he would provide favors, usually in the form of his own labor or that of members of his family, and gifts at traditionally recognized occasions such as birthdays, Christmas, and so on. Ritualistic behavior included the indigenous compadre greeting the ladinos by bowing and kissing his hand. The ladino classically would make the sign of the cross on the child's forehead when meeting. These performances have been mutually reproduced by both indigenes and ladinos, but they are clearly rituals that have been imposed by the Spaniards and ladino descendants. Their rapid disappearance during the 1960s and 1970s is witness to their repudiation by indigenes.

Religious rituals are among the most common ethnic markers. Since the imposition of Catholicism with the advent of the Spanish conquest, one of the major devices for both expression of the faith and for control over the population was the organizations to celebrate the saints. The colonial *cofradías* emerged as organizations that were sponsored either by indigenes or by ladinos, so that membership was separate. The evolution of the two kinds of organizations has, therefore, been distinct. Today the ladinos have entirely shifted to religious societies, retaining little of the paraphernalia of the colonial era. The indigenous *cofradías*, however, served as repositories of indigenous identification and required conformatory in behavior that played an important role in community level social control. Today, as will be related below, their importance has changed.

Periodic ritualistic performances are also a major marker for the Kuna. Howe (1986: 51–52) argues that the "Father's Way and the singing gathering [is] a repository of basic political ideas, . . . a medium of socialization, . . . a tool to be manipulated in a debate, . . . a vehicle of regional alliance, and . . . a charter and rallying point for solidarity in the face of outside threat . . . As the Kuna themselves are quick to point out, it is the religion promulgated in the singing gathering that as much as anything unites them as a single people in opposition to the rest of the world."

Ethnic differences will inevitably have some ritualistic expression. When few differentiating features are in evidence, they become particularly important. In El Salvador, the Indians' concern to camouflage their antecedents led them to forgo some obvious and apparent features such as extensive use of costume. It was, however, much more difficult to shift languages, and that feature apparently remains important today. In the 1950s some ladinoized communities of Guatemala, such as Guazacapán and Chiquimulilla, had effectively lost a distinctive indigenous language and significant territory. What remained were certain Catholic cults, religious groups in which no ladinos participated. These served as self-identity markers for the Indians and, at the same time, as external criteria for ladinos.

In ethnic communities that may otherwise be clearly distinct, such as in many of the highland communities of Guatemala, there will also be certain traits that are selected for special emphasis. The classic case is the *cajas de la comunidad*—small chests carefully hidden in the church or elsewhere in which it is believed that the land titles, often royal grants, are retained.[8]

Biological Reproduction and Expansion

In keeping with the Darwinian model, probably the most successful of the strategies available to the nondominant ethnicities is that of biological reproduction and expansion. Since most such groups in Central America are rural cultivators and laborers, the most effective move in countering the state is the expansion of the agrarian population and, where appropriate, its migratory expansion into frontier areas. It is certainly the case that, while the expansion of the Guatemalan Indian population has placed it in a somewhat precarious position in facing an apprehensive state, its very numbers indicate that in the long run it will occupy a much more important political and economic role than it does now. There is no evidence of any overall indigenous population policy apart from that set by the needs of peasant cultivators. The state, however, for its part has played host in trying to establish population planning programs and has allowed the establishment of clinics and community-level workers to introduce family planning into communities, both Indian and ladino.

It will be recalled that the Miskitu policy of reproduction involves a readiness to incorporate people of whatever genetic extraction; as long as the Miskitu women kept control of the household within the Miskitu community, the need for common ancestry and the inculcation of language and culture were met. The neighboring Sumu, however, have long lived under the coastal hegemony of the Miskitu, and during the seventeenth and eighteenth centuries they, presumably along with other neighbors of the Miskitu, suffered severely from slaving attacks and loss of population.

The "reproductive policy" of the Sumu, however, contrasts sharply with that of the Miskitu. Whereas the latter have easily incorporated alien peoples in contact, no matter what the genetic composition, the Sumu have been more rigorous in retaining biological purity. This has had the Darwinian disadvantage of keeping their numbers low, but it also now allows them an easier basis of ethnic distinction from the Miskitu, who have so extensively Africanized. The separate identity has

allowed them to act independently of the Miskitu in the recent autonomy process in Nicaragua.

The question of reproductive policy, as practiced, certainly can be a
matter of some importance in the retention of identity. Unlike the
problem of lack of territory, fictionalizing reproduction has few selective
disadvantages. Marrying or mating with an outsider provides children
for the inside, no matter what the outsider may be. Since the problem
is common ancestry, it is not a difficult one. The number of ancestors
doubles in every ascending generation, and somewhere the appropriate
individual is likely to be found—or invented.

Economic Expansion

Biological expansion, however, is not the only kind of expansion.
Equally significant is the emergence over the past century of a commer-
cially adept sector of Indians in the western central highlands of Guatemala. Indians of the region that Carol Smith (1976) has called the
"core" of the indigenous western highlands—that area extending from
Totonicapan on the east through Quetzaltenango on the west—have for
years been heavily engaged in commerce. In Quetzaltenango, this has
led to the emergence of an indigenous sector with a life-style clearly
marked by the accoutrements of Western wealth. Along with this,
Indians have increasingly taken up professions, especially as educators.
To characterize this population as an Indian "bourgeoisie" may be true
but also misleading, because, irrespective of their consumption patterns,
some have found a strong nativistic ideology around which a clearly pan-
national Indian identity is currently forming. It was marked by a very
high degree of concentration on commerce. Indians in Quetzaltenango
have become famous for their central position in the municipal and
regional economy, and some have become extremely wealthy, being
known as millionaires and sporting all the symbols of bourgeois wealth.
Equally important, however, has been the economic success that has
enabled some Indians to pursue professional training through university
degrees.

At the eastern end of this region, close to Guatemala City, the Indians
of the Patzicia area have strongly capitalized on the production of
vegetable crops for export. In a region that saw a major massacre of
Indians by ladinos in 1944, the ladinos are now finding themselves
economically uncompetitive with hard-working Indian cultivators who
produce more for less. There is no evidence that this economic success
has thus far provided much leverage to political power, but it seems
likely that this could be a next stage.

The development of indigenous ethnicities is, in many respects, the core problem. Since they are deprived of advantages, special efforts are required to improve their status. If they become weaker, they are more disadvantaged and dependent; to become stronger, they must confront ladinos and ladinoization; they must decide whether to be co-opted into the ladino population or to maintain an Indian identity for the possible benefit of their less successful ethnic relatives.

Third Party Derivative Power

Development in marginalized populations is rarely impressive and, even when it occurs, it is slow. Apart from a rapid and successful revolution, there is only one quick way for a nondominant ethnicity to obtain an advantageous position of power with respect to the state: it must obtain support from a third power, an alternative source that can provide sufficient backing that the state must, in a sense, at least pause and pay attention. In Central America this has been used by both the ethnocratic states themselves and, in one recent instance, by an indigenous population.

Guatemala and El Salvador have both used the argument that the presence of socialist and Eastern European resources, the Communist threat posed by insurgent Indians and guerrilla forces, is sufficient reason to call in all the military and economic aid possible from the United States and Israel. The issue has never been addressed as to whether Indians do, in fact, constitute a Communist threat. It is enough that they are labeled as such.

In Nicaragua, where the positions are reversed, a significant sector of the Miskitu population (and some Sumu) decided to draw upon the military and CIA support of the United States in their confrontation with the Sandinistas. The Miskitu who left the country to oppose the government initially accepted the support of the United States, but then divided in terms of whether they wanted to be really so dependent on what was proving to be a highly self-interested partner.

Clearly, in the 1925 Tule rebellion of the San Blas Kuna, the United States also played a central role, but of a very different kind. In that instance, both Panama and the Kuna accepted the United States as a broker—a role that it played to the advantage of the Kuna.

Nondominant ethnicities in Central America today face unattractive choices among third-party support, since most will inevitably be labeled as coming from the "CIA" or "the Communists." In either case, the label can do more damage than the good that might genuinely be forthcoming from the governments involved. Using such resources frames the ethnicities' political problems into the East-West conflict and thereby obscures the real problems that are confronting the individual members. Moreover, once locked into the competitive dynamics of the major powers, indigenous groups find themselves torn by the demands of the world system with all the lethal potential it implies.

Revolutions and Rebellions

When an ethnicity revolts, it takes on one of the principal strategies usually reserved for the state—that is, the use of force. This is immensely risky, since it requires a whole range of resources that are rarely available to ethnicities; it also requires a degree of centralized decision making that is very uncommon in ethnicities.

Central America has seen many ethnic revolts. Colonial and nineteenth-century history is replete with local and limited regional revolts of Indian communities. The object of these efforts, however, was rarely to displace the center of the imperial or colonial state; much more commonly, they were expressions against the conduct of particular agents of the state—*alcaldes mayores*, priests, and so on.

In the liberal republican era, however, as the state backed the expansion of coffee production and nationalized intervention into the customary practices of the indigenous population, rebellions were more specifically directed against the state. The successful Kuna rebellion in 1925 and the tragically unsuccessful Salvadoran effort in 1932 have already been recounted. In the Guatemalan case, the era since the Depression is too complex to be detailed here, but it has been one of continuing repression (Handy n.d.; see also Adams 1989), including the particularly deplorable slaughter of Indians that began in the late 1970s and lasted into the mid-1980s. The literature on this subject is extensive (see Falla 1983; Manz 1986; Carmack 1988).

In contrast to both the Kuna and the Salvador/Guatemala cases is the case of the military confrontation between the Sandinista government and the Miskitu. This, too, is too complex to explore here, but the emerging result is that after a serious miscalculation and misunderstanding about the nature of indigenous ethnicities, the Sandinista government shifted its position to seek a negotiated settlement, allowing for ethnic autonomy within the Atlantic coastal region. The Miskitu, for their part, after accepting third-party support from the CIA, split over this strategy, and the final negotiation was achieved by those who decided that such dependency entailed more strings than were desirable (Diskin et al. 1986).

Given the state of contemporary military technology and the potential nervousness of the United States in the event of such an action within Central America, the permanent success of an Indian revolt today seems remote. Indeed, only in Guatemala is it possible to conceive of the Indian population engaging in militant action that might have a real chance of success without third-party support. This is suggested not merely because the Indian population composes such a large absolute number and such a major proportion of the total population. It must also be remembered that a large part of the Guatemalan army is made up of Indians who, in the event of a reasonably well-executed revolt, might prove undependable. Whether or not such an effort would succeed, it certainly would be immensely bloody, and it would be years before a stable political state of whatever ethnic product could be expected to emerge.

Social Movements

Revolt is the most extreme recourse to centralized social action. Much more common are proactive and reactive social movements that try to gain coordinated action within ethnicities. Such organizations never include all the members of the ethnicity, in part because the whole ethnicity is too large, fragmented, and widespread to permit effective communication, travel, and economic support.

It is probably safe to say that all identifiable nondominant ethnicities in Central America today have formed one or more organizations for social movement. Omitting for the moment those with explicit revolutionary goals, and to illustrate with a smattering, the Guatemalan Academia Maya Quiché, the Asociación Nacional Indígena Salvadoreña, the Garifuna Organización Fraterna Negra de Honduras, the MISURASATA (to be followed by many others) among the Miskitu of Nicaragua, the Asociación Nacionál Indígena de Costa Rica, "Pablo Presbere," and the Movimiento de la Juventud Kuna. The Garifuna of Honduras have created a dance group and a solidarity group, the Organización Fraterna Negra de Honduras (OFRANEH) that works on community development and issues a monthly publication, *El Garifuna*. The specific purposes of the movements vary somewhat; the significant issue at this level of discussion is that they provide visibility to the ethnicity at both the national and the international levels and serve the members as devices for seeking support for their efforts.

Adaptive Accretion

Strategies are usually conceived of as calculated plans that are laid out in hopes of achieving a specific outcome. In fact, while individuals activate some strategies consciously, the interaction of the social structure and environment often leads to macropatterns of which individuals may be quite unaware. For example, while the Garifuna were clearly aware of their role as a militant coastal buffer between the Spanish and

English in the nineteenth century, the Miskitu were not initially aware they were being manipulated by the CIA.

Cultural change and adaptation, unquestionably central to the survival of an ethnicity, is also a strategy of survival, but one that is practiced unintentionally. The incorporation of Africans into the societies of the island Caribs (producing the Black Caribs) and of the coastal Miskitu (producing what was known colonially as the "Zambo-Miskitu") surely did not begin as an overt attempt on the part of the indigenes to bring foreign elements into their society. On a much more universal scale, the intermixture of Indians, blacks, and whites over parts of Central America for four centuries did not follow a planned strategy of survival for any particular ethnicity. Indeed, the creation of "mestizos," "zambos," and "mulattoes" probably, more than anything else, created a series of individuals who, on the one hand, were deculturated with respect to their parental societies, but who had access to more cultural variety than did either parent.

The problem of acculturation in contemporary indigenous ethnicities is a complex one, both empirically and theoretically. Since identity is spelled out in symbolic elements that are almost inevitably polysemic, the identity value of those indicators may be quite independent of whatever the trait may signal concerning historical continuity and origins. The loss or retention of a particular formal trait, therefore, does not necessarily indicate a change or lack of change in identity. Thus, a group identity can be reproduced through changing formal traits as well as through a resolute adherence to, or observation of, those traits. The *cofradías* established during the colonial era in Guatemala became immensely important as identity features of the indigenous population by the end of the eighteenth century (García Añoveros 1987; Rojas Lima 1988). Following the World War II and the Liberal Revolution of 1944, the Catholic church hierarchy increasingly saw the *cofradías* as a challenge to the authority of the priest, and set about to eliminate them (e.g., Britnell 1979). The Protestants, especially during the holocaust of the early 1980s, also succeeded in gaining a large number of converts, thus dispensing with Catholicism altogether, and these did not give up their indigenous identity (see, e.g., Annis 1987).

The relation between identity and culture is not simple. The Indian population is successfully expanding and reproducing itself and its culture, as the census figures cited earlier indicate. It is also the case that individual Indians are adopting the ladino life-style, or encouraging their children to do so, or are simply finding that the children are doing it in spite of efforts to stay the process (Early 1982). Communities differ in the degree to which they have retained formal traits associated with the indigenous past; they differ in the degree to which they have succumbed to cultural ladinoization; and they differ in the degree to which they apparently are willing to give up Indian identity.

Conclusions: A Map of Ethnic Strategies in Central America

The differing histories of the indigenous peoples of Central America have left highly diverse series of strategies of survival over the region. The region falls into three major areas with quite different paradigms of relations. One major differential lies between Mesoamerica (i.e., El Salvador and Guatemala) and lower Central America (Adams 1989). In the former, the conquest and subsequent colonial and republican societies have yielded *ladinocratic* states that still depend on exercising terror to keep the relatively large indigenous population under political and economic subordination. In the latter, the indigenous populations are smaller and have, at least until recently, been more regionally isolated, and have been less under the direct repression of the state apparatus.

The Atlantic Coast, however, stretching from Mexico to Colombia, as an ethnic area cannot be entirely separated from Lower Central America. In Panama and Nicaragua, it is the locus of major indigenous groups (the Kuna and Guaymí in Panama, and Miskitu and Sumu in Nicaragua) that have never been conquered and that have continuing negotiations with the state concerning their relative autonomy and survival. The Kuna particularly have obtained a rather unusual negotiated reservation relationship (i.e., the *comarca*) with the state that has reinforced their existence. The Costa Rican indigenous population numbers only a few thousand, and survives almost entirely on the basis of reserves.

The Atlantic Coast obtains its unusual quality from the predominance of black populations. The indigenous population is in considerable measure black in Nicaragua, as the Miskitu have a strong admixture of African ancestry, and stretching from Belize through Atlantic Nicaragua there are communities of Garifuna who have historically cooperated in the emergence of the Hispanophone states, adapting to operating within the state structure. They have, however, played a consistently subordinate role to the mestizo/ladino dominated society. Scattered in separate communities along the whole coast, but especially in Panama, Costa Rica, Nicaragua, and Belize, are communities of anglophone blacks, descendants of earlier slave and migrant peoples from the Caribbean. They are known by different labels—"Antillians" in Panama, "Talamancan" in Costa Rica, "Creoles" in Nicaragua and Belize. Everywhere except Panama, they have been playing a political role of some importance, varying with the pressure of mestizo populations that have gradually been moving onto the coast over the past century and a half. In Panama, they arrived principally as labor for the mammoth isthmian

construction projects that began in the nineteenth century. More than
has been the case with blacks elsewhere, they have been subjected to
pressures to give up their Anglo-Antillian identity.

Demographically the indigenous population is everywhere a minority,
except possibly in Guatemala, depending on the definition of "indigenous" that one may choose to use. The dominant ethnicity everywhere
is the mestizo/ladino, although there are some serious identity distinctions within that large category. The term *ladino* in Mesoamerica is
used at different levels of contrast. In a general way, the term may be
used to refer to nonindigenous peoples. This usage, however, does not
accord with the self-identity of all the groups found in the area. Individuals of the middle and upper class who regard themselves as deriving
from European antecedents separate themselves from the "ladinos,"
whom they see as deriving from Indian-white mixture and comprising a
separate population socially.

The state, however, is clearly everywhere run by a nonindigenous
population, and only in Belize is the state apparatus clearly controlled by
blacks. Belize is also the country with the most even balance of ethnic
populations. Nowhere, however, does the indigenous population play a
significant role in the state apparatus. In Guatemala, however, this
situation is clearly changing, although not at a pace that is satisfactory
to the more ambitious indigenous peoples. There are now indigenous
deputies in Congress as well as increasing numbers in the ranks of
teachers and government bureaucrats, and they completely control
many local governments. Nevertheless, the latent ladino fear of a
potential indigenous rebellion continues to be strong. The repeated
slaughters of indigenous peoples (the most recent in November of 1988)
are a continuing reminder that the state is still controlled by ladinos.
The differences in ethnic identity play a critical economic and political
role throughout Central America, but they pose the most serious
problem for peace and development in Guatemala.

Notes

1. Guatemala might be, in these terms, a "ladinocratic" state. Whether
creating terms like this is fruitful is questionable, since ethnic terminology is
itself usually biased in favor of one or another ethnicity.

2. The term *indigenista* in Latin America has been used for over a century
to refer to policies that have been established by mestizo-controlled governments and private interests for dealing with Indians. These policies were argued
to be for the benefit of the Indian. This is the usage of the Instituto Indigenista
Interamericano and the various corresponding national Institutos Indigenistas.
Today, in Guatemala, however, the term is also used to label a particular sector

of pro–Native American activists who favor complete autonomy for the indigenous population and the breaking of all state ties with ladinos.

3. The previous three paragraphs and the three tables are taken from the national censuses.

4. This was introduced by David Maybury-Lewis in his contribution to this volume.

5. The Indians of Costa Rica form a tiny part of the national population and are scattered in what were earlier refuge areas, mainly in the east (Bozzoli de Willie 1986). The government has for some decades provided protective *comarcas*. In spite of considerable beneficent legislation, these small populations are confronting serious incursions by the expanding mestizo population. Too often the legislated lands are of poor quality and, in the event, suffer from indistinct boundaries. Hall (1985: 45) says that 10 percent of the Talamancan reserves are cultivatable. In 1977 the Comisión Nacional de Asuntos Indígenas (CONAI) was set up to provide technical help and legal protection to the Indian groups. According to one study, however, a focus has been to convert the Native Americans into more standard peasants, and to ignore the problem of helping them to find ways to retain their life-style (Murillo 1983: 53).

6. The social anthropological perspective, taken here, seeks to identify consistency between events external to the individual and social collectivity, and those internal, psychological processes, the evidence for which lies solely in the behavior available for external observation. Our interests necessarily lie heavily with these external events, since one cannot directly observe the internal correspondences.

7. In this sense, the family and household reproduces other families, but the community reproduces its membership and thereby retains a separate community structure.

8. Jane Hill (chap. 3, this volume) cites the sacred places for communities of Nahuatl speakers.

References

Adams, Richard N.
  1957   *Cultural Surveys of Panama-Nicaragua-Guatemala-Honduras-El Salvador*. Scientific Publication 33, Pan American Sanitary Bureau. Washington, D.C.
  1989   The conquest tradition in Mesoamerica. In *The Americas*, October, 119–136.
  1990   Ethnic images and strategies in 1944. In *Guatemalan Indians and the state: 1540–1988*, C. Smith (ed.), 141–162. Austin: University of Texas Press.
Anderson, Thomas P.
  1971   *Matanza: El Salvador's communist revolt of 1932*. Lincoln: University of Nebraska Press.
Annis, Sheldon
  1987   *God and production in a Guatemalan town*. Austin: University of

Texas Press.

Bourgois, Philippe
  1989   Conjugated oppression: class and ethnicity among Guaymí and Kuna
         banana workers. *American Ethnologist* 15(2): 328–348.

Bozzoli de Willie, Maria E.
  1986   *El indígena costarricense y su ambiente natural: usos y adaptaciones.*
         San José: Editorial Porvenir.

Britnell, Douglas E.
  1979   *Revolt against the dead, the modernization of a Mayan community
         in the highlands of Guatemala.* New York: Gordon and Breach.

Brooks, David C.
  1989   Marines, Miskitos and the hunt for Sandino: anthropology at war along
         the Rio Coco in 1928. *Journal of Latin American Studies* 21(2): 311–
         342. Cambridge: Cambridge University Press.

Carmack, Robert, ed.
  1988   *The harvest of violence: the Maya Indians and the Guatemalan crisis.*
         Norman: University of Oklahoma Press.

Comité Patrocinador del "Foro sobre el Pueblo Guaymí y su Futuro" y Centro
  de Estudios Acción Social-Panamá, CEASPA
  1982   *El pueblo Guaymí y su futuro.* Panama.

Cruz Sandoval, L. Fernando
  1984   Los indios de Honduras y la situación de sus recursos naturales.
         América Indígena 44(3): 423–446.

Davis, Shelton H.
  1988   Agrarian structure and ethnic resistance: the Indian in Guatemalan
         and Salvadoran national politics. In *Ethnicities and nations,* Remo
         Guidieri, Francesco Pellizzi, Stanley J. Tambiah (eds.), 78–106. Aus-
         tin: University of Texas Press.

Diskin, Martin, et al.
  1986   *Peace and autonomy on the Atlantic Coast of Nicaragua: a report of
         the LASA task force on human rights and academic freedom.* Austin:
         Latin American Studies Association.

Early, John
  1982   *The demographic structure and evolution of a peasant system: the
         Guatemalan population.* Boca Raton: Florida Atlantic University.

Esquino, Adrian
  1987   An Indian with land is an Indian with title. *SAIIC Newsletter* 3(3).
         Oakland, Calif.: South and Central American Indian Information
         Center.

Falla, Ricardo
  1983   *Voices of the survivors. The massacre at Finca San Francisco, Guate-
         mala.* Cambridge, Mass.: Cultural Survival and Anthropology Re-
         source Center.

García Añoveros, Jesús María
  1987   *Población y estado socioreligioso de la diócesis de Guatemala en el
         último tercio del siglo XVIII.* Universidad de San Carlos de Guate-
         mala: Editorial Universitaria.

Gudeman, Stephen
1986 *Economics as culture: models and metaphors of livelihood.* London: Routledge & Kegan.

Hall, Carolyn
1985 *Costa Rica: a geographical interpretation in historical perspective.* Boulder, Colo.: Westview Press.

Handy, Jim
n.d. A sea of Indians. *The Americas,* in press.

Howe, James
1985 Native rebellion and US intervention in Central America. *Cultural Survival Quarterly* 10(1): 59–65.
1986 *The Kuna gathering: contemporary village politics in Panama.* Austin: University of Texas Press.

Lutz, Christopher, and George Lovell
1988 Core and periphery in colonial Guatemala. Paper presented at the symposium on Indian Communities and the State in Guatemala, Latin American Studies Association, New Orleans, March 17, 1988.

Manz, Beatriz
1986 *Refugees of a hidden war: the aftermath of counterinsurgency in Guatemala.* Albany: New York State University.

Marroquin, Alejandro Dagoberto
1975 El problema indígena en El Salvador. *América Indígena,* octubre-diciembre, 755.

Maxwell, Judith M.
1982 Nahual-Pipil: "muy político." *Cultural Survival Quarterly* (6)1: 17–18.

Ministerio de Cultura y Comunicaciones
1985 El indigenismo de El Salvador. Paper prepared for the Organización de los Estados Americanos–Instituto Indigenista Interamericano, Noveno Congreso Indigenista Intermamericano, 28 octubre al 1 de noviembre 1985, Santa Fé, Nuevo México, EEUU. (OAS/Ser. K / XXV.1.9 /CII/ NR-6/86. Original: Spanish, octobre de 1985.)

Moore, Alexander
1983 Lore and life: Cuna Indian pageants, exorcism, and diplomacy in the twentieth century. *Ethnohistory* 30(2): 93–106.

Morellet, Arturo
1861 Viaje a la American Central y el Yucatan. In *Nuevo viajero universal,* Tomo III, *América,* Nemesio Fernández Cuesta (ed.), 602–611. Madrid: Gaspar y Roig.

Murillo M., Maria Eugenia
1983 La reproducción de la fuerza de trabajo en la comunidad de Salitre. *América Indígena* 42(1): 39–56.

Rojas Lima, Flavio
1988 *La cofradía: reducto cultural indígena.* Guatemala: Seminaro de Integración Social.

Smith, Carol
1976 Causes and consequences of central-place types in western Guatemala.

In *Regional analysis, vol. 1, economic systems*, Carol Smith (ed.), 255–302. New York: Academic Press.

Stephens, John Lloyd
  1969 [1841]   *Incidents of travel in Central America, Chiapas, & Yucatan.* New York: Academic Press.

Torres y Arauz, Reina
  1980   *Panamá indígena.* Panama City: Instituto Nacional de Cultura, Patrimonio Histórico.

von Tempsky, G. G.
  1858   *Mitla, a narrative of incidents and personal adventures on a journey in Mexico, Guatemala . . . .*, J. S. Bell (ed.). London: Longman, Brown, Green, Longmans & Roberts.

Wasserstrom, Robert
  1983   *Class and society in central Chiapas.* Berkeley: University of California Press.

Wolf, Eric
  1956   Types of Latin American peasantry: a preliminary discussion. *American Anthropologist* 57: 452–471.

Young, Philip D.
  1971   *Ngawbe: tradition and change among the Western Guaymí of Panama.* Urbana: University of Illinois Press.

8. Becoming Indian
in Lowland South America

David Maybury-Lewis

It was the European invaders of the Americas who, through a famous confusion, started to refer to the inhabitants of the new world indiscriminately as Indians. The Indians for their part had little sense of possessing common characteristics that distinguished them from the Europeans. Their Indianness was a condition imposed on them by the invaders. These newcomers saw the Indians as a source of labor, yet in some parts of the Americas the Indians were so scarce or so recalcitrant that they soon came to be looked on less as laborers and more as obstacles to the acquisition of land by incoming settlers. Such areas became the classic areas of genocide, where Indian populations were eliminated (and in some cases still are being eliminated) in order to "clear the land."

This was the case in Brazil and Argentina and, to a certain extent and for somewhat different reasons, in Chile. In this chapter, I shall therefore compare the different ways in which these three countries have dealt with their Indian populations and examine the emergence in recent years of an Indian consciousness among the native Americans who live in them.

Chile

The best-known of all the indigenous peoples inhabiting what is now called Chile are the Araucanians. There were other Indians in northern Chile who nowadays make up a small part of the local population, and the tiny indigenous groups in the extreme south were all but annihilated at the end of the nineteenth century. It is the Araucanians whose modern descendants, known as the Mapuche, number about a million people (or approximately 9 percent of the Chilean population) who have come to symbolize the Indians of Chile.

This is largely due to their heroic past. It was they who stopped the Spaniards at the Bio-Bio River and who defeated and killed Pedro Valdivia at the time of the conquest. Caupolican, their warrior chief, is

Table 1. Comparative Chronologies

Chile		Argentina		Brazil	
1869	Saavedra's campaign against Mapuche	1865–1870	Paraguayan War	1865–1870	Paraguayan War
1879–1884	War of the Pacific	1879–1880	Roca's conquest of the desert; annihilation of Indians on pampas and in Patagonia		
1882	Final defeat of Mapuche			1888	Abolition of slavery
				1911	SPI founded
1921	FUNDOS: Destitution of Mapuche	1922–1923	Indian wars in Chaco		SPI underfunded—Indians neglected
	Impoverished Indians on reservations excused taxes		Repression of workers on Pampas		
		1924	Suppression of Millennarian Revolt in the Chaco		
1927	Commission to divide Mapuche lands			1930	Getulio Vargas's revolution; growing interest in Central Brazil
1939	Frente Unico Araucano	1939	(Congress of Pátzcuaro in Mexico)		

Year		Year		Year	
				1947	Perón's statutes, Comisión del Aborigen; Dirección de Protección del Aborigen
				1956	Comisión dissolved
				1961	Govt. encourages Indian organizations in Provinces
		1962	Goulart regime (Populist); SPI reorganizing; focus on *campesinos*/Northeast		
		1964	Military government opens up interior		
1967	Frei's land reform	1967	Accused of genocide against Indians; SPI replaced by FUNAI		
1970	Allende's land reform; land seizures			1970	CCIIRA founded; intense Indianist acitivity
1973	Pinochet's coup; Mapuche repressed			1974	Military ousts Isabel Perón; Indianists repressed
			Indian and pro-Indian organizations forming		
		1985	Return to civilian rule; Indian issues become issues of national security		

now a Chilean as well as a Mapuche hero. The Mapuche remember him for his resistance to the white men. The Chileans in general remember him (and the Chilean army celebrates his day annually) as a symbol of Chilean valor in the face of Spanish domination. In fact, the colonial history of Chile was essentially one of costly and inconclusive warfare against the Araucanians. The colony was constantly trying to subdue the Araucanians and worrying about the high cost of the enterprise. Meanwhile, the Araucanians not only succeeded in maintaining their independence, but actually spread out into the pampas from their homeland in central Chile so that by the eighteenth century they controlled much of present-day Argentina.

The wars of independence in the early nineteenth century led to the emergence of Chile and Argentina as relatively weak states that did not at first have the power to deal with the Araucanians. The new nations were in any case riven by civil wars that offered opportunities to the Indians, who could protect their own autonomy by judicious alliances with one or other contending party. As the Chilean and Argentine states became more firmly established, however, pressure on the Indians was steadily increased to the point where they were finally and decisively defeated.

By the middle of the nineteenth century, Chileans were systematically dispossessing the Mapuche who inhabited the Araucanian heartland. Settlers, supported by the army, were seizing Indian land and German colonists were being encouraged to settle in Mapuche territory (Bengoa 1985: 156). This led to a series of Mapuche uprisings. The Indians took part in the abortive Chilean revolutions of 1851 and 1859, hoping that the rebels would overthrow the central government and install a regime that permitted greater provincial autonomy and that might therefore leave the Mapuche alone. When they realized that it had been decided in Santiago to subdue the Mapuche once and for all and to occupy their lands, they desperately sought alliances to stave off the catastrophe. They appealed to Urquiza, then president of Argentina, hoping to gain Argentine help to weaken Chile and preserve their own independence. All these efforts failed. The Chilean army defeated the Mapuche in 1869, in a bitter campaign of extermination, marked by massacres of the Indian population and destruction of their villages and crops (Bengoa 1985: 205–277). The Mapuche were so ruthlessly expropriated after their defeat that they took advantage of the War of the Pacific, when the Chilean army was otherwise occupied in Peru, to rise up again in 1880. In 1882 they were defeated again and were subdued with great ferocity, since the Chileans had now decided to "put an end to the Indian problem." It was at about this time that the phrase "encaminar el indio" gained currency in the Araucanian areas. It meant having an Indian accused of theft or anything else, taken out by soldiers to a deserted spot and killed (Jara 1956: 17).

After 1882 the Mapuche were stripped of their land and their cattle as well as what was left of their autonomy. The Chileans had intended all along to dispossess them. The operational plans of the military who were sent to fight the Mapuche included detailed provisions for the amount of erstwhile Indian land that was to be awarded to the victorious soldiers, according to rank (Lipschutz 1956: 132–133). By 1886 the remaining Mapuche had been confined to 18,300 hectares of poor land. Meanwhile, just one of the people who were given Indian lands, the industrialist Bunster, acquired holdings totaling no fewer than 60,000 hectares (Academia de Humanismo Cristiano 1984: 59–60). The predictable result was to render the Mapuche destitute. They were a people who had traditionally eaten well, since they lived in fertile country, but now they were ravaged by famine, so much so that some Chilean military officers wrote to their superiors, urging that something be done to alleviate the misery of the Indians (Lipschutz 1956: 134–135). Meanwhile, what had been Mapuche country was given over to large estates or *fundos*, a process accompanied here, as elsewhere in Chile, by the pauperization of the rural proletariat. The Mapuche became an especially disadvantaged part of that proletariat.

Nevertheless, Chilean government policy toward the Mapuche at the turn of the century focused on the division of Indian lands, with the express purpose of putting an end to Indian communities. Indians were encouraged to demand their own individual plots of land, and communities were forced by law to divide up communal lands if any of their members requested it. It was assumed that the Mapuche would thus cease to exist as a separate people and would become Chilean smallholders or, better still, part of the landless labor force in this part of Chile. In 1921 President Alessandri's administration did recognize Indian poverty to the extent of exempting Indian communities from paying taxes. Yet only a few years later, in 1927, the government set up a special commission in Temuco to divide up the lands of remaining Mapuche communities (Lipschutz 1956: 155–157).

In the first half of the twentieth century, then, the defeated Mapuche were struggling to survive and to maintain their own way of life in the face of government policies that threatened not only their livelihood but their very existence as a people. Their legendary tenacity did not desert them, however. They maintained their own culture on their dwindling reservations and even contrived to hold their society together through important multireservational rituals in areas where the reservations had been divided up and where their communities thus lacked any official recognition (Faron 1964). Their response to the Congress of Pátzcuaro in Mexico was characteristic.

This congress, held in 1939 under the sponsorship of President Cárdenas himself, is an important turning point in indigenous affairs throughout the Americas. It was the first time that the government of a major American nation had recognized the aspirations of the Indian peoples of the hemisphere and invited Indians and Indianists to gather under official auspices to discuss their plans for the future. The congress not only led to the founding of new institutions, both Mexican and international, to promote more enlightened policies toward indigenous peoples, but it encouraged the Indians themselves to organize on their own behalf.

The Mapuche were quick to respond. In 1939 they founded the Frente Unico Araucano to defend their interests. The agrarian situation in Chile continued to worsen for the poor and for the Indians, but the Mapuche and others were now organizing to try to defend themselves. The tendencies were interrelated. In the decade that saw the formation of the Asociación Nacional Indígena Chilena (1953) and the Foro de Unificación Araucana (1959), the situation of the rural poor was becoming catastrophic. When President Frei took office in 1964, the per capita income in the rural areas was one-half of the per capita income nationwide. The *latifundia* owned 98 percent of the arable land in the country, accounted for 60 percent of rural production, and employed 40 percent of rural workers. Meanwhile, 1.25 million rural poor lived at starvation level (Berdichewsky 1977: 35–36).

It was at this time that agrarian reform became an urgent priority of the government. President Frei's agrarian reform of 1967 was intended gradually to expropriate the excessive holdings of the *latifundia* and to offer guarantees to rural unions, but his slow and "reformist" approach did not satisfy the desperately poor while allowing plenty of scope for the big landholders to resist. He had only succeeded in expropriating the holdings of one-third of the *latifundia* by the end of his term.

When President Allende took office in 1970, he was determined to speed things up. His "revolutionary" reform expropriated the remaining two-thirds of the *latifundia* in three years. This is not the place to discuss the ensuing struggle in the countryside, on which there is already an extensive literature. It need only be noted that the Mapuche, nourishing a full century's worth of grievances against the outsiders who had been usurping their land, participated enthusiastically in the "tomas de tierras" (land seizures) that took place in this period.

Their attempt to redress the balance of past injustices backfired tragically. When Allende's regime was overthrown by the military, the

Mapuche suffered worst of all in the subsequent repression that was aimed against the "radicals" in the countryside (Interchurch Committee 1980). Most of the Mapuche leadership was killed or forced to flee the country and thousands of Indians were killed. Since then the Mapuche have been understandably cautious about forming new organizations, which they fear will only invite further repression.

Nevertheless, the Mapuche started to organize again in 1978 with the help (and to a certain extent under the protection) of the Catholic church.[1] Their purpose was to resist the proposed Law 2568, which provided once again for the breakup of lands held communally by Indian communities. Under the terms of the law, a single individual could request the division of community lands, and all lands would subsequently be divided if such a request were forthcoming. The Mapuche therefore formed an organization known as the Centros Culturales Mapuches, which for legal reasons soon changed its name to the Asociación Gremial de Pequeños Agricultores y Artesanos AD-MAPU.

Once the law was passed, AD-MAPU tried unsuccessfully to have it repealed. Then it tried to persuade Mapuche never to request division of their lands, but it was unsuccessful here too, since it is almost impossible to ensure that no single member of a community will request (or be said to request) division, especially when there is strong government pressure to divide. By now the government was threatening to reimpose taxes on individuals living in communities that did not divide their lands. It is accordingly estimated that the number of Indian reservations fell from about three thousand in 1979 to about three hundred in 1983.

This precipitated a crisis in AD-MAPU, which led to a split in its leadership. On the one hand, some Mapuche leaders, especially those working in or familiar with Santiago and other Chilean cities, advocate stronger alliances with parties of the left. They argue that the Mapuche should make common cause with other segments of Chilean society, such as miners and the non-Indian proletariat, both urban and rural, who share the economic circumstances of the Indians. In this way, they hope to bring about a change of government in Chile that will enable the Mapuche to obtain justice at last. Specifically, they hope eventually to accomplish the repeal of Law 2568 and to recover the lands that have been taken from the Mapuche.

Another group of Mapuche leaders takes a different view. They are skeptical about alliances with the Chilean left who, they suspect, do not understand Mapuche concerns. Talk of recuperating the lost lands of the Mapuche makes them nervous, for this was precisely the tactic that provoked such savage repression directed against the Mapuche in 1973. They feel that the most urgent priority at the moment is to maintain

Mapuche culture in the face of the new threat to it posed by the application of Law 2568. According to this group, which has revived the old title of Centros Culturales Mapuches, its prime task should be to help the Mapuche to retain their sense of themselves and their history, to keep Mapuche tradition alive, and in this way to maintain the Mapuche way of life under changed and adverse economic circumstances.

Argentina

The history of Argentina's policies toward its indigenous peoples shows a number of parallels with the Chilean/Mapuche case I have just discussed. I shall try to postpone my comparative comments until the concluding section of this chapter, however, and will, for the sake of clarity, present the Argentine narrative with a minimum of editorializing.

In Argentina, even more than in Chile, the Indians were at the gates throughout the colonial and early republican periods. Until late in the eighteenth century, the Spanish insisted that trade and other communications between the River Plate region and the metropolis be routed through La Paz to what is now southern Peru and thence via the Isthmus of Panama to Spain. Only the northern part of present-day Argentina was settled by Spaniards who were content to leave the region of the River Plate as a remote colonial backwater. It had no precious metals and no large Indian population to put to work. It was a poor colony, dependent on ranching and farming. Meanwhile, the horses, sheep, and goats that the Spanish had introduced soon produced huge herds that ran wild on the pampas and later provided the basis both for the culture of the gauchos and for that of the Araucanians.

These Indians migrated onto the pampas from Chile, became expert horsemen and stockbreeders, and by the early nineteenth century were firmly in control of the Argentine plains. They were significant actors on the political scene at the time of the wars of independence and the civil wars that followed. As in Chile, the new Republic of Argentina had neither the wealth nor the power to defeat the Indians in its early years. Rosas, the strong man of the republic, actually drew up a plan to move against the Indians with four columns, one coming from Chile in the northwest, two from the heart of Argentina in the north, and one from Buenos Aires, the southeastern outpost of the nation; but the plan was abandoned because Argentina could not afford it (Serres Güiraldes 1979: 170–171). Meanwhile, the Indians traded between Argentina and Chile and could make alliances to affect the balance of power in the region. Some of their chiefs, such as Calfucura, became as famous in Argentina as Caupolican in Chile. Calfucura became a strong ally of Rosas himself and received vast quantities of cattle from the Argentine government to maintain the alliance (Serres Güiraldes 1979: 176–177). Yet, he turned against Rosas later, fighting on the side of Urquiza, who overthrew Rosas in 1852 (Jones 1984: 133).

By the 1880s the cost of annuities paid to the Indians and of defending the frontier against them was felt to be prohibitively high. Besides, when the Indians made war on the settlers, they also carried off captives as well as cattle and put the former to work as herders for the latter (Jones 1984: 161). It was a state of affairs that could not, from the Argentine point of view, be allowed to continue. Once the Argentine state was firmly established and its frontiers to the north stabilized after the Paraguayan war, the government could focus on expansion to the south and the days of Indian autonomy on the pampas were numbered. By the end of the nineteenth century, new technology made the opening up of the pampas for agriculture an attractive economic prospect. Meanwhile the armies of the republic, better organized and equipped than before, were in a position to defeat the Indians. In 1879–1880 General Roca, in his famous "conquest of the desert," defeated and virtually annihilated the Araucanians.

The intention had been to "cleanse the country of savages" while establishing the southern frontier of the nation where it naturally belonged, that is, at the southern tip of the continent. As in Chile, the land to be conquered was promised beforehand to new owners. Some of it was to be divided up among the officers and men of Roca's army. The rest was promised to people already owning substantial amounts of land, who received very large additional holdings on the pampas. So, in 1878, 8.5 million hectares were divided among 391 new owners, who thus received an average of more than 20,000 hectares each. A similar distribution of 3.3 million more hectares took place in 1884. In 1885 another 4.75 million hectares were divided among the officers of Roca's army, who received an average of 8,780 hectares each. The ordinary soldiers serving with Roca were promised 100 hectares apiece but never received it (Cárdenas 1974: 278).

No provision was made for any Indians who might survive the campaign. It was assumed that they would be absorbed, like human flotsam, into the lowest strata of Argentine society. In fact, their defeat led to their virtual elimination as a people. The approximately 44,000 Araucanians that had inhabited the pampas at the time of the campaign simply vanished. They were killed, scattered, or taken into servitude. Nowadays, about 20,000 of their descendants still live on the pampas.

The conquest of the desert prepared the way for the clearing of Patagonia. The Indians of that vast region were very different from the mounted warriors of the pampas. Their tiny and peaceable bands lived by hunting and gathering in regions so remote that they had hitherto not attracted many settlers. Neither their small numbers nor their peaceful tendencies offered them any protection, however. By the early twentieth century, the region was being settled by sheep farmers, many of them foreign and with most of the foreigners coming from Britain. These ranchers took pride in hunting and killing Indians. Some offered bounties for Indian heads. Others organized massacres. A Mr. McLenan provided a feast for a group of Ona on a beach near Santo Domingo, where he and his men killed them all by shooting them with repeating rifles from the sand dunes. On another occasion, Indian hunters invited five hundred Ona to feast on a stranded whale that they had poisoned beforehand, killing them all (Borrero 1957: 44–49).

Meanwhile, the army was dealing with the last groups of independent Indians still remaining in Argentina—the peoples along the northern frontier with Paraguay and Bolivia. In the early years of the century there was constant conflict between settlers and Indians, and the Indians had occasional successes even against the army. By the 1920s the Indians were being forced onto reservations, but this created a problem. Government policy was to establish Indian reservations on lands that no settlers wanted. However, the settlers needed Indian labor at harvest time to pick the cotton that was becoming the important crop of the region. This problem was solved by obliging the Indians to seek permission to leave the reservation and seeing to it that this permission was only given for them to go and pick cotton. Picking cotton was thus the only way in which Indians could legally obtain cash. The needs of the cotton growers were so urgent that Indians were not even allowed to go elsewhere where workers were being offered higher salaries to harvest sugarcane (Cordeu and Siffredi 1971: 55). It was the Indians confined on these reservations in the Chaco who were caught up in the millenarian movements of the 1920s that needed the army backed up by airplanes to put them down (ibid.: 59).

The Indian question was thus "settled" in Argentina at a time when the social framework of the state was being established. It was a state dominated by a landowning elite that controlled beef and wheat production on the pampas and became extraordinarily wealthy in the process. It was a state that protected sheep ranchers in Patagonia and cotton growers in the Chaco. It was a state that was willing to negotiate the notorious Roca-Runciman pact with Britain, that favored the big land-owners by guaranteeing a market for Argentine beef. In return it permitted British control of Argentine meat packing, railways, and utilities, and allowed British exports to enter Argentina free of duty and a British governor to sit on the board of Argentina's central bank. It was a state, moreover, that kept firm control of the working class.

Even when President Yrigoyen came to power, claiming to speak for those segments of the society that had been marginalized by the landed elites, the working classes were expected to know their place. It was during his administration in 1919 that the army massacred the striking workers at the Vasena factory in Buenos Aires, in what came to be known as the semana *trágica*. It was also Yrigoyen who sent general Varela to deal with striking workers in Patagonia in 1922. This time the army killed two thousand of them in a territory whose total population was little more than ten thousand (Crawley 1984: 39).

In this state, there was no place for Indians and they were eliminated, except in the Chaco where the government tried to keep them as a pool of directed labor. Those who could manage it drifted toward the cities where they congregated in the slums. Others remained scattered and all but forgotten in small communities in the countryside.

Little attention was paid to them until Perón came to power, when the Estatuto del Peón became law in 1946. The measure was designed to prevent exploitation of the rural poor, but it also included provisions for granting land titles to Indian communities. This was followed in 1947 by the setting up of a Dirección de Protección del Aborígen. This protectionist concern for Indian rights was short-lived. Perón was ousted after a military coup in 1955, and the Dirección was dissolved the following year. Indian affairs were now the responsibility of the provincial governments, who were unenthusiastic about Indian land rights and did their best to reduce and delegitimize such lands as the Indians controlled. This led to considerable Indian unrest in the provinces, to which the government responded in 1961 by encouraging the formation of Indian provincial organizations. These tended, except in the Province of Neuquen where the governor supported genuine Indian leaders, to follow the government's wishes and acquiesce in the reduction of Indian lands.[2]

By the end of the 1960s, the Indians of Argentina were beginning to organize to defend their interests more effectively. In Buenos Aires, Indians from all over the country could meet and discuss their common problems at the Centro Indígena that was founded in 1968. Meanwhile, the church was working at the grass-roots level with Indian communities. The government established the Comisión Coordenadora de Instituciones Indígenas de la República Argentina (CCIIRA) in 1970 and tried through this agency to control the intense Indianist activity of the seventies. This led to a split in the CCIIRA. It was taken over by the *oficialistas* (those willing to follow the government line), while the *radicales* (who were interested in strengthening grass-roots indigenous organizations and in forging alliances with *campesino* political groups) seceded and worked through local and regional organizations. By the mid-seventies, the bulk of the Indian movement was lined up with those sectors of Argentine society that were critical of the government. It was, through its local organizations, moving toward the creation of a Confederación Indígena Nacional. It was hoped that this national Indian organization would at last give a voice to Argentina's Indians, so that the approximately 200,000 of them still left in Argentina (about 1 percent of the national population) would finally be recognized as an ethnic minority with specific needs to be met by specific programs.

These hopes were disappointed. Isabel Perón's government moved in 1974 to suppress the Indian organizations that it could not control. The military that overthrew Isabel Perón's administration in 1976 nevertheless continued its policy toward the Indians. It insisted that the Asociación Indígena de la República Argentina should be strictly apolitical. Indeed, it accused political parties of both left and right of manipulating the Indian question. The organization was expected to see that Indians and their cultures were respected, that their lands were guaranteed, that their communities were officially recognized, and that they were not discriminated against in the workplace. However, it was stipulated that this must be done without any politics, religion, social science or historical discussion (Serbin 1981: 432)! The activity of the organization, thus freed of all impurities, was to focus on the creation of a national Congress of Indian Leaders. Such a congress never came into being. Meanwhile, Argentina entered the dark days of military government, the "dirty war," and defeat in the Falkland/Malvinas Islands, and the Indians were once again forgotten.[3]

Brazil

In Brazil, unlike Chile and Argentina, Indian wars were insignificant in the nineteenth century. The days were long past when Brazilians hunted Indian slaves to do their work. They had turned instead to black Africans, who were imported in large numbers to toil on the plantations and in the mines. At the same time, the nineteenth century was not, in Brazil, a period of expansion, when the effective national territory was being enlarged and new areas settled. On the contrary, imperial Brazil was a huge archipelago of coastal areas that largely communicated with each other by sea or along one or two major river systems. Beyond that lay the interior, where sparse Indian populations remained relatively undisturbed.

At the end of the nineteenth century, when Chile and Argentina were subduing the Indians on their frontiers, the Brazilians were preoccupied with the issue of black slavery.[4] The important turning point in late-nineteenth-century Brazil was thus the abolition of slavery in 1888, coming almost simultaneously with the abdication of the emperor and the proclamation of the republic in 1889.

The Indians had not been an issue since Father Antonio Vieira and the Jesuits fought the colonists (and lost) in an effort to prevent Indian slavery in the seventeenth century. They reemerged as a question for national debate in the early twentieth century. Settlers, many of them German immigrants, were expanding the effective national territory by bringing new lands under cultivation in the southern state of Santa Catarina. They clashed with the Indians who inhabited the forests of the region and who reacted when their lands were invaded. At the same time, workers extending the railroads in the state of São Paulo, much closer to the heart of Brazil, were also getting into fights with the Indians. These clashes sparked a national debate about how to deal with the problem.

The most famous protagonists in this debate were, on one side, Professor von Ihering, the director of the Museu Paulista, São Paulo's state museum and a prestigious center for scientific research; on the other, a young army officer by the name of Rondon. Von Ihering was the spokesman for those who argued that the Indians were savages, impeding the advance of civilization. It was therefore necessary to remove this impediment—regrettable, perhaps, but necessary nonetheless. Rondon, on the other hand, had led the expedition to set up the first telegraph line connecting the cities of Brazil with the remote regions of the northwest, along the Bolivian border. The success of this enterprise had been due in no small measure to his policy of cultivating friendly relations with the various Indian peoples that his expedition met en route. He therefore urged that Brazil should adopt a policy of protecting the Indians at its frontiers and attracting them to civilization by means of assistance and example.[5]

The issue was a delicate one for the Brazilian government. It was trying to encourage European immigration at the time, and it realized that its plans to attract large numbers of "civilized" immigrants were likely to be undone if the German newspapers carried too many accounts of Indian attacks on German farmers. It seemed likely that the government would be forced to act against the Indians in order to reassure prospective immigrants into Brazil. The debate, however, took on a nationalist tone. Brazilian intellectuals and journalists persuaded public opinion that Rondon's solution of the Indian problem was not only just and effective, but that it was a peculiarly Brazilian solution. It relied on the Brazilian genius for moderation and mediation, especially in the sphere of social and racial relations, that contrasted with the extremist, not to say racist, measures advocated by more uncompromising nations.

This put von Ihering, himself of German stock, and the German immigrants on the defensive. Meanwhile, Rondon persuaded the administration to create a department of the federal government to deal with the Indian question. President Nilo Peçanha signed the legislation in 1910, and in 1911 the SPI, known officially as the Service for the Protection of Indians and the Settlement of National Workers, came into existence with Rondon as its president.

As remarkable as the creation of the SPI itself was the legislation that brought it into being. At a time when von Ihering's views represented the conventional wisdom among educated people and when tribal peoples were being killed off without compunction in various parts of the world by racist invaders who considered them hardly human, the Brazilian congress enacted extremely liberal legislation as it set up the SPI. Under its terms, Indian peoples were to be guaranteed the lands they occupied and the maintenance of their own cultural traditions, as well as a series of other rights. It was to be the task of the SPI to ensure that these guarantees were enforced. The very title of the Indian service implied that such a policy would also facilitate new settlement in areas where the settlers would otherwise have had to contend with hostile Indians.

Why did the Brazilian congress pass legislation concerning Indians in 1910 that would still be considered ultraliberal in our times? It is true that the ideas contained in the law came from Rondon and others who shared his views, but why did the lawmakers approve them? The answer is that Brazil was, at that time, an agrarian country dominated by its landowning elites. In the second decade of this century, these oligarchies controlled state legislatures, jealously defended their regional autonomy (and thus their own interests), and were entrenched in the national congress. I suggest that they passed the new Indian legislation in the spirit of a beautiful gesture that demonstrated the high-mindedness of the Brazilian government. It would have the practical effect of setting up an agency with federal funds to deal with local Indian problems that would otherwise have been a headache for the states. The Indians were few and remote, and the SPI would henceforward protect them and keep them out of the way. It was not expected that this protection would cause much inconvenience to the oligarchies.

Indeed the SPI (which soon lost that part of its title that gave it the responsibility for settling national workers) was from the beginning an agency that could not perform its task properly. If it were effectively to protect and assist the Indians who were scattered throughout the remotest regions of a country as huge as Brazil, it would have needed a big budget and a large number of dedicated employees. Instead, its budget was always much too small for its responsibilities. It has had, over the years, a number of dedicated people in its service, but they have tended to end up frustrated and disillusioned. The agency was already struggling in the 1920s and received even less support after Getulio Vargas's revolution in 1930. Rondon had not supported Vargas, and the SPI suffered corresponding neglect.

In 1934, the SPI became part of a new Special Inspectorate of Frontiers under the aegis of the Ministry of War, which was anxious to secure the national boundaries of Brazil and to turn the Indians who lived near them into good Brazilians before neighboring countries could subvert them (Beltrão 1977: 23). At this time, Getulio Vargas was promoting his "Push to the West" to open up the interior of the country, but the SPI was given no special role to play in exactly the sort of undertaking for which it had been created. It was Vargas's own newly created Central Brazil Founda-tion that was given responsibility for the enterprise. Significantly, the Villas-Boas brothers, who subsequently became famous as the protectors of Indians and the creators of the Xingú National Park, worked for the Central Brazil Foundation and not for the SPI.

Nevertheless, the SPI did establish Indian posts all over the country. While its assistance to the Indians was always minimal and it was not always able to protect them, it did succeed in acting as a brake against those who would simply have ignored and trampled on Indian rights. Meanwhile, it became famous for its "pacifications." These were expeditions carried out by its most experienced people to establish friendly contact with tribes that hitherto had had no dealings (or only hostile ones) with the outside world. These expeditionaries lived up to the proud motto of the Service, "Morrer se preciso fôr, matar nunca" (Die if need be, but never kill), leaving presents on trails where they saw signs of Indians and patiently waiting for weeks and months until friendly contacts could be established. The technique worked and provided good publicity for the Service, but its practitioners soon started to worry about its consequences. What would happen to the Indians so patiently contacted and at such considerable risk? Normally, once they posed no particular threat to outsiders, they would be overwhelmed by the settlers who moved in on their lands, which the SPI was unable to protect.

The push to the west resumed in earnest in 1960 when president Kubitschek inaugurated the new capital deep inland at Brasília. The road-building and developmental euphoria of the early sixties put sud-den and sharp pressure on the Indians, and the SPI was powerless to do much about it. In fact, unlike the situation when the SPI was created half a century earlier, the Indians were not even an issue. Brazil was preoccupied with other matters, notably the festering poverty of the northeast and the rise of populist leaders who threatened the traditional oligarchies. One such leader, João Goulart, became president by accident, and was overthrown by a military coup in 1964.[6]

The military stepped up the development of the interior, and it was thus in the late sixties that scandals erupted and Brazil found itself accused in the world's press of committing genocide against its Indians. There is no evidence of any government policy to eliminate the Indians during this period. On the other hand, the government did encourage development at all costs and took no measures to protect the Indians from the predictable effects of frontier expansion. The SPI too was caught up in the process. A number of its employees were accused of selling out the Indians they were supposed to protect or, worse still, of assisting the frontiersmen who were bent on killing them. The government signally failed to prosecute the people responsible for these acts. Instead, it tried to sidestep the issue by disbanding the SPI, opening a lengthy and inconclusive inquiry into its activities, and replacing it in 1967 with a new agency, FUNAI (National Indian Foundation).

FUNAI was, however, caught on the horns of the same dilemma as its predecessor. Its mandate was to assist and defend the Indians, yet it was an agency of a government committed to development and not squeamish about the rights of those who might suffer in the name of development. The gap between rich and poor widened even during the years of the "Brazilian miracle" at the end of the 1960s. At the beginning of the 1980s, the plight of the poor, especially the rural poor, was becoming desperate, and their numbers had swollen dramatically—and now there was no more miracle, only talk of the country's indebtedness and the problem of paying back its international creditors. As for the Indians, ministers would make statements to the effect that the development of the nation could not be held up by a handful of Indians; that the Indians should be civilized and absorbed into Brazilian society as soon as possible; that the country could not tolerate ethnic cysts within itself; that the Indians should be emancipated as soon as possible. The idea of emancipation has been revived again and again in various forms. It sounds attractive, echoing the emancipation of the blacks, which is such a prominent event in Brazilian history books, and implying some sort of future freedom for the Indians. Yet, it has been regularly denounced by Indians and Indianists as a measure that would simply abdicate the government's responsibility for the protection of Indian rights and leave the Indians to cope on their own with the pressures that threaten them (see Comissão Pró-Indio 1979).

These pressures result from the network of roads built in the last twenty years that have opened up the interior of Brazil. They have brought an influx of people desperately seeking land, while huge mining companies, cattle ranches, and agribusinesses can now operate in regions that were once too inaccessible for them. The Indians, seeing their lands encroached on and their lives threatened by the new invaders, have tried to resist. In remote areas, they have fought back and been crushed. Those more sophisticated in the ways of the surrounding society have tried to fight back politically. In this they were helped by the liberal wing of the Catholic church, whose organization known as CIMI (Missionary Indian Council) helped Indian leaders to hold their first meetings to discuss common problems and strategies to defend the interests of their peoples.

FUNAI did everything it could to prevent the emergence of Indian organizations. At first it claimed that since FUNAI was the legal guardian of Indian peoples, no meeting of Indians could be held without FUNAI's permission. It therefore asked the military police to break up "illegal" Indian meetings. But in the 1970s this policy could not be maintained. International attention was focused on Brazil. National pro-Indian organizations were forming, and they were receiving support from international organizations dedicated to the same cause (see Cardoso de Oliveira 1981 and Maybury-Lewis 1984). FUNAI was acutely aware of the fact that the conflict between the Sioux and the U.S. government at Wounded Knee in 1973 received much press attention in Brazil. Brazilian Indians knew that their American cousins had stood up to the government of the United States and the lesson was not lost on them (Beltrão 1977: 65–70).

For example the Xavante, of whom there are about ten thousand living in Central Brazil, had maintained their relative isolation by means of a warrior reputation that persuaded land-hungry backwoodsmen to avoid them. They came under tremendous pressure when their region began to fill up with ranchers. Their villages were protected by Salesian missions and by FUNAI posts, respectively, but their lands were being whittled away. So the Xavante took to besieging the authorities in Brasília, now accessible to them by bus, to demand a guarantee of their lands. Their combination of truculence and political astuteness—they cultivated allies in FUNAI, in the congress, and among the public at large—paid off. Their lands were finally guaranteed by a special presidential decree, and FUNAI launched a demonstration project in their area to enable them to become tractor-driven rice farmers like their neighbors (Maybury-Lewis 1985).

By this time, the Indians were receiving considerable attention in the Brazilian media. In fact, as the military regime began, at the end of the seventies, to talk of a political opening and a return to democracy, the press took to discussing the plight of the Indians as symptomatic of what happened to those who paid the price of the "Brazilian miracle." Indians were losing their lands to agribusinesses and mining interests, but then so were smallholders. They, like the Indians, did not have title to their lands and could be run off them at will. They would then swell the burgeoning ranks of the rural poor. To write of the injustice being done to the Indians thus became a thinly veiled way of alluding to the agrarian crisis in the Brazilian countryside.

Meanwhile, FUNAI wavered. The government wanted it to keep the Indians quiet while ensuring that they did not "stand in the way of development." But these were contradictory aims, and FUNAI therefore zig-zagged between contradictory policies. At one moment, it was trying to operate the notorious "renda Indígena," according to which Indian areas were to be run by FUNAI as businesses, paying out of their profits for the costs of FUNAI itself. At the next moment, it was pouring money into such undertakings as the Xavante project, in the distant hope that this would eventually turn the Xavante into rice farmers and with the more immediate expectation that it would solve a nasty political problem and get the Xavante out of the news.[7]

Most Indian peoples were not as fortunate as the Xavante. Other FUNAI projects were started but soon abandoned, and the majority of Indians received little protection or assistance. At the same time, Indian efforts to organize and to defend their own interests were increasing. Tribal and regional organizations began to form. At the national level, UNI (Union of Indigenous Peoples) was founded with its major chapter in São Paulo. It worked closely with the pro-Indian organizations of anthropologists and Indianists that had taken up the Indian cause. Meanwhile, the support of the Catholic church continued to be very important.

The Indians, in spite of the government's best efforts, continued to be news. The World Bank was persuaded by international organizations to adopt new guidelines to protect the environment and the rights of indigenous peoples in areas where the bank made loans and to apply these guidelines in Brazil.[8] Now, when the government sought international financing for its large-scale development projects, it was likely to face awkward questions about the Indians. Mario Juruna, a Xavante Indian, was elected as a Federal Deputy from the State of Rio de Janeiro in 1982. He was the first Indian ever to be elected to national office and gave the Indians a spokesman in congress as well as the sympathy of a number of opposition deputies.

The end of the military government in 1985 has not helped the Indians, however. A weak civilian administration has been unable to curb the power of the landowners, whose lobby has prevented any land reform in the countryside. At the same time, this lobby—together with the representatives of the mining interests, both supported by the military—has taken a hard line on the Indian question. In fact, Indian affairs are increasingly being treated as matters of national security and therefore as lying within the special province of the National Security Council, which is dominated by the military.

How has the Indian question, affecting as it does less than 1 percent of the national population, gone from being a nonissue in the sixties to a matter of national security in the eighties? The violent campaign unleashed by Brazil's biggest newspaper, the *Estado de São Paulo* against all those who support the Indian cause, gives us a clue. The *Estado* ran a series of front-page articles for a full week (August 9–15, 1988) accusing the Catholic church of acting in concert with an international organization of churches to manipulate the Indian question to its own political advantage and to the detriment of the nation. Similarly, it accused national and international organizations of using the Indian issue as a pretext for preventing Brazil from exploiting its own mineral wealth, thus forcing the country to buy raw materials from foreign companies.

The Catholic church responded immediately by taking legal action against the newspaper, obtaining a parliamentary commission of inquiry to investigate its allegations and publishing its own response (CNBB-CIMI 1987). The reply showed that the *Estado's* "evidence" was drawn from articles in the world's press that were partially or misleadingly quoted and from documents that were quite simply forged. Moreover, the campaign seemed to have been inspired by the Paranapanema group, Brazil's largest tin mining consortium, whose mining rights on Indian lands (granted by the outgoing military regime) were being challenged in the courts.

The issue has not died down, however. Instead, the Brazilian government is orchestrating a nationalist backlash against the worldwide outcry over the deforestation of the Amazon and the brutality that is accompanying the process. Brazilians and others who protest against the impunity of the large landowners who simply kill smallholders or Indians who get in their way are now being attacked as part of a broad movement to place the Amazonian region under international trusteeship.

The conservatives and the military thus see the attention being paid to environmental and human rights issues in the Amazon as a threat to Brazilian sovereignty. It is no coincidence that the military are now making a concerted effort to secure Brazil's vast Amazonian frontiers for the first time. They also resent the support being given by the Catholic church and others to the rural poor and to the Indians, for this highlights the inequities of Brazil's development policies by drawing attention to the plight of those who suffer for them.

Mineral rights, frontiers, Brazil's development policies, the growing gap between rich and poor, and the ways in which the former keep the latter in their place—these are sensitive issues, and the Indians have the misfortune to be involved, in one way or another, in all of them. That is why the Indian question is now treated by the Brazilian authorities as a matter of national security.

Conclusion

In the three cases presented above, I have compared countries whose Indian populations were not large enough or central enough to provide labor power for the state. The Indian issue in each of these cases had therefore been largely a matter of securing the nation's frontiers, or of consolidating the nation's territory. Hence, the size of the Indian populations concerned is not a crucial variable in determining the treatment meted out to them. Nor, interestingly enough, does the extent of the threat they posed to the frontier seem to have been very important. In the mid-nineteenth century, for example, Chile confronted a comparatively large Mapuche population in the south, but it posed little threat to the frontier. It was settled in its own side of the Bío-Bío river while the heart of contemporary Chile lay to the north. Argentina, by contrast, faced a relatively small number of Indians (about forty thousand) on the pampas, but they did pose a constant threat to the frontiers of settlement. In the early twentieth century, Brazil likewise had to deal with small numbers of Indians who were clashing with settlers at the frontier, but they were more of a nuisance than a serious threat. In these circumstances, Chile and Argentina moved to eliminate their Indian populations. Brazil, on the other hand, resolved to protect its Indians and to bring them slowly to "civilization," although the policy was not carried out very effectively.

It would appear that the national agenda of each country at the time when it focused on its own Indian question is the most important consideration as regards the treatment of the Indians. At the end of the nineteenth century, Chile was entering on a period of national consolidation. It had secured its northern borders through its victory over Peru in the War of the Pacific and was now ready for southern expansion. At the same time, new technology and new markets offered lucrative opportunities for agriculture in the south. There the Mapuche impeded the extension of *criollo* settlement. They could, of course, be bypassed, but Chileans were in no mood to allow their country to be bisected by an autonomous Indian region, especially when the state had at last acquired the military means to defeat the Mapuche. The campaign against the Mapuche and their defeat and dispossession followed inevitably. In that way, the country could consolidate the south and the landowners could profit from the fertile lands that would be transferred to them.

Argentine policy toward the end of the nineteenth century was impelled by similar considerations. The country had come through the war with Paraguay and its own civil wars and was entering a period of national consolidation. Huge new markets for beef and wheat were opening up worldwide, and the pampas, once they were settled and accessible by railroad, promised large profits to the suppliers of these commodities. Landowners, speculators, and railroad entrepreneurs thus had a common interest in opening up the pampas, and the military at last had the power to crush the Indians who controlled them. On the other hand, Brazil at the beginning of this century had no national project to open up new lands either in the west or in the south. The effective national territory was already very large for the population of the country. The big landowners concentrated on coffee and sugar, and the big cattle ranchers produced meat and hides for them in an "interior" that was not far removed as the crow flies from the extensive, settled coastal areas. The Indians, who had been so important as a source of labor as late as the eighteenth century, were now remote from the national life. It is true that they sometimes interfered with people who were building railroads or trying to bring new land under cultivation; but this did not always happen. After all, Rondon's expedition had accomplished a feat of exploration and laid the telegraph line while remaining friendly with the Indians. It was also true that Indian attacks on European immigrants might discourage others from coming to Brazil, but it seemed that Brazil was not so desperate to have them come over anyway. Besides, when they did come, they were smallholders and lacked the political clout of the landed classes. The latter were not particularly interested either in Indians or in expanding the effective national territory.

This was the social background to Brazil's liberal Indian legislation of 1910. Conservative legislators, jealous of their class privileges and their regional interests, were content to pass high-minded laws that made Indian affairs the administrative and financial responsibility of the federal government. The content of the laws, inspired as they were by the ideas of Rondon, seemed to matter little to them at the time. The Indians were simply not an issue. When they became an issue half a century later, measures similar to the ones that the oligarchs had approved so airily in 1910 would be hotly debated and held by conservatives to undermine the very fabric of Brazilian society.

The common element in all three policies at the turn of the century was the treatment of Indians as a marginal category of people, external to the life of the nation. Chile tried to eliminate its Indians socially in the way that had been tried repeatedly throughout the Americas, by taking away their lands, destroying their communities and hoping that this would turn Indians into *campesinos*. Argentina tried to eliminate the Indians physically in the south. Brazil treated them as people outside of Brazilian society who would be eliminated socially as they were taught to become Brazilians.

In all three countries, the first half of this century was a period of amnesia as far as the Indians were concerned. In Chile and Argentina, the Indians struggled to survive in the face of official hostility or, at best, indifference. In Brazil, the frontier was beginning to catch up with the Indians of the interior, but the nation's attention was focused on other issues and other regions of the country. The SPI, underfunded and overextended, could not protect and civilize the Indians as Rondon had hoped, but its very existence prevented them from being casually annihilated at the margins.

In Chile and Argentina the Indians were submerged among the rural poor, so that they eventually began to organize to protect not only their interests but their very identity. This was easier for the Mapuche in Chile. Although they had been defeated and were now separated from one another by a sea of settlers, they nevertheless had their historic sense of themselves, their own traditions and rituals to fall back on. They started Mapuche organizations and then participated in the national Indian association. President Frei's land reform only increased their alienation and their sense of being different from the rural Chileans whose poverty they shared. They were deeply disappointed by the measure, which they felt was "only for Chileans" and did nothing to remedy the historic injustices from which the Mapuche suffered (Berdichewsky 1977: 42–43). It was not till Allende's brief presidency that they threw in their lot with the leftist parties in Chile and took part eagerly in land seizures in their part of the country, which in turn led to their being the targets of savage repression when Pinochet overthrew Allende.

In Argentina, by contrast, the surviving Indians belonged to different tribes, scattered throughout the country. They were given brief recognition in President Perón's legislation for the rural poor, and this seems to have encouraged them. After the fall of Perón, Indians in the provinces were able to react against encroachment on their lands to such an extent that the government felt it worthwhile to encourage the formation of Indian provincial organizations to control and defuse the unrest. But a truly Indian consciousness does not emerge in Argentina until the 1960s, brought about by the Indianist activities of Indians in Buenos Aires and the assistance of the Catholic church in the communities. It was at this stage that the government responded by creating CCIIRA to control the Indian movement. CCIIRA could not control it, but it did succeed in splitting it between the *oficialistas* and the *radicales*, who wanted to throw in their lot with antigovernment opposition parties. It was precisely this association of the Indian movement with the antigovernment opposition that led to its suppression even before the military ousted Isabel Perón.

There is a melancholy similarity between the Chilean and Argentine cases. They proceed through a series of stages: (1) The Indians are defeated at the frontier; (2) they organize to protect themselves; (3) they discover their common Indianness, which distinguishes them from the rural poor whose lot they share; (4) they wonder whether to throw in their lot politically with the parties claiming to represent the rural poor; and (5) they do so and are repressed.

This did not happen in Brazil, because the conservative attack on the populist parties took place when the military came to power in 1964. This was before the emergence of the Indian movement in the 1970s. Yet, the current events that are unfolding in Brazil could well produce results that are structured similarly to the Chilean and Argentine cases. National attention in Brazil began to focus seriously on the opening up of the interior during Kubitschek's administration (1956–1961), but the military regime that took power in 1964 intensified the process as part of its general plan for national development. It was therefore no accident that Brazil was accused of genocide in the late 1960s, for that was when an authoritarian government was pushing ahead with its development plans and dealing summarily with those who stood in its way. The Indians were defined as being "in the way," and they suffered accordingly.

There was, however, no concerted effort to eliminate them, as there had been in Argentina. There are two reasons for this. First, Brazil's own alternative tradition of dealing with the Indians in the spirit of Rondon caused considerable ambivalence in many sectors of Brazilian society, even among the military and the technocrats who were running the country. Second, Brazil's consolidation of its hinterland took place a century later than that of Chile and Argentina. Times had changed and the elimination of tribal peoples was no longer looked upon as a normal part of the process of "civilizing" remote areas. Meanwhile, the Catholic church was increasingly willing to defend the rights of the Indians, as were national and international organizations who supported the Indian cause, and this altered the politics of the situation. Tribal peoples are still regularly dispossessed and killed at the frontiers all over the world, but most governments (Brazil's included) prefer to claim that these are regrettable incidents that they are anxious to prevent.

Brazil tried instead to deal with the issue through FUNAI, an agency that was supposed to prevent atrocities against the Indians (and the bad name they gave Brazil), while simultaneously controlling the tribes and making sure that they either contributed toward development or at least did not impede it. FUNAI was as unsuccessful in controlling the emerging Indian movement as CCIIRA had been in Argentina, but it did succeed in dividing the Indians and delaying the formation of strong Indian organizations.

FUNAI sponsored projects in Indian areas and took to hiring more and more Indians into its service, both in the communities and in FUNAI's regional and national headquarters. Indians have thus been of two minds as to whether they should oppose FUNAI for failing to do its job of protecting their rights or should cultivate FUNAI in the hope of gaining projects for their communities and jobs for themselves. In fact, as the period of military government came to an end and the nation anxiously awaited the empowerment of its first civilian president in more than twenty years, the Indians had high hopes of taking over FUNAI altogether, or at least of seeing it run by people they supported who would put into effect policies they liked.

This did not happen. On the contrary, FUNAI has been decentralized, with much of its decision making devolved to its regional offices. This makes it more susceptible to local influences, which are notoriously anti-Indian, and less susceptible to Indian pressures. The Indian movement and its allies were becoming increasingly skilled in bringing pressure to bear in Brasília. Now such people are told that the matters they wish to discuss are dealt with at regional offices. These may be thousands of miles away in Amazonas. At the same time, it is common knowledge that this is simply a tactic to divert political pressure, for Indian affairs are increasingly becoming the direct concern of the National Security Council, and the Indians have come to regard FUNAI as their enemy.

This is because Brazil's developmental agenda is being set by an alliance of agribusinesses and mining interests, supported by the military. The armed forces have relinquished formal power, but they remain in the wings as a strong and influential presence as Brazil struggles through its current period of economic crisis and political drift. The military is anxious to promote development, which means supporting the big enterprises that have been consistently favored in Brazil's development programs, and ensuring that those who bear the costs of the process do not protest to the extent of overthrowing the system. This means in turn that the military is anxious to defuse the agitation for land reform and to prevent the coming to power of populist politicians. Finally, the military is intent on securing Brazil's frontiers in the vast Amazonian regions and ensuring that these "empty spaces" are appropriately colonized and developed. In this connection, the armed forces are especially concerned about the possibilities of drugs being grown, processed, or run through the enormous wilderness of their continental hinterland.

These concerns all militate against the Indians. Many of the tribes live near frontiers, now declared areas of national security. Others are threatened by enterprises that enjoy the support of the government. If they, or smallholders, or rural workers attempt to fight back, their region is likely to be declared an area of national security, where the military has special powers to keep out outsiders and to maintain order. The Brazilian case is thus a variation, and a telescoping, of the sequence that I traced above for Chile and Argentina. It starts with a similar move toward national consolidation by advancing the frontiers of settlement. The Indians are not simply eliminated, however, at the frontier. Instead, the SPI is replaced by FUNAI, which has a mandate to speed up the social demise of the Indian populations. The Indians organize to defend themselves. The military wants to eliminate them by emancipating (that is, by abolishing their very Indianness) them and turning them into ordinary *campesinos*. It is, however, wary of the rural poor and ready to suppress any signs of revolt on their part.

There is one important respect in which the Brazilian case differs from either of the other two discussed in this chapter. The Indians are currently demanding the right to maintain their own cultures without this implying that they are not Brazilians in the full sense of the term. This was in fact a right that was guaranteed in the Indian legislation, approved with such insouciance in 1910. Yet, such a provision flies in the face both of official ideology and the popular image that Brazilians have of their nation. Brazil, in this conception, is a melting pot; indeed, a peculiarly successful one, where races and cultures have mingled without the nasty extremes of racism and prejudice that have racked other parts of the world. They have mingled, however, by absorption into the mainstream of Brazilian culture. This may be a syncretic culture, as Gilberto Freyre so eloquently argued in *The Masters and the Slaves* (1946 [1937]) incorporating elements from black Africa and the indigenous populations as well as from Portuguese and other European traditions, but it was the culture into which all proper Brazilians were born or absorbed. The Indian demand thus challenges Brazil to change its conception of itself and therefore the premises on which its society is based. That accounts for the fervor with which the Indian desire for cultural autonomy is rejected in some quarters, for it could only be satisfied if Brazil were to acknowledge that it was officially a plural and multiethnic society.

In spite of the apparent contrasts between government policies toward the Indians in Chile, Argentina, and Brazil, there is an interesting similarity between the government agencies that have dealt with the Indians in those countries. All of them have tried to eliminate the Indians. The policy is as old as the conquest. Over the centuries, the conquerors and settlers have been trying to break up Indian communities and abolish the very category of Indian, arguing that Indians should cease to be Indian and become undifferentiated citizens of their respective countries. Over the centuries, the Indians have resisted. The Mapuche case is a particularly poignant example of this. The Chilean authorities have been and continue to be particularly severe in their attempts to eliminate them, yet the Mapuche still maintain their own way of life against all the odds. Meanwhile, in Brazil, the government through FUNAI is now arguing that only unacculturated Indians—those who among other things do not even speak Portuguese—are entitled to protection and to have their lands guaranteed. The others will lose any special rights they may have had as Indians and will have to merge with the local population.

In contrast to the government agencies, the Catholic church has in recent years emerged as a major supporter of Indian rights. It has provided the Mapuche with protection as they struggled to survive. It helped the grass-roots organizations in Argentina and was instrumental in enabling the scattered Indian peoples of Brazil to get together and form their own associations. It is this support, combined with the political and financial assistance that Indian associations now receive from national and international philanthropic agencies, that gives the Indians a chance in what would otherwise be a hopelessly unequal contest.

It is precisely this contest that forges a consciousness of being Indian among the disparate indigenous groups in each country. When the nation decides that it needs what had previously been Indian territory and that the Indians must therefore be eliminated, the Indians are forced to band together in self-defense or be socially and perhaps physically annihilated. This does not, of course, imply that Indian movements form automatically and act with unanimity. We have seen, on the contrary, that their emergence in lowland South America has been hesitant and difficult and marked by divisions over policy among the Indians themselves.

These splits seems to be of two major kinds. There is the split between those who wish to collaborate with the government and those who do not (the *oficialistas* vs. the *radicales* in Argentina; those who would work with FUNAI and those who would not in Brazil). Then there is the split between those who would collaborate with parties in the political arena (normally opposition parties representing the poor) and those who would not. From the evidence of our cases, the results of Indian entry into the conventional political arena have often been disastrous for the Indians. It led to repression directed against them in Chile and Argentina. In Brazil, the growing Indian movement, strongly supported, as it is, by segments of the public that give support to the Indian cause, has provoked a political backlash, whose consequences have yet to be seen.

Yet, if Indians and their supporters do not enter the political arena, how can the Indians defend their ways of life? They cannot rely on the protection of the state, for that is never forthcoming. Even a state like Brazil, which theoretically has a protective and liberal Indian policy, in fact works like the others to abolish Indian cultures. This is the central dilemma of being Indian in lowland South America. The national organizations that deal with Indians regularly seek to impose the national agenda on Indians at the local level. They do not recognize or do not admit that Indians may have their own agendas. Indeed, they cannot admit this possibility, for they work to abolish Indianness and merge the Indians with the rest of the population. The assumption that being Indian is an obsolescent anachronism is often shared by the political parties that cultivate Indian support, or rather the support of Indians whom they see as rapidly becoming *campesinos*. Indians thus gradually become aware of the cruel fact that their interests are on nobody else's agenda. They are therefore forced to become the champions of their own cause, but unless they have allies, they are in a weak position to defend themselves.

The current struggle over Indian rights in Brazil is therefore of more than local significance. In that country, Indians are receiving considerable public support as they pursue their own agenda. They have so far been able to make common cause politically with other segments of the Brazilian public, without having to give up their Indianness in order to do so. It remains to be seen whether this will enable them to defend themselves and their rights in the course of the current Brazilian crisis, or whether they will become scapegoats who are made to suffer for it. Either way, it is clear that becoming Indian in lowland South America is a difficult process of trying to create Indian organizations at a national level that are strong enough and astute enough politically to be able to defend Indian lives and interests locally.

Notes

1. The information on recent events among the Mapuche is taken from Macdonald (1985).

2. My information on the growth of indigenous organizations in Argentina during this century is taken from Serbin (1981).

3. The administration of President Alfonsin has adopted a more liberal policy toward the Indians recently, but a discussion of its tendencies falls outside the scope of this chapter.

4. Note that the United States dealt with both issues, slavery and the Indians at the frontier, in the latter half of the nineteenth century.

5. Much of my information on the debate concerning the Indians and the resultant founding of the Indian service is taken from Stauffer (1955).

6. Under Brazilian electoral law at that time, people voted separately for president and vice president. Goulart ran for the vice presidency and was elected, though his candidate for the presidency lost. He therefore served under his erstwhile opponent Janio Quadros, and became president when the former unexpectedly resigned.

7. The Xavante rice farming project collapsed after a few years, when FUNAI could no longer fund it.

8. My own organization, Cultural Survival, was instrumental in persuading the World Bank to adopt this new policy.

References

Academia de Humanismo Cristiano (Grupo de Investigaciones Agricolas)
  1984   *El pueblo Mapuche: historia antigua e reciente.* Cuadernillo de Información Agraria. Santiago: Academia de Humanismo Cristiano.
Beltrão, Luiz
  1977   *O indio, um mito Brasileiro.* Petropolis: Editora Vozes.
Bengoa, José
  1985   *Historia del pueblo Mapuche (siglo XIX e XX).* Santiago: Ediciones Sur.
Berdichewsky, Bernardo
  1977   *Reducciones Araucanas y su incorporación en el modo de producción capitalista.* Lima: Universidad de San Marcos.
Borrero, José María
  1957   *La Patagonia trágica.* Buenos Aires: Editorial Americana.
Cárdenas, Gonzalo Horacio
  1974   *Las luchas nacionales contra la dependencia,* vol. 1. Buenos Aires: Ediciones Macchi.
Cardoso de Oliveira, Roberto
  1981   Indian movements and Indianism in Brazil. *Cultural Survival Newsletter* 5(1).
CNBB-CIMI
  1987   *A verdadeira conspiração contra os povos indígenas, a Igreja e o Brasil.* Report prepared by the Conselho Nacional de Bispos Brasileiros and the Conselho Indigenista Missionário. Brasilia: CNBB-CIMI.
Comissão Pró Indio/SP
  1979   *A Questão da emancipação.* Cadernos da Comissão Pró-Indio/SP #1. São Paulo: Global Editora.
Cordeu, Edgardo, and Alejandro Siffredi
  1971   *De la algarroba al algodón.* Buenos Aires: Ediciones Juárez.
Crawley, Eduardo
  1984   *A house divided: Argentina 1880–1980.* New York: St. Martin's Press.
Faron, Louis
  1964   *Hawks of the sun: Mapuche morality and its ritual attributes.* Pittsburgh: University of Pittsburgh Press.
Freyre, Gilberto
  1946 [1937]   *The masters and the slaves: a study in the development of Brazilian civilization.* New York: Knopf. Originally published as

Casa grande e senzala.

Interchurch Committee on Human Rights in Latin America
  1980   *Mapuches: people of the land.* Ottawa: Interchurch Committee on Human Rights in Latin America.

Jara, Alvaro
  1956   *Legislación indigenista de Chile.* Mexico: Instituto Indigenista Interamericano.

Jones, Kristine
  1984   Conflict and adaptation in the Argentine Pampas 1750–1880. PhD diss., Department of History, University of Chicago.

Lipschutz, Alexandro
  1956   *La comunidad indígena en América y en el Chile.* Santiago: Editorial Universitaria.

Macdonald, Theodore
  1985   The Mapuche of central Chile. Unpublished Cultural Survival Report.

Maybury-Lewis, David
  1984   Indian and pro-Indian organizations in Brazil. *Cultural Survival Quarterly* 8(4).
  1985   Brazilian Indianist policy: some lessons from the Shavante project. In *Native peoples and economic development*, Theodore Macdonald (ed.). Cambridge, Mass.: Cultural Survival Occasional Paper no. 16.

Serbin, Andres
  1981   Las organizaciones indígenas en la Argentina. *América Indígena* 41 (3): 407–434.

Serres Güiraldes, Alfredo
  1979   *Las estrategia de General Roca.* Buenos Aires: Ediciones Pleamar.

Stauffer, David
  1955   The origin and establishment of Brazil's Indian service 1889–1910. PhD diss., University of Texas at Austin.

ligenism and Nationality

Antonio Carlos de Souza Lima

> *The unconscious of a discipline is its history; the hidden and forgotten social conditions of production are the unconscious: the product estranged from its social conditions of production changes its meaning and exercises an ideological effect: to know what one does when one makes science . . . takes for granted the knowledge of how the problems, the instruments, the methods and the concepts used were originally made—Bourdieu,* Questões de sociologia

The purpose of this chapter is to demonstrate the existence of a relationship between indigenism and nation-building as ideologies in Brazil.[1] The focus is on the crucial first few decades of the twentieth century—the period during which government institutions for protecting the Indians were formed—and on the discourse and practice of what is known as "fraternal protection" (*proteção fraternal*).

"Fraternal protection" is a general cover-term for the set of ideas (and ideals) that guided the formation and operation of the first government agency dedicated to Indian protection. This agency, formed in 1910 under the leadership of Cândido Mariano da Silva Rondon, was first known as SPILTN (Serviço de Proteção aos Indios e Localização de Trabalhadores Nacionais), but since 1918 it has been called by the better-known acronym SPI (Serviço de Proteção aos Indios). It was Brazil's first Indian agency, and it lasted until 1967, when it was replaced by FUNAI (Fundação Nacional do Indio).

The relationship between indigenism and nation-building will be studied through a consideration of the different positions of struggle (Bourdieu 1968, 1974, 1983a, 1983b) within the political and intellectual fields at that time. Those positions may be described in sociological terms as categories of agents, that will be examined here through some concrete individual actors. However, positions are not reducible to individuals. It is necessary to specify not only the discursive elements that define positions, but also the social trajectories that lead actors to participate in them, and, consequently, to produce a specific form of discourse.

In the case of Brazilian indigenism, actors took different stands and disputed who had the right to speak with authority on indigenism, as well as who had the right to act on behalf of the Indian peoples. The main concern here is with the symbolic productions of these actors, and, specifically, with the few individuals who were not only actors but also authors. Some of these authors formulated systematic approaches for helping the Indians, and these approaches may be termed "indigenist projects." An analysis of these projects shows agreements and disagreements on a range of subjects. As a consequence, it is possible to individualize the generic conception of fraternal protection and to show it to be the product of competing discourses within a field of struggle.

Indigenism as a Historical and Analytic Category

Oliveira Filho and Lima (1983), following Nolasco Armas (1981), have proposed that indigenism, as a historical category, can be traced to a specific ideology within the Mexican political field. According to Nolasco Armas, indigenism is rooted in Mexican postrevolutionary romantic ideas of active political participation and welfare for the total population. It is preceded by even older political ideas regarding the need a new nation has to solidify itself by producing homogeneous citizens.

Linked in this way to official thought, the Indian in Mexico became a "problem" and a matter for anthropological action. Applied anthropology found in indigenism a way to induce Indian peoples to participate in "development." Given this local development of the concept as part of the nation-building enterprise in Mexico, it is possible to say that: ". . . indigenism is Mexican, made in Mexico and for Mexican use, so that there is no sense in or need for comparative studies of the situation in other countries. This automatically denies its anthropological essence . . . Our indigenism is only Mexican, Central-American" (Armas 1981: 68). "Indigenism," circumscribed as specifically Mexican, is thus the set of "ideas pertaining to the Indian problem, its cause and effects, etc. . . . The official attitude regarding it is *indigenist policy* and the proposed solutions that go along with it are referred to as *indigenist action*" (ibid.: 69, emphasis added).

Mexican indigenist ideals spread over Latin America after the 1940s with the Pátzcuaro Congress, with the formation of a conception of "interamerican indigenism," and with the establishment of the Interamerican Indigenist Institute (cf. Briones 1973; Caso 1958; and Rojas 1971). Meanwhile, in Mexico itself, indigenism grew in internal consistency during the decade of the 1950s. It reached the stage wherein different positions within the Mexican political field could each regard the concept as their own. Consequently, indigenism came to be seen as the principal policy guiding state interrelations with Indian peoples.

Regarding the Brazilian case, Darcy Ribeiro points out that "the SPI began without knowing the word indigenist. There was a positivist kind of protection activity towards the Indians" (Ribeiro 1979: 91). The word "indigenist," he writes, "came to us from Mexico and from the Hispanic pan-American countries, where it designates those who strive to protect the Indians" (1979: 88).

Discussed in this way, indigenism is taken as a "historical category," developed and used by actors in political fields, and consisting of specific ideas and practices. Its general use throughout Latin America is defined in terms of its Mexican origin (Oliveira Filho and Lima 1983). However, the generalization to contexts other than the Mexican one obscures the specific ideas and different relationships between nation-states and Indians that may obtain there.

If it is possible to understand indigenism as a historical category, it is also possible to treat it analytically. To do so, it will be necessary to introduce the concept of the nation-state, in relationship to which the analytic notion of indigenism will be situated. According to Elisa P. Reis (1983: 2), "the peculiarity of the nation-state lies precisely in the explicit reciprocity between nation and state which precludes sharp conceptual differentiation between them." The attempt to distinguish Weberian authority from solidarity fails, and the two kinds of relationships blend in producing the nation-state. The introduction into the state of "'legitimacy' to qualify the monopoly over the means of violence brings to the fore aspects which pertain to the realm of nation." Legitimacy implies to a certain degree complicity between the dominated and the dominant. This intermingling of "state" and "nation," also mentioned by Mauss (1969) and others, points to the existence of an ideology of nation-building as part of the state's legitimation process.

In fact, according to Reis (1983: 3), "the nation provides for the ideological reconciliation between bureaucratic domination and social solidarity." Correspondingly, the reconciliation constitutes "national-ity," requiring values that shape a sentiment of solidarity (Weber 1974) and that build social identities.

Considering *citizenship* as the political aspect of these social identi-ties, Reis shows how citizens are produced through the articulation of political, economic, and cultural characteristics of a given society in a particular moment in its history. She criticizes the tendency to infer the characteristics of a specific form of citizenship from a universal model, built on the specifically European and North American bourgeoisie historical trajectories.

Within this framework for understanding the nation-state and citizen-ship, it is possible to attempt a tentative definition of indigenism that may substitute for the historical category. *Indigenism* will here be regarded as a set of ideas (and ideals) concerning the incorporation of Indian peoples into nation-states. The ideas focus, for example, on the extent to which there can be "Indian rights" distinct from the rights of citizens, on the borders of citizenship, and on the proposed methods to accomplish the incorporation of Indians into nation-states.

The ideas in question may or may not be formulated within state agencies, although the ideas are most fully *indigenist* when they are produced by the state. Even if the ideas are not state-produced, however, in order to be truly indigenist they must have the state as their principal target, whether the latter is conceived as agent or as mediator of social processes. Indigenism also presupposes the existence of a nation-state independent of the church.

If we take the state as heterogeneous, composed of different and conflicting factions, and (especially in the Brazilian case) intertwined with local power groups, it becomes apparent that the formulation of an indigenist project does not presuppose the existence of power for its implementation. The formulation process can lead to the production of various competing discourses, none of which need have perfect correspondence with actual practices toward Indians.

In keeping with this reformulation of indigenism, it is also possible to redefine *indigenist policy*, by which will be meant any measures taken by the state, through decisions implemented at different levels of public administration, that directly or indirectly affect Indian peoples. In this sense, *indigenist policy* is only apparently based on *indigenism*. In fact, it is possible to have government action affecting Indians that does not draw upon any central plan, let alone an indigenist one. At the same time, despite the ideological aim of integrating Indian peoples into the nation-state, indigenist policy may also be designed to meet other needs. For different factions within the nation-state, the kind of problem posed by the Indians may be different.

In the Brazilian case, indigenist policy seems to be most closely articulated with land policy. At the beginning of the twentieth century, the great task for an indigenist agency was to put an end to conflicts between settlers and Indians in order to permit the opening up and settling of the interior. In any case, these definitions of indigenism and *indigenist policy* are offered as provisional and exploratory. I do not wish to deny the importance of the historical category, but only to provide broader definitions for the purpose of facilitating further research.[2]

The Brazilian Political Field at the Beginning of the Twentieth Century

The Brazilian political field in the early years of the republic can be divided into two important positions: the military and "liberalism."

According to Reis (1983: 8), the military favored a: "unitary form of State, in order to better organize society from above. Strongly influenced by the indoctrination of the military academy, an important group of officers was convinced of the superiority of the resources of authority over those of solidarity in promoting the 'scientific' advancement of the nation-state."

The term used publicly at the time to designate this idea of scientific advancement was "positivism." It should be noted, however, that "positivism" was used to describe a range of proposals, from those of the Positivist Church of Brazil, with its orthodox positions, to those of Pereira Barreto, which were much more liberal.

In any case, within this conception, the agent of scientific advancement would be the military. The idea that the "salvation" of the country was a task for the military had developed within the army, in particular, since the war with Paraguay. The move toward positivism strengthened and helped to institutionalize this development. Positivist philosophy became the basis for military education in the 1870s. In spite of internal divisions within the military, the idea of salvation through progress supplied a unifying theme.

The position of "liberalism," which opposed the military position, was defended especially by the oligarchy of coffee plantation owners from São Paulo. Their proposal argued for: "the superiority of a model which favored society's initiatives over those of the State. The role of authority, they stated, should be mainly to grant freedom and property. They battled for a wide power decentralization through federalism and perceived private initiatives as the most adequate way to foster nation-building" (Reis 1983: 9).

When it came to the Constitution of 1891, liberalism was the clear winner, although the constitution did include some elements of positivism. At the level of the constitution, the nation was represented as a collection of persons. This liberal position was soon abandoned, however. The coffee growers had to confront the crisis of the coffee surplus that forced the Taubaté agreement of 1906 and the subsequent permanent defense of coffee. Little by little, the coffee growers would come to take a position favoring the intervention of the state in the market. They began to think of the state as an actor capable of leading and promoting the nation, and this had serious consequences: "Even though the initial justification for the superiority of the resources of authority over private ones was indeed a rationalization of coffee interests, this ideology, once dominant, imprinted unexpected results upon stateness: it provided crucial legitimacy to public power expansion, even though within an oligarchic context" (Reis 1983: 10). State-building would get significantly ahead of nation-building, since the political field was restricted and was dominated by agrarian interests. The liberal position declined slowly along with the Old Republic, and, with this decline, the nation came to be represented as a collective individual rather than as a collection of individuals.

At the same time, with the formation of a nation-state distinct from the church, and with the expansion of state power to shape and lead a homogeneous nation, a space for indigenism was created. Indigenism arose in an intellectual climate where the central debate was between "positivism" and "evolutionism," a debate that surfaced in fields as disparate as law, medicine, and anthropology.

An "official version" of the 1910 creation of SPILTN is given in Brazilian anthropology in the works of David Hall Stauffer (1955) and Darcy Ribeiro (1962).[3] This history, which emerges from a search for the reasons for the creation of SPILTN, isolates as a principal motivation the growing awareness of vast frontier regions that needed taming. At the same time, in this official version, the land settlement issue merged with pro-Indian reactions stimulated by supposed statements favoring extermination of the Indians (Lima 1989).

This debate would subsequently mature and lead to pressures on the Brazilian government to create an agency for the purposes of mediating interethnic conflict and supervising the incorporation of Indian peoples into the Brazilian nation. Exceptional men would pledge themselves to the task with humanitarian zeal. In the official version, this resulted in a campaign to rouse public opinion in order to alert the government to the need for SPILTN. Notably, in this official version, the state is absent from the debate itself, which occurs among private citizens, and there is also an absence of any conception of a structural conflict that may have stimulated the debate. To mobilize the elite (i.e., the government) was to solve the problem. In buying this official history, we get a ready-made set of "heroes" and "villains."

The approach I adopt tries to rethink indigenism in Brazil within its social and historical milieu, showing that it is driven by structural forces. My analysis regards SPILTN as part of a political field, being an agency of the state and therefore possessing enough political capital to arbitrate one of the great issues of the time, namely, the extent to which the state should intrude into civil society. Simultaneously, it helped to shape the very conception of the Brazilian nation itself.

The characteristics of SPILTN aligned it with the "positivist" position, which saw the nation as a collective individual under the state's tutelage. SPILTN was, indeed, an extension of nation-state services. While it was itself dominated within the broader political field, it assumed dominance in the area of indigenist policy. But SPILTN grew out of the historical needs of the nation-state and out of conflicting forces. Even before the creation in 1906 of MAIC (Ministry of Agriculture, Industry, and Commerce), to which SPILTN later pertained, the idea of an indigenist agency was circulating. Indeed, calls for state intervention in frontier zones go back as far as 1891 in the debates of the the National Congress.

Indigenist Projects: Consensus and "Dissensus"

The general field of debate in which indigenist projects were born consisted of a number of distinct positions, and it will be useful to briefly characterize those positions:[4]

The term *ethnographer* refers to those who claimed legitimacy, by virtue of their knowledge of Indian nature, in the fight over ways of incorporating Indian peoples into the nation-state. They were usually members of legitimate scientific institutions. Hermann von Ihering and Antonio Carlos Simoens da Silva, among others, belonged to this category.

The term *politicians* designates those actors directly linked to agencies of the state. The state tried to define ways to make the expansion of the agricultural frontier compatible with Indian survival. Politicians fought for the establishment of a "place" for the Indians within the nation whose constitution was then under discussion. In this category was Rodolpho Nogueira da Rocha Miranda, Minister of Agriculture, Industry, and Commerce—the agency within which SPILTN was eventually formed.

The *jurists* were those who tried to define the position of Indian peoples with respect to the legal code. The jurists had to decide whether and in what measure Indian peoples had a right to citizenship. The name Antonio Ferreira de Souza Pitanga, among others, is aligned with this category.

The *journalists* participated in this debate also, insofar as they popularized for a broader public indigenist problems and plans. None of them, during that period, formulated an indigenist plan.

The *propagandist* category included those who worked to spread information about indigenist issues among the learned classes, who sought to rouse public opinion, and who endeavored to force the state to take a stand. Among the most prominent propagandists were Leolinda Daltro, Mendes, Jorge, and the Comissão Promotora da Defesa dos Indios.

The term *military-engineer* serves to designate people with a specific kind and level of education who participated in exploratory and telegraph-laying expeditions into the interior. The most prominent figure in this category was Cândido Mariano da Silva Rondon, the founder and first director of SPILTN.

Those who formulated indigenist projects faced some common problems. One was the need for an implicit or explicit conception of the nature of the Indians, which could inform any of their practical proposals. There were no sharp differences among indigenist projects as regards this conception. Each of the projects relied upon what George Stocking (1982) calls the "evolutionist paradigm." The various conceptions of the nature of Indian peoples shared in common the fact of considering the Indians inferior, either with regard to the "national civilization" or "white race," or, as in the case of the positivists, by placing them in an earlier evolutionary phase.

The principal question under dispute was whether Indians were capable or incapable of evolving further. In other words, could they go from "inferior" to "superior," from "wild" to "tame"? The simple binary ordering was later expanded and refined, and passed without criticism into the legal code and subsequently into scientific discourse (Lima 1985: 267–268).

For some scholars, von Ihering among them, Indian peoples were regarded as incapable of evolving. The argument here was that Indians should be left on their own. One should not expect them to contribute to national development, except on a random, case-by-case basis. On the other hand, if they were forced to integrate with the "white race," they would simply retard the latter in its own evolution. The racial admixture would introduce an element of degradation (von Ihering 1911: 132–133). It is worth remembering that von Ihering's education was as a natural historian and that he was born and trained abroad. This no doubt gave him a greater sense of distance in regard to the Indians, whom he could readily see as "others," outside the "Brazilian nation." At the same time, one must remember also that he was the director of the Museu Paulista, an institution located in a state that was promoting private expansion into Indian lands.

For the positivists, in contrast, the "compulsory march of humanity" through the various evolutionary stages would eventually lead the Indians to abandon this "first condition."[5] However, in addition to this evolutionary process, which was ultimately the great equalizer, there were other processes that Indian peoples could undergo that would not change their modus vivendi.

One of these alternative processes was expressed under the rubric of *catechism*. This term, however, had long been appropriated by the religious orders to designate their missionary activity. The term *lay catechism* was established to refer to nonmissionary, indigenist action, either financed or performed by the state.

In addition to these two main positions, there was also a third position, according to which, although the Indians were inferior, they could evolve within limits and contribute to the "nation's progress." They needed only to be educated. The theme of "education" arises time and again in different ways in all of the positions taken throughout this fight.

All indigenist projects had three objectives: (1) to open the hinterland to colonization by putting an end to the conflicts between Indians and whites; (2) to accomplish "the extermination of savagery," an expression used by Jorge; and (3) to confer on the Indians a role within the nation-state.

Regarding the first objective, opinions were unanimous: Indian lands should first be settled, with the wild Indians pacified and protection given to all Indians. All of the major indigenist authors took a stand on the land issue. They wrote that they found it essential to "donate," "grant," "delimit," "concede," "assure possession of," "discriminate," "guarantee," in short, provide land for the Indians. This would be one of the tasks of state protection. The "private owners," "pioneers and *sertanejos*," "industrial entrepreneurs," or "civilized people" would be the potential or actual invaders. The states or federal government would be the land donors.[6]

Insofar as was possible, Indians were to be guaranteed rights to the very same territories that they were already inhabiting or that were theirs previously. Certain exceptions would be made in cases where national interests, such as the need for mineral extraction or running telegraph lines, clashed with occupation sites, as Rondon and Pitanga pointed out. In such cases, Indians would be transferred if consent were obtained from both the Indians themselves and the agents in charge of protecting them. Regarding a specific case, Rondon (1910: 23) wrote: "I have already pointed out to them [the Pareci] that while they lived in the chapadões they would need vast extensions of land to make a living, since the resources there were scanty. *If, however, the Government* granted them more fertile lands and rich pastures, it would be expected that they would be content with less." Of course, in mentioning "more fertile land and rich pastures," there was also an assumption that the Pareci would become cattle-raisers. This kind of subsistence activity was regarded as most appropriate for the "evolutionary level" of Brazilian Indians generally, as Couto de Magalhães (1975) expressed so clearly in one proposal. Though the total amount of land was to be reduced, this was not thought of as interfering with the Indian way of life.

Two authors linked the issue of Indian protection to that of forest protection, aiming to "kill two birds with one stone." These were von Ihering and the Comissão Promotora da Defesa do Indios from the Centro de Ciências, Artes e Letras de Campinas. This was a characteristic theme in both the political and intellectual fields of São Paulo at the time. Several articles concerned with these issues appeared in the *Revista do Centro de Ciências, Letras e Artes de Campinas and in the*

Revista do Museu Paulista. In addition, von Ihering claimed himself to be a "propagandist" for "forest, floral and faunal conservation" (1911: 138).

It was also generally agreed that only the nation-state could have responsibility for the settlement of lands. Among the various authors, von Ihering is the only one who mentions that individual states should also be charged with some responsibility in this regard.

The category of *protection* accommodated ideas common to several authors, emanating from different positions. Everyone agreed that protectionist activity as exercised by the state should secure the possession of land for the Indians and punish any trespassers; it should also guarantee the life and liberty of the Indians and those who worked with them. In connection with protection, moreover, provision should be made for the passage of legislation that would be appropriate for a range of circumstances.

Protection, according to Pitanga (1909),[7] should be designed so as "to reconcile the predominance of civilization with respect for the essential conditions of existence of the Indian peoples." He was here referring specifically to the conditions for *physical survival*, which must be distinguished from the conditions for *ethnic or cultural survival*.

There was also disagreement on a number of issues. Von Ihering, for example, suggested that protection by the state should be extended to pacified Indians, settlers, and *sertanejos* (backwoodsmen), but that it should not be a priority for the "savages." He and the Comissão also used the term *protection* in connection with the forest and ecology more generally.

Von Ihering and Daltro demanded that the state confer rights of citizenship on the Indians, with some restrictions. The Indians would be placed under the effective control of a "tutor," if not by legal right, then at least in practice. Von Ihering had in mind missionaries, while Daltro was referring to the laity. Jorge, on the other hand, thought of protection primarily in terms of legislation that would restore the predominance of religious orders.

Rondon and the Comissão gave to the state the task of inspecting and supervising the activities of other agents involved in indigenist work. In this they were in agreement with von Ihering. The difference between the first two lay in the fact that, whereas Rondon would set up a special state agency called the "Inspetoria Federal de Proteção Fraterna aos Indígenas," the Comissão would assign these state tasks to the "army." The proposals were later merged in the formation of SPILTN.

The term *pacification* was used for the establishment of peaceful contact and relations between the indigenist agents and the "savages."[8] Von Ihering referred to the process as one of "making the Indians more respectful of our civilization." Neither Daltro nor Jorge took any stand on the issue. Teixeira Mendes and the Comissão limited themselves to endorsing Rondon's experience. Rondon claimed that friendship and kindness would be enough to disarm the Indians. The real problem was their aggressiveness with respect to other Indian tribes. It thus appears from these remarks that for Rondon the Indians were capable only of reacting, not of acting, so that they would react to kindness with kindness or to aggression with aggression, but they were not themselves initiators. Everything is dependent on the attitude of the civilized person. After all, the Indians were "fetishists."[9]

For Rondon, pacification would be on the agenda of the "Inspetoria Federal de Proteção Fraterna aos Indígenas," while the Comissão again regarded the army as the agent of pacification. For Silva and Miranda, pacification would be achieved by lay representatives and by Indians who had already undergone their "catechism."

Also, for Silva and Miranda, there would be *centers of civilization* for the Indians, which would serve to attract the scattered groups. Von Ihering and Pitanga proposed similarly that "colonies" would be established in frontier areas so that "tame Indians" could attract, "fraternally seize," and "settle" the "wild Indians." Von Ihering went even further to suggest the organization of *bandeiras*, or expeditionary groups sent off into the hinterlands. These *bandeiras* would consist of civilians, preferably *sertanejos*, rather than soldiers.

Pacification was regarded by both von Ihering and Pitanga as a possible alternative for what was imagined to be otherwise inevitable: the dissolution of these groups when confronted with a "stronger [superior] civilization." Silva's perspective was not altogether different. He wanted the "savage" to be kept alive in order to strengthen the nation as a whole, while the Indian secured his place in the history of Brazil, and also to serve as the subject of research.

In addition to protection and pacification, every indigenist project aimed to solve the problem of transforming the Indian from their evolutionarily inferior stage of "savagery" to the superior stage of "civilization." Proposals in this area were conjoined with suggestions as to the possible roles Indian peoples could play in the nation-state.

The Main Ideas of the Fraternal Protection Position

The agents directly responsible for implementing the state's indigenist action were themselves in dispute. Figures 1–3 outline the positions taken by a cross section of these agents. Viewing these agents in terms of "positions," I propose that there were effectively five positions, identified with, but not restricted to, von Ihering, Daltro, Pitanga, Jorge, and "Fraternal Protection," which includes the other authors shown in the figures.

The "fraternal protection" position was the one officialized in SPILTN. The term should not be confused with "protection," as discussed earlier, which refers to a demand made on the state for a certain type of action. Miranda (1910b) used the term before Congress to defend the creation of SPILTN within MAIC. The term was used by all indigenist agents.

The fraternal protection position was promoted mainly by agents and agencies from the political and intellectual fields, with the state being predominant. The Positivist Church of Brazil, which acted as a "propagandist" primarily through the writings of Texeira Mendes, was itself an agency within the political field. Similarly, although Silva is listed here an ethnographer, in fact he also belonged to an agency, namely, the National Geographic Society. As regards the Comissão, its active participation came to an end at the time SPILTN was create (see the *Revista do Centro de Ciências, Letras e Artes de Campinas* of 1914: 35–36, 103–104).

The scholarly trajectories of individuals linked to these positions was like that of Mendes, Rondon, and Miranda. Generally, these author/actors received training as engineers, since engineering was among the academic programs that most reflected the positivist ideology. Thus, on the whole, they took the view that the nation was a collective individual that must be protected and guided by the state.

In addition to orthodox positivist elements, the fraternal protection position incorporated elements elaborated within the army. The principal idea so incorporated was that of the need for "national salvation," which was regarded as a task for a certain kind of "missionary," namely, the "soldier." The military engineer, "empirical builder" of the nation, was portrayed in virtually religious terms. He was seen as analogous to the Jesuit as a fighter for faith. Among his characteristics were: moral aptness, a firm will, technical knowledge, love of the cause, "constancy/stability, friendship, and suffering," calmness, abnegation, and an easygoing spirit. Such attributes were generalized to all of the agents charged with responsibility for directly interacting with Indians. The prototypical image was that of Cândido Mariano da Silva Rondon himself.

Rondon, indeed, formulated the best and most complete proposal for fraternal protection, which was expressed in his plan for an Inspetoria Federal de Proteção Fraterna aos Indígenas. However, the agency that actually took shape included more than Rondon had originally suggested. It included as well a plan for the "settlement of national workers," something that did not appear in any of Rondon's statements. There was thus within the Ministry of Agriculture, Industry, and Commerce a fusion of agendas involved in the formation of SPILTN.

Figure 1. State Operating Procedures in Indigenist Action and the Agents of Direct Action

Author	von Ihering	Mendes	Daltro	Rondon	Comissão	Pitanga	Silva	Jorge	Miranda
State operating procedure	Supervision of missionaries and laity[a]	Supervision of missionaries and laity	Aid to nonofficial lay action	Supervision of laity and missionaries (creation of a state indigenist agency)[b, c]	Supervision	Aid to catechismal instruction and to nonofficial lay action	Creation of a state indigenist agency	Aid to religious catechism	Creation of a state indigenist agency
Agent of direct indigenous action	Missionaries	Civil servants	Laypersons who do not work for the government	Special representatives (from the state indigenist agency)	Public security forces; the army	Missionaries; laypersons who do not work for the government	Secular representatives (from the state indigenist agency); teachers	Missionaries	(Representatives from the state indigenist agency)

a Von Ihering stresses the role of the state as organizer but not implementer of pacification expeditions.
b In this and other charts, comments in parentheses are my own.
c It is worth mentioning that Rondon's letter, replying to an invitation from Miranda to create a commission for catechism of the Indians, states that Rondon agreed on the condition that he would take part in the commission.

Figure 2. The Aims of Indigenist Action

aim \ author	VON IHERING	MENDES	DALTRO	RONDON	COMISSAO	PITANGA	SILVA	JORGE	MIRANDA
To live together peacefully	+	(+)	(+)	+	+	(+)	(+)	(+)	(+)
To ensure the physical survival of the Indians	(+)	(+)	+	(+)	(+)	(+)	(+)	(+)	(+)
To permit scientific study	+						+	+	
To transmit Christianity								+	
To integrate the Indians with the rural population	+					+	+	+	(+)
To have the Indians acquire civilized manners	(+)	(+)	+	+	(+)	(+)	+	(+)	(+)
To increase the "friendly influence" over the Indians				+	(+)				
To have the Indians become sedentary	(+)	+	(+)	+	(+)	(+)	(+)	(+)	(+)
To populate the interior			+	(+)		+	(+)	+	+
To access economic resources in Indian territory					+				(+)
To increase Indian agricultural productivity		+	(+)	+		(+)	(+)	+	(+)
To use Indian people as labor			+	+		+	+	+	+
To strengthen nationalism		(+)	+	+	(+)	+	+	+	+

Note: Marks placed in parentheses indicate my inference from the text. Where parentheses are not used, the author explicitly stated the aim in his text.

Figure 3. Indigenist Practices of Interference in the Lives of Indian Peoples

practice ＼ author	VON IHERING	MENDES	DALTRO
Method of intervention	Respect for intertribal differences Catechism and learning not compulsory Freedom and supervision for those who want to migrate Proficiency in Indian languages; catechismal instruction to Indians accustomed to rural life Implement catechism gradually	Deal with Indians as independent nations Pacification activity	Organization of Indian centers in areas chosen by whites Dwelling privileges for leaders Encourage the drive for cultural data
Change in cultural habits	Introduce Christian morality	Abolition of anthropophagy and intertribal wars Change in hygiene Introduction of clothing Change in dwelling patterns, musical culture	Change in the areas destined for living quarters Initiation to new orientation to work (tools, habits, conception)
Interference in economic life		Introduction to agricultural and industrial (arts and crafts) techniques Introduction to technology	Supply technology (agriculture, etc.) Introduction to new techniques of cultivation Commerce
Utilization of Indian labor	Work should not be expected from Indians		Development of agriculture, commerce, and industry (trades)
Education	Teaching of "Christian morality" without the imposition of religious doctrine	Respect for free initiative for moral and religious transformation sponsored by missionaries without supporting it	Formal teaching of arts and crafts, fine arts, literature, and science

practice \ author	RONDON	COMISSÃO	PITANGA
Method of intervention	Learning not compulsory Noninterference in family organization Continuity of work Gradual and patient initiation to indigenist practices Affectionate, friendly influence Payment for the use of land owned by the Indians	Freedom to migrate; villages not compulsory Settlement of military colonies along tribal boundaries to supervise and protect No coercion of Indians to change	Organization of Indian centers in selected areas; fluency in Indian languages; gradual passage from cattle-raising stage to sedentary village dwelling
Change in cultural habits	Elimination of intertribal conflicts Introduction of new cultural needs and information Change in living patterns	Initiation to technology Alchohol forbidden	Emphasize the spread of commmon dialects Settle nomadic groups
Interference in economic life	Initiation of new techniques of cultivation Introduction of technology	Exchange of Indian products for civilized products	Introduction of agricultural techniques and technology Introduction of cattle-raising
Utilization of Indian labor	Development of agriculture and cattle-raising; use of natural resources in Indian territory; conservation of railways and telegraph lines; payment for Indian labor on terms better than those for the region	Development of trade	Use of Indian labor in agriculture and cattle-raising
Education	Informal asystematic teaching born from the new needs.		Teaching of common dialects Professional training

Figure 3 (continued)

practice \ author	SILVA	JORGE	MIRANDA
Method of intervention	Organization of Indian centers in chosen areas	Organization of Indian centers in chosen areas; "love" Indian languages	No alteration of traditional religious habits
Change in cultural habits		Initiation into Christian religion	
Interference in economic life	Introduction of agricultural techniques and technology		Introduction of agricultural techniques and technology
Utilization of Indian labor	Agricultural development	Agricultural development	Agricultural development
Education	Agricultural education	Religious instruction	Agricultural education

Although the official history portrays Rondon as having acted in large measure autonomously, the process of establishing SPILTN necessarily involved compromise with other groups, such as the Sociedade Nacional de Agricultura (SNA) (cf. Lima 1985: 271–470).

The fraternal protection position proposed that the state should act through a specific agency (SPITLN) to demarcate Indian lands, to transfer Indians to new territories when necessary, to oversee the protection of Indians, and to pacify wild Indians in accord with the motto of "friendship and kindness." Regarding the discourse and practice of *attraction* and *pacification*, further research would show that there was nothing original about Rondon's methods—the offering of presents, an attitude of nonaggression, and so on—since many of these date back to the Jesuits in the colonial period.

The fraternal protection position also argued that the state should take responsibility for supervising lay and missionary activities with respect to the Indians. In this regard, the Comissão proposed the Army as the active agent of public force in federal but not state areas. Silva specifically mentioned teachers, among the group of lay representatives. In fact, all of these various agents formed part of the original SPILTN.

Thanks to these new indigenist tasks, the scope of state action with respect to the nation was expanding. In some accounts, the "nation" was seen as consisting of local people (e.g., rubber-trappers, farmers, colonists, and rural workers), but specifically in opposition to the Indians, who were regarded as enemies. The purpose of indigenist action would be to overcome this opposition and to fully integrate the frontier regions. Von Ihering (1911: 125) even mentioned the possibility of federal intervention into the state-level oligarchies in order to restrain their actions. The state was clearly growing in power.

Rondon's success in setting up telegraph lines—one vehicle of state control over the interior—and establishing the Indians as guardians of these lines actually accomplished a threefold task: (1) it resulted in the exploration of the interior and the linking up of distant points within the country; (2) it helped to "nationalize" the Indians and turn them into Brazilians; and, consequently, (3) it placed Brazilians on the frontier, securing the wilderness with rural workers who could act as guardians of the strategic supports of the nation, namely, the railways and telegraph lines (Lima 1985: 428).

Within the boundaries of Brazilian orthodox positivism, a whole pedagogical process was conceived for the Indians. As fetishists, the Indians already had a kind of *order*. It was necessary only to provide them with an opportunity for *progress*.[10] If systematic teaching was not proposed, this was due to the fact that the "needs" for technology, for housing, and for a certain kind of work itself had to be introduced first.

These needs, which would be implanted initially even in the first phase of pacification, would subsequently generate demand for the mastery of craftsmanship and carpentry techniques. Systematic teaching could then follow this in at least some posts (cf. Vasconcelos 1939).

It must be stressed that, in withdrawing the Indians from the influence of their "civilized neighbors" by way of protecting them, and in offering them higher remuneration for their work, the state was aiming to increase its power and influence over them. By this means, the state sought to secure a contingent of para-citizens under its tutelage. Indeed, tutelage and protection went hand in hand.

The Indians were generally regarded as lacking any natural right to self-determination. Consequently, they would not bring any prior biases to the task of defending the national frontier. At the same time, they should be kept from the "metaphysical confusion" that results from participation in political controversy and the democratic process.

In sum, the task of Indian education was twofold: to forge out of Indians Brazilians who could populate the interior and guard the frontier, and to "Brazilianize" immigrants (the Indians) who would then no longer constitute a threat to the nation. The SPI would help to mediate this transition from "hostile Indian" to "national worker." Having undergone this kind of transition, the Indian would be in a position to receive a separate plot of land, become emancipated from the tutelage of the state, and acquire full citizenship. This identity transformation would have to be adequately controlled in order to construct the proper citizen and to avoid producing a "demoralized," "addicted," or "low-life" Indian.

I suggest that this transformative process be thought of as a kind of pedagogy, developed out of a certain *conception of the Indian* (as "proud," "free," etc.) and accomplished by means of various *practices* (attraction, pacification, nationalization, education, etc.), which rested upon general *methods* (constancy, the rewarding of success, etc.) and which were effected by *agents* (inspectors, supervisors, doctors, teachers, etc.) linked to institutions.

The SPI was effective not in the "ethnic eradication" of the Indian, but rather in the inculcation into the Indian of a Brazilian being. This proposition may serve as a starting point for a broader investigation of the forms of alienation from ethnic identity that are implicit in reservation life, in what Oliveira Filho (1988) has called "Indianness."

The view of Indians contained in the fraternal protection position was by no means new (cf. Beozzo 1983; Paoli 1983; Farage 1986). What was special about the situation was the fact that the nation-state had to pledge itself directly to the task of fraternal protection and did so by creating a state agency aimed at mediating Indian-white relationships.

In other words, what was unique was the implementation of this ideology in the form of state policy.

The existence of SPILTN implied that Indian peoples, although theoretically capable of acquiring full citizenship, were in reality subjected to a specific mode of domination. The essential facts of the situation have not changed much up to the present day. At the same time, it is important to realize that intellectuals and politicians have not since that time devoted much thinking to the problem of Indian political participation in Brazilian society. It is safe to assume that this is due to a deeply held belief that the Indians must have spokesmen in order to mediate their access to fundamental rights, and that they are bound in any case to disappear (Paoli 1983: 22), the only question being when.

To cast doubt upon the idea of mediation is to question the applicability of concepts such as citizenship, tutelage, and nation to the Indian situation. I suggest that we begin to think about new concepts and tools for understanding and acting upon matters pertaining to the Indian in contemporary Brazil.

Notes

1. This paper represents part of my master's thesis (Lima 1985), submitted to the Graduate Program in Social Anthropology at the National Museum, Federal University of Rio de Janeiro, for which João Pacheco de Oliveira Filho acted as adviser. I am grateful to him and also to Maria Manuela L. Carneiro da Cunha and Luiz de Castro Faria for their critical analyses. I am indebted especially to the latter for the ideas he contributed to the original work. I would also like to thank Jurandyr Carvalho Ferrari Leite, who worked as my research assistant for the dissertation project, which was funded by a grant from ANPOCS in 1984. The ideas presented here have benefited also from the presentation of a first draft of this paper at the Austin "Nation-State and Indian in Latin America" conference, my participation in which was made possible by a travel grant from the Ford Foundation. Last but not least, I would especially like to thank Laurie Graham, Aracy Lopez da Silva, Daniel Lefkowitz, and Ligia Simonian for their warmth and help from Austin through Boston to New York.

2. *Indianism* and *Indianist*, terms sometimes used for similar purposes in other contexts, mean something quite different in Brazil. They refer to a nineteenth-century literary romantic movement that took the "Indian" as symbol of a newborn nation. For more details, see Queiroz (1962).

3. For a critical discussion of this version, see Lima (1985, chaps. 1–3). See also Gagliardi (1985), where the ideas are uncritically reproduced.

4. For a more detailed study of the social positions of agents and agencies in the debate, see Lima (1985: chap. 5).

5. The "three stage law" is described in Comte (1978: 3–4). See Azzi (1980) for the Brazilian Orthodox Positivist view.

6. Until the Constitution of 1946, states were the owners of all free lands in Brazil. The Constitution transferred these lands to the federal government.

7. This is my inference; the author does not actually use the term *protection*.
8. Pacification theory and practice is the subject of an MA thesis being written by Regina Maria de Carvalho Erthal under Prof. João Pacheco de Oliveira. The thesis is part of the Projeto Estudo Sobre Terras Indígenas no Brasil (PETI) being carried out in the Graduate Program in Social Anthropology at the National Museum in Rio. See Erthal (1986).
9. For further discussion of positivist thought on protection, see Leite (n.d.).
10. Orthodox Positivists were responsible for Brazil's flag, where the expression "Order and Progress" is displayed as a national motto.

References

Azzi, Riolando
  1980 *A concepção da ordem social no positivismo ortodoxo Brasileiro.* São Paulo: Loyola.
Beozzo, José Oscar
  1983 *Leis e regulamentos das missões.* São Paulo: Loyola.
Bourdieu, Pierre
  1968 Campo intelectual e projecto criador. In *Problemas do estruturalismo* Jean Pouillon (ed.), 105–145. Rio de Janeiro: Zahar.
  1974 *A economia das trocas simbólicas.* Introdução, organização e seleção de Sergio Miceli. São Paulo: Ed. Perspectiva.
  1983a O campo científico. In *Pierre Bourdieu: Sociologia*, 122–155. São Paulo: Atica.
  1983b *Questões de sociologia.* Rio de Janeiro: Marco Zero.
Briones, José de Jesús Montoya
  1973 Hacia un nuevo planteamiento y fundamentación del indigenismo. *América Indígena* 33(1): 13–43.
Caso, Alfonso
  1958 Ideals of an action program. National Indigenous Institute of Mexico: a report. *Human Organization* 17(1): 27–29.
Comte, Augusto
  1978 Curso da filosofia positiva. In *Comte*, 1–39. São Paulo: Abril Cultural.
Erthal, Regina Maria de Carvalho
  1986 Atrair e pacificar: a estratégia da conquista. Rio de Janeiro: PETI/ PPGAS—Museu Nacional.
Farage, Nadia
  1986 As muralhas do sertão. MA thesis, Departamento de Ciência Sociais, UNICAMP, Campinas.
Gagliardi, José Mauro
  1985 O indígena e a república: estudo a respeito do Serviço de Proteção aos Indios. MA thesis, Departamento de Ciência Sociais, PUC, São Paulo.
Leite, Jurandyr Carvalho Ferrari
  n.d. Proteção e incorporação: a questão indígena no pensamento político do positivismo ortodoxo. *Revista de Antropologia*, forthcoming.
Lima, Antonio Carlos de Souza
  1985 Aos fetichistas, ordem e progresso: um estudo do campo indigenista no seu estado de formação. MA thesis, PPGAS, Museu National, Rio de

Janeiro.

1989 Os museus de história natural e a construção do indigenismo: notas para uma sociologica das relações entre campo intelectual e campo político no Brasíl. *Communicação* no. 13, PPGAS. Rio de Janeiro: Museu Nacional.

Magalhães, José Vieira Couto de, Gen.

1975 *O selvagem.* Belo Horizonte/São Paulo: Livraria Itatiaia Editora/ EDUSP.

Mauss, Marcel

1969 La nation. *Oeuvres* 7: 573–625. Paris: Les Editions de Minuit.

Miranda, Rodolpho Nogueira da Rocha

1910a Carta dirigida pelo Ministro da Agricultura ao Ten. Cel. Rondon. *Jornal do Comércio*, 3 de Março.

1910b Introdução and Exposição de motivos. Decreto No. 8072 e Projeto de Regulamento do SPILTN. In *Relatório do Ministro da Agricultura ... Rodolpho Nogueira da Rocha Miranda, no ano de 1910*, Brasíl, Ministério da Agricultura, Indústria e Comércio. Rio de Janeiro: Of. da Diretoria Geral de Estatística.

1910c Visita ao Museu Nacional. *Jornal do Comércio*, 24 de Janeiro.

Nolasco Armas, Margarita

1981 A antropologia aplicada no México e seu destino final: o indigenism. In *Antropologia e indigenism na América Latina*, C. Junqueira and E. de A. Carvalho (eds.), 67–85. São Paulo: Cortez Edit.

Oliveira Filho, João Pacheco de

1983 Terras indígenas no Brasíl: uma tentativa de abordagem sociológica. Boletim do Museu Nacional, Nova Série, Antropologia, Rio de Janeiro 44.

1988 O "nosso governo": os Ticuna e o regime tutelar. São Paulo/Brasília: MarcoZero/CNPq.

Oliveira Filho, João Pacheco de, and Antonio Carlos de Souza Lima

1983 Os muitos fôlegos do indigenismo. In *Anuário Antropológico 81*, Roberto Cardoso de Oliveira (ed.), 277–280. Fortaleza: Edições UFC/ Tempo Brasileiro.

Paoli, Maria Célia Pinheiro Machado

1983 O sentido histórico da noção de cidadania no Brasíl: onde ficam os índios? In *O Indio e a Cidadania, Comissão Pró-Indio/SP*, 20–43. São Paulo: Brasiliense.

Pitanga, Antonio Ferreira de Souza

1909 O selvagem perante o direito. *O Direito*, vol. 109: 648–649.

Queiroz, Maria José de

1962 *Do indianismo ao indigenismo nas letras hispano-americanas.* Belo Horizonte: Imprensa da UFMG.

Reis, Elisa Pereira

1983 The nation-state as ideology: the Brazilian case. *IUPERJ: Série Estudos*, no. 18. Rio de Janeiro.

Ribeiro, Darcy

1962 *A política indigenista Brasileira.* Rio de Janeiro: Serviço de Informação Agrícola/Min. da Agricultura.

1979   Edilson Martins entrevista Darcy Ribeiro. *Encontros com a Civilização Brasileira* 12: 81–100.
Rojas, Alfonso Villa
1971   Antropología aplicada y indigenismo en América Latina. *América Indígena* 31(1): 5–44.
Rondon, Cândido Mariano da Silva
1910   Carta dirigida pelo Tenente-Coronel Rondon ao Ministro da Agricultura. *Igreja e Apostolado Positiva*, no. 300.
Stauffer, David Hall
1955   The origin and establishment of Brazil's Indian Service, 1889–1910. PhD diss., University of Texas at Austin.
Stocking, George
1982   Race, culture and evolution. Chicago: University of Chicago Press.
Vasconcelos, Vicente de Paula T. da F.
1939   Relatório do Cel.-Chefe do SPI, Vicente de Paula Vasconcelos, ao Ministro da Agricultura e aos membros do CNPI, em 30 de dezembro de 1939. Rio de Janeiro: SPI.
von Ihering, Hermann
1911   A questão dos índios do Brasíl. *Revista do Museu Paulista* 8: 112–140.
Weber, Max
1974   A nação. In *Ensaios de sociologia*, H. H. Gerth and C. W. Mills (eds.), 201–210. Rio de Janeiro: Zahar.

10. The State and Andean Musical Production in Peru

Thomas Turino

Introduction

Many scholars concerned with art and music tend to view them as part of an autonomous aesthetic sphere, or, at best, as texts that reflect a given social formation. In light of a growing body of social theory, however, artistic production and ideologies about art can be reconceptualized as one site where struggles for cultural domination are waged en route to establishing and maintaining social hierarchies (cf. Gramsci 1971; Bourdieu 1977, 1984; Hall 1985, 1988). Musical practice is in this sense not merely a set of texts to be interpreted. It is also a body of resources that are used in the contest to control definitions of worldview and identity, both intrinsically and extrinsically, among antagonistic factions within given historical moments. The importance of music as an index of social identity also makes it a central resource for the creation of imagery underlying the formation of sociopolitical alliances.

Here I am concerned with how policies and activities of the Peruvian state have influenced musical and other cultural practices among indigenous Andeans. A broad historical overview is presented with special attention to three periods that, using Jameson's terms, might be called times of acute *cultural revolution* (those moments "in which the coexistence of various modes of production becomes visibly antagonistic, their contradictions moving to the very center of political, social, and historical life" leading to the dismantling of former cultural styles and modes of discourse (Jameson 1981: 95–96)). "Cultural revolution" is a perpetual process although it is most evident at times of crisis. Only a brief outline of events surrounding three dramatic periods, however, can be attempted here: 1550–1650 during the colonial era; the Leguia regime (1919–1930); and the Velasco, post-Velasco periods (1968–1985).

State and Nation in Peru

Although Peru became an independent state in 1821, it has yet to become a single "nation" in the sense of a group of people with recognized bonds of unity, a common heritage, and shared goals for the future. The situation, however, cannot simply be described as several nations (e.g., indigenous vs. Hispanic) being contained within the Peruvian territory. Indigenous Andeans in the rural highlands perceive their identity concretely in terms of their localized *ayllu* or community, and the notion of a Quechua or Aymara society is not part of their daily discourse (Montoya 1986: 254). Neither a national Peruvian nor a macroethnic consciousness seems strongly evidenced as a basis for unified political or social action among rural peasants or most urban migrants from this background.

The localized purview of indigenous Andeans is matched by the factionalism along lines of economic interest among elite groups since the colonial period. Competition between the colonial clergy and secular state officials is but one example. The social unit defined in cultural and class terms as *criollo* (New World Hispanic) that has directed state operations since the birth of the republic must also be understood in terms of a complex web of competing factions and shifting alliances.

The localized vision of Andean peasants does not imply cultural isolation or "purity" free from *criollo* and mestizo influences. As the following historical outline indicates, sociocultural interaction has been long and profound between the urban-based, Hispanic-oriented state and indigenous rural communities. Nonetheless, I would argue that, surprisingly, in the musical as well as other realms, fundamentally distinct aesthetic and cultural styles have been maintained among some rural Andean groups notwithstanding the centuries-old process of negotiation (Turino 1987, 1989). Central questions arise as to why and how this might be so.

The Colonial Period

Throughout Peruvian history, regional and centralized elites have ruled the indigenous population largely by force through the courts and military. Indigenous populations were incorporated into the colonial system first as part of grants from the Crown to Spanish *encomenderos* who acted as trustees. Tribute was funneled to, and labor organized for, the *encomendero* through community headmen (*curacas*) who comprised an indigenous elite and who often adopted European cultural style (Arriaga 1968: 51; Guaman Poma 1980). After the 1560s, the *encomenderos'* grants and tribute returned to direct Crown control and were administered by colonial state officials (*corregidores*). Under Viceroy Toledo (1569–1581), the dispersed Andean population was concentrated into urban settlements (*reducciones*) augmenting political control, and facilitating tribute extraction and the drafting of forced labor for the mines.

The church officials and missionaries were integrally tied to the colonial state that financially supported them through tribute income.[1] The prime political role of the church was to convert Andeans to a European ideology and modes of behavior, and thus strengthen the ground for an acceptance of Spanish political legitimacy and moral superiority, as well as to subvert the indigenous religious base of the former political system. Conversion was also a major rationalization for colonialization (Wachtel 1973). For Viceroy Toledo, an express purpose of the *reducciones* settlements was to facilitate missionary work, indicating the government's concern in this realm (Marzal 1969: 102; Kubler 1946: 360; Albo 1966: 407).

During the sixteenth century, the Christianization process was largely unsuccessful because of a lack of personnel, the clergy's association with secular elites, and their joint exploitation of Andeans (Guaman Poma 1980: 533–620; Stern 1987: 75), as well as the coercive approaches utilized. As the Peruvian Guaman Poma observed at the time, people cannot become Christians out of fear (1980: 570). Nonetheless, at the beginning of the seventeenth century, repression was stepped up in an "extirpation of idolatry" campaign meant to speed the process of conversion.

Father Arriaga and other clergymen during the sixteenth and first half of the seventeenth centuries accurately observed that Andean cultural artifacts and practices, and even semiotic forms such as names, were central to the reproduction of indigenous worldview:

> No one who saw them performing these celebrations thought there was any malice in it but considered them pastimes, traditional dances, and so forth. If the Indians were thereby indulging in vain superstitions, the fact hardly needed to be noticed. In like fashion, no attention was paid to their names or surnames which were those of the idols or ancestors, used for superstitious reasons . . .
>
> The fact that these activities were passed over and little or no notice was taken of them has led the Indians to keep them up and perform them with impunity. . . . It is from these sources in addition to incest and many other wicked practices that the idolatry of past centuries has arisen. (Arriaga 1968: 70–71)

A basic thrust of the Christianization campaign was thus the assimilation of Andeans into European sociocultural modes of life. Over time, because of Andean resistance, a more realistic attitude became prevalent among missionaries: beliefs and cultural practices that hindered conversion (and thus, implicitly, European ideological control) should be done away with and the rest might as well be tolerated (see Albo 1966: 398–400; Kubler 1946: 401). What constituted "pure idolatry" or a hindrance to conversion and what might be considered merely harmless superstition or custom, however, was inconsistently defined.

The problem of language had to be faced immediately if missionary activities were to go forward. At the beginning of the colonial period it was thought that Spanish would be taught as the language of religious conversion (Marzal 1969: 91; Armas 1953: 90), but by 1567, it had become official policy that missionary teachings and the sacraments were to be given in the native languages to facilitate Christianization (Vargas 1951: 225). Quechua became the most common language used by missionaries and, as in the previous Inca period, it was spread to regions where it had not been spoken previously. While this may have contributed to the abandonment of minority languages (excluding Aymara),[2] it resulted in aiding the conservation of Quechua generally (Albo 1966: 406).

The status of music and dance within the conversion process was more complex. Abundant evidence indicates that from the pre-Columbian period to the present these domains, along with ritual drinking, were directly associated with, and consistently accompanied, Andean religious ritual. Therefore, as a part of the coercive measures to stamp out idolatry, Andean musical performance was officially outlawed and instruments were systematically destroyed beginning in the late 1500s. Article 104 of the Segundo Concilio Limense of 1567 states:

> That the common superstitious abuses that almost all the Indians practice regarding their ancestors [including] drunkenness and [the performance of] *taquies* [songs] and offering sacrifices in honor of the devil at times of planting and harvest and at other times when they begin some affair of importance; all this is totally forbidden, for which the Indians should be warned three times, and after that if they still transgress, they should be rigorously punished by the bishop. (Vargas 1951: 253–254)

Involved in the extirpation of idolatry campaign himself, Father Arriaga describes how the inquisitors would travel from community to community interviewing the inhabitants about their customs and possessions including religious objects, musical instruments, and dance costumes: "When the visitor examines an Indian privately he writes down what he tells him about these things, and at the same time, by his order, they exhibit what they claim to possess. Everything that is inflammable is burned at once and the rest is broken into pieces" (1968: 19). Arriaga states that when the clergy witnessed indigenous festivals where music and dance were performed the instruments would be immediately destroyed, and he lists some of the types involved: drums (probably *tinyas*); *succhas* (trumpets? of deer skulls, see Poma 1980: 295); silver and copper trumpets; "the great coiled horns which they play, called *antari* and *pututu*, and other instruments called *pincollos*, which are bone or cane flutes" (1968: 50, 69).[3] On one trip alone between February 1617 and July 1618, Arriaga mentions that the inquisitors extracted 5,694 confessions of idolatry, 669 "ministers of idolatry" were discovered and punished, and 603 principal *huancas* were taken away from the people, among a variety of other artifacts including musical instruments and dance costumes (1968: 20; see Kubler 1946: 400).

That such repressive measures ultimately failed to root out Andean religious and musical artifacts, practices, and values is attested by the strength of both Andean musical culture and religion presently in the rural southern sierra (Turino 1987, 1989; Allen 1988; Bastien 1978). As is common with the use of force and negative sanctions for sociopolitical control, a reaction of resistance is often augmented, and Andeans simply responded by becoming clandestine in these matters. By the 1660s, the church fathers were satisfied that Christianization had been achieved, and the campaign ceased.

A much more lasting effect on Andean musical practice and aesthetics involved the teaching of European music. It is well known that throughout the Americas, missionaries found music, dance, and pageantry to be, perhaps, the most potent tools for interesting Indians in church activities (Béhague 1979: 1–5; Marzal 1969; Albo 1966; Warkentin 1981: 45). The Third Lima Council (1583) gives official recognition to the power of music, pageantry, and the "external" aspects of worship for the conversion of Andeans:

> Ultimately, because it is certain and well-known that this nation of Indians is attracted and highly motivated to knowing and worshipping God with external ceremonies and aspects of worship; there is much to be gained by the clergy who use divine worship fashioned with as great a level of perfection and splendor as possible, and to this end take care that there is a school and chapel of singers and in addition, music with flutes, chirimias and other instruments in the churches. (Vargas 1951: 374)

Missionaries in the Andes promptly initiated the teaching of European musical forms and instruments to the native population, although the educational process largely focused on children of the indigenous elite.

A typical curriculum included religious doctrine, Spanish, reading and writing, arithmetic, and musical training (Quezada 1985: 75; Marzal 1969: 104). A document from 1575 regarding a mission school in Quito states that the Indians were taught "to play all the [European] musical instruments, [including] keyboard and strings, sakbuts, chirimias, flutes, trumpets, and polyphonic singing" (Vargas 1953: 212). The great diffusion of stringed instruments (nonexistent in pre-Columbian Peru) such as the diatonic harp, the violin, and the guitar, and the birth of Andean mestizo musical culture generally, was initiated to a large degree by missionary activities.

The Andeans' receptivity and great ability to master European polyphonic music both instrumentally and vocally is commonly reported by Spanish observers of the time (e.g., see Stevenson 1968: 277–288). Consistent with the official policy allowing the use of native languages for conversion, religious texts in Quechua were set to music essentially in European style as is exemplified by a piece in four-part polyphony, "Hanacpachap," printed in 1631 (Béhague 1979: 4; Quezada 1985: 76).[4] In addition to the use of European music, Andean melodies with religious Quechua texts also provided a central tool for conversion as is described by the sixteenth-century missionary, José de Acosta:

> Our [clergy] that goes among them [Andeans] have put the things of our sacred faith in their music [*en su modo de canto*], and it is a great thing serving to attract them, because with the joy of singing, they repeat the song for entire days without tiring. Also they have put in their language our compositions and melodies . . . and it is wonderful how the Indians take to them, and how much they like them. (cited in Albo 1966 [1590]: 412)

Besides the attraction music held for Andeans, Acosta's observation regarding the repetitive quality of the singing might indicate another reason why music was particularly useful for implanting new ideas.

The merging of Andean and European cultural resources, fostered because of its utility for Christianization, is evident in these musical practices. The advent of religious, cultural, and musical syncretism is also exemplified in the performance of religious festivals. The Spanish clergy in Peru superimposed Catholic fiestas on preexisting Andean celebrations (see Valcarcel 1946). Since the union of music, dance, and pageantry was central to the celebration of pre-Columbian religious ritual, it is easy to understand why these components were such potent tools for conversion: as modes of representing religious meaning and knowledge, their association with such contexts was already established.

While the performance of indigenous music and dance associated with idolatry was officially banned after 1567, the combining of indigenous and European musical instruments, forms, and dramatic dances in Catholic events is commonly reported even during the years of the extirpation of idolatry campaign (e.g., Marzal 1969; Albo 1966; Schechter 1984). According to Stevenson, in 1610 during a festival in Cusco, indigenous songs and dances traditionally used in praise of the Inca ancestors were transformed to contain Catholic themes, and a statue of Baby Jesus dressed in Inca garments was paid homage. In this event, the use of indigenous drums and trumpets was combined with the performance of European *chirimías* (1968: 298–299).

Indigenous dance dramas that included the use of animal and monster masks and costuming were incorporated into Corpus Christi in Cusco during the early colonial period according to Inca Garcilaso de la Vega (1945: part 2, book 8, chap. 2). This type of costumed-dance tradition later fused with European carnival and fiesta dances to form the mainstay of contemporary mestizo fiesta practice. In a similar manner, European religious plays (*Autos Sacramentales*) such as the "Battle of Christians and Moors" used for conversion during colonial festivals were transformed to include local meaning in extant dance dramas like the "Battle of Atahualpa and Pizarro."

As resources for the reproduction of Andean religious beliefs and worldview, indigenous music, songs, and dance were clearly viewed as a threat to European ideological and political dominance by the colonial state. Official repression of these forms, and the concomitant fostering of European musical practices were central mechanisms by which the state attempted to alter Andean worldview. At the same time, the allowance of indigenous language and musical/dance practices under the guise of Christian trappings proved too tempting as a means for involving Andeans with the European religion.

Thus, both the carrot and the stick were brought to bear on Andean musical culture in a political discourse couched in religious terms. As is indicated by writers of the time as well as contemporary analysts, the use of force resulted in the clandestine maintenance of indigenous values and practices and was an obstacle to Christianization. Coercion, for people who saw no possibility of joining the superordinate group, seems to have resulted in a heightened retrenchment in the original identity unit and in the preservation of its markers as a means of resistance. Hence, the alienating brutality and relative inflexibility of the Peruvian colonial system may have been one cause for the continuity of Andean cultural practices into the present day. Conversely, the positive approach of teaching European ways and the liberal allowance for syncretism had the greater, longer lasting ideological and cultural impact. Indeed, many features of contemporary highland mestizo and indigenous musical culture were initiated by these means.

The Republican Era

The fragile nature of ideological domination in colonial Peru is evidenced by the number and violence of Andean uprisings during the eighteenth century including the famous revolt of Tupac Amaru in the 1780s. Because of the threat that Tupac Amaru and other rebels had posed to colonial rule, the use of Quechua by the clergy for teaching was officially outlawed and "was stigmatized socially and politically" after the 1780s (Escobar, Matos Mar, and Alberti 1975: 61). Thus, the primary Andean cultural domain that had escaped repression during the colonial era finally came under attack. The so-called "Age of Andean Insurrection" (see Stern 1987) underscores the tremendous gulf between the Andean population and Peruvian elites on the eve of the republican era, a gulf that would hinder "nation" building into the present day.

Military leaders tied to traditional land-based elites held sway during the first fifty years of the republic, but in response to heightened international capitalist penetration (1870–1930), rising commercial and agroexporting factions, located on the coast, began to challenge the military caudillos in the 1860s. Colonial patterns of domination over the indigenous population were not altered by either group because of their need for Andeans' labor and land. During the nineteenth century, little official state action regarding Andean cultural practice is evident. *Criollos* continued to look to European cultural models (Iturriaga and Estenssoro 1985: 115), while at the same time, Andean music and other cultural forms were disparaged or largely ignored by national and local elites, probably aiding the persistence of musical pluralism in the highlands.

After the War of the Pacific with Chile (1879–1883), however, new nationalistic currents arose that once again focused attention on Andean cultural forms within the dominant society. Among many explanations for the country's defeat, Manuel Gonzalez Prada echoed a broader sentiment in suggesting that Peru was not a unified nation and hence could not defend itself as one. He observed that the large indigenous population lacked national consciousness because they had been systematically oppressed. This statement intimately linked "national problem"—the lack of sociopolitical, cultural, and economic integration—to the "Indian problem," and foreshadowed the ideological movement known as *indigenismo* that was to have a profound effect on Andean cultural practice throughout the twentieth century (Francke Ballue 1978).

State-Andean Relations during the Leguia Period

The reemergence of an active role by the Peruvian state in the domains of Andean cultural practice must be understood against the backdrop of the *indigenista* movement during the eleven-year government of President Augusto B. Leguia (1919–1930), as well as in regard to his own political agendas. In the years leading up to Leguia's rule, the state was founded on an alliance between the provincial landed oligarchies and major exporting families in Lima, maintaining the gulf between the lower classes and these elite factions.

In the initial stage of his government, Leguia attempted to counteract the fragmented and isolated position of the state by developing a strong centralist government, subordinating these elite factions to the state, and by trying to gain popular support among the proletariat, the indigenous peasantry, and the middle class. According to Cotler, this represents the first attempt during the Peruvian republican period in which a government attempted to represent the national interests of the "popular" classes and, "in Gramscian terms, establish a position of hegemony" (see Cotler 1978: 184–187).

Leguia's populist stance—in the drive to consolidate his own position against the former power bloc—was largely canceled by his heavy involvement with U.S. capital in the move to "modernize" the country. After 1922 he repeatedly had to choose the interests of foreign capital over those of the national popular classes, and repressive measures in response to peasant and worker protest increasingly began to replace his brief attempt to establish hegemony. For example, toward the end of his rule he instituted a law that facilitated the legalization of ownership of land usurped from indigenous communities (Cotler 1978: 199), thereby negating his symbolic gestures toward Andeans.

In addition to moves to consolidate his own power, Leguia's symbolic pro-Indian stance must be understood in the context of the larger ideological climate fostered by the *indigenista* movement. The state's position should be interpreted dialectically both as an effect and a partial cause of this movement.

Indigenismo emerged among middle- and upper-class intellectuals in urban centers, primarily Lima, Cusco, and Puno, between 1910 and the 1940s. Andeans were rarely directly involved in *indigenista* activities themselves, although they were the focus of concern and, in some cases, the recipients of legal aid and moral support. Not to be seen as unified ideology, various currents are evident although all share paternalistic attitudes toward Andeans, and all are concerned with problems of national/regional identity and integration. Identity emblems from indigenous society were chosen because they provided the clearest

contrast with European, U.S., and—for the highland intellectuals reacting against coastal capitalists—*criollo* culture. A conservative *indigenista*
trend suggested forceful assimilation of Andeans into *criollo* society as
a way of solving the "Indian problem." On the opposite end of the
spectrum, mestizo and *criollo* intellectuals with liberal or leftist leanings began to take an interest in the actual political and economic
oppression of indigenous communities.

Despite Leguia's increased use of coercion after 1922, marking a failure
to initiate hegemony, official state policy echoed a moderate *indigenista*
position. Article 58 of the 1920 constitution, for example, states that:
"the state will protect the indigenous race and dictate laws especially for
its development and culture in harmony with its necessities. The
Nation recognizes the legal existence of the indigenous communities"
(Basadre 1968: 44). In 1920, the government established the Comisión
Pro-Indigena made up of well-known *indigenistas* from Cusco and Puno
who were to investigate ways of resolving the "Indian problem." In
1921, the government proclaimed June 24 as a national holiday, Día del
Indio, and the Section for Indigenous Affairs was created under the
direction of the Indigenista Hildebrado Castro. The collusion of moderate *indigenista* intellectuals with the state, and the latter's attempt to
co-opt the movement, is indicated here.

The Patronato de la Raza Indigena was established in 1922 for the legal
protection of Andeans' rights, and in the same year the use of free
indigenous labor traditionally obligated by local authorities was outlawed. Ironically, the central government had already instituted a law
that obliged Andeans to work without pay on the construction of roads
(Cotler 1978: 188–189). While seemingly contradictory, these two laws
underline Leguia's overriding concern with weakening local elites and
strengthening the national government's control.

That the pro-Andean gestures remained ineffectual and largely symbolic has been commented on by a number of writers and by Leguia
himself in a speech made in 1924:

> The Indian is everything in Peru, and in turn we treat him like a
> serf. What have we done to remedy this? We have produced
> ineffectual laws, created bureaucratic organisms to defend him. We
> have . . . responded with sterile declarations [to] the painful echo of
> his complaints. This can not continue. To defend the Indian
> signifies the defense of our economic life. (Cited in Basadre 1968:
> 309)

In spite of such declarations, abuses against indigenous communities
such as land snatching in the southern sierra continued. When indig-

enous communities responded in violent rebellion, as in the Wancho-Lima uprising in Huancane, Puno, in 1923–1924, local troops were sent in to protect large landowners—indicating the state's commitment to defending Andeans (see Tamayo 1982: 229–243).

Indigenistas also focused on Andean society in the spirit of romantic nationalism through academic and artistic activities. Anthropological and folkloristic studies were initiated. Writers began to publish Quechua poetry, and Andean subjects were presented in novels and paintings. Perhaps it is because music and dance were both central Andean art forms, and recognizable as such from a European perspective, that they were granted special attention in the *indigenistas'* quest for nationalistic-regionalistic emblems.

Urban academic composers in Lima, Cusco, Puno, and other Peruvian cities modeled works on romantic interpretations of Andean musical genres in a European idiom (Llorens 1983; Turino 1988). Cultural organizations such as Centro Qosqo de Arte Nativo in Cusco were formed to preserve and diffuse "indigenous" music and dance. These institutions featured urban mestizos performing stylized, costumed versions of rural Andean dances in stage contexts. The musicians, too, were usually middle- or upper-middle-class mestizos. They blended instruments associated with the Andean peasantry such as the *kena* (end-notched flute) and *charango* (small stringed instrument) with guitars, mandolins, violins, and somewhat later, accordions in an ensemble type known as *estudiantina*. In addition to these larger orchestras, *indigenista* musicians also placed emphasis on solo performance with instruments such as the guitar, harp, and *charango*, as well as performed in smaller ensembles that mixed Andean and European instruments.

The musical repertory consisted of: indigenous melodies that were stylized and arranged primarily according to Western aesthetics; new compositions supposedly based on Andean music (e.g., the fox-trot *inkaico*); as well as mestizo genres such as the *wayno, yaravi,* and *marinera*. Performance included the use of European-influenced harmony, timbres, texture, and pitch ranges. Recordings of the style from the 1930s and scores of *indigenista* music indicate that overall it was smoother, with a softer, less strident sound than is typical of indigenous musical performance.

Rather than serving their stated goal of preserving indigenous music and dance, the *indigenistas* created their own new syncretic musical styles (Turino 1984), and initiated the "folklorization" of Andean music. In addition, in rural areas they altered indigenous styles through their involvement with local peasants from a position of greater social power and from their base in Western aesthetics. The most dramatic case that I am aware of in rural Puno is an *indigenista's* creation of a panpipe harmony atypically using parallel thirds (an Iberian trait), and his organization of a peasant ensemble to play the style under his strict direction (Turino 1987: 151–162, 1990).

Consistent with Leguia's attempt to symbolically align himself with Andean society and middle-class intellectuals, the government actively supported *indigenista* musical activities. Whereas previously public performances of Andean music by highlanders in Lima had been rare, in 1927 Leguia and the metropolitan government invited the participation of *serranos* for the Fiesta of San Juan on the Pampa de Amancaes in the capital. Falling on the official Día del Indio, the fiesta provided the first major public context for the performance of sierra-based music by highlanders in Lima. This well-attended event included what was one of the first formal "Andean music" performance contests held in Peru. The winner of the contest in 1927 was a trio from Cusco who performed *yaravis*, *waynos*, and "war dances" with two *kenas* (Andean flutes) accompanied by piano. (The mixture of instruments here is indicative of *indigenista* aesthetics generally.) The musicians were awarded their prize by Leguia himself (Vivanco 1973: 34).

In the fiesta the following year, a contest for unpublished compositions within the category of "Incaic" Andean music was held. The process of inventing a tradition that was clearly divorced from Andean musical culture is underlined by the juxtaposition of "Inca" imagery with the academic tradition of written composition. Indeed, the competitors were well-known *indigenista*-academic composers and musicians of the highland-urban middle-class and elite. Also in 1928, urban-mestizo *indigenista* musical ensembles including Centro Qosqo de Arte Nativo came to represent their departments (Vivanco 1973: 35; Rozas 1985: 265).

Thus, it was clearly not indigenous music performed by rural Andeans that was featured at Amancaes, but rather the emergent mestizo styles of *indigenista* performers—for example, the combination of piano and *kena*, and the *estudiantinas*. Nonetheless, the symbolic importance of "Andean" music for Leguia is indicated by his speech at Amancaes in 1928:

Señores. Nothing better reflects the collective psychology as the music of the people. . . In our Inca music exists the race, the imperial power, the hectatomb of the conquest, the pain of more than three centuries of domination, and the richness of an overflowing glory after this unfortunate event.

The vernacular artists that have come from all corners of the country to take part in this occasion attest to the marvels of our folklore, the riches of our musical sources and original choreographic art. (*La Crónica*, June 25, 1928, cited in Vivanco 1973: 37)

This speech occurred at a time when Leguia had all but abandoned the potential for creating a functioning hegemonic position. But the state, as represented by its head, remained actively involved in the production of nationalistic imagery favoring Andean society, although such gestures were both romantically conceived and were not backed by concrete legislative measures.

The imagery, and the ideology that it represents, however, were significant in themselves and had lasting consequences. Within the dominant society, the orthodox vision of the marginality and "natural" inferiority of indigenous Andeans and their cultural forms had been questioned, at least at some level, by middle-class intellectuals, and such questioning had been validated by the state. This both produced the seeds for further legitimization of Andean culture within the dominant society, as well as provided an impetus for changes in Andeans' self-perceptions as they increasingly moved into the social space of the national society by migrating to urban centers (Bordieu 1985).

After the fall of Leguia in 1930, the state's direct involvement with Andean cultural practice subsided until the 1960s. The entrance of Andean-based music and dance into the mainstream society, however, had been initiated. The trend was fortified after the 1940s by the growing presence of Andean migrants in Lima. The market thus produced led to the establishment of a flourishing highland music industry in the 1950s and 1960s, and to the creation of a new commercial country music style that blended highland-mestizo and urban-Western indices (Llorens 1983; Turino 1987, 1988).

State and Cultural Institutions and the "Folklorization" of Andean Music

The state's official relation to Andean cultural production was reinstituted in 1962 with the establishment of the Casa de la Cultura that, under Velasco in 1972, was converted into the Instituto Nacional de Cultura (INC) assuming the functions and resources of the former. In effect, this state institution became the central umbrella organization both at the national and regional levels directing cultural activities and policy-making. Other cultural institutions were linked to the state through the INC including the National Schools of Music, Fine Arts, Dramatic Arts, Ballet, and Arte Folklórico (Ansion 1986: 145). Worth noting, the emergent message from the taxonomy of these schools is that *music* is defined as European music, and "fine art" is circumscribed by the European tradition, while Andean arts ("folklore") are placed outside of, and I would add, below, these categories. Even so, the Casa de la Cultura stressed the need to preserve and promote Andean "folklore" particularly under the leadership of Peruvian novelist and ethnographer José María Arguedas during 1963–1964. Arguedas's passionate attention to, and profound knowledge of, Andean culture set the tone for, or at least influenced, subsequent directors of the Casa de la Cultura and the INC.

An important difference between the earlier *indigenista* interpreters of highland music and these cultural functionaries was that they fostered musical performance and recording by rural Andeans themselves, thus providing the possibility for somewhat greater auto-control. But the official interest in Andean arts must at least partially be credited to the door opened by the earlier *indigenistas* and the nationalistic concerns that remained. In many respects, Arguedas and those that followed him were still involved with the romantic "folklorization" of Andean arts initiated within the *indigenismo* movement.

The situation is a complex one. Because of their relatively high prestige and their institutional base, intellectuals like Arguedas have been able to effectively work at countering prejudicial attitudes against Andean culture among *criollos*, and feelings of cultural inferiority among Andeans in Lima and elsewhere.[5] With the best of intentions, these cultural administrators were, and are, fighting for the legitimacy, recognition, and preservation of Andean arts through actions such as organizing performance contests, theater-stage presentations, and "folklore" schools. In the very act of doing so, however, they are bowing to the greater prestige of urban-Western values and institutions by suggesting that such contexts are the final proving ground for performers and art forms. Moreover, in such contexts Andean arts are highly influenced by urban-Western aesthetics and *criollo* stereotypes regarding Andeans. Legitimacy is indeed enhanced but on *criollo* terms and within their control. The performance contest (*concurso folklórico*) provides a prime example of the dynamics involved. This type of urban-based context for Andean music and dance, beginning at least as early as 1927 at Amancaes, has been diffused throughout the country and is still central to the INC's efforts to preserve indigenous Andean traditions.

The Velasco Era

Peasant and guerrilla movements for land control in the Peruvian highlands during the 1950s and 1960s (see Handelman 1975), in combination with rising militancy among urban labor, and corruption in the civilian government led to a new crisis within the Peruvian state by the 1960s. Foreign (primarily U.S.) economic imperialism was also drawing increased attention as a structural cause of Peru's problems. The recognition of the need for agrarian and economic reforms to counter instability and future insurgency had become widely diffused by this time, both in military and civilian circles (North 1983). Velasco's "Revolutionary Government of the Armed Forces" (RGAF) emerged in reaction to the crisis proclaiming an anti-imperialistic, antioligarchic, and fervently nationalistic ideology. Emphasis was placed on: nationalizing foreign-held companies (e.g., the International Petroleum Company in 1969); the agrarian reform beginning in 1969; and modernization and increased worker control within the industrial sector.

A relatively large and critical literature exists analyzing the contradictions and failures of the Velasco "experiment" (e.g., McClintock and Lowenthal 1983; Chaplin 1976; Palmer 1980). Central among these was the contradiction between the government's rhetorical stressing of popular participation in the creation of a "new society," on the one hand, and the top-down corporatist control structure that paternalistically directed popular input, often having to revert to coercion, on the other.[6] Little attention, however, has been granted to the Velasco regime's profound impact on state-Andean relations, and on Andean worldview and cultural production.

With the clear understanding that the revolution could not take place without a position of state leadership and popular support, a concerted and conscious effort was made to establish hegemony simultaneously on a number of fronts. By Velasco's own statement, the government conceived of the "Peruvian problematic as a totality. This implies an integral and integrated vision of social, economic and cultural manifestations" (1972: 65). The government's populist position brought increased attention to the indigenous peasantry.

The agrarian reform, more than any other single act by the Velasco regime, redefined the position of the state in the minds of rural Andeans. The reform was strategically proclaimed on June 24, 1969, the traditional "Día del Indio"—renamed "Día del Campesino" by the RGAF because *indio* had derogatory connotations. The government's plan involved the redistribution of all large *haciendas* by 1975. Velasco explicitly stated the goals of integrating Andeans into the economy and, by raising rural incomes, creating a larger consumer market for national industry (1971: 48). The reform dealt the final blow to the hacienda system that had kept Andeans in servitude for so long. Regardless of the reform's failings and underlying agendas, Velasco was, and still is, viewed by many peasants as a liberator and an ally against the landowners (Neira 1974: 105–119), and this can only be truly comprehended in light of the profound hatred Andeans harbored against the local landed elites.

In their conscious attempt to establish a hegemonic position, the government paid special attention to educational reform, and it was under this rubric that pro-Andean cultural policies were initiated. In a speech made in February 1971, Velasco voiced the notion that formerly the educational system upheld the discriminatory social structure, but that:

The educational reform of the revolution aspires to create an
educational system that: satisfies the necessities of the entire
nation; that will reach the great masses of [indigenous] peasants,
always exploited and always deliberately kept in ignorance; that
will create a new consciousness among all Peruvians of the basic
problems of our country; and that will contribute to *forging a new
type of man within a new social morality.* (Velasco 1972: 63, my
emphasis)

During the Velasco period, rural education is said to have expanded,
and figures show that rural illiteracy was notably reduced between 1972
and 1981 (CNP 1984: 102).

A woman in school at the time in Cusco noted that students were
made to study and memorize the government's widely diffused Inca Plan
(Zimmerman Zavala 1974)—the official statement of the revolution's
ideology and objectives—indicating the conscious use of education for
establishing hegemony. In keeping with RGAF's nationalistic position
and as stated in the Inca Plan, another goal of the reform was to bring
education in line with the "Peruvian reality." To this end, educational
materials depicting regional Andean subjects were produced, and Andean
songs and instruments such as the *kena* began to be used in classrooms
in Cusco, augmenting Andeans' pride in their heritage.[7]

Although the use of native languages for teaching had been prohibited
since the 1780s, in 1975, as a part of Velasco's educational reform, the use
of Amerindian languages was reinstituted. More dramatic, another law
(21156) was created making Quechua an official national language on par
with Spanish. The law stated that after April 1976, the teaching of
Quechua would be obligatory at all educational levels, and after January
1, 1977, all legal proceedings involving monolingual Quechua speakers
would have to be conducted in Quechua (Escobar et al. 1975: 61–63). The
law explicitly recognized the cultural plurality of Peruvian society as
well as the most concrete areas where language had been used as a
mechanism of domination over Quechua speakers: in the courts and in
the schools.

In 1975, the government also issued a law in regard to the use of mass
media in accord with its nationalist position and in recognition of the
particular importance of radio as a means for establishing hegemony and
national integration. The Inca Plan states that: "The radio and television
were the pills that put the national consciousness to sleep and infiltrated
it with the lifestyle from foreign countries. [The media] obeyed a
structure of capitalist control and foreign ideology to orient the action of
the masses and the educational criteria of the society." The 1975 law

required all public and private radio stations to dedicate a minimum of 7.5 percent of their airtime to "folkloric music," which was defined as "that which is born directly from the traditions and customs of the people and that, in particular, is the collective creation emanating from rural zones of the country" (cited in Llorens 1983: 127). Although highland-music radio programming had been on the incline in Lima and highland urban centers after the 1950s as a result of urban migration and the consequent commercial market, Velasco's law regarding radio is seen as highly significant by highland musicians as are his other reforms. An interview recorded in 1988 with two musicians of rural-mestizo heritage in Cusco exemplifies commonly stated attitudes:

T.T.: In earlier times were there prejudices against highland music in Lima?

D.F.: Ah! Discrimination. Yes there was, clearly.

E.V.: Yes, but this was erased, not erased, but legitimized [valorado] a bit when Velasco Alvarado, the military president de facto, entered and issued a law giving, (pause) in the first place, making the mother tongue, Quechua, official. Later there came another law giving value to the *wayno* [a major highland musical genre] and to the national music. He required every radio station in the country to dedicate an hour, at least, to the programming of national music including the waltz and the wayno. Thus, this served to give value [to the music], a bit perhaps. It gave it more strength, legality, so that the national music would be maintained and would not be abandoned or transformed.

T.T.: And why was highland music of concern to Velasco?

E.V.: Because his political position was Tupac Amarist. And Tupac Amaru was the first precursor of independence, the first mestizo who went out in defense of the Indian, the campesino. Hence, because he [Velasco] identified with the campesinos, it was necessary for him to give value, not only to the campesino himself, but also to his culture.

Velasco had not been mentioned previously in this interview, and the spontaneous association of his laws regarding Quechua and the radio, as well as the image of Tupac Amaru (a symbol Velasco consciously used— e.g., Velasco 1972: 178), in response to a question about prejudices against highland music in Lima is highly indicative. I received similar responses in a large variety of contexts. For example, in 1985 an older Aymara musician in an isolated rural community in Puno responded to a question about a revival of interest in panpipe music among the youth of his community in the following way:

> The government, when Alvarado, here the president, here in Peru,
> this Juan Velasco Alvarado, this one, he remembered more ours, our
> instrument, we were not able to use foreign [instruments]. "Let us
> issue the law," Juan Velasco Alvarado. After this, recently, the
> young people are playing here and there, the whole length of the
> road, with these instruments of the ancestors. (Interview transcrip-
> tion, tape #80)

This perception regarding actions of the state under Velasco in support
of Andean culture was all the more prominent in interviews (1984–1986)
with highland migrants in Lima, but the statement by this older rural
musician, who is both relatively isolated from, and unconcerned with,
national politics indicates the wide diffusion of such views.

In the end, Velasco did not succeed in establishing hegemony within
the dominant society—among the urban-working, middle and upper
classes, and particularly among intellectuals. Besides the economic
threat posed to more affluent groups, people were alienated by the
RGAF's too frequent reliance on force, and the contradiction between an
ideology stressing participation while simultaneously asserting state
control—among other issues. Andeans in the highlands and in Lima,
however, remember the Velasco era as a major turning point for the
acceptance of their culture.

After 1975, fueled by the presence of ever greater numbers of *serranos*
in Lima and the ideological changes validated by the Velasco state,
Andeans increasingly abandoned their former strategy of attempted
assimilation into *criollo* society and began to assert themselves *as*
Andeans in the economic, political, and cultural spheres in the capital.
More economic autonomy in the huge informal sector and the organized
land invasions for the creation of squatter's settlements are but two
examples. Migrant musical practice is another indicator of the change
in strategy as well as a central resource for strengthening Andean
identity and unity, which is essential to the change.

Previously public performance of Andean music in the capital was
either shaped by Western aesthetics through mestizo-*indigenista* interpretation or was partially controlled and shaped for mass consumption by urban entrepreneurs: a process that also favored the blending of
urban-Western and highland aspects. After 1975, however, a clear trend
of greater regional specificity and Andean migrant control over their own
musical occasions and resources led to the diffusion of traditional
indigenous forms in the city to an unprecedented degree.

Recent data supplied by J. A. Llorens (personal communication 1988) indicate a continual growth of radio time dedicated to highland music in relation to the total number of A.M. radio hours in Lima: from 13.2 percent in 1985 to 15.2 percent by 1987. Even the latter figure is disproportionately low when compared to the percentage of first-generation Andeans within Lima's population. An estimated 40 percent of the urban population was born outside the Department of Lima (Henriquez and Ponce 1985: 13), and a great majority of these migrants are from the highlands (see Dietz 1976: 10). Nonetheless the growth in highland music radio time is still impressive when contrasted with the virtual absence of such programs prior to 1951, and in the context of anti-Andean prejudices that are still prevalent in Lima.

Perhaps even more significant than the mestizo style–dominated radio programs is the increased performance of indigenous music in the capital by migrants after 1975. By the early 1970s, the lower/working-class migrant regional associations had begun to take a greater role in organizing their own performance ensembles, whereas previously there had been a general reluctance to associate themselves with highland, and particularly indigenous, forms. As a prime example, during the 1960s, there were only a handful of indigenous-styled Puneño *sikuri* (panpipe) ensembles in Lima, and these usually played behind closed doors. In contrast, in 1985 I made the partial count of sixty-nine panpipe groups actively performing publicly in the capital. The formation of these regional club-based ensembles in significant numbers begins precisely in 1975 (Turino 1987: 442–444, 1988: 140–143).

Significantly, this same date, falling at the end of the Velasco period, occurs in a statement regarding Andean music by the Peruvian anthropologist Rodgrigo Montoya: "If we observe the records and cassettes of music, one can clearly see that between 1975 and today they began recording Indian music. The music recorded previously was principally *senorial* [of a higher social strata]" (Montoya 1987: 45). Llorens (1983: 122) makes the similar observation that more indigenous musical styles began to be issued on commercial recordings after the late 1960s, paralleling my findings for live migrant musical performance in Lima.

Supporting the increased diffusion of indigenous forms in the city during the 1970s, regional clubs began to take over the organization of their own musical occasions from urban entrepreneurs. The form of these events, however, illustrates that the "Andeanization of Lima" is not a unidirectional phenomenon. For example, the centerpiece of *festivales folklóricos* organized by Puneño clubs is a formally staged performance contest with an urban-styled MC, a sit-down audience, judges, and prizes. Indeed these urban-derived markers, like the term *folklore* itself, have been adopted to define and legitimize the performance frame for Puneño musical events and are particularly important to the participants for the respectability that they provide (Turino 1987: 553–558). This suggests that *criollo* control over the definition of Andean cultural practices is still an issue and internalized feelings of inferiority are still operating. Such feelings have an even greater impact on other cultural domains such as language use and religion among Aymara speakers from Puno (Turino 1987, 1988: 143–144).

The State and Andean Music in the Rural Highlands

As the locus of political, economic, and social power and prestige, Lima exerts a tremendous influence on cultural trends generally within the country. Although space does not permit a detailed discussion of this topic here, it is worth noting that the *indigenista* movement, the commercial-Andean music trend, as well as the more recent diffusion of indigenous musical forms in the city have influenced musical life in the rural Andes. For example, the recent presence and growing popularity of indigenous Puneño panpipe music in Lima augmented the prestige of this tradition and thus inspired similar trends in the departmental and provincial capitals of Puno. This in turn generated a revival of interest and participation in *sikuri* music among Aymara youth in rural communities as noted by the older Aymara musician cited earlier. It is significant, however, that rural young people have largely abandoned the other indigenous instrumental and dance traditions—also because of urban influences.

Since the 1960s, the state's impact on rural indigenous cultural practices in the southern sierra has often been indirect: filtered through the activities and attitudes of migrants in Lima and highland cities. The INC seems to have had little real effect in indigenous communities. The state's most direct influence on rural cultural practice—since the missionaries of the colonial period—resulted from Velasco's cultural politics, whereas Leguia's pro-Indian stance had only diffuse results in the context of *indigenismo*.

There is no doubt that the legitimacy of Andean culture and Andeans' self-images were greatly bolstered during the Velasco years. Paradoxically, however, his policies aimed at reducing the marginalization of Andeans, particularly the educational reform, also partially succeeded in fulfilling the RGAF's goal of integrating indigenous peasants into Peruvian society. Education in conjunction with the vast migratory movements and the advent of the transistor radio have increasingly turned the attention of rural Andean youth toward urban-based Peruvian society. The young Aymara peasants' rejection of the majority of their indigenous musical heritage—thus foreshadowing its demise—is but one result of this.

Conclusions

For much of Peru's history, the cultural forms of Andeans were ignored or repressed by the state and disparaged by elite groups as an element of the orthodox vision of Andean inferiority. This vision, when internalized, bolstered Andean subordination. Social and political domination was required by colonial and neocolonial relations of production. The status of the arts of given groups was structured through homologies with the status of the groups themselves in relation to the state—ideologies about art thus reinforcing social hierarchy and Andeans' negative self-perceptions. But as I have tried to suggest, it may have been precisely *because* Andean arts were ignored or marginalized in the context of a rigid hierarchy that they have been maintained to the surprising degree still evident today. Two issues come to the fore: the use of force to maintain control; and the relative rigidity of the social system in the southern sierra until the mid-twentieth century (Southern Peru Regional Development Project 1959: 13).

Guaman Poma's astute observation around the turn of the seventeenth century, that you cannot make people Christians out of fear, also applies to making people identify with the state. State coercion produced alienation and a reaction of overt resistance as the long history of Andean uprisings attests. Bourdieu (1984: 164) has remarked that creating the appearance of a potential for social mobility is essential for the permanence of social hierarchies. A rigid structure that offers subordinate peoples no hope that participating in the system will improve their lot can only diminish their desire to participate. In the face of state violence or, at best, marginalization, the maintenance of indigenous identity and its markers becomes an obvious course for self-preservation and passive resistance.

Note, however, that when social mobility appeared possible, as, for example, even with local headmen in the early colonial period, the adoption of European social and cultural style increased. Velasco's promise to reduce the marginalization of Andeans had similar results with peasants growing up since the 1960s, as did the expectation of social mobility in the process of urban migration since the 1940s. But the fact that possibilities for peasant social mobility and participation within the state were the exception, not the rule, for most of Peru's history has tended to underwrite the preservation of Andean identity and cultural forms, and has functioned to block the establishment of a hegemonic position (in Gramscian terms) by any governing elite, as Julio Cotler has remarked repeatedly (1983: 4).

On the other hand, state action in regard to Andean arts was undertaken through either coercive or co-optive strategies precisely to reduce

Andean resistance. In the colonial period, both methods were used by church functionaries to legitimate colonial rule. Again, the use of the carrot—music education and the allowance of syncretism in cultural practices—was the most successful course. During the twentieth century, the discourse of cultural politics shifted from its religious guise to a secular-liberal, romantic-nationalist mode. Intellectuals and the state itself adopted indices of "Andeanness" (e.g., "The Inca Plan") as emblems of the state.

In Peru, and perhaps more generally, romantic-nationalism can be viewed as a co-optive strategy to reduce the potency of dominated groups' symbolic means of resistance. That is, the symbolic transformation of the "Andean" into the "national," an appropriation by elites, potentially reduces the power of Andean emblems to mark or unite competing social factions, and nationhood and unity are enacted as a social drama. But as we have seen, this occurs only when convenient to the agendas and needs of a given state configuration. Moreover, during the *indigenista* phase, the transfiguration of the "Andean" took place in a superficial and misinformed manner, resulting in the creation of new mestizo forms and leaving distinctly maintained indigenous musical styles to one side. Hence, the latter were still available to become central components in the competing discourse of Andean migrants in Peruvian cities after the 1960s.

At another level, however, the *indigenistas* created a foothold for Andean legitimacy that was later enlarged upon by intellectuals such as Arguedas within state institutions, and that was developed to a much greater extent by the Velasco government. The fracturing of orthodoxy (the attempt to control the modes and limits of social discourse, and hence what *can* be said and thought) leads to heterodoxy among dominated groups whose self-interest is served by recognizing that their inferior position is by no means "natural" or as it should be (Bourdieu 1977). This is particularly salient when the state itself is involved in challenging the orthodoxy of former power blocs.

What is suggested is that when internalized feelings of inferiority are reduced, even if by the state to advance its own political control, the resulting heterodoxic views gain their own momentum as a basis for new social strategies among dominated groups. Relative to former periods, Andeans in urban centers began to take increasing control over their own lives in the cultural, economic, and political domains during the post-Velasco era. In asserting Andean identity as the basis for social power, migrant groups have significantly altered their position in the social space of Lima, and consequently have affected Andeans throughout the country. Semiotic forms, and particularly music, have been important resources for unification within this process.

I have tried to indicate, however, that the thrust for the legitimacy of Andean identity in the post-Velasco period has not been unidirectional, and it must be understood in regard to specific contexts. Thus, while increasing numbers of Andean migrants are stressing their highland heritage for strategic reasons in the cities, the youth of the rural sierra are rapidly assimilating urban-national styles of interaction and thought, which, by now, are being defined by a new synthesis of Andean and *criollo* components. The crisis of the Peruvian state continues under the present APRA government of Alan García with both the president and the Sendero Luminoso guerrillas balancing the manipulation of Andean imagery against the use of force in their quest for support and control of the Andean population.

Notes

1. The concept of "the state" is amorphous. Here, following Gramsci, Althusser, and others, I have extended my definition beyond the bureaucratic and repressive apparatuses of government to include those whose main function is to influence ideology toward the enhancement of political control and the maintenance of relations of production. Not wanting to expand the conception to all regulatory institutions within society (e.g., the family), only those formally linked to government in terms of support and structural coordination are included (see Hall 1988).

2. The use of Aymara as well as Quechua in conversion work is mentioned in the edicts of the Third *Concilio Limense* in 1583 (see Vargas 1951: 323).

3. *Antari* closely resembles the term *antara* that denoted panpipes in the pre-Columbian period. At the time of Arriaga's observation, *pincollo* (*pinkullu*) may have referred only to end-notched flutes of the *kena* type since the duct flutes known presently as *pinkullus* apparently did not exist in the preconquest period. The mention of bone *pinkullus* clearly indicates the end-notched variety.

4. Part of the score for "Hanacpachap" is provided by Quezada (1985: 76), and a contemporary recorded performance of the piece may be heard on the phonodisc by the Roger Wagner Chorale *Salve Regina: Choral Music of the Spanish New World 1550–1750* (Angel/EMI S 36008).

5. In discussions with migrant musicians in Lima, Arguedas's name came up frequently in explaining the increased pride Andeans were able to publicly demonstrate in regard to their highland cultural heritage.

6. David Chaplin (1976: 19), for example, has suggested that SINAMOS (National System of Support for Social Mobilization) was established to appear as if it was fostering popular participation, while in actuality it was creating a system of vertical segmentation controlled from the top. He goes on to note that the cooperative model of the Industrial Community Program had as a major goal the elimination of trade unions and the threat that they posed. That popular support was not forthcoming from the labor force is indicated by the fact that more and larger strikes occurred during each of the years 1973–1975 than for any

other year in the 1965–1976 period (Palmer 1980: 114).

7. Various friends who worked as rural schoolteachers in the highlands during the Velasco years described the excitement and feeling of mission that were created by the reform. More widely, however, problems of teacher absenteeism and lack of commitment are reported in rural communities regarding the mestizo teachers who felt that they were being banished to a hard life in the rural zones.

References

Acosta, José de
  1964   *Historia natural y moral de Indias.* Madrid: Editorial Mateos.
Albo, Xavier
  1966   Jesuitas y culturas indígenas: Peru 1568–1605 (segunda parte). *América Indígena* 26(4): 395–445.
Allen, Catherine J.
  1988   *The hold life has: coca and cultural identity in an Andean community.* Washington D.C.: Smithsonian Institution Press.
Ansion, Juan
  1986   *Anhelos y sinsabores: dos décadas de políticas culturales del estado Peruano.* Lima: GREDES.
Armas Medina, Fernando de
  1953   *Cristianización del Peru 1532–1600.* Sevilla: Escuela de Estudios Hispanoamericanos.
Arriaga, Pablo José de
  1968   *The extirpation of idolatry in Peru.* Clark Keating (ed. and trans.). Lexington: University of Kentucky.
Basadre, Jorge
  1968   *Historia de la república, Tomo XIII.* Lima: Editorial Universo.
Bastien, Joseph W.
  1978   *Mountain of the condor: metaphor and ritual in an Andean Ayllu.* St. Paul, Minn.: West.
Béhague, Gerard
  1979   *Music in Latin America: an introduction.* Englewood Cliffs, N.J.: Prentice-Hall.
Bourdieu, Pierre
  1977   *Outline of a theory of practice.* Cambridge: Cambridge University Press.
  1984   *Distinction: a social critique of the judgement of taste.* Cambridge: Harvard University Press.
  1985   The social space and the genesis of groups. *Theory and Society* 14: 723–744.
Chaplin, David
  1976   *Peruvian nationalism: a corporatist revolution.* New Brunswick, N.J.: Transaction Books.
CNP (Consejo Nacional de Población)
  1984   *Peru: hechos y cifras demográficas.* Lima: Consejo Nacional de

Población.
Cotler, Julio
1983 Democracy and national integration in Peru. In *The Peruvian experiment reconsidered*, Cynthia McClintock and Abraham F. Lowenthal (eds.), 3–38. Princeton, N.J.: Princeton University Press.
1978 *Clases, estado y nación en el Peru.* Lima: Instituto de Estudios Peruanos.
Dietz, Henry
1976 *Who, how, and why: rural migration to Lima.* Cambridge: MIT Center for International Studies.
Escobar, Alberto, José Matos Mar, and Giorgio Alberti
1975 *Peru: país bilingue?* Lima: Instituto de Estudios Peruanos.
Francke Ballue, Marfil
1978 El movimiento indigenista en el Cusco (1910–1930). In *Indigenismo, clases sociales y problema nacional*, Carlos Ivan Degregori (ed.), 107–186. Lima: Ediciones Celats.
Garcilaso de la Vega, Inca
1945 *Comentarios reales de los Incas.* Buenos Aires.
Gramsci, Antonio
1971 *Selections from the prison notebooks of Antonio Gramsci.* Quintin Hoare and Geoffrey Nowell Smith (eds. and trans.). New York: International.
Guaman Poma de Ayala, Felipe
1980 *El primer nueva corónica y buen gobierno.* Mexico: Siglo Veintiuno.
Hall, Stuart
1985 Signification, representation, ideology: Althusser and the post-structuralist debates. *Critical Studies in Mass Communication* 2(2): 91–114.
1988 The toad in the garden: Thatcherism among the theorists. In *Marxism and the interpretation of culture*, Cary Nelson and Lawrence Grossberg (eds.), 35–73. Urbana: University of Illinois Press.
Handelman, Howard
1975 *Struggle in the Andes.* Austin: University of Texas Press.
Henriquez, Narda, and Ana Ponce, eds.
1985 *Lima poblacion, trabajo y política.* Lima: Pontificia Universidad Católica del Peru.
Iturriaga, Enrique, and Juan Carlos Estenssoro
1985 Emancipación y república: siglo XIX. In *La música en el Peru*, 103–124. Lima: Patronato Popular y Porvenir Pro-Música Clasica.
Jameson, Fredric
1981 *The political unconscious: narrative as a socially symbolic act.* Ithaca, N.Y.: Cornell University Press.
Kubler, George
1946 The Quechua in the colonial world. In *Handbook of South American Indians, vol. 2: the Andean civilizations*, Julian H. Steward (ed.), 331–410. Washington, D.C.: U.S. Government Printing Office.
Llorens, José Antonio
1983 *Música popular en Lima: criollos y andinos.* Lima: Instituto de

Estudios Peruanos.

McClintock, Cynthia, and Abraham F. Lowenthal
1983   *The Peruvian experiment reconsidered.* Princeton, N.J.: Princeton University Press.

Marzal, Manuel
1969   La cristianización del indígena peruano. *Allpanchis* 1: 89–122.

Montoya, Rodrigo
1986   Identidad étnica y luchas agrarias en los Andes Peruanos. In *Identidades andinas y lógicas del campesinado*, 247–278. Lima: Mosca Azul Editores.
1987   *La cultura Quechua hoy.* Lima: Hueso Humero Ediciones.

Neira Samanez, Hugo
1974   *Huillca: habla un campesino Peruano.* Lima: Ediciones PEISA.

North, Liisa L.
1983   Ideological orientations of Peru's military rulers. In *The Peruvian experiment reconsidered,* Cynthia McClintock and Abraham F. Lowenthal (eds.), 245–274. Princeton, N.J.: Princeton University Press.

Palmer, David Scott
1980   *Peru the authoritarian tradition.* New York: Praeger.

Quezada, José
1985   La música en el virreinato. In *La música en el Peru*, 65–102. Lima: Patronato Popular y Porvenir Pro-Música Clasica.

Rozas Aragon, Abel
1985   *Antología de la música cusquena: siglos XIX y XX.* Cusco: Comité de Servicios Integrados Turísticos Culturales.

Schechter, John M.
1984   Diatonic harp in Ecuador: historical background and modern traditions, part 1. *Journal of the American Musical Instrument Society* 10: 97–118.

Southern Peru Regional Development Project
1959   *Human resources in the department of Puno.* Lima: Southern Peru Regional Development Project.

Stern, Steve J.
1987   The age of Andean insurrection 1742–1782: a reappraisal. In *Resistance, rebellion, and consciousness in the Andean peasant world: eighteenth to twentieth centuries*, Steve J. Stern (ed.), 34–93. Madison: University of Wisconsin Press.

Stevenson, Robert
1968   *Music in Aztec and Inca territory.* Berkeley: University of California Press.

Tamayo Herrera, José
1982   *Historia social e indigenismo en el altiplano.* Lima: Ediciones Treintaitres.

Turino, Thomas
1984   The urban-mestizo charango tradition in southern Peru: a statement of shifting identity. *Ethnomusicology* 28(2): 253–269.

1987   Power relations, identity and musical choice: music in a Peruvian altiplano village and among its migrants in the metropolis. PhD diss., Department of Music, University of Texas at Austin.

1988   The music of Andean migrants in Lima, Peru: demographics, social power, and style. *Latin American Music Review* 9(2).

1989   The coherence of social style and musical creation among the Aymara in southern Peru. *Ethnomusicology* 33(1): 1–30.

1990   The history of a Peruvian panpipe style and the politics of interpretation. In *Ethnomusicology and modern music history*, Stephen Blum, Daniel Newman, and Philip Bohlman (eds.). Urbana: University of Illinois Press.

Valcarcel, Luis E.

1946   The Andean calendar. In *Handbook of South American Indians, vol. 2: the Andean civilizations*, Julian H. Steward (ed.), 471–476. Washington, D.C.: U.S. Government Printing Office.

Vargas Urgarte, Rubén

1951   *Concilios Limenses (1551–1772), tomo I*. Lima: n.p.

Velasco Alvarado, Juan

1971   *La voz de la revolución: discursos del Presidente de la República, General de División, Juan Velasco Alvarado, 1968–1970, tomo I*. Lima: Ediciones Participación.

1972   *La voz de la revolución: discursos del Presidente de la República, General de División, Juan Velasco Alvarado, 1970–1972, tomo II*. Lima: Ediciones Participación.

Vivanco Guerra, J. Alejandro

1973   El migrante de provincias como intérprete del folklore andino en Lima. Bachiller en Antropología thesis, Universidad Nacional Mayor de San Marcos, Lima.

Wachtel, Nathan

1973   *Sociedad e ideología: ensayos de historia y antropología andinas*. Lima: Instituto de Estudios Peruanos.

Warkentin, Larry

1981   The rise and fall of Indian music in the California missions. *Latin American Music Review* 2(1): 45–65.

Zimmermann Zavala, Augusto

1974   *El plan Inca, objetivo: revolución peruana*. Lima: Empresa Editora del Diario Oficial "El Peruano."

11. Images of the Indian in Guatemala: The Role of Indigenous Dress in Indian and Ladino Constructions

Carol Hendrickson

Indígena or *natural* (Indian) and *ladino* (mestizo or non-Indian) are the labels most frequently used by Guatemalans to assign themselves a racial or ethnic identity.[1] By local accounts, the terms point to a definition of person according to certain overt markers (dress, language, etc.); blood, heritage, or historical roots; and/or a history of relations between the conquering and conquered that still holds true today. Because of the asymmetrical nature of the two principal categories—Indian is the unmarked or less general one—these defining characteristics are most often used by and applied to the indigenous population and institutions or objects associated with them. Not coincidentally, what people choose to specify as the contents of these terms are also the principal themes used in daily life to help foster, sustain, validate, or criticize notions of ethnicity and, as we shall see, nationality, especially as these relate to being Indian. This should not strike us as unusual for, as Scott (1985: 309) explains about the key symbols of class relations in Malaysia, these "do not constitute a set of given rules or principles that actors simply follow [or, I might add, that reflect a given world 'out there']. They are instead the normative raw material that is created, maintained, changed, and above all manipulated by daily human activity."

In Guatemala, ethnicity is commonly given as a rationale for action. Among those who define themselves as Indian under the broadest of circumstances, a person might consciously and explicitly speak out, act a particular way, or criticize another human being in accordance with a perceived ideal of what it is to be Indian and how this ideal should find expression in the world. Indians and the Indian way of life are seen to be threatened by nonindigenous forces, which are judged powerful, nearly omnipresent, and often opposed to indigenous values. At the local level, ladinos are seen as representatives of these forces, as are the national government and the United States within certain "higher level" contexts.

Judged by its breadth of use and its power to explain the widest range of social phenomena, ethnicity—being Indian or ladino—must be considered one of the fundamental classifiers of the person in Guatemala.[2] Other systems of labeling exist, of course, but many of the more sociopolitically oriented are taken to be subsumed by basic ethnic distinctions. That is one perspective, at least. Thus, for instance, Indians will charge ladinos with prejudicial actions based on ethnic considerations, while non-Indians, talking about the same situation, will disclaim Indian charges and contend that the division is based on contextually appropriate and racially unbiased criteria (often quantifiable "facts") such as wealth, size of land holdings, or the number of votes. Indians, commenting on the latter claims, will agree that criteria other than ethnicity can be used to divide the population. However, as they see it, it is *because* they are Indian that they are kept to the lower socioeconomic rungs and hence can always be separated out by classificatory schemes that divide according to elements of power.

In this chapter, I aim to examine a range of images of the Indian found in Guatemala, images that are constructed, marketed, praised, and denounced by Indian and non-Indian voices at the local, national, and international levels. Among those engaging in such activities are, on the one hand, the national government itself (through institutional actions), individuals representing the government, and members of society whose personal proclivities generally align them with what can be taken to be a government stand and then, on the other, those who see themselves falling outside of or in opposition to the above categories. While "ladino" certainly does not always translate into the former, dominant group and "Indian" into the latter, subordinate group, these terms nonetheless reflect the general polarization of the data to be examined. Refinement will come as I examine not only the range of images—the variety of concrete instances of "the Indian" made public—but also the nature of the representations, the composition of the groups that produce them, the work the images do (or are supposed to do) for those employing them, and the comments these bring from those who define themselves as indigenous under all circumstances.

As the subtitle of this chapter indicates, a particular emphasis will be placed on the role that clothing plays in the various images of the Indian.[3] This circumstance arises from the fact that my fieldwork in Guatemala has focused on *traje*, or indigenous dress, and the construction of social identity by this visual, material means. What is more, the geographic emphasis of the system of categories and perceptions described here tips to the central highlands as I conducted my fieldwork in Tecpán, Guatemala, a town of some six thousand people (approximately two-thirds Indian, one-third ladino) lying fifty miles west of Guatemala City, just off the Pan American Highway.[4]

Because I have generally limited myself to data collected in Tecpán (including local commentary on events and images produced outside of town), I do not deal, for example, with material arising from military campaigns in the northwest departments or from government-directed projects such as the model villages and development posts, both of which reflect and work to create very particular images of indigenous society: I simply lack local commentary on these subjects. Nonetheless, using the details of everyday life in the central highlands during the early to mid-1980s, a system of images and counterimages of the Indian emerges that I feel captures a sense of the larger picture.[5]

Briefly put, the classifications of the Indian with which I will be dealing point to models of the construction of the larger Guatemalan society and, variously, the relation between the two principal ethnic groups or between the indigenous population and the Guatemalan government. Within this set of images, society is seen as composed of interrelated peoples, on the one hand, or autonomous units, on the other. Likewise, it is characterized by the unity created by a common history and heritage or a disunity bred from conflict and centuries of domination. Furthermore, indigenous attributes are seen as natural (even to the extreme of being seen as biologically based), on the one hand, or imposed from the outside by nonindigenous sources, on the other.

Finally, each image of the Indian is seen to have a judgmental or evaluative aspect. Thus, for example, Tecpán youths moving out into the larger social world speak of coming to know "the reality" of life in Guatemala. This coming-to-know speaks of their growing awareness of the political dimensions of highland life and of the full range of classificatory schemes that shape and label Indian existence. This is a knowledge of when, where, and how the "given" of any social situation is likely to be construed as conforming to one particular image or another. What is more, it goes along with an ability to work around or through these stereotypes (i.e., representations recognized as incomplete or somehow untrue) in an effort to control and shape, not only one's personal life as an indigenous person, but the larger construction of the image of the Indian in Guatemala.

The Image and Its Object

In *The Colors of Rhetoric* (1982), Wendy Steiner examines the relationship between the verbal and visual arts, and between each of these and the reality it depicts. In this context she characterizes Charles Peirce's three types of icons—the image as "a sign which *substantially* replicates its object," the diagram as "a sign whose *relations* replicate those of its objects," and the metaphor as "a sign that represents what Peirce terms the 'representative character' of another sign through a *parallelism"* (Steiner 1982: 20)—and adds that Peirce, by labeling these "hypoicons," notes the conventional nature of all three. Thus, the image, far from distinguishing itself from the diagram and metaphor by representing its object in every possible way, instead represents it to a point that satisfies the dictates of a particular time and people. Gombrich (1972: 90), speaking on a similar theme, notes that images (visual images, portrayals, pictures, etc., in his case) represent their objects to whatever degree of accuracy is required for the particular purpose at hand.

While I do not mean to adhere too closely to a technical, Peircean notion of the image for the materials I examine, the implications of such a characterization are valuable nonetheless. An image and what it represents contain within its standing-for relationship a judgment that, for somebody, under some circumstance, and for some particular purpose, the "degree of accuracy" of the representation is adequate or correct. In fact, if the image is accepted as so perfectly representing its object, the line between the two can become largely invisible and the image can be taken (or offered up) as actually *being* the thing. On the other hand, if the criteria for representation are not agreed upon, what is an acceptable image for one group can be a horrible distortion for another and conflict may arise around this point.

The images of which Gombrich and Steiner speak are conventional visual ones (e.g., paintings, woodcuts, etc.) or, in Steiner's work, the verbal images of literature. In the Guatemalan case, I will be concerned with a wider assortment of representations—photographs, descriptions in tourist brochures, performances for public holidays, appearances in beauty pageants, and the like—with the Indian as the common theme. Nonetheless, each of these images has a conventional form, something bracketed or framed off as a separate entity geared for public consumption. What is more, each is put to work as an act of definition or persuasion: defining what it is to be Indian in Guatemala or persuading a particular group that the image being conveyed is an adequate representation of the indigenous people. In the cases where the Guatemalan government or its allies are attempting to maintain cultural hegemony, the notion of an "adequate representation" of the Indian will take on the added dimension of a "natural representation"—one that presents itself as complete and true, for both ladinos and Indians alike. The flip side, of course, is that people, indigenous people in particular, can fail to be persuaded or to agree with the wholeness and truth of one expression and can move to present their own (cf. Hebdige 1979; Scott 1985). Such is in fact the case in Guatemala where a struggle involving images of the Indian is being waged on a number of fronts, not with guns and bullets but with tourist brochures, festival presentations, and beauty queens.

Non-Indian Perspectives

In Tecpán, and throughout Guatemala, "ladino" and "Indian" are referred to explicitly as labels of race (*raza*) or ethnic group (*grupo étnico*). However, non-Indians from the national level on down embrace Indians as "us" in expressions of Guatemalan *national* identity. Despite one Guatemalan author's claim that, among ladinos, there is no such thing as "*nosotros los Guatemaltecos*" (we Guatemalans [Guzmán Böckler 1975: 101]), non-Indian citizens routinely embrace the spirit of the Indian as their own and, in fact, proclaim themselves of the same historical essence (if not always of the same blood). This embrace is often visually marked by the use of *traje* which beautifully sums up their pride in national-cum-ethnic heritage.

On the international level, the use of indigenous (material) culture as *the* image of Guatemalan national identity is seen yearly in the *Miss Universo* contest. Each year, INGUAT, the Guatemalan Tourist Institute, sponsors a local pageant and the (ladino) woman who is elected Miss Guatemala represents her country in the world competition decked out in Guatemala's "national costume"—*traje*. In 1975, Miss Guatemala won the national costume division of the contest and was heralded internationally as having the most beautiful outfit in the world. Subsequent to this, INGUAT distributed masses of posters and postcards showing the young contestant—white-skinned, heavily made up, and posing like a Paris model—radiant in indigenous dress. The point of all the publicity was clear: the honor was something for all Guatemalans to be proud of. Guatemala had been selected above all other countries of the world and recognized for its unique cultural wealth. Its rich Mayan heritage, as symbolized by the clothing, made Guatemala *Guatemala* and presented it in a positive light.

Similar embraces of the Indian occur for strictly national audiences. For example, February 20 is the day the government has set aside to honor Tecún Umán, the Quiché Mayan warrior defeated by the Spanish. Proclamations emanating from the capital herald him as ancestor-to-all: a "symbol of American man" made "without distinguishing between Indian or ladino" (*El Gráfico* 1980b: 6, my translation). While the figure of Tecún Umán appears in highland municipalities as the subject of school plays and a key character in the Dance of the Conquest, it is really only in the capital that February 20 is celebrated at length.

It was also in Guatemala City that three prominent professionals founded the Committee for the Exaltation of the National Hero of Guatemala, their purpose being "to exalt the figure of Tecún Umán" claiming that "to deny him [his existence] is to deny our own national essence" (*El Gráfico* 1980a: 5, my translation).[6] Tecún Umán, therefore, is properly praised each year by public servants, military regiments, and schoolchildren, and editorials appear in the national newspaper proclaiming that:

> Tecún Umán, the warrior prince, is not only a national hero, but the symbol of Guatemalan nationality: he is the image of the honorable warrior who dies in the defense of his territory. But also he is the symbol of American nationality: of the American man— that is to say, of the man who populated this continent before the arrival of Columbus . . . of the mixture [*mestizaje*] produced by the encounter and the fusion of two different ethnic groups: the Guatemalan Indian and the Spaniard. In him we venerate our indigenous ancestor—part of our essence; in him we venerate the heroic defender of the land of his ancestors and his children, in him we venerate the dignity of a people who yielded before . . . a more technically and scientifically developed continent but not without presenting heroic resistance, paying the price with his life. (*El Gráfico* 1980b: 6, my translation)

Although this account of the subjugation of the Indian population carries themes of the subordination of indigenous culture, the irony of the subsequent praise of Tecún Umán is not acknowledged by the author. Rather, the point that is stressed is that Tecún Umán, as a primordial Guatemalan being, may have been "just" an Indian, but through death, the conquest of his people, and resurrection as national hero, he is transformed. By dominating the autochthonous leader, the Spanish, in fact, liberate him from representing the indigenous population alone and elevate him so that he stands for a whole new society, the unity of which is suggested to be the principal product of the conflict.

It is not just at the national level or for foreign audiences that ladinos wrap themselves in *traje* and embrace or "become" Indian as an expression of what it is to be Guatemalan. This symbolic use of the indigenous person and/or traditional dress is also employed in the highlands, in contexts where Indians themselves are present in much greater numbers. Thus, for example, at a ceremony for the regional office of the Ministry of Agriculture in Chimaltenango (a nearby town and capital of the department in which Tecpán lies), stage walls and the table for speech-giving dignitaries were covered with Indian shawls and the cloth indigenous women use for skirts. In this environment, ladino speakers discussing government-supported local projects appealed to an ethnically mixed audience to cooperate "as Chimaltecos" (here meaning residents of the entire department) and "as Guatemalans." Mention of allegiances to bounded geographical units and the visual presence of artifacts that were meant to be taken as unique to Guatemala, in general, and to the Chimaltenango area, in particular, helped stress the unity of those addressed and served to contradict (or camouflage) the growing evidence of sociopolitical tensions and conflicts in that area of the highlands. In addition, it seems to me that because all the pieces had strong associations with women, and women, in turn, are symbolically associated with the domestic sphere, both the Indian population and Guatemalans-as-Indians were portrayed as essentially apolitical.[7] Again, this helped create an atmosphere that removed the audience from the sociopolitical reality of the highlands at that time.

As suggested by the previous examples, the "ritual" use of *traje* (especially women in *traje*) by ladinos can be a powerful means for expressing social unity and ignoring or, as will be seen, repairing tears in the social fabric. This is also the case at the local highland level where the presence of indigenous dress can be even more laden with meaning owing to the larger number of common experiences and shared prag-matic assumptions of members of the audience. For the Tecpán material, a noteworthy example centers on the annual fair celebrations leading up to and surrounding October 4, the name day of Saint Francis of Assisi, the town's patron saint. In 1983 the Tecpán fair committee was a unified body of ladino and Indian members who planned activities together and who, ideally, represented all Tecpanecos' interests. This was also the form of the group up until the mid-1970s. At that time, however, Indian sentiment was that inequalities between the two ethnic groups were being perpetuated by the committee which, as if a microcosm of all society, was dominated by its ladino members. As a consequence, the Indian segment split off into a separate organization with its own budget, planning committee, and events. What were once rivalries within a single group turned into rivalries between groups as each organization vied to hire the best marimba band for fair-time dances or have the best attendance at programs.

The two committees existed separately into 1981. However, in the weeks and months following the murder of the town's Catholic priest in May of that year, a number of Tecpán's Indian leaders were killed and others were forced to leave suddenly. The effect was a decline in the leadership of indigenous organizations (either people with previous experience or those willing to assume power . . . or even participate) to the point where many groups could no longer function. While some organizations ceased to exist (e.g., the cultural organizations founded to allow local Indians the opportunity to come together and discuss current events in light of their Mayan heritage), the Indian Fair Committee simply reverted to its former joint state with the ladino group.

In September 1983, when I returned to Tecpán briefly, the newly reconstituted group was presenting its first major activity: La Primera Fiesta Folklórica de Tecpán (Tecpán's First Folkloric Festival), sponsored by Maybelline (*Cosmético Oficial/Concurso Miss Universo* [Official Cosmetic/Miss Universe Contest]), as a banner over the stage proclaimed). Because the event was largely a queens' competition, the twelve young candidates—six young ladino women, one of whom would become the Queen of the Fair, and six young indigenous women, one of whom would be crowned Queen Iximché and another Princess Ixmucané—were the focus of the show. For their first appearance of the evening, all twelve candidates—Indians and ladinos alike—dressed in *traje*, the former all in the oldest, most traditional Tecpán outfits and the latter in a mixture of pieces from different towns. In retrospect, this differential use of *traje* seems understandable, not only from a practical point of view (the older, traditional pieces are not always part of an indigenous family's possessions let alone those of a ladino family) but also in terms of the different messages each group wished to communicate. While the Indian women showed a respect for their heritage and a knowledge of local customs, the ladino women, in effect, were admitting that their relation to the Mayan ancestors was more superficial or recent. It was enough for them simply to appear in any fine, contemporary outfit in order to show the current solidarity between the two groups. This sentiment, in fact, emerged as the emcee stressed that the goal of the evening was to celebrate *nuestra Guatemalidad*—"our Guatemala-ity" or "Guatemala-ness"—and, as all in the audience understood, a restoration of peace and good relations in the town.

Indians, however, do not have to hand over their clothes to ladinos (as in the example of the Miss Universe contest) or appear in tandem with them (as in the Tecpán presentation) in order to be seen as representing all Guatemalans. In the travel literature produced by the Guatemalan Tourist Institute and other, private enterprises, attractive photographs of Indians introduce us to the warm and friendly people of Guatemala— "pleasant people," "smiling people," as the brochures point out—who welcome foreign visitors to their country and Guatemalan tourists to the exotic reaches of their own land. The Indians in these situations join with images of volcanoes, mountain lakes, ancient ruins, colonial architecture, and weavings, and all of these symbols of national identity are shown to exhibit a passive beauty that the beholder may contemplate in much the same way he or she does an object of art. All, it is also suggested, remain untouched as the visitor passes through their midst.

Photographs that emphasize this friendly manner typically feature head-on faces (often of children . . . a revealing reflection of the producers' attitude toward the larger population (cf. Dumont 1988: 270) or medium-range shots of people ready to serve. Waiters, waitresses, hotel clerks, vendors with mounds of handicrafted items, marimba players, and artisans (some in *traje*, others not) beam out from the page and beckon the visitor. Indians in this context are smiling and alert, though, in my experience, the former manner of presentation would definitely not be one that most would take were the picture for their own purpose. But then, these photographs are not for their subjects' use. They belong to the entrepreneurs behind the camera and are made to appeal to the vacation-seeking foreigner or national. The intent, then, is to have the photographs function publicly as statements that convince outsiders that Indians as "all Guatemalans" are excitingly different and, at the same time, extremely approachable (cf. Albers and James 1983). Another objective of the attractive presentation is to counter news reports of violence in the country and to convince the would-be visitor of the peace of the people and the land.

There is, however, another aspect of the indigenous Guatemalan portrayed in the tourist literature that begins to move us away from the image of the Indian as symbol for all that is Guatemalan—both Indian and non-Indian—to an image of the Indian as a unique being, essentially different from the nonindigenous half of the population. This feeling is perhaps most elaborately, publicly, and positively expressed in tourist literature. In these pieces, the Indians who are not in service roles are shown engaged in what are meant to be seen as culturally specific activities: for example, worshipping at stone altars or in dark, candle-filled churches; weaving on backstrap looms; and carrying water jugs, large baskets, or other unwieldy objects on their heads. Unlike the aforementioned photographs where locals are either shown interacting with tourists in the scene or, by means of eye contact, with the viewer of the photograph, this second type of image is meant to be viewed from afar, like some awesome scenery that is admired but little comprehended.[8]

Perhaps more than in the photography, the texts describe the Indian as being distinct and categorically different from the visitor. Even a single example from an INGUAT brochure will help illustrate how the Indian is portrayed as "different."

[The tropical growth in Guatemala] is an almost human vegetation. Human because it explodes and lives with rapid vigorous movements and with expressions which are similar to the . . . animal world. For all of it is mystery, it is suggestive and provokes myths and legends. In a world like this man becomes an interrogator and believes in god-like answers and myths similar to the nature which surrounds him.

In this environment the Mayan culture was born. It is not a

serene culture as is the Greek which is a product of clear islands and transparent seas but rather baroque in its widest sense, which means to say: confused, full of mystery and dark and terrible legends. (INGUAT n.d.)

The same themes—even the same words, at times—are repeated in other passages and stress the bonds between the Mayans and their mysterious past, the Indian's unchanging quality, the ties between *los naturales* and nature, and the gap between Indians and nonindigenous people.

While some aspects of Indian nature emphasized in the tourist material relate to features Indians themselves note, essential differences exist between the two. For example, ties with the past are stressed in both the tourist literature and by Indians themselves. Yet, while the former emphasizes the unchanging and mysterious nature of this relationship, the indigenous people stress a continuity with the past that is based on a thoughtful, creative reproduction of traditional themes and that fits into a broader, coherent, and culturally rational vision of the social world. By contrast, the image projected by the tourist material is one of mysteriousness akin to irrationality; a spirit closer to nature than other human beings; a lack of awareness of other, nonindigenous forms of being; and adherence to the past that is automatic instead of a conscious and purposeful decision. Indians are not seen as having a vision of society that is equally valid to (although different from) that of non-Indians; rather they are seen as different, puzzling, and essentially limited beings.

At the local level, at least within my field experience, the public expression of such negative sentiments was rather rare (actually much more so than I had anticipated to be the case)[9] and then almost always pronounced in private conversations between persons who already knew the others' sentiments, in more public situations where at least one party (often the outspoken one) was foreign to the area, or in episodes involving intoxicants. That more open or direct statements are absent should not seem entirely surprising in a community where Indians and ladinos live and work side by side, where a certain level of integration of ladinos and indigenous people exists in all aspects of life, where there is genuine friendship between individuals (students, in particular, mention this), and where the general community sentiment is that ethnic relations are better in Tecpán than in many surrounding towns. For these reasons, it was all the more surprising and memorable when, in the late 1970s, Tecpán's ladino mayor publicly proclaimed that Indians are the *escalas* (ladders) for ladinos trying to better themselves. And if the comment itself were not enough, the context of its issuance was the

Indian fair committee's queens' contest. This meant that the speaker made the claim in his official capacity as mayor in front of an audience almost exclusively Indian and one expecting to hear the usual government-sponsored rhetoric in praise of Mayan culture. The violation of the normal etiquette for public appearances (and, some would say, the public admission of what normally lies just below the spoken surface) so jolted the Indian community that years later the episode remains a prime example for Tecpán Indians of what motivates ladino actions against Indians, that is, a desire for wealth, an elevated sociopolitical position, and control over others.

That the mayor's claim has been remembered and retold many times is evidence, I believe, of the uniqueness of such a *public* statement rather than the uniqueness of its sentiment. While such direct public pronouncements of the negative worth of Indians are fairly rare in Tecpán, on the one hand, and by government officials addressing Indian audiences, on the other, the feeling on the part of the Indian population is that discriminatory actions are quite prevalent and far more damaging than "mere" words. An examination of indigenous images of the Indian is the subject of the next section.

Indigenous Perspectives

Indigenous portrayals of the Indian range from a negative self-image that Indians see forced on them by virtue of their position in Guatemalan society, to a positive view of a group of people practicing their traditional *costumbres* (customs), holding responsible jobs, and attempting to create or maintain some sphere of action (albeit one limited in range) dominated by Indian values. Because the former all too often is the reality of highland life and the latter but an ideal, the most positive expressions of being Indian that exist generally appear as individual acts, private interactions restricted to the domestic scene, and small public performances with no overt political themes.

Indigenous Guatemalans condemn the fact that all too often when ladinos appear to embrace the Indian, it is only their words that speak of some true union: their deeds, on the other hand, result in the hierarchical ordering of people. Indians feel that through their actions ladinos attempt to incorporate them into the structure of the larger social world, and inevitably the position allotted the Indian is a low one. Dress, seen in this context, does not function as it does in tourism, that is, as a commodity that is attractive to foreigners and that entices them to come to Guatemala and buy, if not textiles, then at least the whole image of highland Guatemala, which textiles and *traje* are central in creating. Neither does *traje* stand for all Guatemalans as a visually beautiful statement of national heritage. Rather, it points to the class status of the wearer and marks him or her as less than the non-Indian viewers. This idea is made very explicit in an example from Comalapa, a town to the northeast of Tecpán:

> Don't tell me that you don't look down on me, don't lie to me and tell me that my *huipil* [Indian blouse], my skirt, my *tocoyal* [a woven band plaited into a woman's hair] and my sandals don't humiliate you and spoil your splendid gala balls. Don't you remember that you showed me how you felt? Yes, of course, you must remember . . . [my offense was that] I dared to tread on your impeccable floors with my Indian sandals, I committed the sin of mingling with you when I was dressed, not in a beautiful maxi, like yours, but in a *huipil* and *corte* [Indian skirt]. (Maria Alicia Telon Sajcabun, in Jonas and Tobias 1974: 36)

In contrast to women (essentially *all* Indian women), Tecpán Indian men generally do not wear *traje*, and this is especially true of the younger ones. The reason most frequently given for this is that indigenous men are discriminated against in the workplace and that appearing in *traje* only makes the situation worse by making their identity explicit. It seems to me, however, that an explanation must go beyond this since most Indian women who work outside the home continue to wear *traje* in professional roles and do not make the claim that *not* wearing indigenous dress would change their work situation.

I would suggest that the discrimination arises in part because of the differential assessment of *traje* in terms of gender: the image of the Indian man in *traje* is categorically different from that of the Indian woman in indigenous dress. Women's *traje* (thought of in terms of extremely fine pieces) is an admired expression of female beauty. Given that it is painstakingly handcrafted in a bright array of colors and complemented with jewelry, ribbons, and elaborate hair accessories, women's *traje* conforms to (or appears to make reference to) "Western" standards of femininity, female loveliness, and the nonproductive consumption of wealth. And, while ladino women do not wear it on a regular basis, they admire it and even incorporate pieces into daytime or evening wear. Male *traje*, on the other hand, does not contain elements that resonate with the sartorial expression of masculinity according to Western tastes. Outfits incorporating such items as peddle-pusher-length striped pants decorated with bird designs or multicolored woven cloth wrapped around the head contrast sharply with such preferred Western male items of clothing as blue jeans, cowboy boots, and flannel, button-down shirts. The effect, then, is not only to label a man in *traje* as "Indian" but also to see him as one who is less masculine (even less adult) in a world dominated by Western, male values.

But, as we have seen, indigenous men in *traje* are not always portrayed negatively. In tourist literature and special pageants the image of the Indian man in traditional dress gets special attention that is full of praise. However, this positive image, some Indians charge, is not what it seems on the surface. Rather, it points to a victimization of the people being praised such that Indians become commodities in the capitalist scheme of the larger world, an arrangement that benefits the Indianless upper class and not Indians themselves. Thus, *traje* is or is not laudable, beautiful, and unique . . . is or is not dirty, crude, and lower class according to how it suits the money-making situation. *Traje* on an Indian in one of the highland tourist spots is good because it is good for tourism: *traje* on an Indian working as a migrant laborer on the coast is, at best, irrelevant . . . irrelevant to getting the job done but perhaps not to supplying clues about the supposed (lack of) intelligence, sensitivity, and general desires of the wearers.

Indigenous commentators regularly claim to feel the presence and force of negative public images generated, instituted, and preserved by non-Indians, and disagree heartily with these. In Tecpán, the most articulate and explicit pronouncements generally come from younger, more educated, more publicly active, and more nationally aware members of the indigenous population, ones with a high level of awareness of how actions and the physical presentation of self can be perceived and interpreted by a wide range of observers. The most vocal are also those who often take the risk of damning the image-producers and the system that perpetuates a particular image or set of images of the Indian for its own ends. For example, a particularly strong statement was issued by a group of indigenous Guatemalans who joined together at the archaeological ruins of Iximché, just outside of Tecpán, shortly after the massacre at the Spanish Embassy. The massacre—the killing of thirty-nine people on January 31, 1980, after a delegation of Indians and Indian supporters called on the Spanish ambassador to protest Guatemalan human rights violations—became a symbol for the general victimization of Indians by the government and associated forces. In the following portion of the Declaration of Iximché, the authors protest the public portrayals of Indians and label their continued victimization a "massacre." The authors of the statement have a well-developed notion of how indigenous people are being used in the capitalist system, where Indianness is either glorified to turn a profit or debased to turn indigenous people into less-than-humans, good only for their labor:

These rich and their government are the worse liars because they

massacre us in various ways and still try to deceive us, setting up
"fiestas folklóricas" such as the day of Tecún Umán, the [Día de la]
Raza, festivals . . . like those of Cobán, and . . . giving out little
medals, diplomas, pats on the back and little smiles to certain
professionals and "regal" Indians. Their cheating ends in speeches
filled with lies, and, finally, the photographs which the INGUAT
exploits for tourist trade. The INGUAT . . . paints Guatemala in a
very romantic and picturesque way with its Mayan ruins, its
weaving, dances, and traditions. The Indian becomes an object of
tourism, a commercial object. (Guatemalan Information Center
1981: 8)

In this quote, reference is made to several topics discussed earlier in this
chapter (e.g., the holiday commemorating Tecún Umán and INGUAT's
tourist campaign) with emphasis now on the deceitful nature of the
claims and the actual victimization of indigenous people. This theme of
victimization is a common one made frequently with reference to social
policies presented by the government as affecting all Guatemalans
equally when, in fact, Indians claim, they really sort out the indigenous
population. For example, the system of government farm loans purport-
edly available to all citizens with a certain amount of land is seen locally
as discriminating against Indians, the only people in the area with less
than the minimum land who need and want the financial aid.

The question then arises as to what positive steps Indians feel they can
take (or have taken) that would allow them to live as Indians in the larger
world. What would the union between Indians and non-Indians be based
on? And how would it look? The Declaration of Iximché offers a
statement on this subject:

To end all these evils perpetuated by the descendants of the rich
invaders and their government, we must fight allied with workers,
poor ladino peasants, committed students, townspeople, and other
popular and democratic sectors, to strengthen the union and solidarity among the Indians and poor ladinos, since the solidarity of
the popular movements with the Indian struggles has been sealed
with their lives in the Spanish Embassy. The sacrifice of these lives
brings us now closer than ever to a new society and the dawn of the
Indian's liberty. (Guatemalan Information Center 1981: 10)

The passage, then, combines a criticism of the ruling ladino elite—those
affiliated with the "state"—with a vision of a new, Indian-inspired
cultural order that harks back to preconquest ideals. While the Indian
is at the heart of the new order, it does not exclude non-Indians. Rather,

the non-Indians who are included are ones with a similar ideological orientation and who, with Indians, can forge a society run by popular and democratic principles.

But how are these ideals currently played out in a society where, according to Indians, the coming together of the two groups results in the domination of the indigenous segment? As some of the previous materials suggest, actual "solutions" are limited in the present-day world where even the smallest attempt to act publicly in accordance with indigenous ideals may be the cause of death for an indigenous person.

If action within the public sphere is potentially dangerous, the home, by contrast, provides a protected space where the expression of Indian values can be strong and central. It is here, ideally, that children are taught to use *traje*, speak *lengua* (referring to the local indigenous language), and practice *costumbre*. Included in *costumbre* are a number of celebrations that families may organize for the sowing of crops, the harvest of the year's supply of corn, the birth of a child, and so on. All are organized by domestic units for the benefit of the family and, perhaps, close neighbors. Furthermore, the effect of these is rarely felt beyond a certain small set of individuals or seen to intrude upon aspects of life that are of value to non-Indians.

Locally and regionally based organizations with a strictly Indian membership also exist and are involved in attempts to seize control of and separate out of the larger society what is seen as indigenous expressions of ethnic worth. These might be thought of as larger-scale efforts akin to family-based activities, and likewise aimed at strengthening pride in Indianness and fostering the practice of *costumbre*. However, unlike activities centered in the home, these have a public following that extends well beyond the sponsoring group within the indigenous community. Thus, while the professed and, perhaps, most important goal might be to engage indigenous people in the active, public expression of what it means to be Indian, those who organize and participate in the events are also well aware that they are addressing viewers from outside a strictly indigenous circle. The result is that complex patterns of meaning—intended meaning, supposed meaning, perceived meaning, meaning denied—can arise and surround the events. It may also mean that, depending on the larger, political circumstances, certain expressions of Indianness voiced at the community level will be read as public statements of autonomy and, consequently, seen as a challenge or threat to locally dominant ladino or government forces. The following case reveals some of the nuts-and-bolts difficulties indigenous people have in trying to take control of the production of the image of the Indian offered for public consumption in Guatemala.

The festival in Cobán mentioned in the Declaration of Iximché refers to the occasion and site of the national Indian queen's competition. Sponsored by the INGUAT, the Folkloric Festival is billed as a colorful celebration of Guatemalan culture and includes as its events special handicraft exhibits and costumed dances, along with the crowning of the *Rabín Ajau,* or national Indian queen. The competition for the queen sees entries from different highland municipalities vying to represent the entire Guatemalan indigenous population at local, national, and (sometimes) international events. This is the ideal, at least.

Up until the mid-1970s, towns in the Department of Chimaltenango sent contestants chosen and sanctioned by local indigenous groups. However, when participants started coming home with reports that stressed how corrupt things were and how the contestants were being used to further nonindigenous economic ends, the local Indian selection committees began to reassess the matter. They concluded that the festival hierarchy was dominated by ladinos who treated the queen contest like a sideshow rather than as a respectful tribute to the beauty of Mayan women, traditions, and *traje.* Because of this, a number of towns in the Chimaltenango area (Tecpán included) stopped sending locally sanctioned candidates, an action that was soon followed by other groups from other highland towns.

This, however, was not the only reaction to the festival situation. A group of Indians from the towns that boycotted the INGUAT event met in Tecpán to make plans for an Indian-run queen contest. While the event would be similar in form to the Cobán affair, its goal would be to provide the proper context for the appearance of each municipal representative and to focus on Indian culture in and of itself. Instead of subverting the expression of Indianness to monetary ends, the Indian production would match professed goals with actual ends and thereby underscore the purely indigenous values.

Plans for an Indian-run competition, however, never got off the ground. At the start of the first planning meeting in Tecpán, a suspected government *oreja* (spy, but literally, ear) appeared, claiming to want to participate. The meeting was quickly adjourned. Any further thoughts of continuing with plans were dashed as the political situation worsened and key individuals of the young committee were killed or forced into hiding. In the final assessment (and in the privacy of people's homes), Indian commentators charged that this was yet another incident where Indians attempting to participate in the wider Guatemalan society as a group in possession of their own cultural identity are dominated and forced to give over to ladinos and the national government what, at heart, is theirs alone.

The final image I want to mention is that of the professional Indian since it offers something of a bridge between the image of the land-poor *indio* damned to the lowest level of Guatemalan society and that of indigenous Guatemalans doing *costumbre* within the closed ranks of family or small local groups. The professional Indian, by virtue of training, is often able to secure employment in respected community positions (as teachers, home economics agents, agriculture specialists, etc.). At the same time, being Indian means that he or she will have some small influence in the community, as a role model for other Indians or, perhaps, even a policymaker. Being professional *and* Indian, these people redefine the image of the Indian as competent in the ways of the larger world and possessing the "special talents" (e.g., language and familiarity with local customs) to work with individuals who might be, but are not necessarily, Indian.

As with the activities of the Indian organizations, there is an ideal and a real side to being an educated Indian in the work force. While Indian professionals ideally function as examples of intelligent, resourceful human beings in a biethnic world, there is always the threat that the individual will be redefined by the dominant forces as a subversive.[10] There is enough of a history of this redefinition to move some parents to admit to being glad that their sons have not gone on in school. The thought is that a young, educated man (rather than a woman) with a strong character and the tendency to speak out is more likely to hold a public position where his actions are widely known and could be interpreted as having crossed the fine line between balanced participation in the larger social world and advocating Indian interests that run against the dominant national grain.

Summary Comments

Discussion in this chapter has centered on conventional characterizations of the Indian as these relate to indigenous and nonindigenous perspectives. The set of images, in turn, translates into a model of the construction of Guatemalan society and, in particular, focuses on relationships between ladinos and Indians or between the indigenous population and the government. In the cases examined, the images of the Indian shifted dramatically according to the "work" to which each was being put. These shifts, however, are not without their logic.

In figure 1, I present a four-part grid that is meant to summarize important dimensions of the materials just presented. In particular I want to emphasize the fundamental differences in how indigenous and nonindigenous peoples assign values to images of the Indian, images used to characterize the population, on the one hand, as an integrated, interrelated group or, on the other, as autonomous units, unique and

Figure 1. Contrasting Images of the Indian

		Images presented nationally by government, and locally by ladinos	Images presented by the indigenous population
Indians and ladinos character-ized as:	interrelated peoples	+ the notion of "we Guatemalens"; some notion of a common history and heritage	– a utility character-ized by conflict and domination
	autonomous units	– Indians as mysterious others and a source of labor for the market	+ a people practicing *costumbre* in the home or in small groups

distinct from one another. An important, fifth dimension falls outside this neat schemata and has to do with indigenous efforts to build a positive image of their people within the broadest sphere of Guatemalan national life. In the Tecpán case, professional Indians most clearly fall in this group, although the actual status or positive valuation of people in these positions is far from secure.

In closing, I want to focus on a specific example having to do with clothing and examine how Guatemalans acting within a given social moment can contemplate and adjust their own appearance (if only momentarily and on an extremely small scale) and hence the social role assigned to them. It is within such concrete situations that people have to weigh their desires, abilities, and expectations against the expecta-tions and perceptions of others. In these cases, it is also a matter of anticipating how others will react—what image one's presence brings into being—and, in cases that are not purely routine and ordinary, taking the risk of standing out as "different" or, even more extreme, being the subject of negative comments and actions.

This particular instance involves a group of young Indian women in a professional school in Guatemala City who approached their graduation date with the knowledge that they would be obliged to abandon *traje* in order to don *togas* (graduation gowns). Three of the group petitioned the administration for permission to wear *traje*, which they succeeded in doing. The rest of the Indian graduates, characterized as fearing negative comments from the audience, opted for graduation gowns. In the end, however, the audience was an extremely sympathetic one: they gave the indigenous women, so identified by dress, standing ovations in recognition of their special achievements as Indians. The Indian women in *togas*, of course, did not get the same recognition, and later regretted their decision to abandon *traje* for the "safer" act of hiding their ethnic identity behind graduation robes.

As this example shows, the public presentation of self is often precisely calculated, the wearer choosing to emphasize one aspect or another without always knowing the full consequences of the act. This is particularly true when the situation is anything more than routine and when it is not obvious which image of the Indian will come into play for any particular circumstance. Given this uncertainty, individuals working on a day-to-day, personal, local level are, nonetheless, willing to invest a lot of energy (and, when it comes to *traje*, a lot of money) in an effort to create and make stick a new, dominant image of the Indian within the Guatemalan state.

Notes

Acknowledgments: This paper grew out of a chapter of my dissertation and therefore benefited greatly from comments made by my thesis committee: Nancy Munn, Michael Silverstein, and Milton Singer. I would also like to thank Greg Urban for his helpful suggestions on the conference draft of this paper and Charles Briggs for encouraging me to elaborate a bit more on the gender theme. An abbreviated version of the same thesis chapter appeared in *Cultural Survival Quarterly* (1985: 9[2]: 22–23) under the title "Guatemala: Everybody's Indian When the Occasion's Right."

1. The preferred terms used locally are *indígena* (indigenous person) and *natural* (native). The term *indio* (which translates into English as Indian) has derogatory connotations and is not a common word for self-definition. I have chosen to use the English word "Indian" most frequently in this paper *not* as a translation of *indio* but because it is commonly used in the English-language literature and because it has a certain public or popular ring to it that fits well with my discussion of public representations of the group.

2. While *ladino* and *Indian* are generally the terms used to label and divide up Guatemala's population, the two terms are not always enough. Pansini (1977: 138–177) distinguishes between "European Guatemalans"—those with strong, direct ties to families and life abroad—and *Guatemaltecos* (Guatemalans)—a label that goes beyond referring to the person's nationality and indicates group status akin to the *criollos* of Guatemala's past (that is, native-born descendants of foreigners with upper-class socioeconomic ties).

3. See Comaroff (1985) and Hebdige (1979) for related treatments of clothing used as an expression of resistance.

4. I conducted field research for this project for thirteen months between October 1979 and February 1981 and then returned to Guatemala for brief periods in 1983 and 1985.

5. See, for example, Richards (1985) for a complementary treatment of materials from the Ixil region.

6. From what I have read about the founders of and principal forces behind this celebration, they appear similar to those in the Mexican *Movimiento* described by Judith Friedlander in *Being Indian in Hueyapan* (1975).

7. In many important ways, women in Guatemala are associated with the private, domestic sphere and men with the public, juro-political sphere. Thus, while the public is horrified and saddened by the political killings of men, this horror takes a quantitative leap when women are the victims. Because of her sex, it is felt that a woman should be sheltered and protected by her father, husband, or son; and when women are killed in political conflicts, say, that is a signal that something is distinctly wrong in society. That is, in fact, what happened in 1980 when the deaths of a few publicly known women were used as evidence that *la situación* (as the political situation is euphemistically referred to) in Guatemala had escalated.

8. Dumont (1988), in his article on the concept of the Tasaday (Tasadayity, as he puts it), makes a similar distinction between, on the one hand, the gap separating Western "Self" and temporally/spatially distant "Other" and, on the other, the appeal (aesthetic, moral, etc.) of this same Other to the Self.

9. Tani Adams (1978), for example, writes on neighboring San Martin Jilotepeque and has a number of direct statements by ladinos slurring Indian character.

10. Sometimes the line between professional, community-based work and subversive activities is a thin one indeed. After many months of work in Tecpán I asked a few individuals if people from the community were involved in guerrilla activities. While people seemed loathe to use the word "guerrilla," the answers I got mentioned Tecpanecos' involvement with "educational activities." In fact, the first person from the area to be killed in the 1980s was a man who was a teacher and who had spoken out on number of occasion, denouncing social injustice perpetuated by the government on the indigenous population.

References

Adams, Tani Marielena
    1978   San Martin Jilotepequez: aspects of the political and socioeconomic structure of a Guatemalan peasant community. Unpublished paper.
Albers, Patricia C., and William R. James
    1983   Tourism and the changing photographic image of the Great Lakes Indians. *Annals of Tourism Research* 10(1): 123–148.
Comaroff, Jean
    1985   *Body of power, spirit of resistance: the culture and history of a South African people.* Chicago: University of Chicago Press.
Dumont, Jean-Paul
    1988   The Tasaday, which and whose?: toward the political economy of an ethnographic sign. *Cultural Anthropology* 3(3): 261–275.
Friedlander, Judith
    1975   *Being Indian in Hueyapan: a study of forced identity in contemporary Mexico.* New York: St. Martin's Press.
Gombrich, E. H.
    1972   Truth and the stereotype. In *Art and illusion: a study in the psychol-*

ogy of pictorial representation. Princeton, N.J.: Princeton University Press.

El Gráfico
1980a Genesis del movimiento. February 20: 5.
1980b Tecún Umán: simbolo de la nacionalidad. February 20: 6.

Guatemalan Information Center
1981   Iximché: the indigenous people declare unity. *Popular Histories*, no. 5. Long Beach, Calif.

Guzmán Böckler, Carlos
1975   El ladino: un ser ficticio. In *Guatemala: una interpretación histórico-social*, Carlos Guzmán Böckler and Jean-Loup Herbert (eds.), 101–121. Mexico: Siglo XXI Editores.

Hebdige, Dick
1979   *Subculture: the meaning of style.* New York: Methuen.

INGUAT (Instituto Guatemalteco de Turismo)
n.d.   *La democracia, cradle of Mesoamerica.* Instituto Guatemalteco de Turismo.

Jonas, Susanne, and David Tobias, eds.
1974   *Guatemala.* Berkeley, Calif.: North American Congress on Latin America.

Pansini, Jude
1977   El Pilar: a plantation microcosm of Guatemalan ethnicity. PhD diss., Department of Anthropology, University of Rochester.

Richards, Michael
1985   Cosmopolitan world view and counterinsurgency in Guatemala. *Anthropological Quarterly* 58(3): 90–107.

Scott, James C.
1985   *Weapons of the weak: everyday forms of peasant resistance.* New Haven, Conn.: Yale University Press.

Steiner, Wendy
1982   *The colors of rhetoric: problems in the relation between modern literature and painting.* Chicago: University of Chicago Press.

12. The Semiotics of State-Indian Linguistic Relationships: Peru, Paraguay, and Brazil

Greg Urban

> *These considerations show that . . . anatomical type, language and culture have not necessarily the same fates; that a people may remain constant in type and language, and change in culture; that it may remain constant in type, but change in language; or that it may remain constant in language, and change in type and culture.*
> —*Franz Boas*, The Mind of Primitive Man

Boas (1911) long ago demonstrated the separability of race, language, and culture. However, he failed to explicate the mechanism whereby language as an abstract code or grammar—so often assumed to form part of culture—could become detached from the rest of culture and "diffuse" independently. What is going on at the interface of languages in contact such that the grammatical code for referential communication frees itself from clothing styles, behavioral patterns, beliefs, and the rest of culture? It is the purpose of this chapter to reopen that question and to propose a semiotic answer, namely, that whole grammars can function as complex signs, which, while serving the nonreferential communicative needs of social actors, enter into play with the other indexical signs that are deployed in establishing, maintaining, and transforming social relationships. At the same time as they function indexically, however, language and the various nonlinguistic signs also function symbolically: they are interpreted and evaluated by means of discourse. In the contact between cultures, different indices come to acquire distinct interpretations and evaluations, and it is this process of differential interpretation and valuation that leads to their distinct fates.

The chapter focuses specifically on relations between language and culture in the encounter between states and Indians in three cases: Paraguay, Peru, and Brazil. I will argue that the ideological value of Amerindian languages to the state is different in these three cases, and that this ideological value influences their fate. In Paraguay, where an Amerindian language (Guaraní) flourishes alongside Spanish, despite the virtual disappearance of Amerindian culture, society represents itself to itself as held together by "alliance." This alliance is symbolized by the relationship between Spanish and Guaraní, despite the homogenization of various nonlinguistic aspects of Paraguayan culture. In Peru, in contrast, where the persistence of Amerindian culture is considerably greater than that of Amerindian language, Quechua having been steadily on the decline, society was and in some measure still is represented as cemented together by the asymmetrical bonds of governance. The relationship between Spanish and Quechua, correspondingly, has been ideologized in terms of "dominance" and "oppression." Brazil resembled Paraguay until the middle of the eighteenth century. The so-called general language (*lingua geral*), spoken by the majority of the population, was until that time Nheêngatú, originally a trade language based on Tupinamba, which is closely related to Guaraní. However, since then, Nheêngatú has been disappearing; it is now nearly extinct. Correspondingly, beginning in the mid-eighteenth century, society came to represent itself as held together by a "shared culture"—despite considerable diversity. Cultural sharing was in turn symbolized by the sharing of Portuguese.

Types of Meaningfulness

The social meaningfulness of linguistic codes in situations of bilingualism or bidialectalism has been the focus of considerable research interest since Blom and Gumperz (1972: 433) proposed that a dialect may have "social value as a signal of distinctness and of a speaker's identification with others" (see Gal 1987; Auer 1984; Auer and diLuzio 1984; Hill 1985; Hill and Hill 1986; Scotton 1983). At the same time, there has been virtually no attention paid to the semiotic mechanisms through which meaning is produced. There has been simultaneously a perpetuation of certain assumptions about the nature of social meaningfulness of code choice, assumptions that may be valid for a range of situations but that the South American data tend to belie, and that, in any case, seem unable to account for the detachability of language from other aspects of culture.

The key assumption to be reassessed here is that the linguistic code functions as a marker or index of a social group, typically of an "ethnic group" or "nationality." This assumption goes hand in hand with the implicit understanding that a given "people" has one and only one language associated with their culture, what Urban and Sherzer (1988) have called the "one language one culture hypothesis." But this hypothesis is belied by the linguistic exogamy and multilingualism of the northwest Amazon, where linguistic diversity is found amidst homogeneity in the nonlinguistic aspects of culture (Sorensen 1967;

Jackson 1974; Grimes 1985). It is also belied by the situation of the Aymara language in Bolivia, as described by Abercrombie in this volume, where cultural diversity is masked by the sharing of a single linguistic code. And it is belied by the extensive bilingualism in Paraguay, where Guaraní and Spanish are spoken together across a relatively homogeneous culture.

The purpose of this chapter is not to deny the widespread importance of the linguistic code as a signal of social group membership. On the contrary, it appears that social actors tend regularly to interpret codes and code variants as markers of social groups, so that one of the semiotic pressures driving the mechanism operative at the language-culture interface is the tendency to project a one language/one social group interpretation. At the same time, that pressure taken in isolation fails to allow us to understand the possibility of detachment, which is crucial to grasping the nation-state and Indian problem from the point of view of language. The purpose of this chapter rather is to throw light on what other pressures on the language-culture relationship may also be operative through an assessment of the semiotic characteristics of the linguistic code as sign.

From a semiotic point of view, choice of linguistic code need not function for actors as a signal. But when it does so—when the fact of choosing or being able to speak in grammar A as opposed to some other grammar not-A carries meaning—we can distinguish the semiotic pathways through which meaning can be communicated, first, as "indexical" versus "symbolic" or "ideological," and, second, within either the indexical or symbolic mode as "privatively" or "equipollently" meaningful.

A grammar functions indexically insofar as it is actually related by virtue of some contiguity to that which it signals. Thus, it may mark out a group of individuals by virtue of the capability they share to actually communicate by means of the grammar. Or, again, it may signal the presence of certain aspects of the context, as so many studies of code switching have endeavored to demonstrate. The key characteristic of indexical functioning is the one-to-one relationship between the code and the social group or contextual features to which it is linked. But here it must be pointed out as well that when two languages come into contact, as in the case of Spanish (or Portuguese) and the Amerindian languages of South America, there are at least three potential indices formed: there is language A as an index of one social group, language B as an index of another, and languages A+B as an index of a third group of bilinguals.[1]

That competence in A+B can be an indexical signal of social group membership is of importance in understanding the Paraguayan case, as well as, more generally, in grasping the mechanism whereby language becomes detached from other aspects of culture. Although semiotic pressure tends toward a one language/one social group identification, the situation of bilingualism makes possible a two language/one social group identification. Nonlinguistic aspects of culture may be shared throughout the group, which, however, is characterized by competence in two codes. This is not perfectly the case in Paraguay, since approximately only half are fluent in both Spanish and Guaraní, with the majority of the remainder (40–45 percent being monolingual in Guaraní, with only a small portion (<10 percent) monolingual in Spanish. But the extent of bilingualism is sufficient for us to imagine that it could be indexical of "Paraguayaness."

In addition to functioning indexically, however, the language code also functions symbolically or ideologically. That is, its meaning is actually encoded in talk about the code or about code interrelationships, for example, in debates over the language to be used in education, in talk about "oppressed languages," in characterizations of the affective qualities associated with one language as opposed to another, and in references to the socially unifying character of sharing a common language or dialect. In the symbolic mode, the linguistic code is glossed and its meaning discussed within language itself. In this way, what is otherwise a simple index comes to have "connotations" or meanings that can interact with and influence the indexical level.

When language as code enters into this symbolic realm of ideological critique and glossing, in the encounter between cultures, it does so alongside the other nonlinguistic aspects of culture. The various indices in this way assume distinct ideological meanings and, hence, can be subject to distinct fates. For example, in the early encounters between the Portuguese and Amerindians in Brazil, Amerindian clothing patterns were interpreted by the Portuguese not as simple indices of ethnic identity, but rather as "nakedness" within a code of morality that condemned it. Insofar as this belief or symbolic meaning of the clothing index diffused across boundaries and was taken up by the Indians themselves, the result was a self-consciousness—replicated in encounters between Indians and Brazilian nationals to this day—that created a semiotic pressure to modify the identity index itself in the direction of the Portuguese norm.[2] At the same time, the Amerindian languages received a distinct interpretation. The coastal language Tupinamba, for example, was regarded by the Portuguese as a medium for commerce. It became the trade language later known as Nheêngatú.

At an abstract plane, the general mechanism proposed here is this: that beliefs in the form of discourse can, first, interpret indices, supplying them with the symbolic or ideological meaning they have, and, second, "diffuse" across cultural boundaries and thereby differentially affect the maintenance or transformation of different identity indices. One way in which language becomes separated from other nonlinguistic aspects of culture is when it assumes the status of index in this differential meaning-giving process. Belief 1, originating from culture A, interprets the language of culture B as an index 1 and positively values it. Belief 2, also originating from culture A, interprets a nonlinguistic index 2 of culture B but negatively values it. The result is that, insofar as beliefs 1 and 2 become shared by cultures A and B, index 1 flourishes, while index 2 is transformed.

If the interaction between indexical and symbolic meanings of language and other aspects of culture drives the mechanism of historical change, a full semiotic understanding of language requires us to distinguish between privative and equipollent meaning (Trubetzkoy 1939). By privative is meant the meaning accruing to a language A as opposed to all other languages not-A. By equipollent, in contrast, is meant the meaning accruing to language A in relationship to specific other languages. The simplest case—and the one most relevant to the central problematic of this chapter—is the bipolar opposition between two languages A and B. At the indexical plane, the privative functioning of the language code as sign is to circumscribe a positive collection, for example, an ethnic group. The equipollent functioning is to point to a relationship, for example, the contrast between formality/informality, as shown in studies of Spanish/Guaraní code switching, or the social relationship between groups. At the symbolic plane, privative functioning means glossing the linguistic code in terms of positive features, for example, Portuguese as representing the essence of Brazilianness. Equipollent functioning means glossing the relationship between languages in relational terms, for example, viewing the relationship between Spanish and Guaraní as one of "alliance," or the relationship between Spanish and Quechua as one of "dominance."

The Three Cases: A Closer Look

In each of the cases investigated here, Amerindian languages and cultures came into contact with European-based languages and cultures in the sixteenth century, and in each case the military superiority and political dominance of the European-based social organizations became immediately apparent. Moreover, in each case, only one Amerindian language—of the many that were present—emerged as of significance for the state-to-be. Within this matrix of military and political asymmetry, and of focus on a single Amerindian language, however, the differing fates of the Amerindian languages and cultures are striking. How are we to understand these differences? An answer can be found in the differing semiotic roles that the Amerindian languages played in the self-representation of social cohesiveness in the three cases. These roles, which involve the language code functioning at the symbolic or ideological plane and interacting with the indexical levels, can in turn be related to the original New World encounters and to the meanings that took shape at that time.

The basic contrast is between Peru, on the one side, where the relationship between European and Amerindian society was one of *domination*, and Brazil and Paraguay, on the other, where domination was predicated upon a privileged *alliance*. From a semiotic point of view, the social relationship of domination in the Andes was indexed by the linguistic relationship between Spanish and Quechua. Correspondingly, the social relationship of alliance was indexed by the linguistic relationship between Spanish and Guaraní, in Paraguay, and between Portuguese and *lingua geral* (or Tupinamba) in Brazil.

The foundations for both alliance and domination were to be found, in turn, in the pre-Columbian linguistic and social relations. In the case of the Andes, the Spaniards found a situation of dominance already in place in the relationships between Quechua and other Amerindian languages. Edmonson (1983: 90–91) documents that, while the Incas may not initially have endeavored to abolish the local languages, they—in the words of Cieza de León—"ordered and decreed, with severe punishment for failure to obey, that all the natives of their empire should know and understand the language of Cuzco . . . in the space of a few years a single tongue was known and used in an extension of 1,200 leagues; yet even though this language was employed, they all spoke their own." The Spanish language and society thus entered into an already established system of dominance in which domination was indexed linguistically in the relationship between Quechua and other Amerindian languages, or, perhaps, in the relationship between monolingualism in Quechua and bilingualism in Quechua plus other Amerindian language.

Spanish could not move smoothly into this domination relationship, however. By conquering the Incas and establishing a domination relationship between Spanish and Quechua, the Spanish could be viewed as liberating the other Amerindian languages from their oppression by Quechua. In fact, Edmonson (1983: 96) notes that the Spanish conquest "led to the resurgence of some of the local languages, especially in the areas most recently conquered by the Incas." In order to maintain the symbolism of linguistic control, therefore, the Spanish had to first ensure that Quechua remained in place as a "lengua general del Peru."

Within this ideological matrix, Quechua came to flourish in the seventeenth and eighteenth centuries, primarily through the church and missionary orders. Priests were pressured to learn Quechua, and curricula were put into place in the schools and universities. Juan de Balboa established the first chair of Quechua at San Marcos in 1567. Plays were produced and performed in Quechua, including perhaps the best known among them, *Ollantáy*. With the gradual disappearance of the local languages, Spanish came to stand in a direct relationship of domination vis-à-vis Quechua. The linguistic symbolism of domination, however, is correlated with inherent instabilities. Owing to the semiotic pressure to project a one language/one culture/one people relationship, the dominated language can come to appear as a threat and may, indeed, be a real threat as the basis for unification in a class struggle. In fact, in 1781 with the Tupac Amaru rebellion, the monolingual Spanish speakers moved to prohibit plays in Quechua and to mandate Spanish.

The important point here, however, is that the linguistic symbolism of domination was already in place during the late pre-Columbian period. Although the appropriation of that symbolism by the Spanish involved various maneuvers, the basic interpretation of language relationships in terms of domination carried over from the Incaic period through the colonial era and almost into the present. The symbolic glue of Peru, therefore, at least insofar as the symbolism of language relationships is concerned, had ancient roots.

In Paraguay and in Brazil as well, there were also pre-Columbian roots to the later linguistic symbolism, but the nature of that symbolism was wholly distinct. In the coastal regions of Brazil and into Paraguay were found speakers of closely related languages belonging to the Tupi-Guaraní family. These Tupian populations were largely village-level peoples, who, however, were engaged in warfare with one another and with the non-Tupian peoples, and who were accustomed to forming alliances for purposes of raiding. The Portuguese, Spanish, and French insinuated themselves into the existing systems, wherein language was used as one of the indexical tests of ally versus enemy status.

In the Paraguayan area, the Guaraní found in the Spanish an ally in their campaigns, and the Spanish similarly found in the Guaraní useful guides and military allies. Métraux (1946: 200) goes so far as to suggest that "the success of the expeditions that crossed the northern Chaco . . . was due mainly to the Guaraní guides and auxiliary troops." Elsewhere, he observes that the Guaraní:

who understood the aim of the Spaniards and who hoped to make them allies in their raids, were extremely friendly to the Spaniards, and provided them with food and women. Henceforth, the Guaraní served as auxiliaries and porters in all Spanish expeditions . . . When Alvar Nuñez de Vaca fought the Mbayá-Guaicurú in 1542, he was assisted by 10,000 Guaraní, who gathered at Tapuá. Two thousand Guaraní accompanied Domingo de Irala in 1548 and even more followed Nufrio de Chaves in 1558. (Métraux 1948: 76–77)

The Guaraní at this time were also the most numerous tribe in the far east of what is today Paraguay, in a region extending along both banks of the Paraguay River and into southern Brazil. The alliance was thus mutually beneficial, and the linguistic relationship between Spanish and Guaraní came to index and later symbolize it.

It is important to note that the Guaraní who formed alliances and interbred with the Spanish—producing the predominant mestizo class in Paraguay—were only one of three classes of Guaraní. Their plight differed considerably from that of the Guaraní who were forced to labor on the *encomiendas* around Asunción, and also from that of the Guaraní along the Paraná River in what is today southern Brazil who were gathered together in mission stations. The former were ruthlessly exploited and the latter relatively sheltered until 1767, when the Jesuits were expelled from South America. The privileged mestizo class—bilingual in Spanish and Guaraní—stood as oppressors of the *encomienda* Guaraní and of the non-Tupian Indians. So, while the Spanish-Guaraní dyad symbolized alliance, that alliance was a privileged one within a matrix of warfare and exploitation of other Amerindians.

Brazil was until the mid-eighteenth century nearly identical to Paraguay, although commerce—especially in brazilwood during the sixteenth century—appears to have played more of a role in the establishment of the *lingua geral*, based on the coastal language known as Tupinamba, which was closely related to Guaraní. Like Guaraní, however, *lingua geral* spread to the interior as part of a privileged alliance with Portuguese in opposition to other Amerindian languages. Bands of mestizos, known as *bandeirantes*, originating in São Paulo and radiating outward, tamed the frontier during the seventeenth and eighteenth centuries. C. R. Boxer (1964: 31) notes that these *bandeirantes* "spoke Tupí-Guaraní . . . in preference to Portuguese, at any rate when at home with their womenfolk or when absent on their far-ranging expeditions into the interior (sertão)." Emphasizing the prevalence of the Amerindian language in Brazil, he continues: "this preference for the maternal tongue did not, perhaps, apply to those of them who had been educated at the Jesuit Colleges of Santos and São Paulo, but even these men were bilingual."

The positive evaluation of *lingua geral* by the Portuguese, which, in the present interpretation, imbued it with symbolic meaning and value, contrasted sharply with the negative attitude toward other Amerindian languages, as summarized by Teodoro Sampaio (cited in Elia 1979: 177):

"the Tupian languages of the coast, very similar among themselves, were what came to be considered prototypical of our indigenous languages... All of the other languages were disparaged by the Portuguese, just as they were disparaged by the Tupi themselves, and they were included in a general group, called Tapuia, that in Tupi meant 'enemy, barbarian.'" As in the Paraguayan case, and in contradistinction to Peru, the symbolism of privileged linguistic alliance took hold in Brazil. This symbolism was grounded in actual trading, military, and sexual alliances. The linguistic symbolism of the colonial period, therefore, as in Paraguay and Peru, had its roots in pre-Columbian symbolism. In Paraguay and Brazil, this symbolism was grounded in indexical relationships within a system of warfare and alliance between largely village-level peoples. In Peru, the symbolism was grounded in indexical relations of domination based upon conquest.

What differentiates Brazil from Paraguay, however, is that this early bilingualism and symbolic alliance continues into the present in Paraguay, whereas in Brazil it has almost completely vanished. By the mid-eighteenth century, when the coastal regions and portions of the interior of Brazil were settled, the government began making efforts to instate Portuguese as the sole unifying language of Brazil. These efforts included the expulsion of the Jesuits in 1767, who had promoted the spread of the Tupian *lingua geral* to non-Tupian Indians through the missions. *Lingua geral* continued to flourish in the interior, especially in Amazonia, through much of the nineteenth century in the form known as Nheêngatu, but it is now nearly extinct, being found only in isolated pockets in the Amazonian interior.

Race, Language, and Culture

The decline of *lingua geral* may be traced to shifts in the symbolic meaning and valuation of linguistic relations, as constituted through discourse and ideological debate in Brazil. This ideological shift and its social functions will be discussed in the next section. However, it is important to note that in the case of *lingua geral* the one language/one culture/one people hypothesis did not obtain. *Lingua geral* was spoken by Amerindians, even by some whose mother language was unrelated to Tupian; but it was also spoken by individuals of Portuguese descent and, prominently, by mestizos; and it was even spoken by blacks, especially in Amazonia (Elia 1979: 195). A similar situation obtained in Paraguay. But it is not simply that *lingua geral* and Guaraní cut across racial boundaries. It is that in each case the Amerindian language was spoken side-by-side with a European language, despite the relative homogenization of nonlinguistic culture.

Various observers have noted for both Brazil and Paraguay the persistence of cultural elements derived from the Amerindian past. There is,
for example, the use of manioc, which was a staple crop among the
Tupian populations of the pre-Columbian period. And there is the
recurrent use in contemporary Brazilian and Paraguayan literature, and
in the arts more generally, of Amerindian mythological themes and
motifs. But the central point here is that these cultural elements do not
single out a separate group of people associated with the Amerindian
languages in question. Rather, in Brazil historically and in Paraguay up
to the present, two distinct linguistic codes—one European and one
Amerindian—were employed within a broader cultural matrix that was
relatively homogeneous in other respects. The linguistic codes became
in some measure detached from other elements of the cultures and
"diffused" independently of them. How are we to account for this
linguistic spread?

I have already argued that the indexical and symbolic meanings of the
Spanish-Guaraní and Portuguese-*lingua geral* linguistic relationships
have their foundations in historical social relationships grounded in a
privileged alliance. Based upon this understanding, it is possible to
construct an ideal-typic model of actors' strategies under the alliance
interpretation of linguistic interrelations, and to contrast it with an
analogous model under the domination interpretation, such as appears
to have characterized the Peruvian case. While we do not have suffi-
ciently detailed census materials available for the historical periods that
would allow us to test the predictions of these models, it is possible to
examine contemporary censuses for evidence in this regard.

Alliance, unlike domination, is founded upon the mutual interest of
the parties to it in maintaining a social relationship, whether that
interest be military, economic, or sexual-reproductive. When a bipolar
language relationship comes to symbolize alliance, therefore, we can
imagine that it will be manipulated indexically in accord with the same
general purposes. Each party has an interest in learning the language of
the other, so that bilingualism flourishes. When monolingual speakers
acquire the second in a pair of allied languages, they have no desire to give
up the first, since to do so would defeat the very reason for acquiring the
second language. Bilingualism thus celebrates the alliance.

Under such a symbolic model of social cohesion, society is not thought
of as glued together by virtue of sameness, that is, by virtue of sharing a
common culture. Rather, it is thought of as fused together by the
attractive forces of difference, and that self-understanding can serve as
the representation of solidarity so long as there are no de facto fissures
in the collectivity along the lines of the difference as symbolically
encoded. Anthropologists are familiar with such models in exchange

theory. Cohesion results from the mutual attraction of unlike entities, which can interact by means of exchange, as in the classical moiety systems. The irony is that the symbolic self-understanding in terms of difference leads, in the case of language, to homogenization. The limiting case of the model sketched above is the completely bilingual community, in which everyone is in fact like everyone else in speaking the two allied languages. It is thus possible to end up with a single society, as in the Paraguayan case or among the multilingual Tukanoans of the northwest Amazon, which understands itself to be held together by means of linguistic difference, but in which there is in fact linguistic and cultural homogeneity. There is a single shared life-style in the society, but that life-style involves bilingualism.

The ideal type of domination is thoroughly distinct in this regard. Dominator and dominated are at odds, the former wishing to maintain and the latter to change the status quo. Insofar as the bipolar relationship between two languages, such as Spanish and Quechua, comes to symbolize domination, it is possible to imagine the strategies that will be employed in manipulating the languages indexically. From the point of view of the dominated, there are three possible goals: (1) to get rid of the dominator, (2) to transform the relationship, or (3) to become the dominator. Each has its counterpart in linguistic strategies. To get rid of the dominator means to unite socially and culturally around the dominated language, as in fact occurred during various periods of Peruvian history, but most notably in the Tupac Amaru revolt of 1781. Monolingualism in the dominated language is valued, and there is no tendency toward the expansion of bilingualism. To transform the relationship involves a similar rallying around the dominated language, but only to valorize it on a par with the dominating language, as has happened in the recent period, especially in the 1970s in Peru. The trend under this strategy is again toward monolingualism in the dominated language, though bilingualism would appear as acceptable under a relationship transformed in the direction of alliance. The third strategy, however, is to become the dominator, and this means to become monolingual in the dominant language. Here bilingualism emerges as a transient phase in the move toward monolingualism in the dominant language. From the point of view of strategies of the dominated, therefore, there are competing forces tending, on the one hand, to maintain monolingualism in the dominated language and, on the other, to produce monolingualism in the dominant language on the part of dominated parties, with bilingualism as a transitional phenomenon.

The strategies employed by the dominators, correspondingly, reflect an ambivalence toward the dominated language. On the one hand, there is a desire to maintain the symbolic relationship of dominance and hence to encourage the perpetuation of the dominated language. On the other hand, insofar as the dominated language becomes an actual threat to domination by serving as a rallying symbol, there is an effort to prohibit it and instate the dominant language. Such an ambivalence has in fact characterized Peruvian history since the early colonial period (Mannheim 1983, 1984). What remains constant here, however, is that the dominant have no desire to acquire the language of the dominated. Hence, the dominant maintain their language while some of the dominated acquire it. A kind of "semipermeable membrane" develops in situations of symbolic dominance wherein there is a unidirectional flow, over time, toward the dominant language.

Under the dominance model, society is self-represented as held together by the asymmetrical bonds of governance, symbolized by the relationship between two languages. Unlike alliance, asymmetry through domination is not mutually attractive. Rather, it is characterized by conflicting tendencies. On the one hand, both parties wish to remain distinct, though for different reasons—the dominators so as to perpetuate the domination relationship and the dominated so as to be able to throw off the domination or to change the relationship. On the other hand, both parties want the dominated group to become like the dominators, though again for different reasons—the dominated so as to become dominators and the dominant so as to avoid the threat to their domination.

What is the solution to these conflicting tendencies? It is to differentially ideologize the various elements of culture, and, in particular, to remove some of the indices from the sphere of relational symbolization of domination. In the Peruvian case, where domination is symbolized in language, other indices of identity, such as clothing styles, domestic arrangements, and cooking, can be de-ideologized. This accomplishes a twofold purpose. For the dominated, it allows the perpetuation of cultural identity without that identity seeming to be a threat to the dominators, since the latter construe the threat as confined to linguistic identity. For the dominators, it maintains the separateness of the dominated, while allowing the dominated to feel that they have moved into positions of domination by virtue of having abandoned their language. Differential ideologization thus creates a gap between the overt and the covert. Cultural elements other than language can be "covert" forms of resistance, or, correspondingly, domination, depending upon the actor's point of view on the system.

One consequence of differential ideologization is the separation of language from other elements of culture. Due to the semipermeable membrane phenomenon, the language of the dominant group tends to spread to the dominated group, while the dominated language recedes.

However, de-ideologized elements of culture are not subjected to the same pressure. Consequently, they tend to persist even after the language with which they were originally associated has disappeared. The situation is the reverse of that under the alliance model. Under alliance, the two languages persist despite the homogenization of other elements of culture. Under domination, the dominant language tends to spread, and the dominated language to recede, despite the maintenance of heterogeneity in other elements of culture.

In the contrast between Paraguay and Peru—as operating under the alliance and domination models, respectively—the key cultural category is that of the "mestizo," the racial/cultural mediating third term between the main poles of the alliance or domination relationship— "white" and "Indian." Under the domination model, we would expect "mestizos" to be those who have lost the original Amerindian language, but for whom aspects of Amerindian culture persist in covert form. The covert elements are deniable, and this is an important fact since the mestizos wish to see themselves as having moved into the position of the dominant. At the same time, however, the covert elements are in some measure recognizable by the dominant, for whom they reflect a perpetuation of heterogeneity and difference that is simultaneously nonthreatening. In contrast, under the alliance model we would expect "mestizos" to be the bearers of the Amerindian language, as well as of the largely homogenized elements of national culture. The ideal mestizo would speak not only the Amerindian language but Spanish as well, since bilingualism celebrates social cohesion through difference, even though genuine life-style differences have been erased.

In fact, the census data, while less rich than one would like, unequivocally demonstrate this contrast. For Peru, only the 1940 census, among those taken in the twentieth century, included a question regarding racial/cultural categorization. Fortunately, the same census contained as well questions about language, which were also part of subsequent major censuses in 1961 and 1972. The 1940 cultural/racial statistics, while never followed up, have nonetheless been widely reported in various publications as characterizing the ethnic composition of Peru to this day. In these statistics, "blanca" and "mestiza" are lumped together, because "solo fué posible diferenciar claramente a los individuos de raza indígena, negra y amarilla, mientras los nacionales de raza blanca y mestiza se confundían con frecuencia" (Ministerio de Hacienda y Comercio, Peru 1944: CLXXIX). The results show a majority of the population (52.89 percent) in the mestiza/blanca category; 45.86 percent fell into the category of Indian. The corresponding figures for the previous major census taken in 1876 were 38.55 percent and 57.60 percent. What is of interest from the point of view of the present model is that the distribution of Amerindian language (principally Quechua) is roughly coextensive with the category of Indian. Of the population in 1940, 65 percent were reported as speaking Spanish, either as monolinguals or as bilinguals with Amerindian languages, the latter accounting for 16.61 percent of the population. The remaining 35 percent were monolingual in Amerindian languages, primarily Quechua.

It is clear that by 1940 Spanish had spread to considerable portions of the population, and had even made inroads into the group separated out on racial/cultural grounds as Indian. Alternatively, "mestizo" meant generally being monolingual in Spanish, since only 51.61 percent of the population spoke an Amerindian language, either as monolinguals or as bilinguals, a figure barely greater than that for the category "Indian."

The contrast with Paraguay could not be more striking. Here the major Amerindian language (Guaraní) has extended its scope far beyond the bounds of the category "Indian." In fact, census figures confine the Indian population to 1–3 percent of the total population of Paraguay over the last forty years (INDI 1982). While the major twentieth-century censuses have not included questions regarding the mestizo/white category, figures have circulated in the literature. The *Statistical Abstract of Latin America for 1955*, for example, places 97 percent of the population in the mestizo/white category, with 3 percent in the category of Indian. The same publication began in 1957 to omit this statistic, and by 1961 included a note explaining that the "overwhelming majority of the population [is] known to belong in this category, but detailed quantitative distribution is not available" (Committee on Latin American Studies, UCLA 1961: 10). Comparable figures can be found throughout the literature.

The important point is that the Amerindian language, Guaraní, extends vastly beyond the confines of the 1–3 percent of the population regarded as "Indian." The 1950 census figures show that 92 percent of Paraguay spoke Guaraní, with 40 percent of the population actually monolingual in Guaraní, while only 52 percent of the population spoke Spanish. In other words, to be mestizo in Paraguay means to speak an Amerindian language, either exclusively or in conjunction with Spanish. This is just the opposite of the situation in Peru. There to be mestizo means to speak only Spanish, to have distanced oneself from the Amerindian tongue. These data are summarized in table 1.

The contrast is a striking one, and yet it is wholly explicable from the point of view of contrasting models of semiotic process. In Peru, which is much more "Indian" in a cultural sense than Paraguay, the linguistic relationships between Spanish and Amerindian have come to symbolize domination. The expectable set of actor strategies under this symbolic interpretation predict that nevertheless the Amerindian language should be on the retreat, with bilingualism a transitional phenomenon and relatively limited in scope. In Paraguay, which is much less culturally "Indian" than Peru, the linguistic relationships have come to symbolize alliance. The corresponding model of actor strategies predicts an expansion in scope of the Amerindian language, along with Spanish, and a broad, stable base of bilingualism. This is precisely what the data suggest.

Ideology and Ideological Shift

The basic thesis put forth here is that linguistic relationships between European and Amerindian languages congealed into symbolically meaningful and manipulable signs in Brazil, Paraguay, and Peru. The meanings can be traced to the relational indexical characteristics of the languages as signs that took shape during the early years of contact. These linguistic relationships later contributed to the symbolic cement of the emerging nation-states.

But the one key empirical phenomenon that has not been explicated is the linguistic shift that occurred in Brazil, probably beginning in the mid-eighteenth century and continuing into the nineteenth century. Whereas in Paraguay and Peru there has been relative continuity in the linguistic symbolism, in Brazil that symbolism has undergone change. Starting out with an alliance model, by the mid-eighteenth century Brazil was moving in the direction of an interpretation of sociolinguistic cohesion based on sameness or sharing. How are we to account for this shift?

To answer this question, we need to probe further into the semiotic role language plays within state formation, for the key contrasts between Brazil and Paraguay are to be found here. Whereas Paraguay remained relatively isolated from Spain throughout the colonial period—its contacts with Europe occurred primarily overland via Peru—Brazil maintained close relations with the Portuguese Crown into the nineteenth century. Whereas the independence of Paraguay took place swiftly in 1811, the process of separation from Portugal was gradual: Brazil became the seat of the Portuguese Crown in 1808 when Dom João VI fled Portugal; when he returned to Portugal in 1820, he left his son as regent, but the latter refused to accept a reinstatement of colonial status and instead declared Brazil independent in 1822; Brazil remained a monarchy under the descendants of the Portuguese king until 1889. If nation-state formation in these cases meant political separation from Europe, that process was difficult in the case of Brazil because the bonds were so strong. In the case of Paraguay, it was easy because the ties were never close.

Table 1. Statistics on Race/Culture and Language

	Racial/Cultural		Linguistic		
	Mestizo/White	Indian	Spanish only	Spanish and Amerindian	Amerindian only
Peru					
1876[a]	39 %	58 %	—	—	—
1940 [a]	53 %	46 %	47 %	17 %	35 %
1961[b]	—	—	60 %	19 %	20 %
1972[c]	—	—	72 %	16 %	12 %
1981[d]	—	—	73 %	16 %	9 %
Paraguay					
1950	97 %[e]	3 %[e]	5 %[f]	54 %[f]	40 %[f]
1962			4 %[h]	48 %[h]	45 %[h]
1981		1 %[g]	8 %[i]	52 %[i]	40 %[i]

[a] *Source:* DNE (1944: vol. 1, CLXXX, CLXXXIV, 148–151).
[b] *Source:* Myers (1967: 37). Includes a discussion of difficulties in calculating these figures from the census data.
[c] Based on figures in Escobar, Mar, and Alberti (1975). Compare ONEC (1974: vol. 1, 646), where monolinguals are not differentiated from bilinguals.
[d] *Source:* INE (1984: vol. 1, xxxi); 1.4 percent of the population is listed as being bilingual in Spanish and a "foreign language," and 0.9 percent is placed in a category of "other combination."
[e] Estimates cited repeatedly in the literature, for example, Committee on Latin American Studies, UCLA (1955: 3).
[f] Calculated from figures in DGEC (1948–1953: 25).
[g] Calculated from INDI (1982) figure of 38,703 Indians, with the total Paraguayan population estimated at 3,070,000 for 1981.
[h] Based on figures in Corvalan and de Granda (1982).
[i] *Source:* Stark (1983).

But why did the Amerindian language have a distinct fate in these two cases? The proposal discussed thus far has been that language and language relationships, operating at the symbolic or ideological plane, interpret or model the nature of social cohesion in the group in which they are operative. From the point of view of the social group circumscribed by Brazil, that symbolism in the early colonial period was much like the symbolism in Paraguay. Cohesion was seen as resulting from the attractive force of difference. But it is important that the symbolism pertained to Brazil and Paraguay as isolated social groupings, not to the European empires of which they were politically a part. The latter did not symbolize their own internal coherence in terms of alliance. Alliance applied more locally to the internal order of the emerging New World social organisms.

The trajectory under the alliance model, as discussed earlier, is one in which, over time, homogenization tends to occur, not only in the linguistic realm through the spread of bilingualism, but as well in the realm of nonlinguistic cultural indices. As a result of this homogenization, the ideological model of social cohesion as construed through language comes to contradict the model as understood in terms of shared nonlinguistic culture. Whereas ideologically the social order is construed to result from an alliance between different parts, indexically the differences have been erased. A de facto shared culture is put into place.

In both the Brazilian and Paraguayan cases, the models worked well. From the European point of view, however, they worked too well. Brazilian internal coherence appeared to Portugal as a threat, insofar as it meant the distinctiveness of the New World culture with respect to Europe. The relational indexical proportionality was:

Portugal : Brazil : : Portuguese : Portuguese + Amerindian

At a time (the mid-eighteenth century) when the social relationships between Europe and the New World were becoming a focus of concern, the linguistic relationship of Portuguese to Portuguese-plus-Amerindian came to be regarded ideologically as signaling divisiveness and separation, and, consequently, threats to the integrity of the Portuguese empire. By the 1750s, we begin to find ideological pronouncements against *lingua geral*. Mendonça Furtado, Governor of Amazonia at the time of the Marquis of Pombal, for example, indicated his immense irritation at seeing beneath his window "two negroes . . . speaking unabashedly the above-mentioned language [*lingua geral*] while comprehending nothing of Portuguese" (cited in Elia 1979: 195). To eliminate the Amerindian language would, therefore, symbolically at least, neutralize the threat of separatism. To the ideology of cohesion by alliance that had taken hold in Brazil, the Portuguese opposed an ideology of cohesion through sharing. This meant sharing a common language: Portuguese.

In Paraguay, Guaraní played a role in the 1811 independence move against Spain (Rubin 1968: 25). The same might have occurred with *lingua geral* in Brazil, except for the fact that Brazil itself became the locus of the empire in 1808. When independence occurred in 1822, it did so in the form of a schism within the royal family. By this time, the ideology of unification through sharing had had its effect. *Lingua geral* was everywhere in retreat, continuing to function as the primary means of linguistic communication only in the remote interior. As late as the 1890s, the moves to unify Brazil through Portuguese as against *lingua geral* were continuing. Portuguese was "instituted as the official language of Manaos" (Sorensen 1985: 146–147).

While *lingua geral* did not play a major part in the independence move, its precursor, Tupinamba, did during the subsequent period prior to 1889, when the monarchy was finally overthrown and Brazil became a republic. As the historian E. B. Burns (1968: 44) observed:

> The full tide of nineteenth century Indianism swept in between the years 1840 and 1875. During those years, poets such as Gonçalves Dias, in his Poesias Americanas (American Poems), and novelists, of whom the foremost representative was José de Alencar, exalted the Indian over the Portuguese. Alencar advised his fellow intellectuals that "the knowledge of the Indian language [Tupí] is the basis for a national literature." Brazil's first outstanding historian in the national period, Francisco Adolfo de Varnhagen, concurred: "For Brazilian literature, the language of our land [Tupí] is much more important than the study of Greek or other academic languages."

As late as the twentieth century, a chair of Tupinamba studies was established at the University of São Paulo.

The emphasis on Tupinamba as part of the identity of the emerging nation-state was reflected in numerous areas of life, including the Indian surnames that many Brazilians adopted during this period. The Indianist movement was opposed by countervailing classicist ideologies. But the failure of Tupinamba to take root as the actual language of Brazil had to do not so much with this, as with the indexical fact: Tupinamba in its form as *lingua geral* was no longer widely spoken, thanks to the prior ideological shift toward unification by means of Portuguese. The symbolic meaning of the language was out of accord with its indexical value. Brazil was already primarily Portuguese-speaking. From the point of view of bolstering the Amerindian language in Brazil, the

Indianist movement came too late.

It would be incorrect to assume that the linguistic differences between Paraguay and Brazil simply reflect the differing social relationships with Europe that each country maintained. Language as symbol is more than a reflection of social relations. It is one of the devices used in constituting and modifying those relations. The ideological shift toward linguistic unity through Portuguese was part and parcel of the mechanism whereby Brazil and Portugal were cemented together during the late colonial period.

The question of why Brazilians today speak Portuguese, rather than Portuguese plus an Amerindian language, comes down to timing in the interplay between the symbolic and indexical planes of meaning. The Portuguese made an effort to alter the symbolic meaning of the Portuguese language prior to the actual separatist moves, when the Amerindian language was recognized as a useful vehicle for signaling the distinctiveness of the Brazilian nation-state. By the time the symbolic utility of Tupinamba was recognized, *lingua geral* had lost its indexical value. It was in fact no longer widely spoken. In contrast, in Paraguay the Spanish did not move decisively against Guaraní, although they had moved against the Jesuits and, hence, against the Indians. At the time of independence in 1811, the indexical value of Guaraní was in keeping with its symbolic value. It was spoken by a majority of Paraguayans.

Conclusion

To return to the Boasian question of the separability of race, language, and culture, it should now be apparent that the issue is semiotically complex. At the indexical plane, the linguistic code is just one among the numerous markers of identity that can pick out a social group or subgroup, alongside clothing styles, mannerisms, beliefs, ritual practices, and so forth. The problem of separability of language from culture is in this sense no different from the problem of separability of one indexical element of culture from another. Like any other element of culture, the linguistic code can be seized by discourse, glossed at the ideological plane, and given a positive or negative value. Insofar as this symbolic meaning can be disseminated—for example, Mendonça Furtado can get others to share his irritation at the use of *lingua geral*—in that measure can any of the indices wax or wane.

But among all of the cultural indices, language occupies a privileged position. Because of the semiotic pressure to identify a single language with a single culture and people, the linguistic code looms large in defining social relations and cohesiveness. Consequently, when social groups come into contact, the nature of the relationship between those groups can be comprehended and manipulated semiotically through the relationship between languages. The efforts to comprehend and manipulate social relationships in such encounters provide countervailing interpretive pressures to the one language/one group pressure. It is in such encounters that language *relationships* can take on indexical and symbolic meanings, and come to stand for the type of sociability that holds together the emergent collectivity, resulting from the fusion of the two previously isolated ones.

As the new collectivity takes shape, it is the linguistic relationship that symbolizes the nature of cohesiveness. Depending upon what the specific symbolic meaning is, the linguistic codes can have differing fates with respect to the other indexical elements of culture. The present chapter has focused upon two such meanings: "alliance" and "domination."[3] Each has a distinctive historical trajectory, resulting from the actor manipulations that are peculiar to that interpretation. Alliance leads, paradoxically, to homogenization, to a broad and stable base of bilingualism, and to a sharing of other cultural indices. Domination produces a characteristic oscillation, based upon the contradictory strategies of actors. But the long-term result is that the dominated language recedes and the dominant language spreads, despite the maintenance of difference in various nonlinguistic indices.

The relationship between the European empires and the emerging New World nation-states adds an additional dimension to the problem, for the use of linguistic relationships to symbolize social cohesion was confined to the New World social groupings. Consequently, in the separation phase, as the new nation-states were forged, the Amerindian languages played a symbolic role in helping to define what was unique to the New World states. Here the difference between the Brazilian and Paraguayan cases can be traced to timing and to the relationship between the indexical and symbolic planes. Whereas the Portuguese moved to reassert the one language (Portuguese)/one people model well prior to the independence moves, thus effectively attenuating the Amerindian language indexically prior to independence and making it impossible for the pro-Indian movement to reestablish it subsequently, the Spanish through neglect allowed the alliance model to persist in Paraguay, making Guaraní symbolically useful during the revolt and allowing it to be indexically valorized while it was still widely spoken.

At the same time, Paraguay is no more culturally "Indian" than Brazil. The spread of the Amerindian language in the one case, and its retreat in the other, occurred independently of the homogenization of other cultural elements. Ironically, Peru, a country in which the proportion of Amerindian speakers has been steadily dropping, is much more racially and culturally (in covert terms) "Indian" than either Paraguay or Brazil.

The semiotic construal proposed here of the Boasian chestnut is that the separability of language and culture must be understood in terms of two distinct but related actor tendencies: the tendency, first, to put language and culture together, that is, to interpret the linguistic code as an index of one culture and of one people; but also, second, to interpret the relationship between languages as meaningful, and, in particular, as signaling the basis of social cohesion in the newly emergent collectivity formed from the fusion of the two previous ones. Over time, strategic manipulations of linguistic relationships can pull language and culture apart. Simultaneously, however, the first tendency continues to renew their merger, but this time in a distinct configuration. In the broad sweep of time, there thus operates a regular cycle of linguistic attraction and repulsion (or isolation), causing language and the other indices of culture to configure and reconfigure, and this cycle is linked to the formation and transformation of social relationships and power.

Notes

1. There are actually in theory infinitely many indices possible, thanks to the gradations of relative competencies in languages A and B.
2. To show that just the opposite effect can be achieved, a recent ideology of genuine Indianness, held by tourists and other visitors to the Xingu Park in central Brazil, where many different Indian tribes reside, devalues Western clothing and valorizes native dress. Correspondingly, traditional clothing styles have tended there to be maintained as indices of Indian identity.
3. It is interesting that recent scholarly works reflect the different ideological meanings that language has taken on in these countries. In Peru, thanks to the work of Albó (1977), there has developed an understanding of Quechua as an "oppressed language." This accords with the ideology of linguistic domination that has reigned in Peru from early colonial times through the present. In contrast, in Brazil there have been various works dealing with the "linguistic unity" of the country, such as Lima Sobrinho's (1977) *A língua portuguesa e a unidade do brasil* (The Portuguese language and the unity of Brazil) or Elia's (1979) *A unidade lingüística do Brasil* (The linguistic unity of Brazil), which is an effort to deny the importance of regional variation in Portuguese, as well as to deny the impact of Tupinamba and its successor *lingua geral* on the development of Brazilian Portuguese.

References

Albó, Xavier
    1977   *El futuro de los idiomas oprimidos en los Andes*. La Paz: Centro de Investigación y Promoción del Campesinado.
Auer, J. C. P.
    1984   *Bilingual conversation*. Amsterdam: John Benjamins.
Auer, Peter, and Aldo diLuzio, eds.

1984   *Interpretive sociolinguistics.* Tübingen: Gunter Narr Verlag.
Blom, Jan Petter, and John J. Gumperz
1972   Social meaning in linguistic structures. In *Directions in sociolinguistics,* J. J. Gumperz and D. Hymes (eds.), 407–434. New York: Holt, Rinehart & Winston.
Boas, Franz
1911   *The mind of primitive man.* New York: Free Press. (References to 1965 ed.)
Boxer, C. R.
1964   *The golden age of Brazil 1695–1750: growing pains of a colonial society.* Berkeley: University of California Press.
Burns, E. Bradford
1968   *Nationalism in Brazil: a historical survey.* New York: Praeger.
Committee on Latin American Studies, UCLA
1955   [and subsequent years] *Statistical abstract of Latin America.* Los Angeles: Committee on Latin American Studies, UCLA.
Corvalan, Grazziella, and German de Granda, eds.
1982   *Sociedad y lengua: bilinguismo en el Paraguay,* 2 vols. Asunción: Centro Paraguayo de Estudios Sociológicos.
DGEC (Dirección General de Estadística y Censos)
1948– Anuario estadístico de la República del Paraguay. Asuncion: Ministerio
1953   de Hacienda.
DNE (Dirección Nacional de Estadística)
1944   *Censo nacional de población y ocupación 1940.* Lima: Ministerio de Hacienda y Comercio, Peru.
Edmonson, Barbara
1983   The pre-and post-conquest use of Quechua as a lingua franca. *Human Mosaic* 17(1–2): 88–115.
Elia, Sílvio
1979   *A unidade lingüística do Brasil.* Rio de Janeiro: Padrão.
Escobar, A., J. M. Mar, and G. Alberti
1975   *Perú: ¡país bilingüe!* Lima: Instituto de Estudios Peruanos.
Gal, Susan
1987   Codeswitching and consciousness in the European periphery. *American Ethnologist* 14(4): 637–653.
Grimes, Barbara F.
1985   Language attitudes: identity, distinctiveness, survival in the Vaupes. *Journal of Multilingual and Multicultural Development* 6: 389–401.
Hill, Jane
1985   The grammar of consciousness and the consciousness of grammar. *American Ethnologist* 12(4): 725–737.
Hill, Jane H., and Kenneth C. Hill
1986   *Speaking Mexicano.* Tucson: University of Arizona Press.
INDI (Instituto Paraguayo del Indígena)
1982   *Censo y estudio de la población indígena del Paraguay, 1981.* Asunción: Instituto del Paraguay.
INE (Instituto Nacional de Estadística)
1984   *Censos nacionales VIII de población III de vivienda* (1981). Lima,

Peru: Impreso en los Talleres de la Imprenta del Colegio Militar Leoncio Prado.

Jackson, Jean
1974   Language identity of the Columbian Vaupés Indians. In *Explorations in the ethnography of speaking*, D. Bauman and J. Sherzer (eds.), 50–64. New York: Cambridge University Press.

Lima Sobrinho, Barbosa
1977   *A língua portuguesa e a unidade do Brasil*. Rio de Janeiro: Instituto Nacional do Livro, Ministério da Educação e Cultura.

Mannheim, Bruce
1983   Structural change and the structure of change: the linguistic history of Cuzco Quechua in relation to its social history. PhD thesis, Department of Anthropology, University of Chicago.
1984   Una nación acorralada: Southern Peruvian Quechua language planning and politics in historical perspective. *Language in Society* 13(3): 291–309.

Métraux, Alfred
1946   Ethnography of the Chaco. *Handbook of South American Indians*, vol. 1, 197–370. Bulletin of the Bureau of American Ethnology, no. 143. Washington, D.C.: U.S. Government Printing Office.
1948   The Guaraní. *Handbook of South American Indians*, vol. 3, 69–94. Bulletin of the Bureau of American Ethnology, no. 143. Washington, D.C.: U.S. Government Printing Office.

Ministerio de Hacienda y Comercio, Peru
1944   *Censo nacional de población*. Lima: Ministerio de Hacienda y Comercio, Peru.

Myers, Sarah K.
1967   The distribution of languages in Peru: a critical analysis of the census of 1961. MA thesis, Department of Geography, University of Chicago.

ONEC (Oficina Nacional de Estadística y Censos)
1974   *Censos nacionales VII de población II de vivienda* (1972). Lima, Peru: Impreso en los Talleres de la Imprenta del Colegio Militar Leoncio Prado.

Rubin, Joan
1968   *National bilingualism in Paraguay*. Janua Linguarum, Series Practica 60. The Hague: Mouton.

Scotton, Carol
1983   The negotiation of identities in conversation: a theory of markedness and code choice. *International Journal of the Sociology of Language* 44: 115–136.

Sorensen, Arthur P.
1967   Multilingualism in the northwest Amazon. *American Anthropologist* 69: 670–684.
1985   An emerging Tukanoan linguistic regionality: policy pressures. In *South American Indian languages: retrospect and prospect*, H. E. M. Klein and L. Stark (eds.), 140–156. Austin: University of Texas Press.

Stark, Louisa R.
1983   Alphabets and national policy: the case of Guaraní. In *Bilingualism:*

social issues and policy implications, A. W. Miracle, Jr. (ed.), 70–83. Athens: University of Georgia Press.

Trubetzkoy, N.
  1939   Principles of phonology. Berkeley: University of California Press. (Reference to the 1969 English ed.)

Urban, Greg, and Joel Sherzer
  1988   The linguistic anthropology of native South America. *Annual Review of Anthropology* 17: 283–307.

Contributors

Thomas Abercrombie
Department of History
University of Miami

Richard N. Adams
Department of Anthropology
University of Texas at Austin

Martin Diskin
Department of Anthropology
Massachusetts Institute of Technology

Janet Hendricks
Department of Anthropology
Vanderbilt University

Carol Hendrickson
Department of Anthropology
Marlboro College

Jane H. Hill
Department of Anthropology
University of Arizona

James Howe
Department of Anthropology
Massachusetts Institute of Technology

Jean E. Jackson
Department of Anthropology
Massachusetts Institute of Technology

David Maybury-Lewis
Department of Anthropology
Harvard University

Joel Sherzer
Department of Anthropology
University of Texas at Austin

Antonio Carlos de Souza Lima
Department of Anthropology
Museu Nacional
Rio de Janeiro

Thomas Turino
Department of Music
University of Illinois at Champaign-Urbana

Greg Urban
Department of Anthropology
University of Texas at Austin

Index